PRAISE FOR *BECOMING PABLO O'HIGGINS*

"Exhaustively researched, *Becoming Pablo O'Higgins* examines the complex personality of Pablo O'Higgins and his participation in the vibrant and often volatile twentieth-century political art movement in Mexico. Vogel traces O'Higgins's life as an American artist at the center of Mexican politics—an ideal time and setting to serve the leftist ideals in which he believed and to escape a personal past that he held in contempt. Unraveling O'Higgins's true identity, this fascinating narrative weaves together some of the most powerful personalities in international politics and art."

—Donna L. Poulton, Ph.D., Curator, Pablo O'Higgins: Works on Paper, Utah Museum of Fine Arts, 2010; coauthor, *Painters of Utah's Canyons and Deserts*; coauthor, *Utah Art, Utah Artists: 150 Years Survey*; and coauthor, *Painters of Utah's Mountain and Basin Regions*

"A masterful job. This is an ambitious piece of writing, well researched and well done. The research alone is exhaustive and I've no doubt that this book will be a major contribution to the field."

—Diana Anhalt, author of *A Gathering of Fugitives: American Political Expatriates in Mexico 1948-1965*

"*Becoming Pablo O'Higgins* unveils with outstanding skill the real person and the artist behind the legend. With this masterful work, which involved very serious research and a deep understanding of the cultural and political environment that prevailed on both sides of the border in the times of Pablo O'Higgins, Susan Vogel has made a very important contribution for a better understanding between the U.S. and Mexico."

—Salvador Jiménez, former Mexican Consul to Utah

"A fine piece of work with an engrossing narrative."

—John Charlot, Vice President, Jean Charlot Foundation, University of Hawai'i

BECOMING PABLO O'HIGGINS

by Susan Vogel

Pince-Nez Press

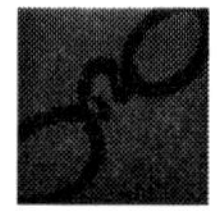

ISBN: 978-1-930074-21-7
Library of Congress Control Number: 2010902147
Copyright © 2010 Susan Vogel

Cover photo by Steve Murin
Cover and page design by Ana Esmee Design, www.anaesmeedesign.com

Pince-Nez Press, LLC
San Francisco/Salt Lake City
www.pince-nez.com
pincenezpress@gmail.com
(415) 267-5978

Printed in the United States

for *my family*

A worker himself, [Pablo O'Higgins's] understanding of mankind is not abstract. Above all, he is interested in depicting man in his daily life and in the social struggle; in that dimension where, as he influences reality, man transforms himself. [1]

CONTENTS

ACKNOWLEDGEMENTS

First, I want to thank my family, especially Ana and Dave, for their patience over the years as I have talked about Pablo O'Higgins, and dragged them to libraries, bookstores, and interviews. Second, thank you to Cynthia Buckingham and the Utah Humanities Council for awarding me a grant to research and write about O'Higgins; thank you as well to the Utah Media Arts Center and Allison Gregerson for sponsoring my grant.

Thank you to Phyllis and Rusty Vetter for joining in the Mexico City adventure. To Amparo Guadalupe Ventura, for the same, and for helping with my research and translating many interviews. To my grant scholars, Professors Joel Hancock, Mary Muir and Rebecca Horn, I express my deep appreciation. Also to artist and grant scholar Irma Vega de Bijou, who has been along for a lot of the ride over the years. Thank you to Tina Misrachi Martin for the many hours we have spent talking about the fascinating period of time in Mexico City in which she grew up. Thank you to everyone who allowed me into their homes and lives to interview them. I want to thank Chad Nielsen for sending me in the right direction in terms of how to shape the story and Beth Gillogly for suggesting the right people to help me get it finished. I am grateful for Rebecca Guevara, my writing coach; Rob Eckman, my research assistant; Julio César Tapia Guzmán and Efraín Méndez, professional interpreters and translators, who, through endless e-mails, texts, late night phone calls, and meetings, helped with the thorniest translations; and Salvador Jiménez, who provided great insight on Mexican politics. My family has been very involved in this project: Dave has graciously allowed this book to take over our house, our vacations, and pretty much our lives and has encouraged me through the challenges of finishing it—thank you! Thank you to my parents, Bill Vogel for his historical research and editing, and Donna Vogel for her editing and overall perspective; to my sister Ann Vogel Palmer, for her editing; to Bernardo Flores-Sahagún, for his help over the years and assistance with translations; to Ana for her amazing graphic art talents and patience (she was two when I started and is now applying to grad school). My gratitude to Abuelita for her years of hospitality including great food. Thank you to art historians Mary Muir, Ph.D., Donna Poulton, Ph.D., and James Swensen, Ph.D., for their insights into Utah art. In Hawai'i, John Charlot, Bronwen Solyom, and Rae Shiraki, were so generous with their time and hospitality. Many thanks to Steve Murin for sharing his beautiful photographs and his stories (the best sixty-dollar cab ride in my life!). Thank you to Carol Wells at the Center for the Study of Political Graphics in Los Angeles, to art historian and Mexican graphic art expert Noah Bardach, Ph.D., and to Carol Cuenod of the Labor Archives and Research Center at San Francisco State University. I greatly appreciate the help of the Utah Historical Society and Anthony Castro. Special thanks to those who read the latest drafts of my manuscript and offered excellent suggestions: Joel Hancock, Irma Vega de Bijou, Dave Valenti, Diana Anhalt, John Charlot, David Betz, Cynthia Maw, and Salvador Jiménez. My gratitude to Sue Anderson, who suggested I finish this project; my opera friends, for showing me that Wagnerian-length projects can be completed; to Donna Poulton, for recognizing the importance of Pablo O'Higgins and prodding me to completion of this book, and to the Utah Museum of Fine Arts, especially Donna Poulton, Gretchen Dietrich, and Shelbey Peterson for their enthusiasm. And to Lisa and her wonderful team who provided me draft after draft as well as abundant encouragement. And finally to copyeditor Jane Ludlam for her steady "pen."

PROLOGUE

This book is the result of many years of research, and some may say obsession, trying to learn how a blond-haired, blue-eyed young man from Salt Lake City, Utah, my hometown, became a celebrated Mexican muralist.

I learned about Pablo O'Higgins in 1985, on a trip to Mexico City. It was just months after the 8.1 earthquake had flattened multistory buildings, leaving piles of bricks, rebar and, sadly, as I recall, children's shoes. I was walking down Calle Juárez, after stopping in Galería Misrachi, which had been my favorite place for a respite from the crowded buses and subways years earlier when I had studied for two semesters in Mexico City. I had bought a paperback book called *Mural Painting of Mexico*, by Rafael Carrillo Azpeitia, and was paging through it as I walked down the street, enjoying the familiar pictures of the murals that I had studied years earlier with Dra. Moreno, my favorite professor at the National Autonomous University of Mexico (Universidad Nacional Autónoma de México, or UNAM). The images and names were all familiar to me, as Dra. Moreno had sent her students through all the subway tunnels in Mexico City to see what I thought was every important mural. But I nearly jumped when I saw the words "Salt Lake City, Utah," on a page of the book. "Pablo O'Higgins, born 1904, Salt Lake City, Utah." I had never heard of him. I lived in Salt Lake City. I was at the time married to a Mexican architect, Bernardo, and we were involved in the arts. How had I not heard of Pablo O'Higgins?

I started researching O'Higgins through books published in English and in Spanish, newspaper archives, and magazine articles. I found many consistencies in my research. He was a serious artist who adopted Mexico as his home and was deeply committed to bettering the lives of poor Mexican peasants and the working class. He was loved by all who knew him. He was a simple man who did not care about money or possessions. He was kind, modest, genuine, and sincere. Repeated over and over was Diego Rivera's statement that if he had a son he'd want him to be like O'Higgins, and his prediction that O'Higgins would one day be as admired as Vincent van Gogh.[1] In everything I read, Pablo O'Higgins was described as a hero, if not a saint. His art was powerful and alive. He received much admiration in Mexico. A book published in Mexico shortly after his death has four chapters with the title, "*Pablo. El hombre de corazón puro* [Pablo, pure of heart]." (Rivera had referred to him as "limpio de corazón," pure of heart.)[2]

But there were also inconsistencies: was he born in Salt Lake City or San Francisco? Did he grow up in Utah or California? Was he Irish? Did he study in art school for two weeks or two years? Was his mother a *campesina* (farm woman), or an art-loving upper-middle-class housewife? Very little had been written about Pablo O'Higgins's life before he arrived in Mexico in 1924.

And, I had found nothing that answered my original simple question, one that almost everyone asks when learning about Pablo O'Higgins: how did a blue-eyed, blond-haired young man from Salt Lake City, Utah, without a drop of Mexican blood, become a renowned Mexican muralist, and indeed, as I later learned, a Chicano?

Over twenty years, I have interviewed people who knew O'Higgins and I have read everything I could find about him. I have spent many months in libraries and archives. Over these years, I have also watched as O'Higgins's fame in Mexico has skyrocketed, mainly through the efforts of his widow, María. In the past few years, several beautiful coffee-table books have been published about him in Mexico, all with the cooperation of María. One is titled *Pablo O'Higgins, Voz de lucha y de arte* (*Voice of Struggle and of Art*). Another is called *Humanidad recuperada* (*Humanity Regained*).

Twenty years ago, I had expected I would write a simple story about an artist whose work I found powerful. But my research revealed a story that is more complex, and indeed a person more complex who cannot be described simply as an "artist of the people" who was kind, gentle, and generous, although he was all those things. This is the story of how Paul Higgins transformed into Pablo O'Higgins. It is not an art history book, it does not attempt to be a complete discussion of his art and does not include images that would require me to seek permission from his widow, who midway through my project became very antagonistic and denied me access to materials she had previously allowed me to review.

Out of necessity, as O'Higgins spent nearly thirty-five years in Mexico creating political art, this is also a story of the transformation of that country.

I understand that this book may raise more questions than it answers: my friend David Betz, an art dealer and writer, used the same words to describe O'Higgins as Churchill used in October 1939 to describe the Soviet Union: "a riddle wrapped in a mystery inside an enigma." I hope this book initiates more critical discussion about O'Higgins.

For simplicity, I refer to O'Higgins as Pablo (he signed some works only "Pablo"). I sometimes refer to the United States of America as "America" and residents thereof as "Americans." My apologies to other residents of the Americas.

CHRONOLOGY: PABLO O'HIGGINS (1904 – 1983)

1890: Higgins and McAfee families arrive in Utah
1896: Parents, Edward V. Higgins and Alice McAfee, marry
1897: Brother Roger born
1904: Paul Stevenson Higgins born, Salt Lake City, Utah
1906–07: Family lives in San Diego, California
1915: Pablo's father, as assistant attorney general, urges the Utah Supreme Court to uphold the conviction and execution of miner and now labor martyr Joe Hill
1916–18: Family lives in San Diego, California
1922: Paul Higgins graduates from East High School, Salt Lake City, Utah
1922?: Studies briefly at San Diego Academy of Art
1924: Travels to Mexico City; six months later begins assisting Diego Rivera on murals at Ministry of Education
1926: Assists Rivera on murals at Agricultural College at Chapingo; name change to Pablo O'Higgins begins; father dies in Palo Alto, California
1927: Joins the Communist Party
1928–29: Serves as cultural missionary in rural Mexico where he encounters violence of the Cristero Rebellion; paints first mural in open-air theater; involved in organizing miners' strikes against mines owned by U.S. companies
1928: Sixth International leads Communist Party to take a hard-line approach; Pablo's brother dies in Salt Lake City, Utah
1929: Communist Party banned in Mexico (through 1934); abandons cultural missionary post to help Tina Modotti, who has been arrested for murder; begins working with Rivera on National Palace murals; leaves Rivera over political differences
1931: Lives with Jean Charlot in New York City; has an individual exhibit at John Levy Gallery there; sketches for *Daily Worker*
1931–32: Studies art in Moscow on a scholarship from the Communist Party
1933: Paints fresco murals at Emiliano Zapata School in Mexico City; assists Marion Greenwood with murals in Taxco and Michoacán
1934: Cofounds League of Revolutionary Writers and Artists—LEAR
1934–36: Paints fresco murals at Abelardo Rodríguez Market, Mexico City
1936–47: With LEAR, paints fresco murals at National Print Shops, Mexico City
1937: Cofounds the People's Graphic Workshop (Taller de Gráfica Popular or TGP)
1937–39: Produces anti-fascist art
1939-41: Complies with Nazi-Soviet Non-Aggression Pact and drops anti-fascist message
1939–40: Paints murals in Michoacán School in Mexico City honoring President Cárdenas's expropriation of the oil industry and depicting soccer players
1940: One of two U.S.-born artists whose work is included in New York's Museum of Modern Art exhibit "Twenty Centuries of Mexican Art"
1941: Renews anti-fascist art after Nazis invade Soviet Union
1942: Mural commission in Mexico City revoked on grounds he is not Mexican
1944: Creates poster for Roosevelt's Office of Inter-American Affairs, *Good Neighbors, Good Friends*, showing friendship between the United States and Mexico
1944 or 1945: Travels to the United States during Tehran Accord, purportedly feeling a "moral duty to fight fascism from his country of origin"; paints fresco mural for Ship Scalers Union in Seattle.

1947: Leaves Communist Party; joins People's Party (Partido Popular); along with Leopoldo Méndez paints fresco mural, *Maternity*, for a hospital in Mexico City
1949: Teaches at California Labor School, San Francisco and Los Angeles; paints a fresco mural for the Gabriel Ramos Millán School in Mexico City; is one of several dozen artists who form Mexico City's Salon of Mexican Plastic Art (Salón de la Plástica Mexicana)
1950: Begins teaching at La Esmeralda, Mexico City. Paints a fresco mural for the state of Michoacán; individual exhibit at the Salon of Mexican Plastic Art. Created portable mural, *Veracruz 1914*, depicting the U.S. invasion of Veracruz, Mexico
1951: Named a Communist Subversive by the U.S. State Department; mother dies in San Jose, California
1952: Paints mural for International Longshoremen's and Warehousemen's Union in Honolulu; being watched by U.S. State Department
1955: Wins acquisition prize, Salon of Mexican Plastic Art
1956: Second individual exhibit in the Salon of Mexican Plastic Art; Diego Rivera compares him to Vincent van Gogh
1957: Wins acquisition prize, Salon of Mexican Plastic Art
1958: Name appears on deportation list in Mexico City
1959: Wins first prize in Bellas Artes Annual Salon; creates ceramic mural for municipal palace in Poza Rica, Veracruz, Mexico; meets María de Jesús de la Fuente, marries in May.
1960: Paints mural, *Tenochtitlán libre* (*A Free Tenochtitlán*), University of Michoacán, Morelia, Michoacán; leaves TGP
1961: Becomes a Mexican citizen by decree of Mexican President Adolfo López Mateos; paints mural, *Mercado interior indígena* (*Inside Indian Market*), National Bank of Foreign Commerce, Mexico City
1962: Visits Havana, Cuba; individual exhibit at the Salon of Mexican Plastic Art
1963–64: Paints murals, *Boda indígena en el pueblo de San Lorenzo* (*Indian Wedding in the Town of San Lorenzo*), *Paisaje Tarahumara* (*Tarahumara Landscape*), and *Dios del fuego* (*God of Fire*), at the Museum of Anthropology, Mexico City
1965: Retrospective at Salon of Mexican Plastic Art
1968: Travel to USSR
1969: Death of Leopoldo Méndez, cofounder of TGP
1971: Is awarded Elías Sourasky prize by Mexican government; homage at Palace of Fine Arts, Mexico City
1975: Travel to Seattle, Washington, teaches class; exhibition and unveiling of restored Ship Scalers mural
1976: Retrospective of his work at Diego Rivera's Anahuacalli museum and Dolores Olmedo Patiño museum
1983: Dies of kidney failure July 16 in Mexico City; given State funeral at the Palace of Fine Arts (Palacio de Bellas Artes) in Mexico City

NAMES

Beals, Carleton: U.S. writer in Mexico on Guggenheim; correspondent for TASS, the Soviet news agency
Brenner, Anita: Mexican writer focusing on Mexican art, culture and travel
Catlett, Elizabeth: African-American artist, member of TGP
Caughlan, Goldie: Wife of John Caughlan
Caughlan, John: Seattle-based immigration and civil rights lawyer
Charlot, Jean: Paris-born artist of part-Mexican descent
Charlot, Zohmah: Wife of Jean Charlot, grew up Mormon in Salt Lake City
Eisenstein, Sergei: Soviet Russian filmmaker
Freeman, Joseph: Party member, founder of and writer for *New Masses*, husband of Ione Robinson
Goldblatt, Louis: Secretary-Treasurer of International Longshoremen's and Warehousemen's Union (ILWU)
Goldblatt, Terry: Wife of Louis Goldblatt
Guerrero, Xavier: Muralist, Party member, lover of Tina Modotti
Higgins, Alice McAfee: Pablo's mother
Higgins, Charles: Pablo's uncle
Higgins, Edward V.: Pablo's father, mining attorney and judge
Higgins, Gladys: Pablo's half sister, daughter of his father and his aunt, Lida
Higgins, Roger Chapin: Pablo's brother
Higgins, Will: Pablo's father's brother, married to Pablo's mother's sister
Jenkins, David: Longshoreman, head of California Labor School
Kahlo, Frida: Artist, wife of Diego Rivera
Maestas, Roberto: Founder of El Centro de la Raza, Seattle, Washington
Marin, Guadalupe (Lupe): Wife of Diego Rivera before Frida
McAfee Higgins, Alice: Pablo's mother
McAfee: Isabel: Pablo's mother's sister, married to Will Higgins
McAfee, John: Pablo's grandfather (Jr. his uncle)
McAfee, Lida: Pablo's father's first wife and Pablo's mother's sister
McCormick, Kathryn: daughter of Goldie Caughlan; lived with O'Higginses in 1976
Mella, Julio Antonio: Cuban revolutionary, lover of Tina Modotti
Méndez, Leopoldo: Mexican printmaker, cofounder of TGP
Mérida, Carlos: Guatemalan muralist and artist
Modotti, Tina: Italian-born photographer who lived with Edward Weston in Mexico
Orozco, José Clemente: Guadalajara-born Mexican artist and muralist
Orozco, Miguel: Indian servant to Pablo in 1970s
Packard, Emmy Lou: San Francisco Bay Area artist; assistant to Rivera
Porter, Katherine Anne: Texas-born writer on Guggenheim Fellowship in Mexico
Randall, Byron: Bay Area artist from Portland who worked at Taller de Gráfica Popular
Remba, Luis and Lea: Printers in Mexico City and later Los Angeles
Rivera, Diego: Mexican muralist
Robinson, Earl: Composer of the "Ballad of Joe Hill"
Robinson, Ione: Artist, Rivera assistant, married Joe Freeman
Siqueiros, David Alfaro: Mexican muralist, militant
Toor, Frances: Californian, publisher of bilingual magazine *Mexican Folkways*
Weston, Edward: California photographer living in Mexico with Tina Modotti

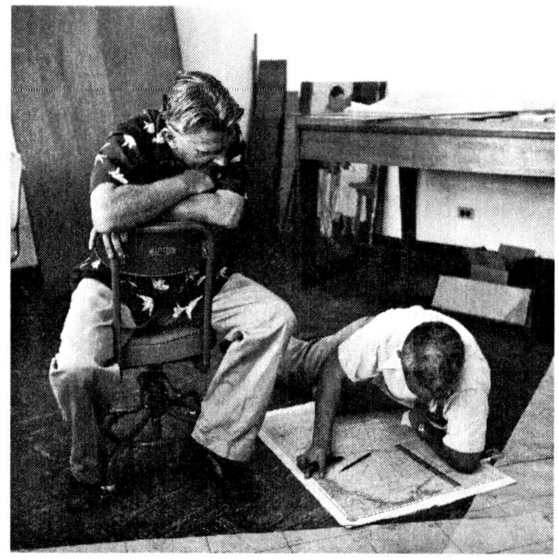

1

SEATTLE, 1975

Pablo watched out the car window as the lush green woods of the outskirts of Seattle turned to tight beige bunches of houses and then to the gritty gray of the waterfront. So much had changed since he had last been in the United States twenty-three years earlier, but so much had not. He was used to having to explain, justify, and defend himself, but not María. It wasn't fair what they had done to María.

It was September 30, 1975. Pablo and María were staying for a month in Seattle at the University Motel as guests of the University of Washington.

Pablo had been drawn into the center of the storm of the Chicano student movement at the university.[1] Earlier that year, the university had fired two Chicano administrators, prompting Chicano faculty and staff to resign in solidarity. Nearly two thousand students protested at the administration building and Chicano students called a two-day boycott of classes.[2]

Pablo's involvement in the controversy began when Roberto Maestas, the director of Seattle's El Centro de la Raza (Latino Center), "out of the clear blue sky," got a call from John Caughlan, a civil rights lawyer who had known Pablo in 1945. Caughlan said, "A Chicano janitor has informed me that he has seen some murals that are somehow related to the culture of Mexico and that they are being warehoused and are decaying." [3]

Maestas rallied students to find out what had happened to a mural titled *The Struggle Against Racial Discrimination* that Pablo had painted at the headquarters of the Ship Scalers, Drydock and Miscellaneous Workers Union 541 in Seattle in 1945. They found the mural panels at the university's Corporation Yard No. 1.[4]

On February 26, 1975, the mural panels were uncrated in the presence of Maestas and university representatives and later that day were examined by Maestas's class. The panels were found to be disfigured "by the deposits of salt that had risen to the surface and by the warping of some of the panels." [5]

The students learned that in 1955 (at the height of the anti-Communist McCarthy era in the United States), when moving to another building, the union had offered the mural to the University of Washington's School of Architecture. The School of Architecture had the mural cut off the wall of the union hall, and crated and stored "under plywood and tar paper" at the Union Bay Corporation Yard and then at the Corporation Yard No. 1.[6] With Caughlan's encouragement, Maestas turned the mural into a university community political issue and a class project in activism. The mural was described as "painted by a Chicano artist," "found by a Chicano janitor," and suppressed for its political message. Caughlan said, "due, perhaps, to the emphasis of the mural on international labor solidarity, anti-fascism, and anti-racism, the storage at the University became something of a 'deep freeze' . . . ." [7]

Maestas and his students sent a demand letter to the university accusing it of hiding the mural because of its political message—it contains a hammer and sickle and includes the faces of Marxist Mexican labor leader Vicente Lombardo Toledano and Chinese Communist leader Mao Ze-dong. The students insisted that the university "return the mural to the people." The Ship Scalers Union joined in, demanding that the mural be returned "to the working class" because it was "a work of art by a Chicano depicting the history of the Ship Scalers union." [8]

The university's position was that it had not deliberately hidden the mural but simply had misplaced it. The controversy received front-page coverage in the *Seattle Post-Intelligencer*.[9]

The university agreed to pay for the restoration and to mount the mural in a temporary, secure location on campus. The students demanded that the university bring Pablo to campus to oversee the mural restoration. The university agreed but required that he also teach a class on mural painting. The package expanded to include the university exhibiting his work, and Pablo teaching a class, overseeing the mural restoration, and attending a dedication.

Pablo, who was living in Coyoacán, an upscale suburb of Mexico City, said he was busy working on two murals but agreed to the trip. He began selecting art for the exhibit and completing the paperwork for the crating, insuring, and shipping of four drawings, twenty-four lithographs, six photographs, and seventy-three sketches, collectively valued (likely for insurance purposes) at $7,435.

By 1975, after many years of dedication to Mexico and its people, Pablo seemed truly to have become a Mexican artist. In the 1920s he had worked alongside many of the artists of the mural movement, gaining their respect and friendship through his passion for Mexico and the struggle of the social movement, his devotion to art, and his quiet, modest personality.

Pablo had been a founder of the Taller de Gráfica Popular (most often translated as the People's Graphic Workshop or People's Graphic Art Workshop, and referred to in this book as the TGP), which documented and protested worldwide injustices through the 1930s, '40s, and '50s. He had worked with many of Mexico's best-known printmakers. In 1992, Helga Prignitz, author of a comprehensive book on the TGP, referred to Pablo as the "most important lithographer in Mexico in the 20th Century." [10] Pablo had produced more than ten murals in Mexico, including for Mexico City's famous Museum of Anthropology, and had taught at La Esmeralda (the Escuela Nacional de Pintura y Escultura, or National School of Painting and Sculpture), Mexico's prestigious art school. Pablo was described as the only U.S.-born artist included in a blockbuster 1940 show at the Museum of Modern Art in New York City, "Twenty Centuries of Mexican Art."

Underlying Mexico's adoption of Pablo as a Mexican artist was Pablo's dedication and unwavering concern for the common Mexican people, the worker, the peasant. His art, his opinions, his pastimes, all reflected his deep love for and dedication to Mexico. His art depicted the struggle of the Mexican worker for the basic necessities of life, and even in his dramatic landscape paintings of later years the worker was almost always present.

Pablo's acceptance in Mexico had not come easily. For many years he struggled to define himself and to fit into a group of radical, revolutionary, and mainly well-educated artists whose enemies were often "Yankee imperialists." That a blue-eyed blond-haired young man who grew up in an affluent, conservative Republican family in Salt Lake City, Utah, could become a Mexican artist—and be presented by a La Raza group as a Chicano—was an amazing and paradoxical feat requiring some adjustment of his life and family history.

On their 1975 trip to Seattle, as Pablo and María came off the plane in California (where they would visit friends prior to going to Seattle), they were met by immigration officials. Pablo had been prepared for this—he knew he might be questioned because of his past membership in the Communist Party. But it was María they were after—they had identified her as a Communist Party member or past member. Why are you in the United States, they wanted to know. What were you doing in Cuba? María was livid. It took hours for her to straighten things out, recalled Terry Goldblatt, the friend with whom Pablo and María were staying in the Bay Area.[11] Incensed, Pablo vowed never to return to the United States.[12]

Days later, at the University of Washington, Pablo and John Caughlan walked among old, Gothic cathedral-like buildings and new, boxy concrete-and-brick structures. "We're right at home here, Pablo," said Caughlan, a Harvard Law graduate and Communist who had represented the party as an attorney. "They call this Red Square." Tables lined the redbrick-paved plaza, wet from the morning's drizzle, where students sought recruits for their organizations. Despite the gloomy weather, there was something inspiring about being on a college campus among university students whose activism had played a large role in ending the U.S. involvement in the Vietnam War earlier that year.

The students and the press referred to Pablo as a Chicano artist. By 1975, at the age of seventy-one, Pablo was very experienced at adapting himself. He seemed to know the need to explain his background to a reporter from the student newspaper:

> I was born in the States, in Salt Lake City, but my father left very early. My family lived near the border, in El Cajon, near San Diego. And as a kid I met Mexican friends and studied Spanish. I spoke Spanish, I guess, when I was seven or eight years old. I'm a Mexican citizen. I went to Mexico in 1924—fifty years ago.[13]

Pablo was accustomed to having to defend his Mexicanidad (Mexicanness). During the thirty-seven years he lived in Mexico but retained his United States citizenship, he had difficulty arguing that he was Mexican. He could travel in and out of the United States with ease and return at any time to live in the wealthiest country in the world. There was no dual citizenship during Pablo's lifetime. But by 1975, he had relinquished his United States citizenship and could say he was a Mexican citizen.

At the University of Washington, Pablo went to work overseeing the restoration of the Ship Scalers mural. Seventy feet long, the mural was a fresco painted on thirteen reinforced concrete panels, up to seven feet high and each weighing three to four hundred pounds. He described the mural as depicting the unity of races during the Second World War when the "allies were together" and "there was a unity with the Soviet Union," in the war against fascism.[14]

Pablo fulfilled his duties required by the university but didn't have his heart in it, according to Caughlan.[15] In an interview with the student paper, Pablo said he was not an art teacher—though he had taught lithography at the California Labor School in San Francisco and in Los Angeles and, for more than ten years, taught painting at La Esmeralda.[16] At the University of Washington, Pablo discussed techniques of fresco painting but didn't take his teaching terribly seriously. He seemed to be going through the motions required to get the mural restored, Caughlan recalled.[17]

A friend, Viola Patterson, who had known Pablo in Mexico in the mid-1930s and had assisted him on a mural, was amazed at his transformation when she saw him in Seattle. She recalled him, as many others did, as a poor artist who didn't care about money and gave away his paintings.[18] Until Pablo met María, he had lived in a rooftop studio in a rundown area of Mexico City and hung his clothes from nails in the wall. Patterson said that by 1975, Pablo "had become an elder statesman. . . . He married a very wonderful person. She was a well-known lawyer in Mexico City. And he was now so established and so well off, really, I think, both financially and socially and every other way, that he was a different Paul than the Pablo we'd known in Mexico. He'd become pretty much part of the establishment, I'd say." [19]

In 1975, Pablo played the role of the outsider, as he had for much of his life. At the exhibition of his art in Seattle, he had the opportunity to sell his pieces, but didn't make any effort.[20] He hated selling his work and had a disdain for galleries. With a "devilish smile," he quipped that art galleries take the value of an inch of a painting and multiply it. He called galleries "dangerous." [21] María had taken on the role of sales agent when they married, but in Seattle, since she spoke only limited English, she was quiet and out of her element.[22]

By 1975, Pablo was at the height of his career and indeed an "elder statesman" of the Mexican art world. The following year, decked out in evening wear, Pablo and María attended the inauguration of Mexican President José López Portillo. Ambassadors would visit their home and governors would call on the phone.[23] The wealthiest art collectors in Mexico City, such as Dolores Olmedo, were regular visitors to their home.[24] Both Pablo and María considered Pablo the heir to Diego Rivera—perhaps because Rivera had said that Pablo eventually would become as important as van Gogh.[25] But despite Pablo having achieved his dream of acceptance as a Mexican painter, and having received high honors as a Mexican artist, such as the prestigious Elias Sourasky prize, his art of these later years, according to one of his students, reflected something other than calm—"anguish." [26]

Had Pablo, in becoming a Mexican, a Mexican artist, indeed a national treasure connected with the most powerful people in Mexico, in some way lost an important part of himself, the humble painter who hung his clothes on nails pounded into the walls?

I

CHILDHOOD

What baggage did this solitary traveler bring? Nothing more than his heart, in the passionate adventure of beauty, and his thoughts as he searched for new realms of truth. — Gilberto Bosques, former Mexican Ambassador to France (re: Pablo O'Higgins)[1]

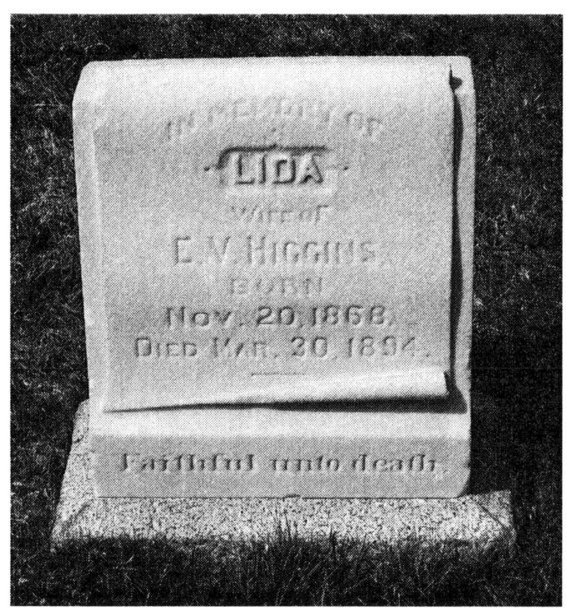

2

PURITANS & COVENANTERS

Pablo is known for depicting the close bond between human beings and their environment. Author Helga Prignitz says that what attracted Pablo to Mexico was the unity of its people with their surroundings. His artwork, she notes, depicts people who blend with the landscape.[1] In many of his works, nature and those who inhabit it become one. With Pablo seeing people so much a product of their landscape and place of origin, it is interesting to look at his feelings about the places he came from and the effort he undertook to separate himself from the place where he was born and spent most of his childhood—as well as from the heritage of his father and his father's *Mayflower* ancestors.

In her 1929 book *Idols Behind Altars*, one of the first books published in English on Mexican art, Anita Brenner referred to her friend Paul Higgins as "a sincere and extremely sensitive and gifted Irishman 'gone Mexican.' " "He . . . has changed shoes for sandals and an overcoat for a serape," said Brenner, a journalist born in Mexico who attended high school and college in the United States.[2] Patricia Albers, author of a biography on photographer Tina Modotti, called Pablo a "husky blond Irish-American." [3] The University of Washington's website refers to Pablo as a "world renowned Irish Mexican Muralist." [4] Pablo O'Higgins was generally thought to be Irish or Irish-American. One person, who met him in 1945, thought he had an Irish accent.[5]

In his early years in Mexico, Pablo, who was born to Edward Higgins and Alice McAfee, began using the surname O'Higgins, giving the impression that he was of native Irish descent.[6] He once described his father as an "unprosperous Irish lawyer." [7] Another time Pablo said, "The O'Higgins family was always on the move. One of the ancestors came from Ireland and did his bit in the Revolutionary War and then as generations went by moved westward. . . ." [8] Close friends in Mexico believed he was a direct descendent of Bernardo O'Higgins, liberator of Chile and "the George Washington of Latin America." [9]

The Higgins family, however, was English. A Higgins family history provided by Pablo's nephew traces both sides of the Higgins family to pre-American Revolution New England and many relatives to the *Mayflower.*

Pablo's paternal grandmother, Harriet Ward Chapin, was a descendent of John Alden and Priscilla Mullens, who came to Massachusetts on the *Mayflower.*[10] Her history can be traced to tenth-century England. Pablo's paternal grandfather, Corydon Webster Higgins, a Presbyterian minister, was related on his mother's side to Mary Ring, a widow who sailed on the *Mayflower* with her three children. Corydon Higgins's father, Luther Higgins, came from a long line of English Higginses going back to Richard Higgins, who was born in 1613 in England and died in 1634 in Plymouth, Massachusetts.[11]

Pablo's father, Edward V. Higgins, was a proud member of the Sons of the American Revolution.[12] A 1914 yearbook from that organization lists Edward V. Higgins as a new member and his lineage as:

> Edward V. Higgins, Salt Lake City, Utah (25980). Son of Corydon Webster and Harriet Ward (Chapin) Higgins; grandson of Moses and Lucy Terry (Barton) Chapin; great-grandson of William and Mabel (Terry) Barton; great-grandson of William Barton, Colonel Rhode Island Militia and Continental Troops.[13]

Pablo's middle name is often listed as Barton, the surname of one of his Revolutionary War ancestors, rather than that of his maternal grandmother, Margery Stevenson.

Pablo's father's family was typical of New Englanders who tired of life in the eastern United States in the nineteenth century and joined the great adventure into the American West. Pablo's grandfather, Corydon Webster Higgins, was born in Massachusetts and attended Auburn Theological Seminary, in Auburn, New York. There he received an education designed to prepare him for work in the expanding American West—much as students today are educated to live and work in a world made smaller by globalization.[14] In Auburn, Corydon Higgins met Harriet Chapin, who would become his wife. They had six children: three sons and three daughters.

Consistent with Reverend Higgins's education, in 1868 the couple moved their family to what was then considered the gateway to the West, Kansas City, Missouri. It was the launching point for prospectors seeking quick fortune, young couples looking for adventure, families pursuing a better life, and freed slaves seeking to build their own lives. Due to a shortage of ministers, the Presbyterian Church at the time was losing members on the frontier to the Baptist and Methodist churches, which did not require trained clergy. Reverend Corydon Higgins was likely sent "out West" to Missouri to try to keep Presbyterians in the fold.[15]

In 1872, Harriet died, leaving Reverend Higgins with children ages eighteen, sixteen, fourteen, eleven, eight, and three. He did not remarry. He sent his three sons, Will, Edward (Pablo's father), and Charles, to Park College, near Kansas City, a new college cofounded by a Presbyterian minister with the mission of "cultural leadership to advance the westward movement." [16] The students studied in the morning and built the college's buildings in the afternoon. They were trained to take on the spiritual and professional challenges offered by the newly opened West, including Christian moral values and a strong work ethic. These values of responsibility and hard work drove the lives of not only the Higgins sons but Pablo as well.

Pablo's mother's father, John McAfee, was born in Ireland. But he was a Presbyterian from Protestant Northern Ireland, which had joined the British crown in fighting against the autonomy of native Irish Catholics. McAfee, born in 1914 in Antrim, part of Ulster, was thus Scots-Irish, his ancestors, from Scotland, having come to Ireland after 1603, when the Protestant James VI of Scotland became King James I of England, Scotland, and Ireland (and the King James of the Protestant version of the English Bible). King James confiscated land in Ulster belonging to native Irish chieftains in an attempt to tamp down the unruly Catholic native Irish who had fought against the crown. He offered the Ulster land to Protestant Scottish immigrants who he believed would be loyal to him. Many Scots immigrated to Ireland in search of a better life. They were rewarded with privileges, including education and desirable jobs–benefits that the crown denied the native, Catholic Irish, whom they considered ignorant, overly fecund idolaters.

John McAfee's family came to the United States when he was eight years old and they settled in Philadelphia, the most popular city for the Scots-Irish.[17] At twenty-five, John McAfee moved to Chicago and took up his father's trade, brick making. John married Margery Stevenson, also of Scottish descent.

Devout Presbyterians, the McAfee family joined a religious temperance community, the St. Louis–Western Colony, in Ayers (now Oakdale), Illinois, founded by a reform Presbyterian minister in November 1870. The minister recruited residents from members of his church, who were called "covenanters" after the Scottish Covenanters of the seventeenth century who pledged support of the Presbyterian Church over the Anglican Church. John and Margery had ten children, four of whom survived: Alice, Isabel, Lida, and John Jr. Alice, Pablo's mother, was born in Sparta, Illinois, in 1865.[18]

In the early 1870s, John and Margery McAfee moved their family to another Presbyterian colony in Evans, Colorado, which was modeled after the nearby Union Temperance Colony, a Utopian community founded by Horace Greeley, owner of the *New York Tribune*, and editor Nathan Meeker.[19] The Union Temperance Colony required prospective residents to fill out applications and be financially solid. It promoted agriculture rather than mining as the basis for an economy. (The quote, "Go west, young man, go west and grow up with the country!" is attributed to Greeley.[20]) The McAfee family grew up in a town whose inhabitants were moral, religious, and believed in temperance, even if not all practiced it.

In saying he was Irish, Pablo could have been referring to John McAfee, who died in 1888, sixteen years before Pablo was born, though this would not explain Pablo's saying his own father was Irish. He might have heard that his mother's father was born in Ireland, but must also have known that John McAfee was Protestant Scots-Irish from Northern Ireland, not native Irish. In fact, some family death certificates list John McAfee as born in Scotland.[21] It is doubtful that this family of devout Protestants headed by a Presbyterian minister would have misled Pablo to believe his grandfather was an Irish Catholic. In a play about the life of Harry Bridges, the founder of a union for which Pablo painted a mural, the Bridges character points out this difference: "You try writing home to an Irish Catholic mother and telling her you're living in sin with a Scottish Protestant girl." [22]

As discussed more fully in Chapter Twelve, Pablo chose to make his name unequivocally Irish, likely out of a wish that his ancestry more accurately reflect his compassion for the oppressed and their struggle for independence and a better life. In later years, in his art and his words, he would attempt to reconcile his father's Sons of the American Revolution heritage with the struggles of the Mexican people.

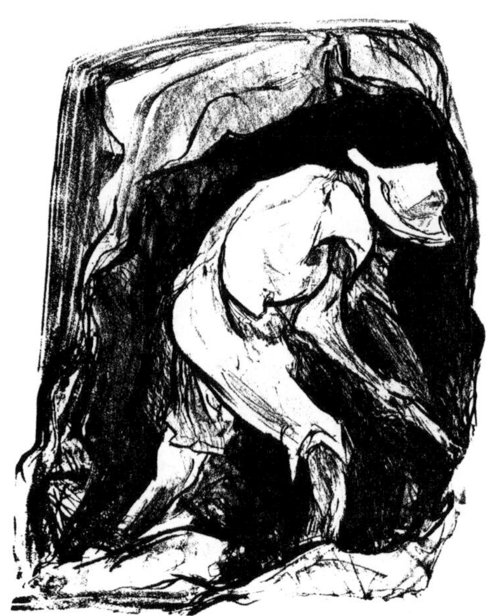

3

MORMONS AND MINERS

Salt Lake City, at the time Pablo lived there, was dominated by Mormons (members of the Church of Jesus Christ of Latter-day Saints) and mining. Both had an impact on Pablo: Mormons in making him feel like an outsider and not a part of the culture in which he mainly grew up and miners in teaching him of the struggle of the working class. John Caughlan said that Pablo subscribed to the concept that "the world should belong to the working class and that workers are people who sweat and work in mines." [1] Likely because of his childhood experiences in Utah, miners came to symbolize the working class for Pablo.

But Pablo's father's involvement in the mining industry and in a criminal prosecution of one of the world's most famous miners caused Pablo to further distance himself from his father and from Salt Lake City: he often said he was from San Francisco, California.[2] His birth certificate, however, says he was born in Salt Lake City and there is no evidence that the Higgins family, or Pablo, ever resided in the San Francisco Bay Area during Pablo's boyhood, though his half-sister, Gladys, who was fourteen years older than Pablo, possibly lived in the Bay Area beginning around 1910, when she married.[3] Sometimes, such as in Seattle in 1975, Pablo would say he was born in Salt Lake City, Utah, *por circunstancia*—by circumstance.[4] When he did mention Salt Lake City, it was usually followed by a quip about polygamy. [5]

In Mexico, Pablo produced many works of art depicting the struggles of miners. He painted an oil painting of a miner at work and produced numerous prints depicting miners. He made a print denouncing the Mexican government's declaration of a miners' strike as illegal. [6] His support of miners did not end with his art: in the late 1920s he organized miners against their American bosses.[7]

Pablo knew about mining: he grew up in a very close extended family entrenched in mining—but not on the side of miners. His family came to Utah to take advantage of the opportunities that the mining industry created. Pablo's father was an attorney for mining companies and became a judge; his uncles were investors in mines and publishers of newspapers for the mining industry. In Mexico, Pablo never revealed to anyone the extent of his family's involvement in the business of mining.

THE STORY OF HOW EDWARD HIGGINS came to be Pablo's father and Alice McAfee Higgins his mother begins when the Higgins family arrives in Salt Lake City in the late 1800s. Salt Lake City at the time was populated by two separate and only occasionally overlapping populations: mining people seeking fortune, and Mormons seeking to be left alone to live in their agriculture-based cooperative society. The Mormons were still involved in their fight over polygamy with the federal government. The U.S. government, in 1866, had abolished one of the "twin relics of barbarism" —slavery; now it sought to eliminate the other—polygamy. [8] Coincidentally, the Higginses and McAfees had lived in the same states where Mormonism grew—New York, Illinois, and Missouri.

Polygamy in the United States was practiced by members of the Mormon Church, founded by Joseph Smith in New York in 1830. Encountering hostility in New York, Pennsylvania, and Ohio, Smith and his followers settled in Jackson County, Missouri, near Kansas City, in 1838. They were not welcomed, especially when they revealed that God had promised them the entire county. The state governor issued an order to "exterminate" them.

Escaping to Illinois, they founded, on a bank of the Mississippi River, the town of Nauvoo, which provided temporary respite. There, in July 1843, Smith revealed the doctrine of polygamy to a small group of his closest followers. He said that polygamy was essential for a man to attain the "fullest exaltation in celestial glory." [9]

The following year, Smith, who was town mayor, was killed in a raid on the jail where he was being held on charges that he had muzzled an opposition newspaper. Brigham Young became Smith's successor and organized the group's arduous journey west, hauling their belongings and families across seemingly endless plains and steep mountains. They wanted to be left alone and they found the perfect place. Descending through what is now Emigration Canyon, Young looked out at a vast valley with mountains on three sides and an inviting blue lake on the other (it turned out to be saturated with salt), and declared, "This is the place," meaning the place God had chosen for them.

Faithful male Mormons dutifully married their wives' sisters, their brother's daughters. Brigham Young eventually had twenty-seven "official" wives; some count the number of wives at fifty-six.[10]

Their solitude was short-lived. Gold was discovered in 1847 in California and miners began traveling through Salt Lake City. The U.S. government passed anti-polygamy legislation in 1866 and refused to grant Utah statehood. Federal troops raided the homes of polygamists, jailing the men. The polygamist raids brought additional misfortune to the Mormons: miners. The top army commander in the area recruited his troops from the gold mines in California and encouraged them to stay and prospect in Utah.[11] Gold, silver, zinc, and copper were found and soon prospectors flowed into Utah faster than pioneer handcarts.

In 1869, the golden spike was driven at Promontory Summit, Utah, completing the transcontinental railroad and opening the doors to Utah even wider. Gold and silver were within the reach of anyone with a dream and an adventurous spirit. Fortunes were made literally overnight. One mine in Utah, the Horn Silver, paid out fifty million dollars in silver between 1875 and 1885. Its treasure was found fortuitously by a prospector resting on a rock near his camp. These stories, as well as pictures of the mansions being built from gold and silver mining, filled the newspapers of the East and created a powerful westward lure. The valley was flooded with men and sometimes women interested in quick cash, not in joining a new and seemingly odd religion.[12] After twelve-hour shifts underground, the men looked forward to strong and abundant beverages and the company of dancing girls, not women in prairie clothes.

To shield its members from the bad influences of mining, the Mormon Church discouraged mining activities in Utah and forbade its members from engaging in mining.[13] It further created distance between Mormons and non-Mormons (whom they refer to as "Gentiles") by establishing separate schools and businesses. It even had its own political party, the People's Party, which oddly had the same name as the Mexican socialist party that Pablo would later join.[14]

This separation between the Mormon and non-Mormon community in Salt Lake City continued well into the next century. As late as the 1960s, public elementary school teachers, at the beginning of the school year, asked their students to identify themselves to the class as Mormons or non-Mormons. In the 1970s, at East High School, the same high school Pablo attended, Mormons were told not to date anyone they wouldn't marry, in other words, non-Mormons.[15]

By the 1880s, mining was growing into big industry, creating jobs for educated men like the Higgins sons, in conditions that were not as gritty as the mines themselves. Mining companies needed lawyers to sort through the claims, courts needed judges to resolve disputes, and towns needed newspapers to announce the results, report the gossip, and advertise the new businesses.

The Higgins family's move west began when Will, the oldest son, took a job at the *Evans Reporter* in Colorado. There he met the three McAfee sisters through their brother Charles McAfee, age fifteen, who worked at the newspaper as an apprentice. This meeting would forever bind the three Higgins brothers (Will, Edward, and Charles) with the three McAfee sisters (Isabel, Alice, and Lida), and result in three marriages, as well as in tragedy.

Will and Isabel McAfee married in 1880 in Greeley, Colorado, the county seat. Their lives revolved around newspapers. Will Higgins was the turn-of-the-century equivalent of the cable-TV entrepreneur of the 1970s or the Internet mogul of the 1990s.

Seven years later Edward Higgins, who had graduated from law school, married Lida McAfee in Syracuse, Kansas, near the Colorado border, where he had set up his practice and was co-owner, along with Will, of the Republican-oriented *Syracuse Sentenial.*[16] His father, Reverend Corydon Higgins, officiated the marriage. That same year, Charles Higgins, who had been working for the *Caldwell County Sentinel* in Kingston, Missouri, met and married Blanche Barton Brelsford (not a McAfee) who was seventeen. That left all three Higgins boys and two of the three McAfee girls married. Only Alice McAfee, the middle sister—who would become Pablo's mother—remained unmarried.

The families made their way to Utah in 1890, after Will got a job as the telegraph editor of the *Salt Lake Tribune*, then called the newspaper for "non-Mormons, anti-Mormons and thinking Mormons."

Salt Lake City was a dirty, muddy mess. It was experiencing a boom that would transform it over twenty years from a quiet town with modest adobe homes and orchards to a busy city with horse-drawn streetcars and later electric trolleys and, thanks to the wealth from the mines, spectacular stone mansions with turrets and multistory columns outside, and elevators, shooting galleries, and bowling alleys inside.[17] The newspaper reported who had telegrams awaiting them at the Western Union office and who had checked into local hotels.[18]

When the Higginses arrived, streets were unpaved or cobblestoned. In both cases, they were covered with the droppings of horses pulling wagons and streetcars. Plumbing was a luxury; open ditches still supplied much of the culinary water for the city and open-air latrines were common.[19] Houses were going up everywhere as the city, now with 44,800 inhabitants, had more than doubled its population in ten years.[20]

Edward Higgins and his wife, Lida McAfee, moved in with Will and Isabel McAfee Higgins, their children Marjorie and Corydon, and John McAfee Jr., at a house on First Street (now First Avenue) between L and M Streets. The house had running water and, unlike the homes in Evans, a telephone. The houses in the Avenues, the city's first real residential neighborhood, with the streets lined up perfectly from west to east and north to south, were substantial, built of brick on concrete foundations, and meant to last through freezing winters and hot summers. Fragrant lilac bushes and fragile dogwoods separated them. All ten members of the Higgins and McAfee families lived in a house that was likely no more than seventeen hundred square feet. The families were close: the married Higgins and McAfee families often lived together, just next door, or a few blocks apart, and the single adult members of their families sometimes moved among their homes. They seemed to move often. The Salt Lake City directories list eight different homes as Edward Higgins's residences between the time Pablo was born in 1904 and when he graduated from high school in 1922. They ranged from one-story brick bungalows to foursquare Victorians, all in the desirable northeastern section of the city.

Soon, Will quit his job at the *Salt Lake Tribune* and, operating as Higgins & McEwan, began publishing two newspapers, the *Salt Lake Advertiser* and the *Salt Lake Stock Exchange Journal.* Will put Alice to work as a typesetter and her brother, John, as a printer.

In September, 1890, a few months after Edward Higgins and his family had arrived in Utah, Mormon Church President Wilford Woodruff issued the so-called "Manifesto," telling church members that he had had a revelation from God that they must stop practicing polygamy. This cleared the air between the Mormons and the federal government, and the Deseret territory was finally allowed statehood in 1896.[21] But the church left the mandate to practice polygamy in its scriptures, where it exists to this day.[22] Many Utah polygamists moved to Northern Mexico, where they set up colonies across the Rio Grande in the border state of Chihuahua. Others continued to practice polygamy, some secretly, others openly in Utah. At East High School in the 1970s, students who were children of polygamists called their siblings "cousins," but everyone knew—by the way they dressed, their names, or where they lived—that they were from families of practicing polygamists.[23]

The Higginses' and McAfees' attitudes toward Mormons were likely shaped by their experiences in both Illinois and Missouri and consistent with *Harper's Magazine*'s description of the reputation of the Mormons in the East:

> In the year 1830, one Joseph Smith, an idle person who had lived upon the credulity of his acquaintances, associated himself with other knaves, and pretended to have discovered, through the aid of divine revelation, the 'Book

> of Mormon' which was a sort of supplement to the Bible. Joseph Smith like other imposters, found dupes, and planted his new sect at Kirtland, Ohio.[24]

New York–educated Reverend Corydon Higgins, who soon joined his sons in Utah along with their unmarried sister, Lucy, likely would have put the Mormons in the same category as the spiritualists who had preyed on people in New York—smooth-talking folks who promised to bring back the spirits of dead relatives and who charged for their deception. Like other non-Mormons in Salt Lake City, they viewed mining, not the Mormon Church, as the reason Salt Lake City was on the map. In Will Higgins's words, "Were it not for mining, Salt Lake City would be a whistle and water tank stop on a transcontinental railroad." [25]

It is no wonder that Pablo, in adulthood, did not want to discuss Mormons, avoiding the subject by saying he was from California. In doing so, he also, intentionally or unintentionally, diverted attention from the labor scandal and execution his father was involved in—another event that put Utah on the map.

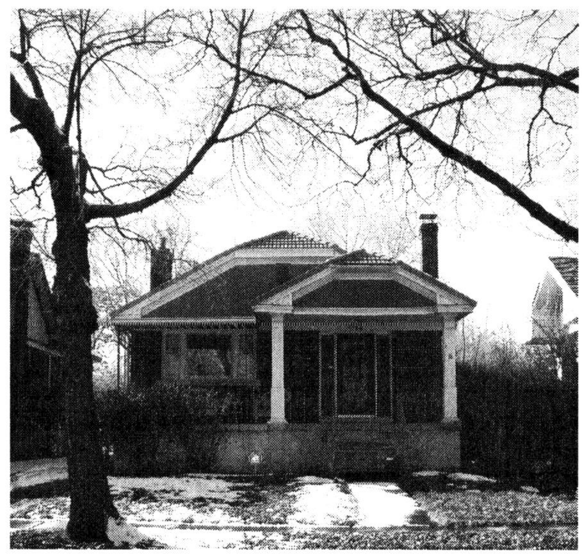

4

ALICE MCAFEE

Pablo and his mother, Alice McAfee Higgins, were very close. She was responsible for encouraging his interest in music and the visual arts. They kept in touch throughout her life with visits and many letters, which they both wrote in long, elegant, slanted handwriting, Pablo beginning the letters he wrote her every Sunday with "Dearest Mother." [1] Pablo held onto his U.S. citizenship until 1961 because, according to many friends including John Caughlan, "he didn't want problems coming to the U.S. to visit his mother." [2]

Although Pablo would later describe his mother as a farmer, she was a refined woman who loved music and the visual arts. The daughter of family friends had a recollection from her childhood of holding Alice's gloved hand as Alice led her through museums and took her to concerts. Prior to Alice's cousin getting married, Alice sent her a letter advising her on how a lady should behave. [3]

Pablo's parents' marriage began not with romance but with a double tragedy. Just before Christmas in 1890, Hazel, the daughter of Charles and Blanche Higgins, Edward Higgins's brother and sister-in-law, died twenty-two days short of her second birthday. She was buried in Salt Lake City Cemetery.[4] The death of a child was not uncommon in her time: one out of five children met Hazel's fate.[5] Currently at the Salt Lake City Cemetery, among row after row of Ostlers, Cannons, and Taylors, a few little stubs of marble stick out of the ground like lone teeth. A lovely creamy marble headstone, softened by 110 years of wind, rain, and snow, stands alone and behind it, with letters so soft they are barely visible, a tiny black tower memorializing the little girl.

Three years later, it seemed the family was recovering. Charles and Blanche had a new baby, Helen. The economy in Salt Lake City was booming. Real estate speculators were making fortunes and the city had eight new banks downtown. Will and Charles Higgins started the *Daily Stock & Mining Journal*, a sixty-page, semimonthly newspaper reporting on the mining industry.[6] The paper's offices were at 52 West 200 South, on the same block where the Alta Club, the prestigious men's club, then stood.[7] (Streets in Salt Lake City are laid out on a grid beginning at the Mormon Temple, and are named based on how far in each direction they are from the temple.) Just doors away, Edward Higgins had his law office. He advertised in the *Journal* as specializing in mining law. [8]

Spring of 1893 was welcome after a hard winter destroyed many crops in the valley. The crocuses came first, followed closely by tiny violets. A month later the maple trees burst into green and tossed their winged pods all over the ground.

But even before the lilacs had spent their clusters of blooms, there was trouble. Everyone sitting in the Silver Palace Restaurant on 200 South on May 4 with a copy of the *Salt Lake Tribune* was quiet. The far right column: "Panic on Wall Street. Prices go down with a jump. Brokers make a wild rush to sell even on a falling market. . . ."

It would get no better. The next day, "Crash on Wall Street, Brokers Thrown into a Frenzy."

This was a time when the Higginses and the McAfees would square off, with Edward and Will Higgins, Republicans, lamenting the Democratic administration of President Grover Cleveland, blaming it for the economic troubles. The McAfees would have supported President Cleveland and Vice President Adlai Stevenson. Both the president and the vice president were Presbyterians of Scots-Irish decent.

The Panic of 1893 and the worldwide depression that followed was the most serious economic crisis in the United States to that date. Some blame India's decision no longer to buy U.S. silver to use for coins, but most believe it was a direct result of the repeal of the Sherman Silver Act in 1893. The Silver Act, passed in 1890, required that the U.S. government buy large quantities of silver with notes that could be redeemed in either gold or silver. People began redeeming them in gold, depleting the country's gold reserves and making investors squeamish. In 1893, the Silver Act was repealed, and silver prices plummeted.

With the economy of Salt Lake City dependent on silver, the Higginses looked at moving elsewhere. Alice had limited options. At twenty-eight, her chances for marriage were dimmer every day. She depended on relatives for a roof over her head. According to the *Salt Lake City Directory* (these directories collect information during a certain year and publish it at the beginning of the following year, so the information would reflect the previous year's status), Alice lived in Brighton, a resort in a canyon near Salt Lake City founded by Scottish immigrants in 1871.[9] It's not clear why, but she may have worked and boarded at a hotel. Supporting herself and living on her own was not a practical option: in 1900, only nineteen percent of women held jobs. A front-page story in the *Salt Lake Tribune* asked whether "newspaper women" should marry, and if so, to newspaper men? [10] Women who worked outside the home commonly lived with family members. Only five percent of households in the U.S. in 1900 consisted of people living alone.[11]

With her relatives moving out of Salt Lake City to smaller towns, Alice could move away with her relatives and earn her keep by helping with the household. Respectable Victorian women could work at home, doing cooking, laundry, ironing, and sewing for boarders, or others, without losing social status.[12] Or Alice could stay in Salt Lake and try to get a job, but in a bad economy no one would hire a woman over a man. She could have worked in a mining town, earning good money cooking and looking after boarders. She may have tasted life in a mining town by visiting Charles and Blanche when they lived in the boomtown of Eureka, Utah. In a mining town—with a ratio of approximately one hundred men to every woman—she was sure to find a husband, but Alice likely would rather not marry a miner, and even the mining engineers seemed a lot like the miners—rough around the edges. She was likely happy to leave the mining towns to Blanche.

It is hard to imagine Alice not having some jealousy toward her sisters, as well as her sister-in-law Blanche. Wife and mother were the primary roles for women, and the only roles that many people were comfortable with. Women could work, but they rarely had careers. And "spinsters" were pitied.

Alice had a family who loved her, but she was not at the center of it, as were the other women. She helped out. She supported them. Occasionally her mind must have wandered to the question of which of the Higgins men she would have chosen had it been her place to choose. Charles Higgins had endless energy and enthusiasm. The next bonanza was always around the corner. And he was the perfect broker, which is what he called himself, bringing investors (in the city directory they called themselves "capitalists") to projects. A mining claim is nothing until you find a capitalist to invest in it.

Will Higgins was a man everyone loved. When he spoke, everyone listened because he always had something dry and witty to say. He would tell stories that never ended, and they usually involved an old prospector, a burro, and some unimaginable things happening. He often printed these in his newspapers. His wit would later earn him the title, "the inimitable Will C. Higgins." [13]

Edward Higgins was the serious one. Generally he was pondering the ramifications of what Charles was proposing or Will was critiquing. But he had a steadiness and evenness to him that was comforting. Alice could see Charles or even Will investing his life's savings in a hole in the ground, but not Edward. He was the most stolid of the three, and the most conservative. Because he represented mining companies, he was the one who would have clashed most with Alice's brother, John McAfee Jr., who always spoke up for the worker.

By July 1893, the newspapers were laying off their employees. Banks in town had closed and some of the owners of the grand homes on South Temple street had gone bankrupt. Unemployment rose to 18 percent in 1893 and 22 percent in 1894. Railroads started going under.[14] Silver mines closed and more than one hundred banks in the West went into receivership.[15]

All of the extended Higgins family moved out of Salt Lake City. Charles and Blanche Higgins moved to Lewiston, Utah (later called Mercur), a gold mining town that had the first cyanide plant in the nation, which allowed gold to be extracted from ore more efficiently. Charles Higgins launched the *Lewiston Mercury*. Will and his family moved to Cedar City, population 100, and started the county's first newspaper, the *Iron County Record*, on December 8, 1893. Alice chose to join Edward, Lida, and their daughter Gladys in Nephi, eighty-six miles south of Salt Lake City, in Juab County.[16]

Edward practiced law in the small town while Lida and Alice looked after Gladys and took care of a house that would have been small and without running water. Their time together in this remote outpost accessible only by stagecoach (the railroad didn't come until 1923) would have cemented their relationships, but this was cut short.[17]

At the Salt Lake Cemetery, the white marble headstone in front of Hazel's is that of Edward's wife Lida. She died on March 30, 1894, at age twenty-six. There is no death certificate listing the cause of her death.

Lida was buried next to Hazel, and the two of them remain there, between strangers, the Brookses and the McAllisters. Lida could have died in childbirth (though there is no record of an infant's death). Lida's headstone reads: "Lida, wife of E.V. Higgins. Faithful unto death." Other stones for wives read "Beloved," or "Rest in Peace."

Perhaps as a hedge against the economy, Edward, who was in private practice, ran for public office as a district judge for the Fifth District in Cedar City, Utah. Will Higgins, whose nickname was Judge since he'd served a term as a probate judge in Kansas, encouraged Edward to run and endorsed him in his newspaper. Edward won and was sworn in in January 1896 at the same time Utah grandly celebrated becoming a state. Higgins was one of the first judges of the new State of Utah.[18]

Nineteen months after Lida's death, on November 9, 1896, Edward married Alice.[19] Edward had no duty to marry Alice, but certainly it was a convenient thing to do. In some cultures, a man whose wife dies has the right to marry her unmarried sister in order to have someone to look after the children.[20] Some men are required to marry their sister-in-law and take care of her children if their brother dies.[21] And it would have been in the best interest of Gladys to keep the household as intact as possible and not subject her to more change. But Alice must have felt that she was Edward's second choice—because she was. In many families of that time, the younger daughters couldn't marry until the older ones had. Alice had been passed over twice by Higgins men: once when Will Higgins had married the oldest McAfee girl, Isabel, and again, when Edward had married the youngest McAfee girl, Lida.

Edward Higgins was extremely knowledgeable about mining. As a judge based in Cedar City, he presided over the trials of mining cases, including the original jury trial of *Mammoth Mining Company v. Grand Central Mining Company*, a landmark case that established the ownership of mineral veins that meander beyond boundaries when different mining companies claim rights to them.[22] The opinion he wrote demonstrates a deep understanding of a highly technical area of mining law, including the geological issues involved in determining what constitutes a vein of ore. His opinion was affirmed by the Utah Supreme Court and again by the United States Supreme Court.

In August, 1897, Edward and Alice's first son, Roger Chapin Higgins, was born in Nephi, Utah.[23] (Chapin is the name of a Higgins *Mayflower* ancestor.)

In 1900, Edward, Alice, Gladys, and Roger returned to Salt Lake City. Edward established a partnership with another mining attorney, Edward Senior.[24] In an ad, Higgins advertised his specialties as mining law, corporate law, and irrigation law.[25] Will Higgins, meanwhile, had worked as mining editor for the *Salt Lake Herald*, and, in 1899 founded the *Salt Lake Mining Review,* whose masthead read, "devoted to mining, milling and kindred industries." Its readers were "men who make mines and equip them." [26] Several newspapers around the state announced the launch of the publication, calling Will a "well-known newspaper man" and "ablest writer on mining in the state." [27] Will also was an investor in mining claims, including around Bingham Canyon.[28]

Paul Stevenson Higgins was born to Edward V. and Alice McAfee Higgins on March 1, 1904, at home in a brick bungalow in Salt Lake City, near Liberty Park, the city's largest park. Pablo's brother, Roger, was six, and his half-sister, Gladys, was fourteen. His father was forty-five and his mother was thirty-nine.

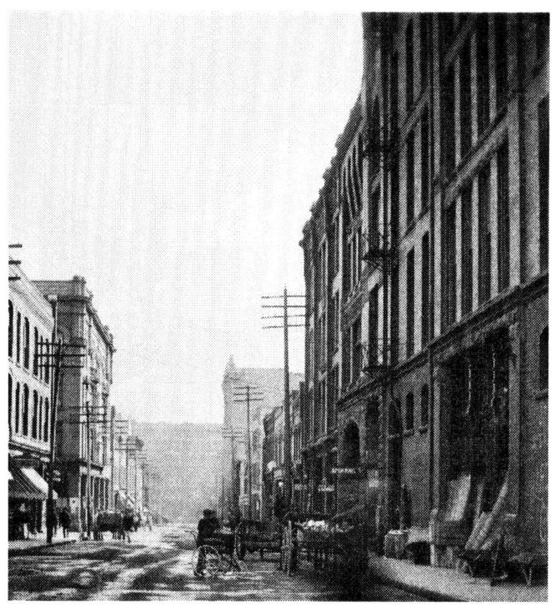

5

SALT LAKE CITY AND EL CAJON

A book of Pablo's drawings and sketches published in Mexico in 1987 says that by the time he met Diego Rivera at age twenty, Pablo had "dedicated his life to the cause of the worker." [1] An exhibit catalog from 1995 says, "His social commitment and his goal upon arriving in our country were the same as those he fought for in the United States." [2] An article published by a museum in Mexico said Pablo "always identified with the marginalized sectors of the population." [3]

If by age twenty, Pablo's heart was already with the worker and he identified with marginalized people, it would have been based on two childhood experiences that may have opened his eyes to the plight of the worker and the *campesino*: one he spoke of all the time, and another he never spoke of.

Alma Reed, in *The Mexican Muralists*, said that Pablo's "identification with Mexico came about as the result of childhood experiences in El Cajon Valley, San Diego County, California, where his parents established their home." [4] When he painted a mural in Hawai'i in 1952, all of the publicity materials referred to Pablo as "raised on his father's ranch in El Cajon, California." [5]

In 2004, at an exhibit in Hawai'i, one of the captions for the pieces read, "Having been raised on a ranch in the El Cajon Valley of California, O'Higgins sympathized with the common laborer." [6]

When Pablo was two, his family may have moved to El Cajon, San Diego County, California, for two years.[7] The *Salt Lake City Directory* says, "moved to El Cajon," but his family is not listed in the city directories for San Diego or El Cajon for those years.[8]

They are not listed in the San Diego County directories at all until 1917.[9] But whether his family lived in El Cajon, lived in San Diego and spent weekends in El Cajon, or just visited El Cajon, it was the place that captured Pablo's heart and that he emphasized when speaking of his childhood.

Today it is difficult finding any open space in El Cajon, much less the ranches or vineyards that drew people to El Cajon during Pablo's childhood. It is a sprawling suburb of mostly 1950s homes, some from Sears Roebuck kits.[10] Its main street has the look of many other Southern California towns, with beige stucco buildings that normally house chain stores. But El Cajon's storefronts have locally owned businesses. On the corner of Main and Avocado stand the Ali Baba Family Restaurant and La Pita. Down the street, coming soon, the Baghdad Market.

While Pablo suggested that he almost grew up in Mexico, saying it was just fifteen (actually twenty) miles north of the Mexican border, in 1909, El Cajon was not a lot different from Utah in terms of demographics.[11] In 1900, its population of 563 was 98 percent white, mainly middle class, conservative, and religious.[12] The town had two churches, Presbyterian and Episcopal. In spite of its proximity to Mexico, it was heavily populated by Midwesterners. A historian wrote, "It was as if a whole town from Nebraska or Illinois had moved to this agricultural suburb of San Diego." [13] The 1900 census had no category for Mexicans, but recorded ten "Indians," four of whom were members of the family of a Mexican laborer. One hundred percent of El Cajon residents spoke English and 99 percent read and wrote English. In 1905, travel between El Cajon and San Diego was by stagecoach.[14]

In 1908, El Cajon's residents listed their occupations as ranchers, butchers, and clerks. The town, whose name means *drawer*, sat in a small valley with dirt roads winding around homes—many grand homes of doctors and army majors—and through acres of vineyards and olive trees. Pictures in the county's historical archives show families in formal dress sitting on verandas or playing tennis on makeshift courts among vineyards. Others show workers "picking raisins" or olives.[15] Having a ranch in El Cajon for well-to-do people living in San Diego was like people in San Francisco having a small vineyard in Napa.

Two years later, the Edward Higgins family was back in Salt Lake City, this time living in a two-story brick foursquare Victorian home at 144 South 1100 East, one block from the mining mansions of South Temple street.[16] They lived in this house when Pablo was four and five years old.[17] Pablo remembered it; in a letter to his mother many years later he wrote, "Do you remember how I used to lie under the living room table on 11th East and think?" [18]

In Salt Lake City, Pablo's family's life continued to involve his large extended family whose professions centered on mining. Pablo's father had a law practice in the Boston Building—at the non-Mormon end of the three-block downtown—specializing in mining law.

The *Salt Lake City Directory* lists Edward Higgins as a resident of Salt Lake City and working in Salt Lake City for every year since Pablo's birth, except 1907 and 1908, when Pablo was three and four years old, and in 1917, 1918, and 1919, when he was thirteen through fifteen years old (though these directories reflect the previous year's status). School records indicate that Pablo attended elementary school in Salt Lake City at Irving School during at least one of the earliest grades, and then at Longfellow Elementary School from third through sixth grades.[19]

During the first three years after returning from El Cajon to Salt Lake City around 1909, Pablo's family was hit by three tragedies. Two months after marrying, Corydon, the son of Will and Isabel, returned home from work early one day and within minutes was dead. Corydon's new wife had arranged to have the apartment fumigated and had not told him.[20] On a good day, the family saw the new wife's actions as careless, on a bad day as suspicious.[21] Just a year later, another blow: Corydon's sister, Marjorie's, son, Thaddeus Ireland, died. He was just one year old and was Will and Isabel's first grandchild. Uncle Will took Isabel to Ocean Park, California, to recover, but she too died, of heart failure, at age fifty.

By 1912, Alice Higgins had lost her two sisters. Alice, at forty-nine, was the last of the McAfee girls.

Alice was the greatest influence on Pablo. A chronology of Pablo's life by Mexican art critic Francisco Reyes Palma says that Edward Higgins's job as a judge required that he temporarily reside in San Francisco and San Diego and that Pablo's childhood was spent closer to his mother.[22] The first talent she helped develop in Pablo was for music. She had Pablo study piano from age six and wanted him to become a concert pianist. He practiced every night after he and his brother had washed the dishes and cleaned the kitchen so that their mother could rest.[23] Years later, he didn't have a tolerance for Beethoven because it reminded him of all the repetitious drills he had to play as a child.[24] He loved Chopin and Bach, however, and he gave his first public recital at age ten.[25]

Pablo was extremely sensitive to music. In August 1915, his mother took him to the Mormon Tabernacle at Temple Square in downtown Salt Lake City to hear Ignace Jan Paderewski, concert pianist and later prime minister of Poland, play Chopin. Paderewski was on a three hundred–concert tour in the United States to raise money for Polish relief efforts.[26]

Before he began playing, Paderewski spoke to the audience sitting on the hard wooden benches of the long dome-ceilinged auditorium. He vividly described the war in Europe, which had begun the year before, and how millions of Polish families were wandering homeless and hungry, their only food bark from trees and decomposing horses from the battlefield. The concert tour sought to raise a million dollars for the Polish people who were facing certain starvation and death with the winter approaching.[27]

Even without the backdrop of the story of the suffering of the Polish refugees, the music conveyed struggle and futile attempts at resolution. The Chopin nocturnes must have had a tremendous power for a child who had recently experienced tragedies in his family and who had just heard of the profound suffering of innocent victims of what turned out to be one of the world's most horrific wars.

As Pablo waited for the bittersweet ending of the piece, the crowd burst into thundering applause. That was it for Pablo. He began sobbing. His mother, frightened, took his arm and excused them as they pushed past knees and left the hall, hurrying past the tables of bisque dolls that were being sold to raise money.[28] For an eleven-year-old who was very attuned to music, the combination of powerful music and vivid images of suffering could have been painful and frightening.

Later in Mexico, he had a similar response to a performance. At the end of August Strindberg's play *Miss Julie*, which he saw with writer Elena Poniatowska, the audience began clapping before the actress was finished speaking and Pablo became paralyzed with anger and had to be helped out of the theater. He later told Poniatowska about his experience as a child at the Paderewski concert.[29]

Pablo's emotional connection to music is reflected in his visual art. Critics often refer to music when talking about his work; one called his oil paintings "visual symphonies." [30] A fellow painter described Pablo's landscapes as paintings that "could have been produced only by someone who knew music." [31]

Pablo and his mother shared an appreciation for art and music, and a sense of wonder at the simplest things. When Pablo became involved in something, he lost himself in it. He could go for hours drawing or examining something that interested him, oblivious to time passing or people around him. As a child, he wandered away from a school field trip because he was interested in studying some plants he'd seen. When he returned home after dark, his parents did not punish him, but were simply glad he had been found.[32] But Alice and Edward themselves were practical, not dreamers. In the letter he wrote to his mother about lying under the table when he was five, he recalls she would "accuse me of dreaming and send me off to bed."

Around the time he was ten years old, Pablo's interests began shifting to art. He won a prize for an urban landscape drawing, and he became interested in acid etching while reading a book on Rembrandt. Alice encouraged him and he spent hours in the kitchen experimenting.[33] Pablo said it was Alice, who, ten years later, sent him the article that led him to Diego Rivera.

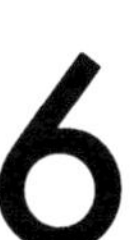

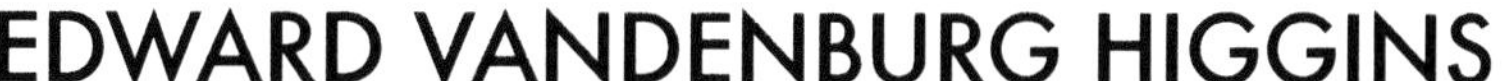

6 EDWARD VANDENBURG HIGGINS

Edward V. Higgins appears in a photograph along with Pablo, at around age five, and his older brother, Roger. The three stand alongside a stream in what appears to be Little Cottonwood Canyon in the mountains east of Salt Lake City. The two boys are dressed for a hike, with boots and a camera or canteen. Both are solemn-faced. Other than wearing boots, Edward Higgins, a serious-looking and imposing figure, could be dressed for a day at the office. He wears a white dress shirt, tie, and jacket, and is smoking a pipe.

Pablo's father influenced him, but in a different way than his mother. While his mother's influence can be seen in his love of art and music and his caring nature, his father's likely led to Pablo's values of hard work and responsibility.

Edward Higgins was described by a relative as a "conservative Republican, dry in every sense of the word." [1] Rather than being itinerant or "unprosperous," as Pablo once described him, he was a respected and successful member of the Utah legal community. In the extended Higgins family, Edward Higgins was held out as a model for other lawyers who actually were unsuccessful. Edward McKinley, Pablo's nephew, said, "my father *was* an itinerant lawyer, and he thought that Edward V. Higgins was a cut above the rest. My father idolized him." [2] Upon his death, the *Salt Lake Tribune* lauded Pablo's father as "one of Utah's most esteemed pioneer jurists," referring to his having been one of the first judges for the state of Utah.[3]

In 1911, Edward joined the Utah attorney general's office as an assistant attorney general. In 1914, he was assigned to the case of a lifetime, one that received international attention, put Utah on the map worldwide, and gave Pablo a secret he kept throughout his life.[4] Art historian James Oles has suggested that Pablo changed his last name from Higgins to O'Higgins so that no one would make the connection between him, his father, and the Joe Hill case.[5]

The Joe Hill saga began the night of January 10, 1914, when two men entered a Salt Lake City grocery store as the owner and his two sons were preparing to close. Moments later, the grocer and his older son were shot dead.

Joe Hill (born Hillstrom) was a miner who had recently lost his job in the silver mines of Park City.[6] He was also a songwriter and a member of the radical Industrial Workers of the World (IWW or the "Wobblies"), which had established a presence in Utah mining communities.[7] At 11:30 p.m. on the same night as the murders, he appeared at the home of a physician friend with a bullet wound in his chest. He explained that he had been shot during a quarrel over a woman. As he left the physician's home, a gun dropped out of his coat. Two days later, Hill was arrested and charged with the murders. The case became a labor cause when the IWW provided Hill with a defense lawyer from the Western Federation of Labor. Soon Hill, already well known for his labor organizing songs, became a symbol of the worker helpless to defend himself against the powerful capitalist mining companies and government.

Hill offered no details or corroboration for his story. No one stepped forward to offer him an alibi. A jury found him guilty, and, on July 8, 1914, he was sentenced to die the following September. Hill appealed his conviction to the Utah Supreme Court. Edward Higgins was one of two assistant attorney generals for the state of Utah who, along with the attorney general, argued that Hill's conviction be upheld.[8]

Throughout the Hill controversy, public officials and the press typically depicted the IWW as an anarchistic, undesirable "element" that had "infested" Zion (the term Mormons use to refer to Utah, their "promised land").[9]

When Utah Governor William Spry granted Hill a temporary reprieve at President Woodrow Wilson's request, the *Salt Lake Tribune* carried a statement by Utah Supreme Court Justice William McCarthy warning that "hundreds of this undesirable element will swarm to this state and, using Hill as an excuse, will undoubtedly attempt to create a reign of terror." [10] Governor Spry was quoted by a New York newspaper as saying:

> This fight has just begun. We will not stop until the state is free of the lawless element that now infests it. . . . I am going to see that inflammatory street speaking is stopped, and at once. They can call it free speech or by any other name if they wish. It must be stopped, and if the proper officers do not stop it I will get a force here in Utah that will stop it.[11]

It is not surprising, given Utah's history, that religion also became an issue. Hill supporters complained that he had been treated unfairly because he was not a Mormon. This accusation deepened the ever-present rift in Utah between Mormons and non-Mormons. Pablo's family was near the center of the storm as they lived just blocks from the Governor's home and Pablo's father worked for the state.[12]

The case put Utah in the international spotlight. The controversy pervaded the press, the schools, and the general activities of the community, from Hill's trial in summer, 1914, through his execution in November 1915. The events of the case were reported extensively in the three local newspapers. The extended Higgins family, mostly Republicans, would have been interested in the case not only because of Edward's role in it, but because it involved the mining community.[13] Pablo's uncle John McAfee

Jr., a lifelong union member, would have discussed it from the point of view of the worker. Union members were drawn into a controversy surrounding the position of the unions—it was first reported in the newspapers that the Utah delegates to the American Federation of Labor (AFL) convention joined the AFL in condemning the execution, but the delegates later denied they had done so.[14] If Pablo were sensitive enough to cry in response to clapping at a piano concert in August, surely he would have been aware of the tension in the city, and possibly in his own family during the autumn of 1915.

Nearly everyone in Salt Lake City picked a side in the debate—even school principals, who officially expressed their support for the death sentence.[15] Mining company executives supported the actions of the state, congratulating Governor Spry on his "manly" stand in not succumbing to pressure from those motivated by "cheap sentimentality." [16]

In the weeks before the execution, death threats were directed toward Governor Spry and members of his administration. Bomb threats targeted the Spry home at 368 First Avenue, only three block away from the Higgins home at 37 H Street, and four blocks from Longfellow Elementary School, where Pablo was a sixth grader.[17] Bomb threats were also directed to the new State Capitol building, where the attorney general's and governor's offices were located, and where Edward Higgins worked.[18] Pablo's brother, Roger, a seventeen-year-old student at the time, may have been working at the attorney general's office as well, and certainly would have shared his experiences with his brother.[19] Both buildings were protected by armed guards and bathed in arc lights for several nights before the execution. The *New York Tribune* reported that Salt Lake was "terror stricken" by IWW threats. On November 19, 1915, Hill was taken to the yard of the Salt Lake State Prison next to what is now Sugar House Park. A red heart was pinned to his white shirt. A phalanx of men stood ready to shoot. Hill's last word was "Fire!" Pablo never spoke of his father's involvement in the Joe Hill case.

This does not, however, mean that he was unaware of his father's participation in the appeal that sent Hill to the firing squad. He generally did not speak about his past, and when he did, he usually emphasized aspects of it that were consistent with his politics, rather than those that revealed the bourgeois or conservative nature of his family.[20]

Pablo may have alluded to the case, or at least what it came to represent, in his art. In 1951, Pablo produced a lithograph called *Justice* (see p. 182). It depicts a skeleton or *calavera* dressed in a judge's robe dancing with a prostitute. The lithograph is titled *Justice is a farce of the rich, the gringo and comparsa*—that last word, meaning extras, like movie extras—making a rhyme with *farsa* (farce). Tossed to the ground is a document titled "Rights of the Working Class." This commentary on the judiciary could apply to much of Pablo's family, as Pablo's father and his uncle Will had served terms as judges, and his brother Roger was a candidate for judge at the time of his death. (Oddly, the *calavera* wears a mortarboard, like a graduate at a ceremony.) It also could have referred to the abuse of the judicial system during the McCarthy era: the year Pablo made the lithograph, he was listed in a report by the House Un-American Activities Committee investigating activities of alleged Communists in Mexico.[21]

Throughout his life in Mexico, Pablo identified with marginalized people. He never took the side of power, industry, or the state over that of the poor and powerless. This suggests where his sentiments would have been in the Joe Hill case. As he sought the acceptance of the Mexican workers and *campesinos*, Marxists, and Communists in his new life, logically he would have never mentioned his father's role in the Joe Hill case. Keeping this a secret would not be difficult. His father and brother died during Pablo's early years in Mexico. His mother spoke no Spanish and was fiercely devoted to him. He kept the existence of his conservative sister a secret from his wife, María, and he maintained no friends from Utah after he left.

Even if Pablo had been oblivious to the Joe Hill controversy at age eleven, he obviously learned about it later—he sang the popular folk song, the "Ballad of Joe Hill," and was a houseguest of its composer, Earl Robinson. He must have linked his father to the case, as it would be an irresistible coincidence to learn of a labor martyr executed in one's sparsely populated home state at the same time one's father was a lawyer for the state prosecutor.

Edward Higgins represented much of what Pablo, as an adult, came to denounce both personally and politically.[22] As a professional, Edward was, in the eyes of the Communist Party, a member of the hated bourgeoisie; as a judge, he was part of the "farce" called the judiciary; and as an attorney for the mining industry, he was a participant in the capitalist exploitation of the worker.

From all indications, Edward Higgins and his son Roger were two of a kind and Pablo was different. Pablo does not seem to have found a close companion in Roger or in his half sister, Gladys. His lack of closeness to Gladys may be explained by their age difference—she was fourteen when Pablo was born, and had married and moved away by the time he was six. Roger, however, was only six years older than Pablo and the boys grew up together.

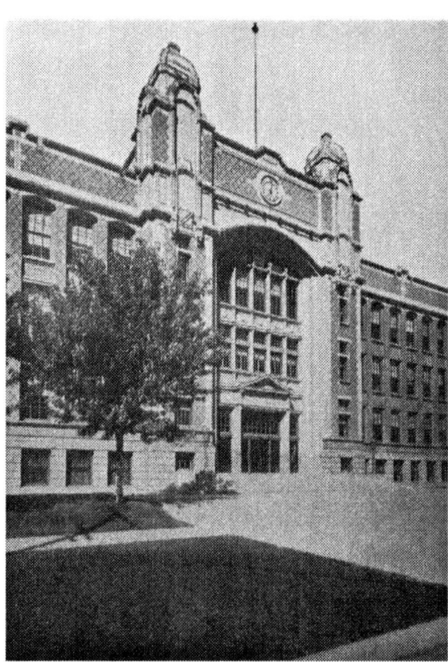

7

WORLD WAR I

The war quickly replaced Joe Hill on the front pages of the local newspapers. World War I was one of the deadliest wars in history, involving more than seventy million troops and killing more than fifteen million people. Pablo spent the years of the United States' involvement, 1917 to 1918, in San Diego, a major naval center.

The end of the Joe Hill case must have been a relief for the Higgins family. They caught up on family events—Edward's fifty-eighth birthday had taken place two days before the execution—and Uncle Will had married Eva I. Cook on December 16, 1916, four years after his wife Isabel's death.

At the end of 1915, the war still seemed far away from the western United States, but it had edged closer with Germany's April torpedoing of the passenger ship *Lusitania*, killing one thousand people, including 128 Americans traveling from New York to England.[1] Rumors spread that Germans were cutting off the hands of Belgian babies. Utah's German immigrant community was unfairly punished. One store owned by a German immigrant was defaced with angry black letters, "Death to Huns." Salt Lake City's large Greek community was also harassed until July 1917, when Greece joined the Allies. Pablo most certainly had friends in school who were of German and Greek ancestry and may have seen them treated poorly by other students. The Presbyterian Church the Higginses attended also would have included members of German descent.

Babe Ruth, pitching thirteen shutout innings in game two of the World Series for the Boston Red Sox, provided some distraction, but still the war stayed on everyone's minds. Alice must have dreaded the possibility of the United States entering the war. She had seen what Will and Isabel had gone through when their son Corydon died. Her son Roger was nineteen years old and a college student. As a member of the Reserve Officer Training Corps (ROTC), he would be obligated to go to war.

In April 1917, the United States joined the Allied forces, including Russia, the United Kingdom, Italy, France, and Japan, in the war against the Central Powers of Germany, Austria-Hungary, the Ottoman Empire, and Bulgaria. For the next nineteen months every page of the *Salt Lake Tribune* was filled with war news. "Salt Laker Bags His First Teuton," read a headline. The paper printed approved "War Menus," such as codfish balls and stewed prunes, to help families survive "meatless Monday." It announced the "death knell" of the Industrial Workers of the World (IWW), and ran ads for tonics (mostly alcohol) for nervous women.[2] German immigrants were interred at Fort Douglas under suspicion of being spies.

When the Joe Hill case ended, Edward quit his job at the Utah attorney general's office and spent two years in San Diego. The San Diego County directories for 1917 and 1918 list Edward and Alice living in San Diego at 3360 30th Street.[3] They may have rented this home.[4] Edward practiced law in San Diego during these years, first as "Wood Higgins and Wood" and then on his own.[5] The family may have had a ranch in El Cajon at this time, though they do not appear as residents of El Cajon in the *San Diego Directory*, but rather of the city of San Diego.

El Cajon had changed dramatically since the Higgins family had been there in 1909. By 1912, half of the valley had been developed. El Cajon Boulevard stretched fifteen miles from El Cajon to San Diego; the tracks of the San Diego & Southern Railroad paralleled the highway. Eight trains a day carried people from San Diego to their "beautiful country home[s]." [6]

The city was self-governing. Its main issues were "the liquor question" and public utilities.[7] Indeed, the sale of liquor was prohibited "in any way excepting by druggists under medical orders."

Pablo completed his eighth-grade year in San Diego in 1918 as Roger was graduating from Westminster College, a Presbyterian college in Salt Lake City.[8] Upon graduation, Roger entered the U.S. Army as a first sergeant in the 145th Field Artillery of Utah and began his training at Camp Kearny, eleven miles north of San Diego.[9]

In San Diego, Pablo, who was fourteen, could visit Balboa Park to get a taste of what Roger was experiencing. The park was a center of activity for San Diego's massive war efforts—a major port city, it was home to naval, army, and marine bases during World War I.[10] The park's exposition grounds, the venue of the Panama-California Exposition from March 1915 to January 1917, had been turned over to the navy. (To the dismay of the horticulturists, its lily ponds were being used to teach sailors to swim.)[11] The park hosted dances and concerts nearly every weekend. On June 12, Madame Shumann-Heink sang "O Danny Boy," "a mother's farewell to her son," to a crowd of five thousand men in uniform. Other activities were less welcoming, such as the navy's mock gas attacks.[12]

The comfort of Roger being nearby was short-lived: his regiment left for Europe on September 2, 1918, just as Pablo was starting his freshman year of high school at San Diego High School, "Old Grey Castle," not far from the family's new home at 422 Brookes Avenue, near Balboa Park.[13] Developed between 1910 and 1920, the neighborhood, called Hillcrest, is now very trendy and the center of San Diego's gay community. Edward and Alice both registered to vote in San Diego County as Republicans.[14]

Although Pablo's high school was made up mainly of Anglo-Americans, San Diego had an increasing population of immigrants from Mexico. San Diego, of course, had been part of Mexico until 1821. During the Mexican Revolution, between 1910 and 1920, nearly one million legal immigrants came to the United States from Mexico, as well as tens of thousands of illegal immigrants.[15]

Pablo's family depended on Uncle Will and Aunt Eva for news of their family and friends in Salt Lake City. In the spring, they began hearing about a crazy flu that was appearing in the Midwest. The children's taunt of the day became, "I had a little bird, his name was Enza, I opened up the window and in-flu-enza."

The epidemic of what came to be called the Spanish Flu (because it was first reported in the uncensored Spanish press) began in the United States in military bases on the East Coast in March 1918, and had worked its way westward by fall. It would kill as many as one hundred million people worldwide—more than all the wars of the twentieth century combined.[16] It killed 20 percent of those affected and, oddly, it claimed a disproportionate number of healthy people between twenty and forty years old, rather than the very young or elderly, who are usually the main flu fatalities.

San Diego public officials thought the city's climate was too temperate for an epidemic of la grippe. Yet in October, just as in Salt Lake City, the flu hit San Diego hard. Camp Kearny was put in quarantine. On October 11, all theaters, "moving picture houses," dance halls, churches, and bathhouses were closed, and two days later "all public places" were closed. On October 18, residents working indoors in factories or offices were required to wear gauze masks.[17] Women set to work sewing them. Had the Higgins family had a ranch in El Cajon, they likely would have moved Pablo there: any family who had the means to move to the country did, but the flu could sweep over a town in a few days via a mail carrier's delivery.

On November 11, 1918, the war was over. Roger was coming home.

The flu ended as abruptly as it had started. Crowds poured into the streets to celebrate and, based on *Salt Lake Tribune* headlines, in Salt Lake City the flu seemed to disappear overnight.[18] In San Diego, it lingered until December, the month in which it took its greatest toll of 2,039 cases and 188 deaths.[19]

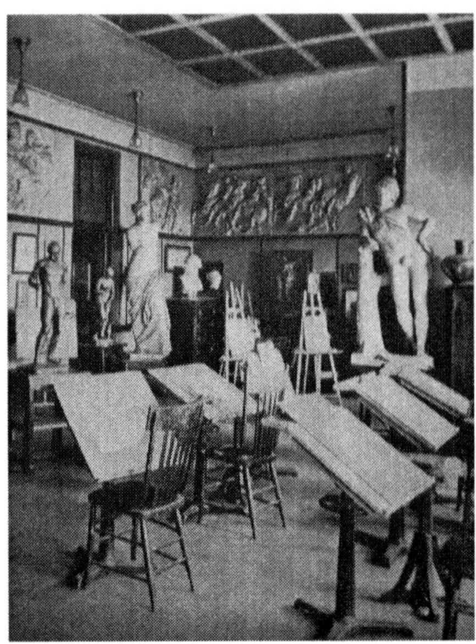

8

AN ART EDUCATION

As much as Pablo downplayed his childhood in Salt Lake City, he was influenced by the art education he received there. Ironically, his first exposure to mural painting may have been in Utah during his childhood: the Mormon Church was busy constructing temples and training and hiring artists to paint murals on their walls.[1] In 1890 the church sent a delegation of "art missionaries" to Paris to study painting so they would be better trained to paint murals in the Mormon Temple in Salt Lake City.[2] The Utah painter who most influenced Pablo, LeConte Stewart, though not an "art missionary," had painted murals for the Mormon Temple in Hawaiʻi.

During his sophomore and senior years of high school in Salt Lake City, Pablo studied under two of Utah's best-known artists, James Taylor Harwood and Stewart. Stewart seems to have modeled the kind of artist Pablo wanted to be; from Harwood, he may have learned what path he did not want to take.

In fall of 1919, back from San Diego, Pablo enrolled at East High School.[3] He earned excellent grades, ranging from 83 to 98. During his second semester, his art teacher was Harwood, who was the first Utah painter to study in Paris and the first to have a painting accepted in the Paris Salon.

Harwood, who was born in Lehi, Utah, in 1860, was classically trained. He had studied under Virgil Williams at the San Francisco School of Design (now the San Francisco Art Institute) and in Paris at the Académie Julian and the competitive École des Beaux-Arts.[4] At the Julian and École, students drew from plaster casts of the human body, and then from live models of both sexes and of various ages. The professor visited twice a week to critique student work. The courses also included excursions to paint landscapes.[5]

At the time he taught Pablo, Harwood painted mainly impressionistic, romanticized landscapes.[6] Harwood's 1893 *All the World's a Stage, Liberty Park*, depicting family members strolling and relaxing in Salt Lake City's Liberty Park, evokes Georges Seurat's *A Sunday Afternoon on the Island of La Grande Jatte–1884*. One of Harwood's students, Lee Greene Richards, said that he learned as much from Harwood as he had from his teachers at the Julian in Paris.[7] Harwood advised promising artists that they should study in Paris.[8] Harwood also taught mural painting including to Lee Greene Richards, who later painted murals in Utah's public buildings and Mormon facilities.

Harwood achieved mastery in etching; in the mid-twenties he was teaching what is said to be the only course in color etching in the United States.

Pablo may have learned from Harwood how he did not want to study. He had no interest in or patience for spending hours and hours indoors drawing from statues of the human body. And unlike even the most devout Mormon "art missionary" being trained in Paris to paint religious paintings, he never painted a female nude.[9]

Pablo returned to San Diego High School as a junior in the 1920–1921 academic year where he studied "Music-Harmony" and journalism as well as Spanish and his required subjects, earning 85 to 90 in all his classes. During this time, Pablo would have gotten his first education in Communism through the so-called "Red Scare" of 1919 to 1920, when the United States feared that the Bolshevik Revolution that had just taken place in Russia could be replicated here.[10]

San Diego High School was as homogenous as East High in Salt Lake City: only about five or so students in his class had Hispanic surnames. The yearbook lists Pablo as a member of the Musical Society but not the Spanish Club. [11]

Moving back and forth between Salt Lake City and San Diego every few years might have taken a toll on Pablo. During his childhood, Pablo did not establish any close friendships that he maintained over the years, or even that he spoke about later.[12] He was introspective and, aside from the Musical Society, not interested in the social life at the large public high schools he attended. His high school yearbooks reveal schools whose social life focused on sports and personality.

Pablo returned to Salt Lake City's East High for his last year of high school.[13] The *Salt Lake City Directory* lists Pablo and Roger as living at 265 Fifth Avenue with E. V. Higgins (wives were not listed unless living alone). The house, a foursquare Victorian approximately eight blocks from downtown, still stands. Pablo studied art with LeConte Stewart both semesters and, during his last semester, it was his only class.[14] Stewart made a great impression on Pablo and his art.

LeConte Stewart is one of Utah's best-known regionalists. Stewart taught many well-known Utah artists and, after teaching at East High, headed the University of Utah art department for eighteen years.

Stewart was born in Glenwood, a small town in Utah. He began his studies at the University of Utah in 1912, and in 1913 and 1914 studied at the Art Students League Summer School in Woodstock, New York.[15] While many other artists of the time were doing their mandatory studies in Europe, Stewart felt European study was unnecessary, and in 1924 he enrolled in the Pennsylvania Academy of Fine Arts in Chester Springs.[16] Stewart, who described himself as a "tonal impressionist," is best known for his paintings of the countryside and small towns of Utah.[17] His paintings include dilapidated barns, rusty trucks, and billboards. He did not believe in romanticizing the outdoors or rural life but portraying life as it is. Stewart's choice of subject matter, as well as his decision to study art in the United States rather than Europe reflects, in the view of James Swensen, assistant professor of art at Brigham Young University, "an important shift in the 1920s and 1930s when American Isolationism following WWI begins to change not only what American artists were painting but where they were studying." [18]

Stewart had just returned from Hawai'i, where he'd spent two years painting large murals for the Laie, Oahu, Mormon Temple. He also painted murals for the Mormon Church in Cardston, Alberta, Canada, in 1919. Mary Muir, a professor of art at the University of Utah and biographer of Stewart, sees Stewart's influence in Pablo's commitment to the integrity of the object, to social realism, and to paint "what is in your world, what you know." Stewart taught students to "paint what you love. He believed you have to love something to paint it," she said.[19]

In the years he taught Pablo, Stewart never glorified his landscapes and rarely included humans in them. Instead, they depict empty buildings and long shadows. His buildings reflect themes of alienation similar to those of Edward Hopper. Stewart may have taught Pablo printmaking, a medium Pablo worked in for most of his life.

Stewart enjoyed taking students out to paint en plein air. On an outing to Kaysville, where Stewart lived, the students would have followed Mr. Stewart through knee-high grasses until he slowed fifty feet or so away from an abandoned farmhouse whose roof was marked with the long afternoon shadows of towering poplars. Stewart would tip his fine brush in black and create an outline—like Cezanne's and van Gogh's paintings, which Stewart had seen at the 1913 Armory Show and discussed with his class.

Stewart's father, like Pablo's, was a lawyer. Stewart was expected to become one as well, according to Muir. Instead, he studied art in New York because at the time there was a belief that to be an artist you had to study in New York or Paris. But Stewart came to believe that artists can get a good education at any number of art schools and then move into what they want to do, what they love doing. Stewart would have advised Pablo to go where his heart took him. Muir also says that Stewart would have told Pablo that he could study on his own, that there was no rule that an artist had to graduate from an art school. Stewart believed in learning art by creating art. Pablo came to share this belief of Stewart's, as well as his absolute dedication to art. Once, at a friend's house, Stewart saw one of his own paintings on a wall and, without an explanation took it down and took it home with him. Several months later he brought it back, having made some "corrections" to aspects of the painting that had been bothering him for years.[20]

Pablo graduated from East High School in 1922 with good grades. He moved back to San Diego, and began distancing himself from his birthplace. A woman who would become a friend in Mexico, Dorothy Day, also distanced herself from Utah. Dorothy Day grew up in Salt Lake City around the same time Pablo did and felt she never fit in. Her family was Mormon at the time (her immediate family would later leave the Mormon Church), but she felt like the odd one out, in part because she had dark skin and brown eyes among blondes. She said that one day some American Indians came to her door and she saw people who looked like herself for the first time, and connected with them. At age twenty, Day, who had changed her first name to Zohmah, took a ship to Mexico. She married Pablo's closest friend at the time, Jean Charlot, and lived her life in the art world. Yet, in her seventies she was still concerned her family did not fully accept the unconventional decisions she had made in life, choosing a world of art over what was more acceptable in the Utah culture.[21]

Pablo too, as young artist expressing interest in painting outside of religious or religiously condoned art, might have felt disconnected from the mainstream in Utah and even from the men in his own family, who were lawyers, judges, journalists, and engineers.

In San Diego, Pablo enrolled in the San Diego Academy of Art, in Balboa Park, just blocks from where his family had lived.[22] He is said to have enrolled in art school because there was no music composition school in San Diego.[23] This would indicate that his main interest was in being in San Diego. Had he wanted to study music composition, he could have enrolled in the San Francisco Conservatory of Music or another music school.

Despite Pablo's decision to abandon the study of music, it continued to play an important part in his life. In his early years in Mexico, Pablo earned money by giving piano lessons. But his own playing waned. During their twenty-four years together, María heard Pablo play the piano only three times.[24] He did not want a piano in their house.[25]

The city directories for 1924 list Edward Higgins living in an apartment in Salt Lake City and a Mrs. Alice Higgins living in La Jolla, California. Alice may have moved back to California with Pablo while Edward remained in Salt Lake City, moving from the large Victorian on Fifth Avenue to the French Apartments on 600 South.[26]

The San Diego Academy of Art was founded in 1912 by Maurice Braun, who had studied at the National Academy in New York City under teachers trained in the French academic tradition and for an additional year with William Merritt Chase.[27] Braun became the best-known landscape painter in San Diego during the first part of the twentieth century. His was a traditional art school, but not one that would draw students from other regions of the country. [28] This also indicates that Pablo chose the San Diego school not for its art program but because he wanted to be in San Diego. Had he been looking for an art school based on its program or reputation, he might have chosen what is now the San Francisco Art Institute or a less traditional school than the San Diego Academy of Art.

The San Diego school taught drawing using live models, commercial art, and painting, including painting outdoors.[29] When Pablo enrolled, in approximately 1922, Braun was absent, working in a studio in Connecticut, and the school had moved from the Fisher Opera House in downtown San Diego to the old Sacramento Building in Balboa Park. It was under the direction of Eugene De Vol, with his wife, Pauline Hamill De Vol Rea, who were more progressive than Braun in their approach.[30]

Interestingly, although Pablo usually listed his study at the San Diego Art Academy in his biographical data for exhibits and publications, he rarely spoke about his art classes there except to indicate that he found the formal study of art a waste of time. He would say that his true art teachers were Mexican workers and peasants. In an interview in 1939 with the Communist publication *People's World*, Pablo, then thirty-four, talked about how he was having trouble with a mural he was painting in Mexico and so he asked a worker for advice and took it.[31] This attitude would appeal to a Communist readership: Chinese Communist leader Mao Ze-dong, during his infamous Cultural Revolution, required that educated "intellectuals" live in work camps and be "reeducated" by peasants, who were considered more advanced in revolutionary principles.[32]

Pablo surely benefited from the art education he had in U.S. schools, but he never admitted it. He did mention winning a prize for a drawing when he was a child, but said nothing of any art instruction that might have helped him along the way. Oddly, Pablo also acted as if he had never heard of the prestigious New York Art Students League, the well-known art training program that many of his friends had attended. When Pablo lived with his good friend Jean Charlot in New York for six months, Charlot taught at the Art Students League. Yet, when asked, in 1974, whether Jean Charlot had attended it, Pablo shrugged it off, saying that he didn't know what "clubs" he belonged to, even when told it was an art school.[33] In the end, Pablo become an art teacher, and always mentioned his teaching at La Esmeralda in the biographical statements created during his life.

According to BYU art professor James Swensen, an interesting parallel can be made between Utah culture and the Communist ideals Pablo pursued for a good part of his life. Mormon pioneers, persecuted in Missouri, fled in 1848 to Utah—which was a part Mexico until it became a U.S. territory. Mormon pioneers, upon their arrival in Utah (then Mexico) lived under the "United Order," a communal society, working lands owned by the church and sharing in their bounty. Their goal was a self-sufficient society free of the poverty and inequality that plagued the capitalist, industrial world.[34] In his childhood, Pablo would have learned about the hardships suffered by the pioneers as they attempted to live an agrarian life in Utah's often harsh climate. The natural obstacles they faced—an arid climate, drought, starvation, disease—were similar to those facing the *campesinos* Pablo witnessed in the Mexican countryside and portrayed in his art.

In the interview in *People's World*, Pablo also gave the impression that he had been unable to attend college because of a lack of money and that he worked as a longshoreman to support his art studies in San Diego. He said:

> [W]hen it was time for Little Paul to appear on the scene, [my family] had reached San Francisco. My father left 'Frisco and moved around from the Rockies to the Pacific. I didn't have a chance to attend college, but my early crayon drawings convinced me I wanted to go to art school. But there was bread to earn and I worked as longshoreman [sic] and at other odd jobs and went to drawing school at night.[35]

Pablo said that he did not attend college because he wanted to spare his parents the expense.[36] Surely college was an expense Edward Higgins would have been happy to pay for Pablo, as he must have for Roger, who attended a private college, the University of Utah, and University of California. It is possible, though, that practical Edward would have conditioned paying for college on Pablo's studying something "serious."

Pablo's statement to the *People's World* that he worked as a longshoreman would have appealed to the publication's Communist and working-class readership (the longshoremen's union, led by militant Harry Bridges, was always accused of having ties to the Communist Party), but likely was not accurate. Vittorio Vidali, possibly the most radical Communist Pablo ever met, and his rival for the affection of a radical woman, had worked as a longshoreman. In a biography published in 1949 by the Taller de Gráfica Popular (People's Graphic Workshop—TGP), a group Pablo helped found, Pablo says that while at San Diego Academy of Art he worked as a surveyor's assistant.[37]

Had he worked as a longshoreman while in San Diego, he certainly would have revealed this in 1951, when he sought a commission to paint a mural for the International Longshoremen's and Warehousemen's Union in Hawai'i.[38] Letters and other documents in the union's archives contain extensive descriptions of the efforts Pablo undertook to get the commission and then to understand the work of the longshoremen, but say nothing about Pablo having worked as a longshoreman.[39] Pablo's friends in the United States who had been longshoremen, the wife of the union official who got Pablo the longshoremen's mural commission, the wife of the union member who assisted Pablo on the Hawai'i mural, and the artist who touched up the mural in 1968 had no knowledge of Pablo having worked as a longshoreman.[40] Perhaps when he was interviewed by *People's World* in 1939, he felt the need to portray himself as more working class: The American Communist Party was very interested in knowing members' social origins and required them to fill out forms stating what class their parents and grandparents were from.[41] Lawyers were considered bourgeois.[42]

Accounts differ as to how much time Pablo spent in art school. One says that after only two weeks of study at the San Diego Academy of Art, Pablo became dissatisfied with the method of teaching and left to set up a studio with classmates Kennedy Slaughter and Miguel Foncerrada.[43] Perhaps Pablo was influenced to quit art school by the article about Rivera that he read before coming to Mexico, which described how Rivera had turned his back on the formal, European-based study of art, preferring to learn art from "the people"—the indigenous people of Mexico who had been creating art without formal education.[44]

Other biographies created during Pablo's lifetime lead one to believe that Pablo studied at the San Diego Art Academy for a year or two.[45] His biography for a 1949 publication of the TGP, says, "1922–23, studied at the San Diego Academy of Art." [46] An article that appeared in the *San Francisco Chronicle* in 1975, when he stopped there after painting a mural in Seattle, says he studied at the San Diego art school for two years.[47] Art historian James Oles, however, was told that Pablo studied at the San Diego Academy of Art for two months and then was expelled because he was not interested in learning art in order to make a living as an artist.[48]

If Pablo sought to give the impression that he studied art in San Diego longer than he did, he may have been motivated by a desire to match the educations of those around him in hopes of being accepted by them. Although the "revolutionary artists" with whom he worked in Mexico publicly eschewed formal art education, many of them had studied in Paris, New York, at the Academy of San Carlos (which later became the Escuela Nacional de Bellas Artes), La Esmeralda, the Free School of Guadalajara, or abroad.[49] Unless one was a talented peasant artist, having an art education helped one's credibility. Indeed, thirty years after his death, people assumed that Pablo knew certain things because he went to art school in the United States and were surprised to hear that he had studied for only a short time.

At the San Diego Art Academy, Pablo met Miguel Foncerrada, who was his age.[50] In a photograph of Pablo and Foncerrada, Pablo is perched on a fence, leaning away from the camera with a practiced look of seriousness; Foncerrada has his legs crossed and a fedora tipped down over one eye. Foncerrada wears a shirt and tie, whereas Pablo wears the denim work clothes that became his trademark in Mexico. In photographs Pablo often is seen in denim overalls, jeans, and a work shirt, or at most formal, a Western-cut jacket—clothing that would set him apart from the "bourgeoisie"—even when other men are wearing suits.[51]

It was during a visit to the Foncerrada home near Guaymas, Mexico, that an exchange of letters occurred that brought Pablo to Mexico City and to the center of one of the most important artistic movements of the twentieth century. Alice Higgins had sent her son an article on Diego Rivera from the October 1923 issue of *The Arts*, a magazine published in New York.[52] Written by Mexican poet Juan Tablada, the article described how Rivera had tired of the academic study of art and had returned from Paris to Mexico to paint the walls of Mexico.[53] It described how Rivera had become bored of the rigidity of studying art in Paris and had returned to his native Mexico to participate in a mural renaissance that was sweeping the country.

Since Pablo recently had left the traditional study of art in favor of self-study, he was immediately attracted by Rivera's attitude.[54] He said, "[It showed] a strong contrast to European characteristics. . . . And I was so happy to see something rather unusual and different. And very well done, it seemed to me." [55]

Pablo wrote a letter to Rivera expressing his admiration. Though Pablo never expected an answer, Rivera wrote back and "said that it would be very fine for a young painter to know what we're doing here and the character of the Sindic[ato] . . . how do you say? our group of painters working on walls or something like that. So I invite you to come down." [56]

Pablo worked for several months to save money for his trip.[57]

It was just that—a trip, rather than a move. Rivera had invited him only to see the murals. Pablo probably never dreamed Rivera would ask him to become an assistant just a few months after he had arrived in Mexico.[58] In an interview in 1939, Pablo described why he went to Mexico:

> I went to Mexico in 1923 [sic]. I went there because I was an artist and because I had heard that it was a country full of wild beauty and color worthy of an El Greco canvas. But I didn't go there as some American writers did when they fled to Paris around that time. I wasn't bored with my country; I wanted to visit my neighbors.[59]

Pablo's father accompanied him to the border and gave him one hundred dollars, a substantial sum at a time when the average income in the United States was twelve hundred dollars per year.[60] This was likely more an act of paternal responsibility than a showing of enthusiasm for the trip his son was embarking upon. In 1924, in the eyes of North Americans, Mexico was still in turmoil. The U.S. press in both San Diego and in Salt Lake City had carried detailed accounts of Pancho Villa's ravages in Northern Mexico and New Mexico. Marines had been sent to San Diego. Pablo's friends and his father warned Pablo of the dangers of Mexico, with its bandits, bullets, and derailed trains. (Three years later, the train that thirteen-year-old Emmy Lou Packard, who would become an assistant to Rivera, was riding through Northern Mexico was blown up near San Luis Potosí, killing three.)[61] Even with Villa dead and the revolution over, travelers were often ambushed by thieves.[62]

Edward Higgins was not to see his son again.

II

THE REVOLUTIONARY YEARS

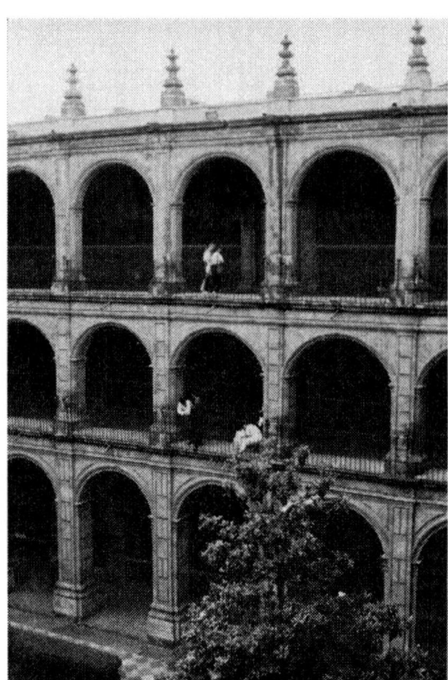

9

POST-REVOLUTIONARY MEXICO

As Pablo and Foncerrada rode the train across the border into Mexico, it seemed to Pablo as if "all of the fragrance of Mexico came in through the window." [1] He saw women outdoors cooking in pots, and noticed how beautiful they were with their shawls, their dark hair, full skirts, and the slow way in which they walked and moved.[2] He later would capture this impression in sketches and paintings.

Two days later, the train pulled into the station and Pablo stepped off the platform into Mexico City. One of his first impressions was that there were no cars, only trains, streetcars, and *carruajes*—carriages pulled by horses.[3] Mexico City, an urban area of five hundred thousand, had no skyscrapers, as did New York and Chicago, or subways, as did Paris, though it was laid out like a European city with wide boulevards and neoclassical palaces. Sitting in outdoor cafés with French names were men in dark suits with hats and canes, older women in flowery hats and cinch-waist dresses flowing to the ground, and young women in the newest, short, drop-waist flapper styles. They would leave food on their plates so no one would think they were hungry. Next door, men in overalls, who actually were hungry, stood while eating street vendors' fresh tortillas, smoky *carnitas*, and cinnamony *café de olla* (cinnamon coffee from a clay pot), which sent a fusion of scents through the streets. Sitting on the street, atop blankets, were peasant women, who spoke no Spanish, only their native Indian languages, in richly embroidered *huipils* (white cotton tunics) selling fruit and clay pots. The disparities between the European-emulating rich and the peasants and working class are part of what underlay the Mexican Revolution of 1910. Mexico's population of fifteen million was 30 percent Indian. Two million Mexicans spoke no Spanish.

The Spanish conquered the Aztecs "with the sword and the cross" in 1521, and rather than decimate them, as the Spanish had attempted with the Mapuche in Chile, under direction of the pope they converted them to Catholicism and intermarried with them (those who did not die of the smallpox the Spanish brought). By the time Mexico fought and won its war of independence from Spain in 1810, 60 percent of the country was Indian, and the remainder mostly mestizo, mixed Spanish and Indian.[4] Yet in spite of intermarriage and independence, a colonial hierarchy persisted that placed Indians at the bottom of the social structure, followed by mestizos and topped by Europeans. The Spanish conquerors instituted a land grant system to reward themselves and their friends with vast tracts of the best land in Mexico, and forced Indians into servitude under the feudal hacienda system.

President Porfirio Díaz, who took office in 1876 and held power for more than thirty years, guided Mexico into the industrial era, bringing steel and beer factories to Mexico and replacing mule-drawn cars with a countrywide system of railroads. Mining and cattle exports boomed.[5] He transformed Mexico City into a magnificent European-style city with wide boulevards and monuments to the country's heroes of the independence.

The system relied on wealthy foreigners, mainly from the United States, to provide the technical knowledge and capital for production; they in turn bought the products Mexico produced. This gave foreigners a great deal of power in the country. Industrialization took its toll on the poor of Mexico as it did on the poor throughout the world, creating a large urban working class toiling twelve hours a day, often in unhealthy conditions. In the country, the peasants who had farmed for centuries continued to lose their land by having to prove they held legal title. The consequence was that by 1910, 1 percent of Mexicans owned 87 percent of Mexico's land. Ninety percent of the population was landless.

Díaz sold off much of Mexico's mineral wealth, rigged elections, muzzled the press, and enforced a system of land ownership that favored the Catholic Church and wealthy foreigners. By 1910, he had peasants, liberals, and the middle class willing to take up arms to end his power. The middle class wanted access to power, the working class wanted limits on child labor and hours worked, and the peasants wanted the return of the land Díaz had seized from them.

An idealistic liberal and now revolutionary hero, Francisco I. Madero, president of Mexico from 1911 to 1913, promised to bring democracy, with free and fair elections and voting rights for all. The revolution he started sought to accomplish what independence from Spain in 1810 had not—the self-rule of the Mexican people. The revolution began on November 20, 1910. Pablo, growing up, would have heard of the bloody battles that spilled from the Mexican state of Chihuahua into New Mexico, and of the United States sending troops into Mexico.

Those who sought change in Mexico were encouraged by the ongoing revolutions in Russia and China, where the efforts of workers and peasants were ending the rule of dynasties, with the goal of replacing them with just and fair democracies of the people inspired by the ideas of Karl Marx and Friedrich Engels.

For many, socialism seemed like a reasonable solution to the inequities brought about when societies changed from farm-based to factory-based economies. Proposed solutions to these problems ranged from the enactment of labor laws and the establishment of unions, to revolution or the expropriation of industry for the good of the people.

With the help of Emiliano Zapata in the state of Morelos and Pancho Villa in the north, the revolutionaries took down the Díaz administration in 1911, but the country did not achieve stability until November 30, 1920, when Álvaro Obregón took the presidential oath of office, marking the official end of the revolution.

The socialistic, antireligious, and antiforeigner stances of the Mexican Revolution were codified in the Agrarian Reform Act of 1915 and the Constitution of 1917. Much of the work of the muralists of the 1920s centered on bringing Mexico's new constitution to life through art, in a way that Mexico's mainly illiterate population could understand. One of Pablo's first assignments as an assistant to Rivera was to paint words summarizing the principles of the constitution on Rivera's murals at the Ministry of Education building in downtown Mexico City.[6] Unlike the U.S. Constitution, which focuses on individual rights, Mexico's 1917 Constitution, still in effect today, focuses on social justice. It sets the workday at eight hours maximum, six days a week, and gives workers the right to form unions and to strike. It guarantees Mexicans the right to a good job, decent housing, and health protection and care. It contains anticlerical provisions designed to curb the historical abuses of the Catholic Church in Mexico, including preventing public worship outside of church buildings. It also decrees that all church real estate is national property. The constitution, to this day, requires that primary education be free, compulsory, and secular.

The new constitution gave the government control over privately held land and the right to expropriate it whenever it deemed necessary. Article 33 restricts foreign interests, including the capacity of non-Mexican nationals to own land and to engage in political activities and allows deportation of them without a hearing and for nearly any cause.[7]

Article 27 of the constitution decrees that the wealth contained in the soil, the subsoil, the waters, and seas of Mexico belongs to the nation and gives it power to control the activities of mining and oil companies and to expropriate and redistribute private land to the *campesinos* for the common good. This concerned the United States the most. Granting the nation the ownership of Mexico's mineral wealth, Article 27 allowed the expropriation of the vast oil and silver mined by U.S. companies.

American investors had significant money invested in Mexico. U.S. Senator Albert Fall (a Republican from New Mexico) had a $75,000 interest in a mining company in Mexico. He reported that forty thousand U.S. citizens were "developing the farming resources, the stock industry and other natural resources of Mexico, building railroads, opening mines, constructing irrigation and power plants and building electrical tramways." He said that U.S. investments in Mexico represented 50 percent of "the entire tax paying and revenue producing wealth of Mexico . . . ."[8]

Fall intended to get U.S. President Woodrow Wilson to break diplomatic relations with Mexico, overthrow the Mexican government, and install a new government more protective of U.S. interests.[9] Fall's comments reflect the Manifest Destiny ideas of Corydon Higgins's generation, who believed that their mission was to conquer the natural and indigenous challenges of the West, to tame, civilize, Christianize, and industrialize. They would not have understood that Mexico might want to forgo "progress" in exchange for self-rule.

When the United States refused to recognize the new government of President Obregón, he worked out a deal, the 1923 Treaty of Bucareli, in which the United States agreed that Article 27 would not apply to lands from which oil had begun to be extracted before 1917, and that for any expropriation of more than 4,335 acres from U.S. citizens, Mexico would pay cash.[10] When Pablo arrived in Mexico in 1924, the majority of Mexico's inhabitants were indigenous, and 90 percent did not read or write Spanish. The government of Obregón was returning land to the *campesinos* via its *Agraristas*, federal agents who retook haciendas from wealthy owners. The country was experiencing a wave of nationalism and antiforeigner sentiment in the process of changing its identity from one that placed the greatest value on European ideas, art, and culture, to one that embraced its own indigenous heritage. Like Pablo himself, Mexico would struggle with how much of its past to abandon.

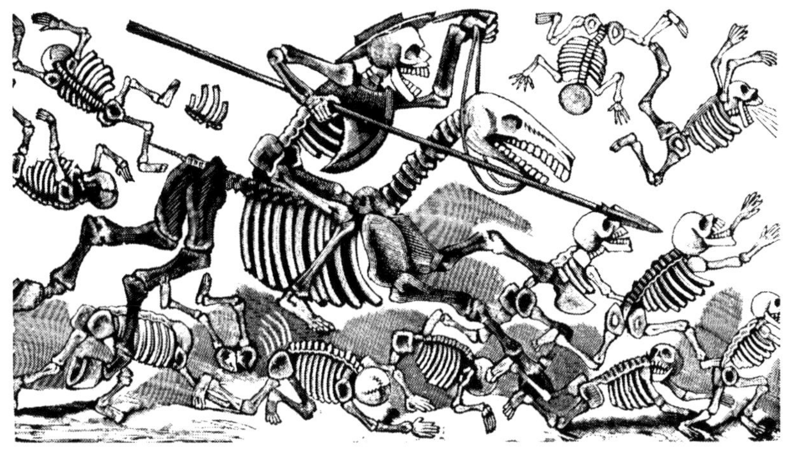

10

THE ARTISTIC REVOLUTION

Pablo and Miguel Foncerrada checked into a hotel, paying for it with the gift from Edward Higgins. Later, Pablo stood at the house at 10 Mixcalco Street and knocked.

Would Rivera be there? Would he remember the letter? What if he didn't? Pablo formed the words he would say. Gracias por la carta (Thank you for the letter). Mucho gusto conocerle (It's nice to meet you). The Spanish he practiced as a child in El Cajon for several years had limbered his tongue; his high school Spanish had taught him grammar; and his stays with Miguel Foncerrada's family had given him some confidence. Yet even when totally fluent, Pablo always would speak slowly and deliberately both in Spanish and English.

Guadalupe (Lupe) Marin, Rivera's wife of two years—and the third woman to bear his children—opened the door. Pablo told her that Rivera had written to him asking him to come. Lupe yelled to her husband. Gordito! (Tubby!) She told him that a tall (Pablo was around five ten) blond man was looking for him. Rivera was just heading out the door. He invited Pablo into the house, which was decorated with Rivera's cubist paintings. Rather than having the European furniture of many Mexico City homes, the house had rustic Mexican wood and leather furniture; woven mats were used as rugs over the red terra-cotta tile floors.[1] Singer Concha Michel was playing the guitar on a patio full of geraniums. Rivera warmly introduced himself to Pablo and apologized that he had to leave for a meeting. Rivera left Pablo with some drawings that he had made in Italy and asked him to look them over, and when finished to close the door behind him and plan to meet him Monday at the Secretaría de Educación Pública (the Ministry of Public Education).[2]

Rivera was born in Guanajuato, Mexico, in 1886. A child prodigy by his own account, he studied art from age three, and at age eleven, began studying at Mexico City's Academy of Fine Arts of San Carlos, founded in 1785, the oldest art academy in the Western Hemisphere. In 1909, Rivera went to Europe to study. For the next twelve years, he lived mainly in Madrid, Paris, and Italy, and worked in the midst of Picasso, Mondrian, Modigliani, Braque, Klee, Dérain, and Cézanne. In Europe he began to question why Mexico's art, like its politics, should be dominated by Europeans.

In colonial times, the Spanish had imported their own artists to Mexico; Porfirio Díaz relegated Mexican artists to unimportant assignments and had all significant projects, such as public buildings and monuments, designed by French, Italian, and Spanish artists and architects. During the time of Díaz, the Academy allowed only European artists to be department heads and required strict adherence to European methods.

For the 1910 celebration of one hundred years of independence from Spain, Díaz held an exhibition not of Mexican art but of Spanish art. Seeing the irony of this, future muralist José Clemente Orozco and artist Gerardo Murillo ("Dr. Alt") organized an alternative exhibit of Mexican art. The following year, students at the Academy, including Orozco and Siqueiros—the other muralists who, along with Rivera, became known as the *tres grandes* of the mural movement—began a two-year strike in protest of the stifling curriculum, which involved hours of copying European artwork and anatomical charts. [3] The Mexican artistic revolution had begun.

Mexican artists, several of whom, including Siqueiros, personally had experienced the bloody Mexican Revolution, were committed to establishing a new direction for art. Orozco, Siqueiros, and Rivera formed the Sindicato de Trabajadores Tecnicos, Pintores y Escultores (Union of Engravers, Painters, and Sculptors). Its manifesto laid the foundation for social realism—art realistically depicting social struggles—that would dominate Mexican art for the next forty years. It condemned easel painting as "aristocratic," favoring "the expression of Monumental Art because it is a public possession." It declared that "the ideal goal of art, which is now an expression of individualistic masturbation, should be one of beauty for all, of education and of battle." [4]

The artists who subscribed to the Sindicato principles considered themselves workers. They were paid the same wages as masons on some mural projects. But although their art depicted the peasant and manual laborer as superior in culture to formally trained artists and people of the middle and upper classes, very few peasants or untrained artists were hired to paint or direct the mural projects. In later decades the artists with the Sindicato orientation would be challenged on how much these projects really did to improve the lives of the *campesino* and worker.

The Sindicato applied for membership in the Communist International, the organization of Communist parties dedicated to creating an international Soviet state. The Sindicato's newspaper, *El Machete*, an oversize publication sometimes printed on brightly colored newsprint, later became the newspaper of the Partido Comunista de México (Mexican Communist Party or PCM).[5] Rivera, Siqueiros, and Xavier Guerrero all joined the PCM. Guerrero's woodblock print of a hand grasping a machete became the newspaper's trademark.

The mural movement officially began in 1922 when President Álvaro Obregón hired José Vasconcelos, a writer, lawyer, and philosopher, as Minister of Public Education with the mandate to bring education and culture to all people. Vasconcelos was a brilliant, well-read man who loved the Greek and Roman classics. His influence can be seen today in the markets of Mexico where vendors sell cheap editions of Dante's *Inferno*.[6] Vasconcelos faced the challenge of uniting Mexico after years of the Díaz-imposed caste system, and chose to do it by "rebuilding a national culture" through a concept of Mexicanidad.[7]

The Mexicanidad growing out of the revolution is enormously significant in Mexico's history. Salvador Jiménez, a thirty-year veteran of Mexico's diplomatic corps, maintains that the revolutionary heroes are essential for Mexican identity. "They gave us the legacy of Mexico. They fought against the risk of Mexico becoming Europeanized. They made us proud to be descendants of both Indians and the Spanish and helped Mexico gain a position of dignity in relation to the U.S.," he says.[8]

Vasconcelos recruited artists to paint the walls of public buildings as a way of educating and communicating the ideology of the revolution to Mexico's people. The murals have been compared to medieval art that sought to teach Christianity to the masses.

In the Soviet Union, the new revolutionary government was seeking to achieve the same goal through film: between 1925 and 1927, Russian Sergei Eisenstein, on a government commission, made a series of three films, *Battleship Potemkin*, *Strike*, and *October*, to bring the message of the Russian Revolution to Russia's mainly illiterate population. Eisenstein would later work in Mexico and Pablo would visit him in Moscow.

John Charlot, whose father, Jean Charlot, was one of the first artists to work on the murals, said:

> The first artists to accept mural commissions were the only ones who dared—the young artists. Vasconcelos carefully avoided giving them themes and was embarrassed when they turned out to be so political. He himself liked non-political, allegorical works. The young artists painted political themes because they backed Obregón's policies. Only later was politics a criterion for commissions.[9]

As the mural movement became more political, so did the government's selection of artists to receive these desirable commissions, and mural commissions came to be granted based on who was in the good graces of the government. In Mexico this changes every six years. Rivera's status changed regularly; his only consistency was his desire to dominate, even if it meant being a tyrant. Tina Martin, whose father, Alberto Misrachi, was Rivera's art dealer from 1935 to 1945, remembers how large and intimidating Rivera was. She once saw him push someone out of a room with his big belly.[10] (Rivera was six feet tall and over three hundred pounds.) When Rivera was commissioned to paint his 1931 mural at what is now the San Francisco Art Institute he painted himself right into the middle of it. That's where he liked to be: on display at the center of everything.

Rivera was notorious for sleeping with American women who visited the projects and "mixed his paints"—a euphemism for someone he had sex with—according to Siqueiros, and for having an entourage of followers, often young artists from the United States, and eager assistants whom others cynically referred to as *Dieguitos* (little Diegos).

The first mural Vasconcelos awarded Rivera was the allegorical *Creation* for the amphitheater of the Preparatory School. Four young artists, the only ones brave enough to accept Vasconcelos's general invitation, were given other walls in the same building. Charlot's *Massacre in the Templo Mayor* was the first mural finished and the first in fresco.

The next project Rivera took on was seventeen thousand linear feet of the Court of Labor at the Secretaría building. Again, young artists, including Charlot, were assigned walls in the same building, but Rivera would gradually take over, leaving only a few walls of their work.

The Rivera home was a gathering spot for many of those involved in the murals. At a typical party, Rivera was at center stage—immense, garrulous, entertaining adults and horrifying children with stories of eating cats in Paris and, recalls Tina Martin, women's ribs. Lupe, her pale green eyes flashing, her voice and gestures as abundant as Rivera's size, entertained guests with animated stories, and occasional abuse when she felt they were too cozy with her husband.[11] Surrounding them were their friends, dressed in extravagant flapper clothes, throwing back tequila. Everybody was drinking and singing while someone played the guitar. Lupe would be leading a raunchy song about getting borracha—drunk, and running an amazing show, keeping young female fans of Rivera in check. Whenever one of them gushed over him, Lupe would interject something about his bowel movements or his warts. Lupe kept the most beautiful women in the house running back and forth to the kitchen fetching things for her: ¡Más salsa! ¡Más tequila!

The cast of characters in the Rivera circle was vast. But Mexico City was still a small town. Everyone knew everyone, at least if they were in the arts, the Communist Party, or the intellectual community. Frida Kahlo had not yet found her way to this group of artists and writers who called themselves "the family." [12] She was sixteen, in high school at the Preparatory, and dating her classmate Alejandro Gómez Arias. It would be six more years before she and Rivera would get together, and first Rivera's marriage to Lupe would be shattered by his affair with the most desirable woman in Mexico City, one of the women Lupe was shuttling into the kitchen to keep away from Rivera.

At the center of what has been termed the mural renaissance in Mexico in the 1920s, and often living it up in the Rivera home, was a group of idealistic, talented, artistic and, in many instances charismatic people who were passionate about Mexico. Many were foreigners but all were captivated by Mexico's indigenous culture and determined to document it, promote it, and to varying degrees, live it.

Tina Modotti, an actress, photographer, revolutionary, and eventually fugitive, was a woman with whom nearly every man in Mexico was in love. Pablo would fall in love with her. Modotti would transform herself from one of the most beautiful and legendary women in Mexico to a tired, burdened woman who would die a sad, untimely death.

But in 1923, she was at her best: turning heads, causing whispers. Modotti immigrated to the United States from Italy as a child and worked in the textile mills in San Francisco before moving to Los Angeles. Her husband Robo, an artist, died in 1922. Modotti arrived in Mexico in 1923 with her lover, California photographer Edward Weston, and his son Chandler. Weston left his wife and three other children behind in California.

Modotti had grown up in bohemian San Francisco and epitomized the new woman that the flapper craze was promoting: one who refused to wear corsets, smoked and drove cars, drank and wore makeup, cut her hair short, and made her own decisions about life and love. Modotti wore blue jeans at a time when women wearing pants were not allowed to cross the U.S. border into Mexico and when priests in Mexico refused to give communion to women who had cut their hair into fashionable flapper "bobs." [13] She lived openly with a married man and modeled nude for him. Modotti had dark hair, deep, heavily lidded eyes, and full and sensuous cupid lips. At a party she would wear a tight blue suit that hugged her tiny waist and seemed to make her walk with a heavy swing. But then she also walked like that in jeans, and had men, and women, too, mesmerized.[14]

At these parties, the small-boned and diminutive Edward Weston, with his sharp nose and receding hairline, would be defending his right to photograph women's asses for his own artistic pleasure to anyone in the group who spoke English. Who should tell him otherwise; why should he be required to photograph sombreros, cacti, and rifles? Weston and Modotti had an "open relationship" that allowed them to bring lovers into their home, even when the other was present.[15] Their Saturday night parties became legendary.[16]

Paris-born artist Jean Charlot was handsome and sophisticated in his suit and his round glasses. Charlot's mother was from a French family that had immigrated to Mexico in the 1820s. Her grandfather had married a woman who was half Aztec.[17] Charlot's father was half French and half Russian. Charlot had grown up in Paris surrounded by Aztec art and was learning Náhuatl, the Aztec language. Vasconcelos had assigned to Charlot, Xavier Guerrero, and Amado de la Cueva walls of the Secretaría's Court of Fiestas, in what Charlot called "a first try at communal painting." [18]

Charlot would be instrumental in developing mural technique in Mexico and reviving interest in nineteenth-century printmaker José Guadalupe Posada.

Flirting with Charlot was a woman with short curly dark hair and a striking profile. She was stylishly dressed and highly animated. The lively Anita Brenner, though she didn't look any older than Pablo, would step right in and begin challenging Diego, first in perfect English, then in rapid-fire Spanish, chastising him for not respecting other artists' work on the Secretaría murals. Weston didn't understand Spanish and would just wander away.

Brenner, only nineteen years old, was a journalist who was writing about Mexican art. She ultimately published a best seller about Mexican Indian culture, *Idols Behind Altars*, when she was twenty-four. A year later, she earned a Ph.D. from Columbia University in New York. Born in Aguascalientes, in central Mexico, of an American mother and a Latvian father, Brenner, as a child, was moved between Mexico and Texas as her family attempted to avoid the violence of the revolution. She arrived in Mexico City in 1922, and was welcomed into the city's tight Jewish community. Anita Brenner was one of the few women in Mexico who would take on Rivera intellectually.[19]

Frances Toor, a Berkeley-trained anthropologist, had come to Mexico to study for a summer, but stayed and with a stipend from the Mexican government published a magazine about Mexican culture, *Mexican Folkways*.[20] The bilingual magazine documented indigenous cultures throughout Mexico through drawings, paintings, accounts of their rituals, and even printed the music and lyrics of their songs. In the 1920s and '30s there were no art galleries in Mexico; Toor was one of the first to begin buying and selling art. [21] Toor lived in Edificio Zamora, where her neighbors were Carleton Beals, writer for *The Nation* and future correspondent for TASS, the Soviet news agency; Bertram Wolfe, in Mexico to establish the Communist Party; and his wife Ella Wolfe, an agent for TASS.[22]

Xavier Guerrero, a handsome artist with dark Indian features, brought mural technique from his home state of Coahuila, Mexico. Guerrero, one of the few pure Indians in the group, was self-taught as an artist. In his native Northern Mexico he had painted murals for the owners of mines.[23] Quiet and stone-faced, he would become one of the most fervent Communists in the group.

David Alfaro Siqueiros, from the state of Chihuahua, on the border with the United States, had fought in the revolution. He was the most militant of the artists of the Mexican School. U.S. artist and Rivera assistant Ione Robinson described Siqueiros as a "green-eyed Mexican, very handsome with white skin and black, curly hair." [24] His "in your face" murals got him the label of an "ugliest." Rivera's and Siqueiros's strong personalities and extreme political positions resulted in intense clashes between them.

José Clemente Orozco, quiet and antisocial, and not a Communist, would not have been at Rivera's party.[25] Born in Jalisco, Mexico, in 1883 and educated at the Academy of San Carlos, Orozco created art containing some of the most heart-wrenching images of suffering. Calmer than Siqueiros's, Orozco's paintings convey strong messages with more subtlety and delicacy, like Chopin nocturnes—beauty and sadness. He had painted numerous murals in the Preparatory, including *Christ Destroying his Own Cross* and *Maternity*.

The 1920s sometimes are referred to as the golden age of the mural movement in Mexico, but the movement was never without dissent and conflict. By the time Pablo arrived in Mexico in August 1924, some of the murals had been mutilated or destroyed. Some members of the public truly felt ownership of the art projects in public buildings and believed they had the right to comment on the murals' content, even to destroy murals they deemed ugly or irreverent. At the Preparatory, a Catholic women's group, the Damas Católicas, nailed a cloth draping over Orozco's mural depicting a naked Madonna and Christ.[26] And, in mid-1924, conservative students at the Preparatory who were opposed to President Obregón scratched and threw stones at murals by Orozco and Siqueiros and demanded that all mural painting stop.[27] Orozco said sixty people shot at the murals.[28] The Orozco and Siqueiros murals were targets because, unlike Rivera's ephemeral, allegorical *Creation*, they were sharp commentaries on society. Orozco's mural contrasted the gluttony of the rich to the condition of the worker, and portrayed a drunken judge and a winking god. Siqueiros included a dead worker. Members of the artists' union staged a counterattack via pamphlets.[29]

By October 1924, Mexico had a new president, Plutarco Calles, who removed Minister of Education Vasconcelos and replaced him with J. M. Puig Casauranc. Puig Casauranc dismissed Siqueiros and Orozco from their government positions as mural painters.[30] Rivera, seeing the political danger of expressing solidarity with his fellow painters, resigned from the artists' union.[31]

Rivera's expressions of solidarity with other artists, of course, didn't mean much. "Rivera worked against all," said one artist.[32] Rivera wrestled control of the Secretaría Court of Fiestas murals to himself, recasting Amando de la Cueva, Xavier Guerrero, and Jean Charlot, who had originally been assigned to paint the larger courtyard, to the role of assistants. Rivera destroyed one of Charlot's murals, *Danza de los listones*, to make room for his own, *Market place*.[33]

The artistic movement took the position that the formal study of art was bourgeois, and that untrained, indigenous Mexicans inherently had a better understanding of art than trained artists. Yet few of the artists in the movement were full-blooded Indians. Most were of mixed Mexican–European heritage, such as Jean Charlot, Juan O'Gorman, Rufino Tamayo, and Frida Kahlo.[34]

In terms of education, at the time, Rivera eschewed the traditional study of art, yet he himself had the finest classical art education both in Mexico and in Europe. Carlos Mérida, who would be referred to as "the Guatemalan," and Charlot had both studied in Paris.[35] Some of these artists downplayed their formal education and dressed in a way that would cast them in the role of worker in order to appear better qualified to carry out their mandate of bringing the revolution to the people. Tamayo, primarily an abstract painter, dressed in a serape and had his wife, Olga, dress in Indian clothes on a trip to New York.[36]

The way artists were treated by the government—their employer—reinforced the idea that the artists were workers. Rivera assistant Ione Robinson, a friend of Pablo, described the difference between the way artists in Mexico and the United States were treated. She said the artists in Mexico were "serious and sure of what they do." [37] The fact that the artists received the same pay as the masons meant that they "were sure of" earning money, just like a worker. "I don't believe in painters living on air anymore," she said. "For the first time, I feel like a real human being, and not a queer artist, and it all has to do with earning a fixed amount of money and working every day." [38]

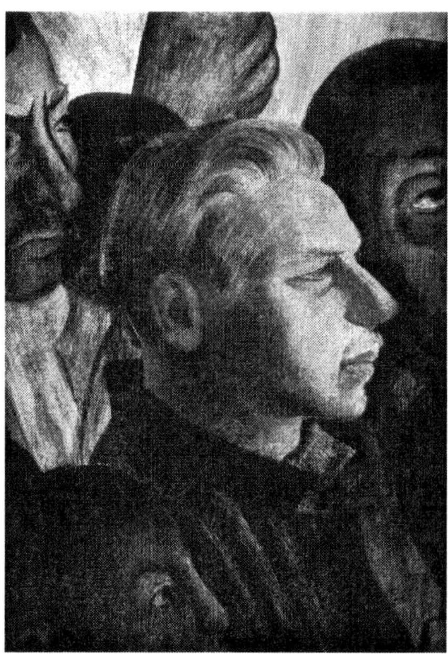

11

RIVERA'S ASSISTANT

The morning after Pablo's arrival in Mexico City, his education in Mexican history and politics began as he stepped through the huge doorway of the Secretaría, where he was to meet Rivera.

Once inside the massive neoclassical building, Pablo could see the murals Rivera had already painted on three stories of walls circling the Court of Labor. They told the history of Mexico's labor struggle in a way that the simplest person could understand. The first floor depicted the problems faced by the indigenous people of Mexico, the second floor the struggles of the working class, and on the top floor, the position usually reserved for the gods in Italian Renaissance murals, the joining of the peasant and the worker and the emergence of "Revolutionary Man," liberated through education and technology.

In the lower stairway was a new mural, *Pearls Before Swine*, satirizing Puig Casauranc's firing of Orozco and Siqueiros (Rivera later removed this image when Puig Casauranc was to give him a mural commission).

Pablo saw, laid out next to the walls to be painted in the Court of Fiestas, large pieces of brown paper with the outlines of images drawn exactly to size for the fifteen-foot-high walls. Men in overalls were preparing a vat of plaster. The fresco technique, first used in Mexico by Charlot (Rivera first used encaustic), involved painting on a wall of wet plaster. The paint permeates the plaster, becoming a part of it. Another technique is to paint on plaster after it has dried—easier and less stressful than having to paint relatively quickly on wet plaster. The paint, however, is more likely to flake using this method.[1]

Viola Patterson, an artist from Seattle who became a friend of Pablo and assisted him on a mural project, described the process beginning in the early morning when the plasterers would prepare the walls:

> [T]hey were craftsmen of the highest order themselves. What they could do in the final troweling of a wall was unbelievable; they left a surface that was so luscious you couldn't believe it. Well, after they'd finished then the wall had to sit for, depending on the atmosphere, on the humidity, an hour or two or three. If it was very dampish, it would be a fair length of time. . . . The artist would have come along, and he'd be chatting. It was all so informal. They'd be looking at each other's work, and so on. But when the moment had arrived when it was ready to work on, they would attach their paper cartoons, which had already been pricked through, and with their pounce, this little bag with the powder color, usually sort of a deep sepia or umber or something, over the lines and so there was an indication of the drawing. Then they'd begin to work, to build their tones. They already knew the color scheme . . . . The whole gamut of the colors. And it's a beautiful range. There's a marvelous blue, just the most piercing blue. And the greens are somewhat earth greens, and all the other colors are colors!
>
> They're very, very fine colors. And then using the soft—I've forgotten—camelhair brushes or what the hairs are. They're soft brushes . . . [a]nd you can work over and over and it's a marvelous feeling to put a brush loaded with color to the surface, because it pulls the liquid away out of the brush immediately, leaving the color on the surface. Just vanishes like that. There's something (chuckles) very special about the feeling of the way it goes on the surface. And you can build from a faint tone up to a deep tone. Some of the very assured ones paint what they want very quickly, but there's often a building process of adding color, and you can work over a fairly good-sized surface. You don't have to do all your blue area at once, or all your green area at once, and so on. [2]

If Pablo had felt special having been invited by Rivera to Mexico City, upon seeing all the other people at the Secretaría, he would have wondered if Rivera had invited all of California. The building was always filled with tourists and journalists who traveled to Mexico City to see Rivera in hopes that he would be engaging in the high jinks for which he was known. These sometimes involved guns and always attractive women whose intentions would be cut short by the arrival of Lupe Rivera, voice booming, coming to check on her famously untrustworthy husband.

Pablo and Foncerrada rented a studio in the center of Mexico City.[3] Two twenty-year-old young men were in the biggest city they had lived in: San Diego had been a city of seventy-four thousand and Mexico City was reaching a half million. To earn money, Pablo began giving piano and English lessons.[4] He would play at the home of Bodil Christensen, an ethnographer from Denmark who traveled around Mexico on horseback researching papermaking and pre-Columbian witchcraft.[5]

Pablo began spending his time at the Secretaría, watching Rivera work. After approximately six months Rivera asked Pablo to assist him. During these months, Pablo must have demonstrated to Rivera that he was different from the many tourists and artists from the United States who came to watch him paint.

One day not long after Pablo had arrived in Mexico, as he watched Rivera work, Rivera said to him, "You ought to get in touch with Jean Charlot. Go down and see Jean. Jean is a fine person and can tell you many things. And he's doing important work." Pablo asked for his address.[6]

The French-born artist was two years older than Pablo. Before coming to Mexico in 1921 with his mother, a widow, Charlot had studied art in Paris in the corridors of the

Beaux-Arts, had one of his pieces included in an exhibit of religious art at the Louvre, and had served in the French army.[7]

Pablo rang Charlot's doorbell at around nine one morning. Jean was shaving, and asked him to come back at around four p.m. When Pablo returned, he was surprised to see Luciana (Luz Jiménez), a very beautiful Indian woman whom Rivera would use as a model for his murals in Chapingo, "sitting on a *petate* [woven mat], completely nude, very beautiful, and Jean was painting her . . . talking Náhuatl [the Aztec language]." Even fifty years later, in describing the event, Pablo's laugh and voice expressed the surprise that this twenty-year-old Presbyterian from Utah experienced when he entered Charlot's house.

Charlot was fascinated with Mexico and very knowledgeable about its history and art. Luz was teaching him Náhuatl.[8]

Sharing an interest in learning about the country that was new to both of them, Pablo and Charlot began exploring Mexico together, with Charlot showing him the places he loved and painted. Two trips stood out. On one excursion, they traveled to a village for the baptism of Luz's first son. Charlot was to be the godfather. Charlot and Pablo traveled by horseback and Luz met them. When they arrived in the mountains of Ytapalapa (probably Ixtapalapa) they started walking. It turned dark and began raining, so Luz took them to Xochimilco and they spent the night with a friend of hers. Early in the morning, they took the streetcar to the end of the line at San Gregorio. Finally, they rode on horseback to San Pedro, where the baptism took place. Then they got on the horses again and went to Milpa Alta, where Luz lived.[9] (Neither Pablo nor Charlot drove.)

On another trip Pablo and Charlot took the train to the outskirts of Cuernavaca to visit an Indian family Charlot knew. They stayed for three days, sleeping on *petates*. Jean spoke Náhuatl with the family.[10]

"We wanted to know not what one sees in Mexico," said Pablo about his travels with Charlot, "but the Mexican life, the roots of the Mexican." [11] Pablo carried little sketchbooks with him, as had LeConte Stewart, and made quick sketches and notes whenever he was inspired, often nearly jumping out of the car to draw something.[12]

Sometimes Anita Brenner went along. She and Charlot seemed in love and they were collaborating on several writing projects. Evenings, Pablo often attended parties at Anita Brenner's, almost always with Miguel Foncerrada and Brenner's cousin, Abel Plenn.[13]

Pablo's job for Rivera was to grind the colors for the Secretaría paint in a metate—the course stone slab used to grind corn—and mix them with distilled water.[14] If he earned what Charlot did, he would have made eight pesos a day.[15]

Pablo worked all day, meeting Rivera and the other artists at the Secretaría at seven a.m. He worked until afternoon siesta time, when the city shut down for workers to eat the leisurely main meal of the day with their families and perhaps take a nap, before returning to work until eight p.m. or so. Every evening he went to Rivera's home to grind the colors for the next day's work. Eventually he was painting backgrounds and calligraphy.[16]

As Pablo worked, Rivera spoke passionately about the history of Mexico and argued eloquently that Communism was the only way to ensure the dignity of workers and peasants. He learned how the Mexican people had suffered under the rule of foreigners. Rivera spoke of how the rich hacienda owners had stolen land the Indians had worked for centuries, killing or enslaving those who protested, and how the abolition of private property and the disappearance of classes would end the exploitation of man by man.

Pablo painted, above a panel contrasting a miserable night of the poor with a decadent night of the rich, the "Ballad of the Agrarian Revolution"—"the land is for everyone like the air, the water, the light and the warmth of the sun"—a concept foreign to anything he had heard in Utah, where his father dedicated his career to protecting private claims on the earth's natural resources.[17]

Pablo soon fell under Rivera's spell politically. Rivera was a forceful presence, both physically and dogmatically. To Rivera, Pablo was a serious, intense student of his art and his politics. In the mural *May Day Meeting*, Rivera painted the light-skinned, mustached Pablo in profile, emphasizing his straight, prominent nose, heavy brow, and thick, blond hair. Pablo's expression is one of concentration and intense absorption in the activities surrounding him.

Pablo likely had an experience similar to that of Ione Robinson, who in 1929 at age twenty became a Rivera assistant on Mexico City's National Palace. Her letters to her family overflow with enthusiasm for Rivera's teachings: "Diego says that the only intelligent thing a person can do is to be a Communist." "According to Diego . . . ," "Diego thinks . . . ." [18]

BY LATE 1924, Rivera had begun work on a new mural project at a Spanish baroque estate that had been nationalized as the National School of Agriculture in Chapingo, near Mexico City.[19] The college was established to teach *campesinos* about agriculture.[20] Pablo and the other assistants worked three days a week at the Secretaría, three at Chapingo.

Cinching the Chapingo commission was a coup for Rivera. The end of the government-sponsored mural projects was already in sight. Mexico's new president, Plutarco Calles, was an extreme conservative and was appalled by the radical nature of the murals. Rivera demonstrated loyalty to the new administration by lampooning Vasconcelos, the creator of the mural projects, in a mural depicting him as a dwarf straddling a white elephant. This, as well as Rivera's removal of Puig Casauranc's face from the *Pearls Before Swine* mural, convinced the new administration that any murals Rivera created would be consistent with the government's ideology. It is no surprise that the Chapingo murals are Rivera's least political in terms of subject matter.

Three days a week, Pablo boarded the train to Chapingo at seven a.m., along with Rivera and his other assistants, who would listen as Rivera spoke with workers about politics, the land, cultivation, and seeds.[21] The murals were to have an agricultural theme and Rivera wanted to learn about agriculture from those who were closest to it. Pablo learned from Rivera to seek out the people whom he would be depicting in a mural and learn as much as he could about their lives.

The Chapingo project covered two buildings, a conventional one and a vaultlike former chapel with high, narrow walls and a cupola. The chapel murals, begun in 1926 and finished in the fall of 1927, are considered by many to be Rivera's masterpiece, an art deco Sistine Chapel.

Rivera painted two huge nude female figures wrapped into a Rivera cosmology that includes the elements, manual labor, and machinery. The murals depict the social development toward revolution as a progression as natural and inevitable as the germination and growth of a seed. Lupe, now postpartum, modeled for the first figure representing "The Liberated Earth With Natural Forces Controlled by Man." Tina Modotti modeled for the figure of germination and Luz Jiménez for a third female figure.[22] Pablo worked with Xavier Guerrero, Alva Guadarrama, and Máximo Pacheco. Depicting seventeen female nudes and two male nudes, the Chapingo chapel murals have been described as not inspired by politics, but by sex.[23]

Pablo became passionate about learning everything he could about Mexico. He spent days in the Museum of Anthropology, where he saw the massive stone sculptures of the Aztecs, Mayans, and Teotihuacanos. Following Rivera's and Charlot's example, he traveled through the countryside, visiting peasants who lived in grass huts furnished only with hammocks and a stove; and he spoke with everyone, from *campesino* to university professor, who would discuss the problems facing Mexico and its people. These excursions to the country became a habit that Pablo would keep to the very end of his life.

Pablo, Texas-born artist Emily Edwards, Charlot, and others began attending informal, free classes Rivera taught at his home. Edwards recalled Rivera spreading a big piece of paper over the dining room table and getting out a compass and rulers. He placed tracing paper over a reproduction of a famous painting and, with the tools, showed the students the structure, the bones, of the painting. Edwards said, "it was pure and simple geometry . . . based on the Golden Section or Mean. Rivera spoke of art history and music as well. Pablo or Charlot would interpret what Rivera said into English." Edwards recalled that Rivera once became furious with Charlot's interpreting when he thought he hadn't translated accurately something Rivera had said about the Catholic Church banning an ancient god.[24]

Pablo's top-floor studio at Belisario Domínguez 43, in the center of Mexico City, became famous. A visitor in the late 1920s might have found Pablo instructing a visitor on where to find the plumpest figs in the *mercado*, or asking a *campesino* to critique his latest sketch. An article described his studio: "[A]mong blue walls, white market stands, and happy swallows, workers, women of the plaza, veritable pilgrimages of *campesinos*, are roaming around." [25] Among those who visited Pablo's studio over the years were D. H. Lawrence, American poet Hart Crane, Soviet filmmaker Sergei Eisenstein, and writer Katherine Anne Porter.[26] Porter knew Rivera and reportedly "mixed his paints." [27]

In groups such as these, Pablo would listen more than speak, observe more than participate. He was just twenty years old when he arrived in Mexico, did not speak Spanish with proficiency, and was suddenly among a group of people who had fought in revolutions and in World War I, lived in Europe, traveled extensively, and risked their lives. The artists and intellectuals in Pablo's circle knew Marxism in and out and could argue their points with conviction and eloquence, often in several languages. (Rivera spoke Spanish, French, and some English and Russian; Charlot spoke French, German, Spanish, English, and some Náhuatl; Frida spoke Spanish and English.) But listening and observing suited Pablo since he was never comfortable with being in the spotlight. He was not talkative and didn't enjoy parties, dances, or society.[28] Even at parties in the United States in the 1950s Pablo would sit quietly, listening with a smile, but he seemed to be in another world. He was said to be "drawing with his eyes" as he took in the activities and people surrounding him.[29]

This is not to say Pablo failed to make an impression. He was handsome, blond, fit (he swam every morning), carried himself well, and had a "radiance" about him.[30]

Universally, he was adored and respected by those who came to know him. He had a reputation for being honest, direct, and incorruptible. He was intolerant of gossip and superficialities; if he felt people were being insincere or pretentious, he would leave the room. The words most often used to describe him by those who knew him were "gentle," "modest," "pure," and "kind." [31]

One friend, Yvonne Templin, whose husband, Ernest Hall Templin, was a Spanish professor at University of California, Los Angeles, and who arranged shows for Pablo at the Freymart Gallery in Los Angeles in the 1940s, said Pablo was "almost Christ-like" in his goodness. She said, "He was so good that he couldn't conceive of evil." [32] In some situations, she said, this trustfulness became naïveté—a quality that can be both endearing and annoying. Byron Randall said the only thing that irritated him about Pablo, who was in general "a very easygoing guy," was his "political naïveté, his innocence." [33]

Templin recalled Pablo as intelligent, but not "sophisticated intellectually." According to Templin, "Pablo was not highly educated, and people did not give him credit for being intelligent." "Though he lacked formal education," she said, "he was very intelligent—but his intelligence came through his feelings." [34] Goldblatt said, "He was slow and deliberate, with a gentle spirit. Never rushed. He had a strong sense of fairness and justice. He wasn't sophisticated." [35]

Pablo's unpretentiousness and directness sometimes came across as simplicity. Goldblatt described him as "simple," and Templin said he was "simple, but with the complications of the human heart." [36] The impression of simplicity was also conveyed by his manner of speaking slowly. He refused to use certain words, even English words, if he didn't like the sound of them. María recalled his dislike of the name of a certain medicine. Only after he renamed it with a word that was more pleasant to him, could he again refer to it.[37] George Gutekunst, an American who met Pablo in 1943, summed up Pablo's character in describing him as a "sweet, modest, tender guy with great steel underneath." [38]

Pablo's friends also came to know his idiosyncrasies. They learned of his extreme sensitivity to sound and knew to tiptoe into his studio because loud, harsh, or abrupt noises would put him outside himself.[39] The smallest sound would make him jump.[40] He believed that jazz was harmful.[41] He wanted to be treated as a Mexican, and became angry when waiters offered him potatoes and everyone else rice and tortillas.[42]

Rivera told Pablo to study the work of Orozco and see what other artists were doing, but the sketches he made in his early years in Mexico show mostly Rivera's influence. In a 1924 sketch of a hill with maguey plants in the foreground, the hill is a perfectly shaped, rounded line, showing a Rivera-like voluminousness (*El cerro*, page 89). Maguey plants, arranged in front of the hill, are orderly and benevolent, their leaves reaching skyward like little outstretched fingers. Later, as Pablo came to know life in Mexico, and, as his own life played out, these shapes would change, becoming sharp, ominous, and threatening (see *Quiero vivir*, page 219).

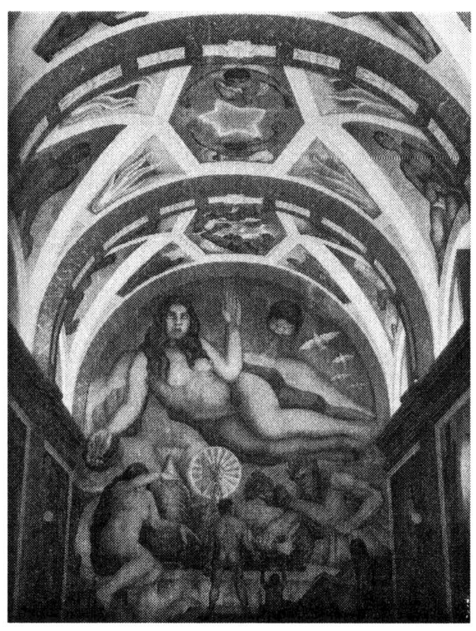

12

PAUL BECOMES PABLO

Pablo joined the Communist Party in 1927, three years after he'd arrived in Mexico, and while he was working for Rivera.[1] Pablo remained a member until 1947, when he switched over to the Partido Popular—People's Party (later the People's Socialist Party).[2]

The Communist Party played a big role in Pablo's life. Many of the decisions he made in his first decades in Mexico are explained by his allegiance to the Communist Party. This includes choices in his study of art, his travel, and the content of his art. He also seemed to be drawn to women who were also party members, some dangerously political.

When Pablo arrived in Mexico in 1924, the Communist Party of the Soviet Union was only two years old. Formed after the Bolshevik Revolution of 1917, it was the only legal political party in the new Soviet Union. In 1919, at its first congress, the party established the Communist International (the Comintern) to fight for the overthrow of the international bourgeoisie and create an international Soviet republic. Even in its infancy, the Comintern was interested in Mexico. Just out of its own revolution, Mexico seemed an ideal place for the party to keep an eye on the extensive imperialistic activities in the Americas. According to historian Daniela Spenser:

> Although [Lenin's] knowledge about Mexico was rudimentary, he was interested in the Mexican peasant movement, the national and indigenous question and the strength of anti-imperialist sentiments more than in Mexican socialism, which he said was bound to be rudimentary. For Lenin, what was most important was Mexico's strategic location in the Western Hemisphere as a neighbor to the United States.[3]

In 1919, the Mexican Communist Party (PCM) was formed. Early artist members were Rivera, Guerrero, Siqueiros, and Máximo Pacheco.[4] In 1924, Rafael Carrillo, who became a close friend of Pablo, became its international secretary. Bertram Wolfe, a Brooklyn-born member of the Communist Party of the USA (CPUSA), became its delegate to the June 1924 Fifth Congress of the Comintern, in Moscow.[5] Wolfe also became the editor of *El Libertador* (*The Liberator*). After Wolfe was deported from Mexico for his Communist activities, Rivera took over.[6]

The United States was also interested in Communist Party activities in Mexico. To its dismay, the government of President Álvaro Obregón, whose "enthusiasm . . . for the Bolshevik revolution stemmed from its own ideological commitment to social justice," had just established diplomatic relations with the Soviet Union.[7] U.S. Secretary of State Frank B. Kellogg said that the Communist Party in the United States intended to use the party in Mexico to overthrow American imperialism.[8]

Membership in the Communist Party was common among the artists with whom Pablo worked. Mexican artists who believed strongly in the revolutionary movement felt a closeness to the Soviet Union, which had also suffered a bloody revolution. Even those who didn't have an affinity for Communism found it necessary to play the role in order to secure a coveted position as a Rivera assistant. Artist Ione Robinson, newly arrived in Mexico, and, at Rivera's suggestion, a houseguest of Tina Modotti, wrote to her family in the United States, "A constant stream of people is coming to see Modotti—writers, musicians, and painters who all wear overalls with a red star pinned on the front. Everyone is a Communist, a 'red' as you would say; it is evident that one must take sides in Mexico, and the side that the painters are on is red, so I have decided to be red, too . . . . Don't get angry—it is only to help me to work with Rivera." [9]

The Mexican Communist Party and the government were close. Art historian David Craven says that between 1924 and 1929 the government, granter of the mural commissions, was "covertly subsidiz[ing] the Party." [10]

The formation of the artist's union in Mexico in 1922 was contemporaneous with the formation in the Soviet Union of the Association of Artists of Revolutionary Russia, whose manifesto stated: "As citizens it is our duty towards humanity to engrave the greatest moment of history in its revolutionary surge. We shall depict the present day: the everyday life of the Red Army, of workers and peasants, of revolutionary figures and heroes of labor. We shall offer a true picture of events and not abstract fabrications that discredit revolution before the world proletariat." [11]

In 1919, when the PCM was formed, Communism was an untried dream, full of hope and the promise of fairness, equality, and a good living for all workers. Communism had attracted many people in the United States who were fed up with the power of monopolists and supported the trust-busting of President Theodore Roosevelt in the early 1900s. Even in Utah, Mormons, whose history included communal ownership of property, were attracted to Communism.[12] Among other Americans drawn to Communism was John Reed, from a wealthy Portland, Oregon, family. Reed, a Harvard graduate, visited Mexico as a journalist covering the Mexican Revolution. He met with Pancho Villa and saw the mistreatment of Mexican workers by the huge American mining companies. Reed immediately identified with the Mexican people and their struggle for a decent life.[13] Reed's experience in Mexico solidified his commitment to Communism; he became the first American to be buried in the Kremlin.

A practical reason existed for party membership. In post-revolutionary Mexico, as in much of history, art and politics were inseparable. The Mexican middle class and the private art market it created did not yet exist. Consequently, artists who wanted to be paid for their work had to stay in the good graces of the government—the only source of mural commissions—and to paint using the prescribed visual language of realism, simplistic symbolism, and exaggeration to the point of caricature that the illiterate masses were expected to understand. As Ione Robinson noted, in the eyes of artists who did not participate in the mural movement, the revolution had not freed artists from the confines of European standards, but had simply confined them to a new prison. Artists who refused to join the movement and adhere to "Revolutionary Realism" in the style of Rivera, Orozco, and Siqueiros felt forced to leave the country.

There was pressure, therefore, to appear to be a worker.[14] "Maintaining a personal style of dress which clearly identified one's allegiance to the working classes was de rigueur," says art historian Noah Bardach. [15] Core to the artists' beliefs was the idea that they were *trabajadores* (workers), just as were brick makers, plasterers, and housepainters. A young man who had felt at odds with the conservative, Mormon society in which he had lived as a child, Pablo wanted to be accepted in Mexico. He immersed himself in the Mexican culture. By the 1930s he was using the name Pablo.

Involvement in a working-class and agrarian revolutionary movement presented a dilemma for Pablo. As an American, he already would be associated with the American capitalists shown in the Secretaría murals emerging from bank vaults or resting their heavy moneybags on sickles held by workers. If the Mexican arts community, most of whom were Communist Party members or sympathizers, learned that his background included *Mayflower* ancestors and privilege, this would only add to what he had to overcome in order to be accepted. And his father's involvement in the Joe Hill case would raise questions of his motivations.

It was in this context that Pablo began saying he was born in San Francisco or grew up in San Diego: "At three years of age my parents took me to live in San Francisco. Three or four years later we moved to San Diego. There I met many Mexicans and learned Spanish." [16] He avoided references to Utah.[17]

In 1933, the *San Francisco Chronicle* described Pablo as a San Francisco native.[18] The reference to San Francisco as his birthplace appears often over the years, including in publications he would have had the ability to edit, such as catalogs for solo gallery shows.[19]

It is said Pablo added the O to Higgins because it is easier to say Pablo O'Higgins than Pablo Higgins, but the addition of another syllable makes the name more difficult to pronounce.[20] (Paul Higgins in Spanish has three syllables, Pablo O'Higgins has five, including an awkward double o followed by an i sound, since in Spanish the h is silent.) Adding a consonant to the beginning of his surname would have made it easier to pronounce, but adding a second vowel does not.

There is a more plausible explanation. In "becoming" Mexican, Pablo was burdened with an English surname, Higgins. Alfredo Zalce, who knew Pablo for decades, said, in an interview in 1971:

> Pablo Higgins is blond and has the misfortune of having such a non-Mexican name as Higgins. But if you live with him, you see he's very Mexican. All his friends are Mexicans. I never thought of him as a foreigner.[21]

A simple solution to the English name was making it Irish. Describing his father as an unprosperous Irish lawyer, and changing his English name to an Irish name would make Pablo appear less blue-blooded and draw on the goodwill enjoyed by the Irish in Mexico because of the countries' common religion and history of oppression. If one had the burden of being a U.S. citizen of European heritage in the Mexican art world in 1924, one would be better off being an Irish Catholic than an English Protestant, or even a Scots-Irish Protestant.

Changing his name to O'Higgins led people to believe that Pablo's father was of native Irish heritage (since the O designates native Irish heritage), like the father of one of his contemporaries, artist and architect Juan O'Gorman, who later designed the famous mural on the library of the Universidad Nacional Autónoma de México, and Bernardo O'Higgins, the emancipator of Chile.[22]

In his early days in Mexico, Pablo would have learned of the affection Mexicans have for the Irish Catholics and their struggle in the 1916–1920 civil war for independence from Great Britain, a struggle that paralleled Mexico's struggle for autonomy. Pablo would have learned that among Mexico's martyred heroes were Irish Catholic citizens of the United States who changed sides in the Mexican-American War of 1846–1848 to fight for the mainly Catholic Mexicans against the United States—the highly honored Los Patricios (St. Patrick Brigade). A monument to the brigade stands in Mexico City. Mexican President Álvaro Obregón, was said to be of Irish heritage, with O'Brien having become Obregón.[23]

In Latin America, the name O'Higgins was and is auspicious: Bernardo O'Higgins liberated Chile from Spain in 1818. Jules Heller, with whom Pablo stayed in Los Angeles in 1948, said, in 1999, "[I]t seems reasonable to believe that the man's surname was, somehow, related to that of that great Chilean liberator, Bernardo O'Higgins." [24] Diego Rivera may have believed this as well: he referred to Pablo as having "*sangre de libertadores americanos* [blood of American liberators]," meaning liberators of the Americas, not of the United States.[25] Pablo's close friend Jean Charlot, with whom he lived in New York in 1931, believed the same: Charlot, who became a well-known art history professor and author of numerous books on Mexican art, told an audience at Wayne State University in 1965 that Pablo was a "direct descendent" of Bernardo O'Higgins, "the liberator of Chile and the George Washington of Latin America." [26] Charlot's son, John Charlot, said that his father had said this to many people and that he would not have done so if he had not been told this by Pablo.[27]

There may be another, sad, explaination for the name change: Pablo told his wife, María, that O'Higgins meant "bastard son of Higgins," indicating that Pablo may have felt unworthy of his father's name. [28]

Thus, Pablo was routinely referred to in Mexico as Irish or as Irish-American.[29] Sometimes, he was separated even further from his European heritage in statements such as, "He was the youngest child of a middle class family of distant European origin." [30] Interestingly, Jean Charlot, clearly European as he was born and educated in Paris, didn't face such an uphill battle in being accepted as Mexican: a myth developed around him that he was a "descendent of Aztec royalty." [31]

Pablo's characterizing his mother as a peasant or a farmer also would have helped him establish a more working-class background more in line with party membership than a middle-class background.[32] Party member and TASS correspondent Joseph Freeman complained to his new wife, Ione Robinson, that the Mexico TASS reporter "never really covered the news well in Mexico because of his bourgeois background." [33] When Rivera behaved in a way unfitting a Communist, Pablo attributed it to his "middle class" background.[34]

Pablo wasn't the first artist to seek to create his own identity, independent of that of his family, on arriving in a new country. When Archile Gorky, an Armenian, immigrated to the United States, he allowed people to believe he was Russian and related to the famous Russian novelist Maxim Gorky. Other artists of the century, such as Bob Dylan (born Zimmerman in Minnesota), tried to roughen up their backgrounds to appear less middle class and more "of the people." Johnny Cash led people to believe he had been in the real prisons he sang about in his deep baritone laments, not just in jail drunk tanks.

Pablo also avoided talking about himself, instead deflecting inquiries and changing the subject to something that could not be questioned: his passion for Mexico. After his death, longtime friends looked back over the years and realized they had never discussed anything personal with Pablo, only the problems of Mexico.[35] In this sense, consciously or unconsciously, he may have used his concern for Mexico to avoid answering questions about his personal life and his past.

TWO YEARS AFTER he had said good-bye to his son at the Mexican border, on August 5, 1926, Edward V. Higgins died of kidney disease at the home of his daughter, Gladys, in Palo Alto, California, where he and Alice had been for the past two months.[36] It appears that Pablo traveled back to the United States around the time of his father's death, a five-day train ride each way.[37] In an application to register as a U.S. citizen in Mexico dated March 1930, Pablo stated that he had last left the United States in August 1926.[38] It would seem that any visit around that time would have been precipitated by his father's death or illness. Rather than bury him near his first wife, Lida, his niece, Hazel, and other family members in the Salt Lake Cemetery, Alice had Edward buried in Palo Alto. Had Pablo attended the funeral and discussed his father's life with family and friends, it seems the famous case of Joe Hill would have come up.[39] Edward V. Higgins's obituary in the *Salt Lake Mining Review* describes Pablo as "an art student in Mexico City." [40]

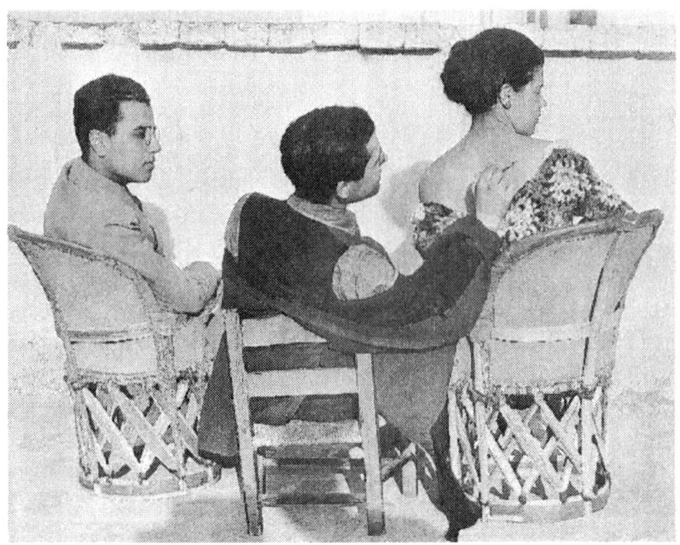

13

TINA MODOTTI

Tina Modotti was one of the most important women in Pablo's life. He would fall in love with her, draw her, abandon his job to help her, follow her to Russia, and perhaps, in the words of one of her biographers, become her lover. Years after her untimely death, Pablo confided to a friend that he had "been carrying a torch for Tina Modotti." [1]

From Rivera's scaffold at the Secretaría, where Modotti was photographing the murals he was painting, Rivera introduced Modotti to Pablo as a "magnificent photographer." [2] (Today her photographs fetch some of the highest prices on the international photography market.) When Modotti finished her work, Pablo walked her to the house she and Edward Weston shared and she invited Pablo to see her art.[3] He described his first impressions of Modotti:

> Naturally, I was just another person, but she impressed me immediately as a beautiful woman. I mean beautiful—not trying to be beautiful—but born beautiful. Very much of Tina was always like that—never pretending to be anything she wasn't. Very open and frank. I told her that I would like to see some of her work and she invited me to where they were staying . . . she was living with Weston on Calle Lucerna, and so when I went there to see Tina, I met Weston too. We talked of many things and the next time I went I made a sketch of Tina that I liked very much because I liked the way she was sitting.[4]

The drawing he made shows not the famous face of Tina Modotti, but the outline of her forehead, cheek, and jaw, her hair, her shoulders, and her hand, in which she rests her chin. A portrait Pablo painted of his cousin Lillian McAfee while he was in high school shows only the back of McAfee's head, neck, and shoulder, yet anyone who knew her, even forty years later, immediately recognized it as McAfee.[5] Just as in the portrait of McAfee, Pablo was able to convey the sense of Modotti without including her features.[6]

Pablo must have also been somewhat in awe of Modotti. Pablo was twenty, Modotti twenty-eight. She was gorgeous, famous, sexually daring, and scandalous. In his mother's world of white-gloved women pouring tea, Pablo had never met anyone like Tina Modotti.

Modotti surely appreciated that Pablo was interested in her art. She spent much of her life attempting to be taken seriously as an artist and later as a revolutionary. It upset her when others spoke of her only in terms of her beauty, such as when, for a joint exhibit of her and Edward Weston's photographs in Guadalajara, Mexico, Weston was called "The Emperor of Photography" and she "la Bellisíma Italiana." [7] Not everyone was sympathetic with Modotti's plight, however, and for good reason. Once, when a group of friends were describing themselves on slips of papers, Modotti reportedly wrote, "Tina Modotti—profession—men!" [8] Anita Brenner had a special set of barbs for Modotti, most related to her steady stream of suitors. Brenner kept a list of people she marked as "friend," "enemy" or "both." People moved between the columns; Modotti's name was often under "both." [9]

Pablo quickly fell in love with Modotti.[10] They went on outings together to Alameda Park, where they marveled at the colorful handcrafted *artesenías* the vendors sold. They traveled to the village of Chiconcuac to see Indians weaving serapes. Modotti would photograph the children who crowded around them trying to sell whatever they could.[11]

At the end of 1924, Weston left for the United States for several months, leaving Modotti in charge of their new house at 42 Avenida Veracruz and photography studio, maid, and cat. Modotti was trying to establish herself as a photographer and took photographs of her social circle, including Carleton Beals, the young, preppy-looking correspondent for *The Nation*; artist Natui Olin; songwriter and feminist Concha Michel; Dolores Del Río, who would become Mexico's most famous actress; and Frances Toor.[12] Modotti also produced graceful and delicate photographs of flowers, including her iconic photograph of a pile of slightly faded white roses resting one on top of another.[13]

With Weston away, Modotti gravitated to political causes. The Mexican left was strengthening following Calles's victory in the presidential election of fall 1923. Modotti, whose Italian family had rallied against Mussolini, joined the Communist International Red Aid and was called on to talk about the threats of Italian fascism. She, along with other leftists in Mexico, were elated when Mexico became the first country in the Americas to recognize the newly established Soviet Union. One of her photographs from 1925 is of the Soviet Union's first ambassador to Mexico, Stanislov Pestkovsky, who infused money into the Artists Union's publication, *El Machete*, and, on May Day, 1925, turned it into the official publication of the Mexican Communist Party.[14]

When Weston returned to Mexico, it was obvious that the political schism between him and Modotti was widening—on a train between Guadalajara and Mexico City, Weston rode in a first-class sleeping compartment and Modotti chose to ride in second class, sleeping on the benches with the Indians.[15]

In mid-1926, Modotti began appearing on the seven a.m. train from Mexico City to Puebla, which carried Rivera and his assistants, including Pablo, to Chapingo. Lupe Marin, Rivera's usual model, was pregnant and housebound, caring for their young daughter, Guadalupe. Over the next year, Modotti modeled for Rivera at Chapingo.[16]

On May Day, 1926, Pablo, Modotti, and Weston watched the May Day parade from Pablo's roof. Tina shot her photograph, *Workers Parade.* [17] Edward had plans to return to

California and Modotti had recently spent two and a half months in San Francisco, where she had met with photographer Dorothea Lange in her cottage on Russian Hill, worked in her studio on Union Street, and had dinner with Frances Toor in Berkeley. It would be interesting to know how Pablo would have responded to any questions from Modotti about where in San Francisco he had grown up and what his experience had been, and what he might have said if she had spoken of the factory where she worked and learned songs about Joe Hill.[18]

Modotti had impeccable radical credentials. She was from a poor, militant immigrant family who fled a fascist regime; she had toiled in sweatshops in San Francisco as a youth; she had no formal education. Aside from Weston, she gravitated to militant men. Around Modotti, Pablo would have wanted to appear more working class.

Weston's return to California was delayed when Anita Brenner commissioned him to take photographs around Mexico for her upcoming book *Idols Behind Altars.*[19] On June 3, 1926, Modotti, Weston, and Weston's son, Brett, left Mexico City to travel by rickety train and sometimes horseback to remote areas of Mexico.[20] When they returned four months later, Modotti wrote in her diary, "Weston fini!" [21] Weston left Mexico for good in January 1927, and Modotti moved into an apartment down the hall from Frances Toor's apartment in Edificio Zamora at Abraham Gonzáles and Atenas streets. [22]

Modotti continued to photograph murals at the Secretara, where Rivera was completing the third floor of the Court of Labor with its depiction of Revolutionary Man. Brenner had hired Modotti to photograph Orozco's murals as well. Newly single with Weston gone, Modotti revived the weekend parties she and Weston had, moving them to Friday nights. She would make large quantities of her inexpensive standby, spaghetti with butter, for crowds, and Frances Toor, Anita Brenner, Carleton Beals, and of course, men interested in filling the space Weston had left vacant, would stay late into the evening.[23] Did Pablo vie for the vacancy? Patricia Albers, in her biography of Modotti, described their relationship:

> We know that, in their long walks and over cups of tea on the roof of Pablo's shabby colonial-era building near the Zócalo, the two forged an enduring friendship based in art, politics, and music. Perhaps they were intermittent lifelong lovers, more tender than passionate. Lacking machismo, steadfast yet intense, Pablo was to reappear in Tina's life at various times, and, so mutually trusting were they, she invariably found solace in his arms. [24]

One of Pablo's closest friends from the United States, Byron Randall, who first met Pablo in 1940, says that Pablo was very much in love with Modotti.[25] Mildred Constantine, who wrote a biography of Modotti, said that Pablo "loved her, but never claimed to be her lover." [26] Another Modotti biographer, Margaret Hooks, says that Modotti's later lover, Vittorio Vidali, was unhappy when Pablo visited Modotti and Vidali in Moscow because he suspected that Pablo was "enamored" of her.[27]

María O'Higgins said that Modotti and Pablo had a very good relationship and that he was crazy about her.[28] Modotti was always "after him" and this made other artists jealous. Modotti would arrive at his apartment early in the morning when Pablo was still in his pajamas and it would shock his landlady that Pablo would let Modotti in. María denied, however, that Pablo and Modotti were anything more than friends.[29]

Pablo and Modotti had several things in common. Both had lived in the United States but felt more comfortable in Mexico. Modotti said she felt Mexican, that in the United States she felt like a foreigner.[30] Neither had any formal art education beyond high school, unlike most of the members of their group. Modotti was self-conscious about her "meager education." [31] Pablo may have been as well.

Both Pablo and Modotti were taken by Soviet Ambassador Alexandra Kollontai, an elegant, high-born Bolshevik feminist who criticized the traditional family structure, and "bourgeois sex morals" that expected women, but not men, to be "spotless." [32] Kollontai arrived in Mexico in 1927 and, in English and French, advocated for women to be respected and valued not for their "good morals" but for carrying out their duties to their class, country, and humanity as a whole." [33] Her views—and her love life—were considered, in Mexico, on par with those of Tina Modotti.

Pablo said he admired Modotti because she never pretended "to be anyone she wasn't." He made a similar comment in 1974 about Jean Charlot, saying, "He is what he is. You see what I mean? There are some people who pretend to be what they're not, you know. But Jean is a sincere person from the top to the bottom." [34]

Pablo was popular with women, though he did not marry until he was fifty-five years old. Friends would joke that there were lots of blond-haired Pablitos (Little Pablos) in the Mexican countryside.[35] Byron Randall remembers being in a village with Pablo and seeing several small children run up to Pablo and call him Papa.[36] But the general perception of Pablo was that he was a bachelor whom women loved to care for but who was generally oblivious to women.[37] Seymour Kaplan said, "It didn't take long for women to get interested in him," but "they had to work hard to get his attention." [38]

Pablo's lack of interest in the women who doted upon him, the fact that he sometimes lived in his studio with other men (such as Foncerrada and Charlot), and his longtime bachelorhood led some people to believe that he was homosexual.[39] Other friends totally disagreed, mentioning relationships he had with women throughout his life, but conceded that he was "asexual," that he simply didn't exude sexuality.[40] Randall, whose paintings of nude women were celebratory, felt it was strange that Pablo was not interested artistically in the female nude.[41] A statement Pablo once made to a friend, however, indicates he took his romances and the responsibilities they created seriously. Pablo told this friend that he was not happy with a woman he was seeing. The friend suggested he simply break off the relationship, to which Pablo replied, "But I slept with her." [42]

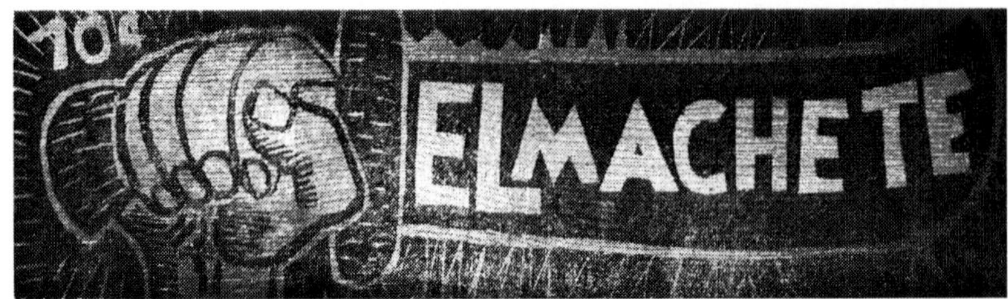

14

MEXICAN COMMUNIST PARTY

By mid-1927, everyone knew. After a few months of modeling for Rivera, Modotti and he began having an affair.[1] It apparently continued for nearly a year, until mid-June 1927, when Lupe Rivera gave birth to their second daughter, Ruth, and Rivera confessed.[2]

Lupe was irate, reportedly not only because of the affair but because she had to suffer the indignity of permanently sharing a wall with the image of a nude Modotti.[3] Modotti was irate that Rivera had told Lupe.[4] Rivera and Lupe separated, although he and Modotti had broken off their relationship.

Word spread quickly through the artist community. Although the Communist Party took the position that a couple should not "own" each other, many still believed in fidelity, at least in name. Relationships like that of Dr. Atl (Gerardo Murillo) and his mistress, Nahui Olin—in which they were both married to other people yet lived together and took other lovers—were considered very daring and bohemian. Modotti would later vow to give up her lovers only when it became too distracting to her party work.[5]

Pablo could not have been happy to hear the news. Anita Brenner expressed satisfaction when she learned that Modotti had been the latest recipient of one of Lupe's angry missives, which Lupe sent to any woman she felt was too close to Rivera. (Modotti was moving to Brenner's active "enemy" list because Modotti was selling copies of the photographs Brenner had commissioned her to take.)[6]

Rivera hightailed it to the Soviet Union, where he attended the celebration of the tenth anniversary of the 1917 October Revolution. He was a delegate of the Mexican Peasant League at the Moscow Peasant Conference and general secretary of the Anti-Imperialist

League.[7] (Lupe wrote to Rivera that he needed to send someone to collect his things from her house, that his sister did not want to store them and "Pablo does not want to either," suggesting that Pablo was not inclined to do any favors for his friend.)[8] Modotti continued to photograph Rivera's murals and to offer the photos for sale. She also worked as a contributing editor of *Mexican Folkways*, as did Pablo.[9]

After Weston was out of her life, Modotti seemed to change. She began spending time with Xavier Guerrero, who many thought was married to the party (although he had proposed marriage to Katherine Anne Porter).[10] Modotti traded her pretty sundresses for worker's overalls and no longer wore flowers in her hair.[11] At a reception for Soviet ambassador Alexandra Kollontai, Modotti allowed Guerrero, who had "renounced his art out of dedication to the Communist Party" to criticize her photographs of flowers, saying it was irresponsible and self-indulgent to create art that served no political purpose.[12] Ione Robinson was getting the same advice about her art: She said her new husband, TASS correspondent Joe Freeman, made her feel that she had "committed a crime by painting flowers." He showed her pictures from *New Masses*, in which everyone was "being hit over the head, hung or starved." She was "certain a worker would like to look at a beautiful flower more than at a picture of a policeman hitting him over the head."[13]

Guerrero moved in with Modotti and they spent much of their time at party headquarters and working on *El Machete*.[14] Guerrero took her to the slums of Mexico, the *ciudades perdidas* (lost cities), to show her the "real Mexico," far from the parties and exhibits she had experienced with Weston and Rivera. Modotti's more political art began appearing in publications such as *El Machete*, and *Forma*, a Latin American art journal published by Gabriel Fernández Ledesma.[15] Their house became the meeting place for the Central Committee of the party.[16]

On one of Guerrero's "evangelizing" trips, novelist John Dos Passos watched Guerrero talking with Indians. The Indians would bring up their problems with their *enemigos* (enemies), and Guerrero kept trying to explain, "*los enemigos* were the capitalist oppressors" not "the Indians on the other slope of the mountains."[17]

In late 1927, Modotti met two men who would complete her transformation from a talented and vibrant independent artist to a worn-down slave to Communism: Julio Antonio Mella, a Cuban revolutionary, and Vittorio Vidali, an Italian member of Stalin's secret police who was known for his many aliases and disguises. By late 1927, she had become a member of the party.[18]

Modotti's work took a turn. She began photographing the prescribed symbols of the revolution, the hammer and sickle, bullet bandoliers, and peasants.

Modotti's relationship with Guerrero was cut short when he was called to the Soviet Union by the Central Committee of the party, which included Vidali. Some have suggested that Vidali cleared Guerrero out of Modotti's life so he could step in. But before he could, someone else slipped through the door.

Pablo joined the party was well, a year after his father died, and the same year that Tina joined. Pablo believed in Communism.[19] But he was not dogmatic and never forced his opinions on others. A student of his recalled how Pablo responded when pressed for his opinion on the revolution in Cuba, which, according to John Caughlan, Pablo was very much in support of.[20] Pablo answered that the student should go to Cuba himself and form his own opinions.[21]

Pablo's commitment to Communism was more humanitarian than doctrinal. It was an emotional response, arising from a strong compassion for the people in general and the oppressed in particular, and from a strong sense of fairness and justice. Marxist scholar and art critic Alberto Híjar, who serves on the board of María O'Higgins's foundation, established to promote Pablo's work, described Pablo as a "militant" and an "exemplary Communist," whose commitment was based on a belief that the social relationships created by Communism were more humanitarian than those of other systems.[22] Pablo's militancy was strongest in his early years of party membership.

Pablo's party membership was not accepted by many of his family members and certainly would not have set well with conservative attorney and judge Edward V. Higgins. Perhaps this is why he did not join until after his father died. But joining the party was a benefit for Pablo in terms of putting him firmly in the middle of the artistic community. It also put him close to Modotti.

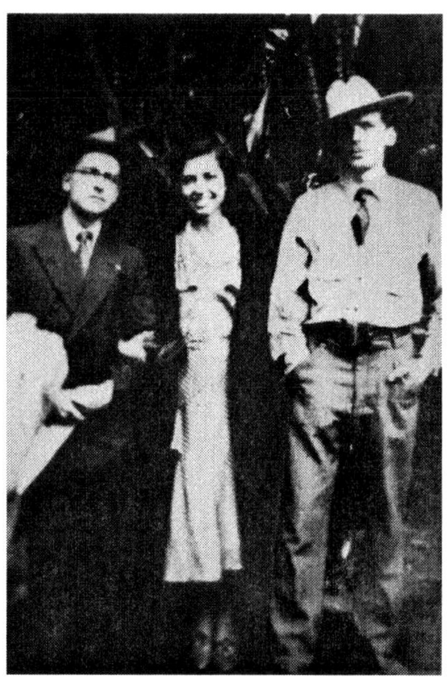

15

CULTURAL MISSION

One of the country's most beautiful colonial cities, Zacatecas, sits high in the Sierra Madre Mountains of central Mexico. Its hilly streets are lined with limestone facades so intricately carved they appear to be dripping with jewels. At the city's center, a massive eighteenth-century Churrigueresque cathedral presides over a large plaza, where vendors sell *paletas* (fruit ice pops) and children play while dark-clothed *abuelitas* watch them closely.

Zacatecas became an important colonial city when silver was discovered shortly after the conquest. Up until the nineteenth century it produced one-fifth of the world's silver.

After completing his work on Rivera's mural at Chapingo, Zacatecas was one of three places Pablo worked earning three pesos a day as a "cultural missionary" charged with bringing art to the rural areas.[1] This job confirmed his growing Mexicanidad, and his becoming Pablo O'Higgins rather than Paul Higgins.

Pablo was among many Communist and leftist artists who fled Mexico City—and indeed Mexico—in the late 1920s when President Calles cracked down on the Communist Party. Orozco left for the United States in 1927, where he would paint murals at Claremont College in California, the New School in New York, and Dartmouth College in New Hampshire. Siqueiros would work for three years in Los Angeles. Rivera stayed in the Soviet Union for nearly a year.

Many artists who remained in Mexico, including Leopoldo Méndez and Alfredo Zalce, opted to join the Misiones Culturales (Cultural Missions) a program of the Ministry of Education that sent artists into rural areas to teach art to schoolteachers and *campesinos*.[2] It was part of an effort to assimilate Mexico's indigenous peoples into the rest of the country, and to reduce the influence of the Catholic Church on that population.[3]

The Cultural Missions were established by the Mexican government in the early 1920s. The Constitution of 1917 requires that the federal government provide free public education, including constant "economic, social, and cultural betterment of the people." Beginning in December 1933 it mandated a "socialist education." [4]

Mexico's rural states did not have a tradition of schools; the schools they did have were staffed by teachers "whose training probably averaged less than three years of elementary education." [5] The government conceived of a comprehensive program that would establish more schools and train teachers. By 1924, one thousand federal schools and six thousand state schools had been established. This was met by considerable opposition from the Catholic Church, which feared the government's secular education would affect the religious education imparted by the church.[6]

In the fall of 1923, temporary Cultural Missions were established in rural areas and staffed by individuals trained in social work, agriculture, hygiene, midwifery, mechanics, music, and art. These groups would spend several weeks teaching Indians and *campesinos* in each town and then move on. By 1930, fourteen missions were spread over nineteen states with 2,482 teachers attending them.[7]

The cultural missionaries took advantage of the revolution's "awakening" of the rural people to try to interest them in education.[8] The teams of cultural missionaries were touted as experts in their fields, but being simpatico was also a requirement.

> "[A]s a matter of actual practice, a misionero is an individual with some training and experience in his particular field of endeavor and whose outstanding qualification is his complete devotion to the cause and his sympathetic understanding of the people among whom he is to work. There are many individuals available who are far better prepared as 'experts' but who, lacking this all-important personal qualification, could not possibly serve as missioners.[9]

For Pablo, an American who had been in Mexico for only four years, to be chosen to teach Mexican revolutionary principles to the very people for whom the anti-imperialist, anti-American revolution was fought, was a great honor. In the early days of the missions, the teachers had to be people who "knew or would learn the Indian language of the area where they were working." [10] The most successful teachers were "men of campesino origin with little formal education who were technically competent and adapted to the conditions of rural life . . . [and who] demonstrated rather than taught"—a pedagogy that Pablo believed in.[11]

Pablo had to have proven himself both to be competent in art but, even more, to have great compassion for the rural people and enthusiasm for revolutionary principles and the Indian cultures they valued. George Sánchez, who visited the missions, wrote, "Through improvisation, guided by an ingenuity born only of devotion and faith in their patriotic undertaking, and because of a deep-rooted belief in the ideals of the Revolution, the missioners carry on as a spearhead of the cultural revolution." [12]

The missionaries quickly assimilated into the Indian communities:

> In a period of ten or fifteen days the missioners lose their status as strangers, they adapt their dress to local custom, they worm their way into the confidence of officials and citizens, they become accepted members of the community. I was dumbfounded at the complete change that had occurred in misioneros whom I had known in Mexico City and who had fitted into the cosmopolitan sophistication. As they worked in the rural village, it was difficult to distinguish them from the peasants of the community." [13]

For an American to become so close to and accepted as a teacher of the Indians and *campesinos* was an amazing feat. Frances Toor, Bodil Christenson, Anita Brenner, and even Katherine Anne Porter and D. H. Lawrence were documenting Mexican culture around this time. But Pablo was teaching Mexican culture to its indigenous peoples.

Pablo was nearly six feet tall, and, according to Miguel Orozco, a Zapotec Indian who lived with Pablo and María for four years in the 1970s, he was "enormous." "He was tall. The Indians would be three-quarters of his height. And he was very blonde with deep blue eyes. He always had a big smile. He was very noticeable. If you didn't know him, his stature was intimidating," said Orozco. [14] Mariana Yampolsky also described him as "*enorme, guerro, con pelo abundante que peinaba con sus manos* [enormous, blonde, with lots of hair that he combed with his hands]." [15]

What made Pablo less intimidating and allowed him to capture people's hearts, according to Orozco, was his manner. "He was very innocent," said Orozco. In dealing with the Indians, he "saw their humanity." He "brought the person into him" through his warmth, his innocence, his facial expressions. "It was not easy," said Orozco, with the obstacle of his physical presence. Many people have described Pablo as a "saint," and many, including Miguel Orozco, said he had a radiance or a glow about him.[16] One called it a "halo of light." [17] The Aztecs, four hundred years earlier, had accepted the tall, light-skinned Spanish conqueror Hernán Cortés, as their god Quetzalcoatl. Since the conquest and their conversion to Christianity, Mexican Indians had gazed daily in reverence at the light-skinned Jesus on the walls of every church and home in Mexico with a halo of light around his head. Former Mexican consul Salvador Jiménez, a native of Zacatecas, has suggested that this may have influenced their impressions of Pablo.[18]

For the *misioneros culturales*, success was measured by activities as simple as a round of basketball after work rather than a round of drinks. Sports competitions among villages were encouraged to "[break] down centuries-old feuds and prejudices." [19]

Chronologies of Pablo's life say that he was first posted in Hidalgo, and then in Zacatecas, and finally in La Parilla, Durango. In Zacatecas, Pablo lived in shacks with the miners and learned of the dangerous conditions in which they worked, their long hours and low pay. Most of the boys would leave school to work in the mines. Accidents would claim many of their lives.

This story must have sounded familiar to Pablo. Growing up in a family involved in mining, conversations around wages, strikes, and safety issues were familiar. From his father's family, he might have heard that no one was forcing the miners to work these jobs; they should be happy to have work. From his mother's brother, John McAfee Jr., the union position—that mining companies should hire only adults, educate workers, use safety precautions, pay fair wages, and that strikes are the only way for workers to get management to pay attention to them—may have resonated with him.

Pablo needed to see the mine for himself. The foreman agreed, under the pretense of allowing Pablo to look for *cal* (calcium oxide) needed to prepare walls for murals.

Entering a silver mine involves a tooth-chattering trip in a small cage into the deep, dark mine shaft. At the bottom, the cage shudders to a stop. In the deep catacombs Pablo saw men and boys, naked from the waist up and covered in dust, laboring with pickaxes at the walls of the tunnels, the candles in their helmets sending licks of light dancing like the devil on the walls.

Pablo learned that an American company owned the mine, and the miners urged him to speak to the owners about working conditions *Americano a Americano*. Pablo would remember the same position of the mine owners his father had represented: "Not let those kids work? How do you expect them to support their families? Their dad is drunk or dead, and their momma has eight younger kids to take care of. You think I'm doing them a disservice by giving them work?" If not blinded by youthful enthusiasm, he may have felt awkward, being a U.S. citizen on a "cultural mission" to teach Mexican Indians about a revolution that had at its heart the ousting of the foreign interests that had "stolen" the mineral wealth of Mexico.

Publications about Pablo differ as to what happened next. One report states that eventually the miners began organizing a strike and Pablo supported them in this effort.[20] A priest attempted to circumvent these efforts by appealing to the wives of the miners. The miners were able to accomplish their goals of higher wages and expel the priest.[21] The army was called in, and, for some reason, Pablo was suspended from his post and sent to Mexico City. Decades later, María O'Higgins, Pablo's widow, said that Pablo had organized the miners' strike.[22]

After three months, the strike was still on but the cultural missionaries were scheduled to leave for another location. Pablo felt he couldn't abandon the miners so he stayed, even though this meant he was fired.[23] (This does not explain how he came to work at his next cultural missionary post, in Durango.)

La Parilla, Durango, is a small, hilly, dusty mining town with one-story adobe buildings surrounding a plaza with a small plaque dedicating it to José María Morelos y Pavón, the hero of the war of independence after whom the state of Morelos and the city of Morelia are named. Laid out next to a small stone church with a Moorish doorway is the plaza that was the site of Pablo's first mural, in an open-air theater in 1928. He painted it with revolutionary themes marking secular civic and school holidays to counteract the emphasis the church placed on religious holidays.[24]

In Durango, Pablo witnessed a dark chapter of Mexico's history: the Cristero Rebellion. When eighteen-year-old Ione Robinson attempted to travel by train from El Paso, Texas, to Mexico City in June 1929, U.S. border officials discouraged her from entering the country because of the violence of the Cristeros. She learned that the rebels had control of Northern Mexico and that, although the shooting had ended, the train tracks to the capital had been blown up in places. She was told Americans were not being allowed to enter Mexico and was questioned extensively about her plans. She convinced the officials to let her travel but once in Mexico saw that "No one seems pleased to see an American, and for the first time I know what it is like to be hated for my nationality." [25]

The Cristero Rebellion was caused by Mexico's rather schizophrenic relationship with the Catholic Church. By the time of the revolution, the *campesino* class that formed the base for the revolution was primarily Indian and Catholic. One of the goals of the revolution, however, was to end the Catholic Church's abuse of power, so the 1917 Constitution contains the anticlerical provisions mentioned in Chapter Nine. In 1926, when an archbishop published an article that criticized the Mexican government, President Calles unleashed these laws and added some of his own. The Law of Calles, ratified by Congress on June 14, 1926, prohibited priests from speaking adversely against the government, from teaching in primary schools, and from wearing clerical garments in public.

While the *campesinos* had happily picked up arms to fight in the revolution, they were less happy with the thought of not being able to worship their *virgencita*—the beloved Virgin of Guadalupe, the dark-skinned virgin who appeared to a poor Indian, Juan Diego, near Mexico City on December 12, 1531. But the government did not relent, and on July 31, 1926, all churches in Mexico closed and most nuns and priests left the country. Those who stayed rallied bands of devout followers, including many *campesinos*, who roved the countryside in packs ambushing and killing any government employees they could find, including schoolteachers:

> The Catholic guerrillas burned down the new government schools, murdered teachers, and covered their bodies with crude banners marked VCR (for their battle cry "Viva Cristo Rey!"). In April, 1927 the Cristeros dynamited a Mexico City–Guadalajara train, killing over a hundred innocent civilians. Not to be outdone, the government troops tried to kill a priest for every dead teacher.[27]

The rebellion left eighty thousand dead. Several chronologies of Pablo's life state that when a town of Tepehuano Indians in Nayarit was attacked by the Cristeros and the inhabitants fled to an area near La Parilla, Durango, the site of Pablo's last mission post, Pablo was able to remove a bullet from the leg of a boy. The Indians asked Pablo what they could give him in thanks. He gave them paper and asked them to draw for him. Several days later, the Indians invited him to a cave in the mountains, where he was presented with drawings by the old men of the group. Upon his return to Mexico City, Pablo presented the drawings to the government because he believed they belonged in a museum where everyone would be able to see them.[28]

In another version of this story, Pablo said that he was on a cultural mission in Nayarit and he described the people who shot the boy not as Cristeros but as Sinarquistas, a similar group that did not form until the 1930s. He said that five to six hundred Tepehuano Indians came to thank him.[29]

The Cristeros are responsible for one of the tragedies of Mexican history: the assassination of former President Obregón. Obregón had survived several assassination attempts, but on July 17, 1928, four years after leaving office, while he was enjoying music in a restaurant after a banquet with his supporters, a fanatic Catholic approached him seeking permission to draw a sketch of him, then opened fire on him.[30]

In early 1929, while still on his mission, Pablo received a postcard from Modotti informing him that she had been arrested.[31] He immediately left his post to travel by train to Mexico City to help Modotti, thereby losing his job.[32]

Just months earlier, on November 5, 1928, Pablo's brother Roger had died. Roger had returned home from the war and enrolled in law school. Upon his graduation, he entered private practice with his father, who, after two years in San Diego, had returned to Salt Lake City. They practiced as Higgins & Higgins. In 1928, four years after Pablo moved to Mexico, Roger announced he would run as a Republican candidate for judge, an office their father had held. One fall day during the campaign, Roger died of an apparent heart attack on a streetcar traveling on First South street in Salt Lake City.[33] He was thirty-one years old and "one of the most prominent young attorneys in the city." [34]

Pablo did not return to the United States as he had when his father died. He may not have gotten word of his brother's death in time to travel to the United States. His receipt of a postcard from Mexico City about Modotti's January 1929 arrest indicates, however, that he had the means of receiving news while on his cultural mission, but it is possible that letters from the United States may have been delayed.

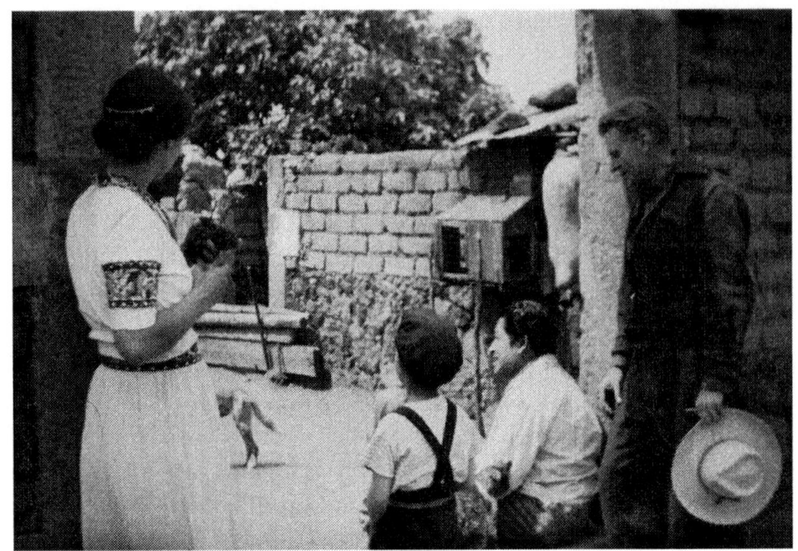

16

MODOTTI TRIAL

On January 10, 1929, Modotti was walking with Julio Antonio Mella from the office of *El Machete*, the Communist Party newspaper, toward a bar two blocks away when Mella was shot at close range and killed. Modotti, the only person with him when he was shot, was arrested and charged with murder.[1] Mella died at the Rivera home in the presence of Modotti, Rivera, Carleton Beals, and Frances Toor.[2] When Pablo had left Mexico City for his cultural mission, Modotti had been living with Xavier Guerrero. Pablo knew Mella from the party: he was a Central Committee member and reported to Rafael Carrillo. Híjar called Mella Pablo's compadre (friend). Carrillo says Pablo had thought that Mella and Modotti were just committed comrades, but she was living with Mella, who still had a wife in Cuba.[3] Had Brenner's assessment of Modotti as a loose woman made its way into Pablo's mind, he would have pushed it out. Modotti needed him. It didn't matter whom she slept with. She had been arrested and needed his help.

In Mexico City, Modotti's and Rivera's faces were plastered on the newsstands, with the *Excelsior* calling her a harlot.[4] The party put Rivera in charge of her defense, an assignment that gave him the opportunity to place himself in the spotlight.[5]

During Pablo's cultural mission, a lot had happened in Mexico City. Charlot and Brenner had broken up. A poem Brenner wrote suggested that after much inner struggle she had realized she wanted to marry a Jewish man; Charlot was a devout Catholic throughout his life.[6] Brenner moved to New York and enrolled in Columbia University. Rivera returned to Mexico from the Soviet Union in June of 1928, after the party asked him to leave Moscow. In September, Modotti and Mella moved in together on Abraham

Gonzáles Street. At one of Modotti's parties, Rivera met the diminutive, twenty-three-year-old Frida Kahlo, a German-Mexican artist who eventually expressed her Mexicanidad by dressing in the style of Indian women, with shawls and flowing skirts and ribbons winding through her intricate hairdos.[7] Her trademark ankle-length skirts covered her bad leg, disfigured from polio as a child, and obscured her limp a bit.[8] Shortly after meeting Frida, Rivera painted her into the Secretaría murals he was completing, showing her distributing arms alongside Modotti.

While Pablo was on his cultural mission, his art had been included in the first large group exhibit of Mexican art in the United States. Organized by Frances Flynn Paine, representing the Rockefeller interests in Mexico, the show at the Art Center Gallery in New York exhibited the works of twenty-two artists, including Rivera, Orozco, Siqueiros, Pablo, Jean Charlot, and Carlos Mérida. It was cosponsored by Mexico's National University and the Mexico Ministry of Education. It was not well received, according to Orozco, who wrote to Charlot from New York in 1928:

> I have heard that up to now there was a very receptive attitude toward everything Mexican as a result of the publicity that had been given it (based on Rivera). It all but came to an end with the Art Center show and I am happy about that because it will be the beginning of a new era in which each person will be judged for himself alone and not for his exotic-picturesque-renascentist-Mexican-Riverian quality. . . . The /Mexican fashion/ or mode de Mexique, whatever you want to call it, that farce, is now passing.[9]

Orozco's attitude may have been based in part upon his animosity toward Rivera—in the same letter he refers to Rivera as "Diegoff Riveritch Romanoff."[10] Modotti's arrest was directly tied to the government's increased hostility toward the PCM and its members. Although President Calles left office in 1928, he maintained his power through 1934, effectively circumventing the Mexican constitutional prohibition on reelection by controlling weaker presidents.

The government-controlled press found Modotti's life and lovers fascinating material for reporting and moralizing. The *Excelsior* claimed to have nude photographs of Modotti and of Mella and labeled her a prostitute and a pornographer.[11] The government considered Modotti a liability to all of Mexico for her revolutionary activities and open sexuality, which seemed to be on trial as much as her alleged involvement in the murder.

Journalists and spectators converged on Modotti's trial. During breaks they gathered at Sanborns, the famous restaurant and bookstore in the Casa de Azulejos (House of Tiles) on Avenida Juárez, which was, according to Anita Brenner, the only place to get a decent cup of coffee, and the most popular restaurant in the city.[12] Its upholstered booths were filled with reporters and friends of Modotti, including Frances Toor, who lived down the hall from Modotti's apartment, where Modotti was under house arrest with armed guards outside her door.

Writer Elena Poniatowska describes a thin and weary Modotti testifying about her relationships with Xavier Guerrero and Mella.[13] The room got hot; Rivera was muttering to those around him and shifting his huge body. He noisily took out a notepad while the guards looked on with dismay. Soon, there was tittering behind him—people watching a caricature of the judge appear on his notepad. Modotti's friends were annoyed that Rivera was once again trying to make himself the center of attention when Modotti's freedom was at stake.

But Pablo likely missed the drama and the opportunity to help Modotti. Within a week of her arrest, she had been exonerated of the murder charges. The government arrested a Cuban, José Magriñat, alleging that the Cuban government had ordered him to murder Mella because of Mella's criticism of the government. Mella had scrawled Magriñat's name on a piece of paper before dying. No one was ultimately convicted but some people suspect Rivera and Vidali of involvement. In the mural at the Secretaría, Tina is shown handing a bullet bandolier to Mella, who is wearing a white hat, while Vittorio Vidali, wearing a black hat, sinisterly looks on. Some suggest this indicates Rivera was complicit with Vidali in the murder of Mella.

Following Modotti's release from house arrest, Pablo went to Modotti's apartment every night, often with Louis Bunin, an artist from Chicago who was also an assistant of Rivera.[14] Pablo and Bunin would sit and watch the other guests, Bunin smoking a pipe. One night, Modotti admired Bunin's hands and talked to him about photographing the marionettes he made.[15] One of her famous photographs is of his expressive, veined hands working a puppet.

Modotti now looked rested. She was enjoying a surge in the demand for her photographs from the United States, Europe, and Mexico. Once again, she was surrounded by her friends, Diego, Jean Charlot, Carleton Beals, Vidali, and friends Pablo hadn't known before, including Manuel Alvarez Bravo, a shy young man from Oaxaca who was interested in photography.[16] Pablo again was amazed at the people Modotti attracted. "All men, as usual," Brenner would have said. But Frances Toor was there, and Vidali's girlfriend.

When he went alone, Pablo sat with a sketch pad. He observed more than participated; he listened to others speak of the Communist Party and the rising fascism in Europe but he avoided the theoretical discussions that got Brenner, Rivera, Vidali, and Modotti so worked up. Other women would come over and talk to Pablo; he always left alone.

In September 1929, Modotti threw her wildest party ever, celebrating Rivera's marriage to Frida. Modotti's rooftop was decorated for the event, including lingerie hanging on clotheslines. It is said that Lupe Rivera came to the wedding party, pulled up Frida's dress, and shouted, "You see these two sticks? These are the legs Diego has now instead of mine!" before storming out.[17]

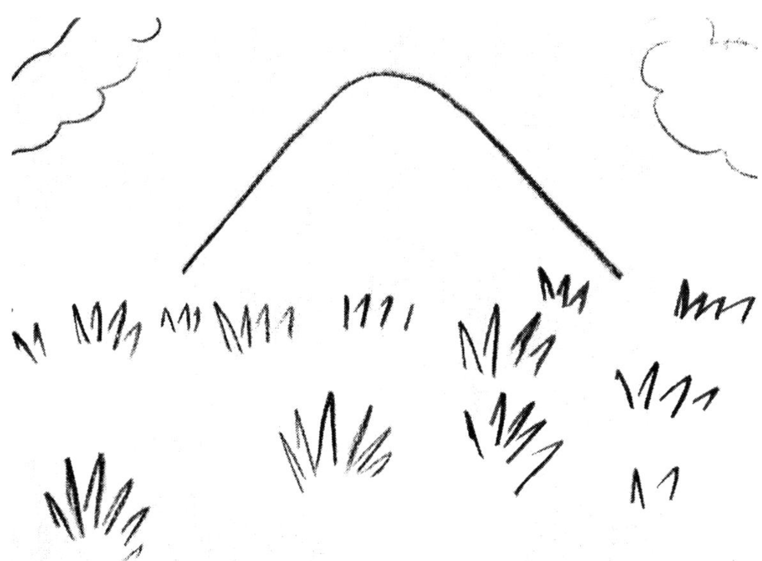

17

SPLIT WITH RIVERA

As Rivera's relationship with Kahlo flourished during 1929, his relationship with the party eroded. In April 1925, during the work on Chapingo, Rivera resigned from the party, saying he would devote himself to Marxism through art. A year later he sought readmission. Throughout his life, he would be criticized for not being revolutionary enough, as demonstrated by his acceptance of mural commissions from Mexico's often conservative government, his working for Yankee imperialists such as the Rockefellers, his being protechnology, and his unwillingness to dismiss people based on their class.

The party went through drastic changes in 1929 following the Sixth Congress of the Comintern (Sixth International) in Moscow, in 1928, which adopted a class-against-class position.[1] By 1929, the Mexican Communist Party was calling for a "revolutionary uprising." [2] Siqueiros described the mandates of the PCM under the new sixth congress: "(O)ur party has no alternative but to take up arms, to organize the armed uprising. At the same time we must sabotage the imperialist menace which would attempt to crush our revolution. Should the Yankees attempt to stop us we can destroy their industries, set fire to their oil wells and then take refuge in the mountains where they will never find us." [3] Vidali was said to be one of the members in charge of this operation.[4]

With this mandate, in 1929, the PCM made a bid for power "in the midst of the turmoil" caused by the assassination of former President Obregón.[5] It formed a "Workers-Peasant Bloc" with its aim "the substitution of workers' and peasants' soviets for the Chamber, the Senate and the Cabinet." Diego Rivera became president of the bloc, Ursulo Galván, its secretary general, and Rafael Carrillo its secretary of information.

The results were disastrous.[6] In response, President Calles outlawed the Mexican Communist Party in March 1929, and broke diplomatic relations with the Soviet Union.[7] Calles condoned a band of fascist-imitating terrorists, Acción Revolucionaria Mexicanista (Mexican Revolutionary Action), commonly called the Camisas Doradas (Goldshirts) after Mussolini's Blackshirts, who attacked Communists and Jews. Calles was demonstrating increasing right-wing militancy. He was undaunted by the wave of fascism spreading through Europe. Indeed, fascism—advocating for a strong, authoritarian one-party state, dictators, repression of opposition, extreme nationalism, and war for expansion of empire—was consistent with his anti-Communist, antiliberal, antiparliamentary, and anticlerical beliefs.[8] Not surprisingly the government took the opportunity to arrest Siqueiros at a May Day rally the next year and imprisoned him for six months for being a member of the outlawed Communist Party.

Yet Rivera was happy to accept the patronage of the same government that was oppressing workers. He accepted the directorship of the Academy of San Carlos and a major commission for the walls of the National Palace, a building in the center of Mexico City housing the offices of the president, the treasury, and other federal government agencies. Rivera began work on the murals in July 1929.[9]

Party members were outraged and on September 10, 1929, just weeks after marrying Kahlo, Rivera was expelled from the party.[10] Scholar Alberto Híjar explained:

> Diego . . . was responsible for the Pan American Anti-Imperialist League and specifically its organ *El Libertador*, and was also the leader of the Worker and Peasants' Bloc in the years 1927–29 when the Communist Party is experiencing difficulties in Mexico and ends up, along with its paper, *El Machete*, being outlawed. In this situation Rivera asks the Party for permission to finish his many [art projects for the government], and the Party responds by not giving him permission but by expelling him, because they had adopted the Sixth Congress of the International Communist's line of 'class against class' calling for the liquidation of all the little bourgeois tendencies inside of the parties as well as what they called social-fascism [liberals, intellectuals and socialists]. . . . Rivera met all of the requirements for expulsion from the Party. Obviously this had an influence on his relationship with a militant like O'Higgins. [11]

Rivera, Híjar said, went on to "accept the patronage of the U.S. Ambassador Dwight Morrow for the murals of Cuernavaca [just] a year after Rivera accused Morrow of being the one who organized the repression" of the May Day rally at which Siqueiros and other activists were arrested. Pablo, in contrast, said Híjar, "didn't have anything to do with this type of project." Emphasizing their allegiances, Híjar said, "Diego goes to the U.S. and Pablo goes to Russia." [12]

At the time Rivera was expelled from the party, artist Ione Robinson was dating TASS correspondent Joe Freeman.[13] Robinson said that Freeman "presided over" the party meeting when it made the decision to expel Rivera, and that Rivera was expelled because he accepted too much money from an "imperialist capitalist," because he was painting the National Palace for the rightist Mexican government, and because he had accepted the directorship of the art school from the same government, one that was persecuting Communists.[14]

Robinson noted that after marrying Frida Kahlo, Rivera "discarded his khaki" clothing for "a grey salt and pepper American business suit" and "[Frida] . . . changed from *huaraches* [sandals] to bright orange leather high-heeled slippers!" [15]

Pablo, in contrast, was extremely close to the party. According to Modotti biographer Patricia Albers, Modotti and Pablo both engaged in "undercover work" for Soviet intelligence, passing supplies to imprisoned party members and shuttling messages between them.[16] This was dangerous work. The PCM was illegal, and many of its leaders and members were beaten, sent to prison, or killed. One of those beaten was Benita Galeana, whose memoir Pablo would later participate in illustrating.[17] Galeana was a Communist "street fighter" who engaged in clashes between Communists and the government and Communists and fascist groups. She told Mexican writer Elena Poniatowska that Kahlo "was always with the artists; she never stood with us, the soldiers on the front line, not even by mistake. Now Tina Modotti, the photographer, she did join us." [18] Galeana, who was from the southwestern coastal state of Guerrero, felt Kahlo was bourgeois and that her dressing in "beautiful and jeweled" Indian clothes was contrived.

As Híjar pointed out, Rivera's expulsion from the party had an effect on Pablo, who, at this time was a "hard-core Stalinist." So did Rivera's sympathies for Trotsky, which he began expressing around the time of his expulsion from the party.[19]

Since Trotsky was considered a traitor to Stalin and the Communist Party, Trotskyistas (Trotskyites) like Rivera were also seen as traitors by party members. Pablo's separation from Rivera began "when Rivera gave Pablo a book to read about Trotsky," said Pablo's friend Byron Randall. "Pablo took it home and never went back to work with Rivera." [20] Most accounts of Pablo's life list Chapingo as the last mural project on which Pablo assisted Rivera. But records of Joseph Freeman indicate that Pablo and Louis Bunin were both assistants to Rivera in the early stages of the National Palace murals.[21]

By the late 1920s, Rivera was beginning to support Leon Trotsky in his struggle with Joseph Stalin over who would lead the Soviet Union after the death of Soviet Head of State Vladimir Lenin. Rivera adopted Trotsky's view that revolution should be worldwide over Stalin's view of developing "socialism in a single country." [22] Rivera shared his developing interest in Trotsky with Pablo, whom he had found to be a willing pupil on social, political, and artistic matters. Híjar concurred that "the political differences between Diego and Pablo were obviously the Trotskyism of Diego." María, however, denied politics had anything to do with Pablo's break with Rivera, and said it was simply time for Pablo to do his own work.[23]

This split did not affect the friendship between Rivera and Pablo in the long term nor affect Pablo's ability to benefit from having been Rivera's assistant. Pablo already had Rivera's blessing. Having worked for Rivera and having had him as his mentor would open many doors for Pablo throughout his life.

The late 1920s and early 1930s, however, were a low point in Pablo's relationship with Rivera; during these years, Pablo would draw closer to Siqueiros. Over the decades, Pablo suffered the same frustrations regarding Rivera as did many other artists who dealt with him. Pablo at one point referred to Rivera as *desecho* (worn out, used up).[24] In 1945 he referred to Rivera as "*ese sin vergüenza Rivera* [this shameless Rivera]." [25]

Despite their political differences, Pablo and Rivera remained friends; Pablo may have been a pallbearer at Rivera's 1957 funeral.[26] Rivera was a lifelong supporter of Pablo. He had great fondness for him and thought highly of both him and his work. He contributed introductions to exhibition catalogs and sponsored Pablo on his application for a Guggenheim Fellowship, a prestigious award given to people who "have already demonstrated exceptional capacity for productive scholarship or exceptional creative ability in the arts." [27] Pablo's years with Rivera had given him the experience of working with a great artist and teacher, status among fellow artists, as well as a good friend.

Apart from politics bringing an end to their relationship as muralist and assistant, it was important for Pablo to find his own means of expression. Although Pablo's work shows the influence of Rivera, especially the restrained rounded shapes and subtle shading of Pablo's early murals, he ultimately departed from Rivera in concept, subject matter, and style. Later, Pablo's lines loosened and became less restrained, sweeping and curving with boldness and confidence.

Breaking with Rivera was a big step to take and risky. Many artists from the United States, including Ione Robinson and Emmy Lou Packard, worked as assistants to Rivera, but Pablo was the only one who sought to be considered a "Mexican artist."

HUNDREDS CAME TO the only major exhibit of Modotti's work in her lifetime, in December 1929 at the National Library. While it included her early flower studies, its focus was on her political work, showing the peasant and worker as heroic. Her iconic photograph of Mella hung above the rest of the work.[28]

Following the exhibit, Pablo wrote a letter that, according to Ione Robinson, resulted in a "hornet's nest" of bad press against Rivera. Pablo wrote to Robinson's then husband, TASS correspondent Joe Freeman, who had been in New York since at least November, reporting to him "and Tass" events of the late fall.[29] This letter, according to Robinson, caused Freeman to write a diatribe against Rivera that kicked off a firestorm of criticism of Rivera later deemed "The Battle of the Century." The letter Pablo sent reported that Carleton Beals, TASS's correspondent in Mexico, was "lukewarm and had shown reactionary tendencies of late." [30] Pablo reported that at least thirty Communists had been arrested in Mexico City and were in jails, and more arrests and "deportations of aliens" were likely.[31] According to Robinson, Pablo appeared to be in hiding, along with "Gaston L." Pablo, according to Robinson, wanted Freeman "to write an article exposing the persecution unless it cut in on Beals," and Pablo added that "Siqueiros made a speech at the close of Tina's exhibition which expressed frankly what the Party thought of Diego—and called him an opportunist and a collaborationist." This letter did what Robinson predicted: It stirred up "a hornet's nest" of criticism of Rivera.[32]

Two months after her exhibit, on February 6, 1930, Modotti was rearrested and charged with an assassination attempt on Mexico's new president, Pascual Ortiz Rubio. This time she was deported. She set sail for Europe, having turned down the United States' offer of a passport if she renounced Communism.

On March 26, 1930, Pablo registered with the U.S. Embassy in Mexico as an American citizen. He was described as five feet six and one-half inches in height (he was actually more like five feet ten inches) with blue eyes and the occupation of artist. He stated that he had last left the United States in August 1926 and gave his legal residence as 1624 S. Arlington St. in Los Angeles. As references, he gave the names of his mother and Lucretia Van Horn of Berkley [sic], California. Horn, whose full name was Lucretia Blow Le Bourgeois Van Horn, was an artist friend of Emily Edwards from San Antonio, who had assisted Rivera on the Secretaría murals.[33] Frances Toor, residing at Abraham Gonzáles, No. 31, signed an affidavit identifying him and saying she had known him for six years. His application was approved on April 8, 1930. This was likely the certificate of citizenship that he needed to get a U.S. passport.

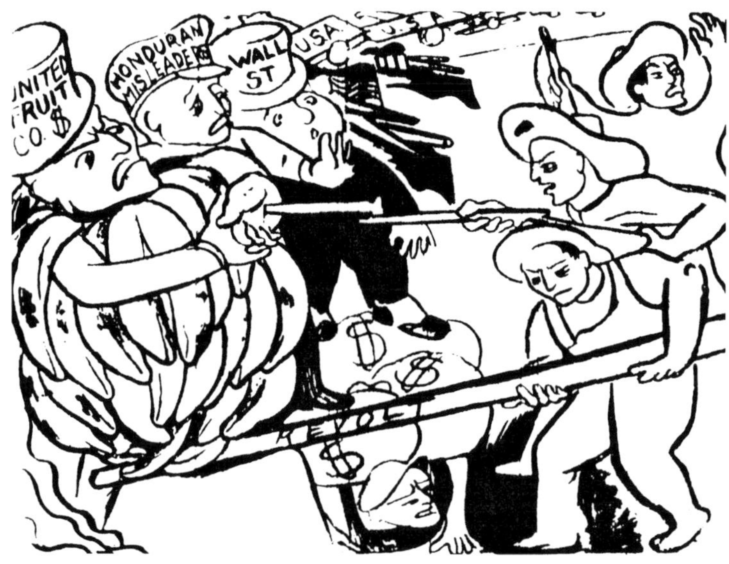

18

MEXICO/U.S. LOVE AFFAIR

Katherine Anne Porter blew a long blue ribbon of smoke into the still air of her Mexico City patio. The cocktails after the lessons were as important to her as the piano instruction Pablo gave her for six weeks in 1930, "teaching her the principles of harmony and explaining the system of balance and weight in getting tone, and showing her how to read music." [1]

It was a hot, languid afternoon, the welcome hour when Porter switched from coffee and cigarettes to martinis and cigarettes. Gene Presley, her lover with whom she shared the big house, walked about the garden, looking comfortable even in his suit, inspecting the flowers and calling in the servant if he found an imperfection in the cutting.

Porter's hair was pure white though she was only forty-one years old. The Spanish flu had done that in 1918, before she became one of the United States' most renowned writers. Now, she was at a standstill, frail because of tuberculosis, waiting to hear if she would be awarded a Guggenheim Fellowship.

Porter gave Pablo a hard time about his militancy, telling him he should be playing the piano rather than playing politics.

Porter took another drink from the tray the servant placed in front of her. Pablo couldn't help but smile at the woman with the sweet Southern voice and arched eyebrows, sitting like a queen in the garden with the servants and her dapper young lover waiting on her. She looked archly at Pablo. "You need to go to Russia and get your bottom paddled." [2] Porter believed Communism would become a world power and was hoping for a Guggenheim to allow her to travel to Russia, but was skeptical.

Porter was one of many artists, writers, and tourists from the United States who lived in Mexico during the 1930s. The economic depression after the stock market crash of October 1929, made Mexico, with its lower cost of living, very attractive. The widespread ownership of cars and the popularity of road trips brought a wave of tourism Mexico had not seen before.

Porter was typical of American artists living in Mexico at the time. Several, like Hart Crane, Ione Robinson, and Anita Brenner, had Guggenheim Fellowships that provided some income. Others brought savings from the United States, knowing dollars would last longer in Mexico. Many of them began their adventure of living in Mexico at Pablo's studio on Belisario Domínguez.

Anita Brenner was back in Mexico writing a travel guide for tourists called *Your Mexican Holiday.* She had been away for more than three and a half years, getting her doctorate at Columbia University and publishing the successful *Idols Behind Altars*, her first of book on Mexico.[3] With her was her new husband, David Glusker, a Jewish medical student from Brooklyn. Brenner had a Guggenheim to write about Aztec art that paid for her and David to travel around Mexico.[4]

Brenner would not be looking to Frances Toor to help her publish her book. Brenner had moved Frances to her "active enemy" list after Frances had cut her out of a project that she and Charlot had planned on doing together, cataloguing the works of nineteenth-century printmaker José Guadalupe Posada. Posada provided inspiration for the graphic art workshop that Pablo was involved in for much of his life.

Posada was one of Mexico's first real "artists of the people." A self-taught mestizo printmaker best known for depicting gruesome events such as rapes and murders, and using calaveras—skeletons—his accessible, highly reproduced work was in the nature of political cartoons, but with very few words, thus appealing to the uneducated masses. Posada's art was particularly "Mexican" in the sense that it defied European traditions and reflected the peculiarly Mexican (Indian) interest in death.

Posada produced more than fifteen thousand woodcuts, lead-cuts, zinc-cuts, and lithographs in his life. At death, he was buried in a common grave, which was later washed away in a storm. Whenever his work was published it was credited to Anonymous. Artists at the center of the mural movement vied for credit in rediscovering him; Rivera claimed to have studied under him.

Jean Charlot is generally recognized as having "discovered" Posada, in terms of reviving interest in him, after finding his prints being sold on street corners in 1922 and then finding his printing blocks in the offices of Posada's former publisher, Blas Vanegas Arroyo.[5]

Anita Brenner said that she was with Charlot when he located the blocks and that she planned to write a book about Posada with Charlot, but that Frances Toor conceived of a project on Posada and cut Brenner out of it.[6] The result was a special edition of *Mexican Folkways* that Toor published in 1928, which was devoted to Posada.[7] These publications piqued the interest of both artists and the public in Posada.

Toor took on another publishing project, which she planned as a catalogue raisonné on Posada, containing more than four hundred images. She retained Pablo, Charlot, and Blas Vanegas Arroyo, the son of Posada's publisher, to catalog the prints, and had Rivera write an introduction. Pablo and Jean spent hundreds of hours researching and cataloguing them.[8] *Monografia: Las obras de José Guadalupe Posada, grabador Mexicano* (*Monograph: The Work of José Guadalupe Posada, Mexican Printer*) was published in 1930, by Mexican Folkways and the National Print Shop.

With the outlawing of the Mexican Communist Party, the left deserted Mexico City. *El Machete* was published underground.[9] The new faces that showed up at Pablo's studio were artists from the United States who were in Mexico not to participate in a revolutionary art movement but to stretch their money, paint, and write.[10] As Pablo and Brenner caught up on news, Brenner's eyes widened when the subject turned to Modotti. She couldn't believe what she had missed when she was gone. If Brenner had asked Pablo if he had seen Modotti off, Pablo would have been sad to say no. By the time Modotti was ready to leave she was seeing practically no one but Manuel Bravo and his wife, Lola, party official Luz Ardizana, and Modotti's Italian compatriot Vittorio Vidali.

Brenner said, "Tina is again a martyr." [11]

Just as Mexico welcomed U.S. artists during the 1930s, the United States opened its arms to Mexican artists. Mexican art, with its realistic images, "filled a cultural and ideological vacuum" existing at a time when U.S. artists were "still trying to figure out what happened at the [1913 New York] Armory Show," where canvases were filled with confusing, flat geometric images.[12] Mexican social realism also appealed to the country's economic crisis. Images of rich bosses and poor Mexican workers easily translated into rich bosses and U.S. workers or out-of-work workers. Intellectuals in the United States were forming writers' and artists' groups much like those in Mexico to counter the rise of fascism in Europe.[13] Mexican revolutionaries enjoyed great status among them. The 1930s were the "heyday of American Communism." [14] Pablo is said to have had his first solo exhibit in the United States in New York in 1930 at the Bonestell Gallery.[15]

Still, in the United States you could go only so far. Months after their marriage, Rivera (newly expelled from the party) and Kahlo left for the United States, where they lived from 1930 through 1933. There, Rivera painted murals that, in the eyes of the party, glorified capitalism, and in the eyes of the capitalists, glorified Communism. In the San Francisco Bay Area, he painted a mural at the San Francisco Stock Exchange, another in what is now the San Francisco Art Institute, and a third in the Atherton home of Rosalie Stern. In Detroit, Rivera painted a mural at the Detroit Institute of Arts, and in New York at the New Workers' School and at Rockefeller Center. Angered by its depiction of Lenin, the Rockefellers jackhammered down the mural (he later recreated it in Mexico City).

Siqueiros painted three murals in Los Angeles. The two that were visible to the public were destroyed or whitewashed for their political content. The U.S. deported Siqueiros back to Mexico in 1932 when his visa expired. Of the tres grandes, only Orozco did not displease his host country during the four years that he painted murals at the New School for Social Research in New York and at Dartmouth College in New Hampshire.

In 1930, Frances Flynn Paine, an art dealer who managed a Rockefeller fund to sponsor Mexican artists, invited Pablo to have a solo exhibit of his work at the John Levy Gallery in New York in May 1931. Previously, Paine had shown the work of Jean Charlot and had a joint exhibit of Rufino Tamayo and Joaquin Clausell. She would soon arrange for Rivera to have an individual exhibit at the New York Museum of Modern Art.

Two years earlier, Frances Toor had tried to get the Weyhe Gallery in New York interested in Pablo's work, commenting that he had been an assistant to Rivera "for two to five years," but the gallery's director, Carl Zigrosser, had responded in August 1930, "He seems like a nice person but his art is without distinction. Whatever virtue there is in it, it is derived from Diego." [16]

Pablo arrived in New York in December 1930, to prepare for his exhibit at the John Levy Gallery in early 1931.[17] He stayed with Jean Charlot in his small unheated apartment at Union Square and Fourteenth Street.[18] Charlot had moved to New York with his mother in 1928.[19] In January of 1929, Madame Charlot had died of pneumonia.[20] Pablo stayed with Charlot for at least four months.

The gallery produced a small, four-page brochure for the exhibit, "Paul O'Higgins May 16th until May 30th." It includes a biography of Pablo by Frances Flynn Paine, which gives Pablo's birthplace as San Francisco.[21] Paine described Pablo's work as "reflect[ing] the soundness that results from [training with Rivera]," and "present[ing] under an unassuming appearance important conclusions both social and esthetic and [making] a genuine contribution to an American continental plastic."[22] The next day, May 17, 1931, *The New York Times* published a review of the previous day's opening.[23] It praised Pablo's depictions of workers and compared him to seventeenth-century Flemish painter Pieter Bruegel (the Elder) for his ability to capture with detail the life of the common person.[24]

Indeed, Pablo's painting of a May Day demonstration in New York with protesters being assaulted by police reflects a Bruegel-like quality. The painting depicts a melee of bodies from a bird's-eye view, much like Bruegel's village scenes in which the artist looks down at a crowd. The story Pablo repeatedly told of this painting is that Charlot had booked tickets for the two of them to return to Mexico on May Day (May 1). On Pablo's way to catch the ship back to Mexico, he came across a May Day workers' rally at Union Square (in a 1974 interview he said it was Battery Park) in which the police had intervened fiercely. He stopped to sketch it and nearly missed his ship. Pablo said that it was nine thirty a.m. and Charlot was waiting on the ship, which was to leave at eleven thirty a.m. Pablo got the sketch then took a cab and barely made it to the ship before it set sail.[25]

This story is used in books about Pablo to show that he was willing to take risks and make personal sacrifices to be the voice of the worker. One account concludes from this story, "Pablo never minded taking risks to get a direct sketch."[26]

The ship records of Charlot's departure (all foreigners were listed on a log) and Charlot's very detailed diary, however, reflect that Charlot and Pablo left New York not on May 1 but on May 16 at noon. They spent Sunday, Monday, and Tuesday on the ship, which stopped in Cuba on Wednesday, May 20. When they arrived in Mexico, Pablo and Charlot moved into Pablo's Belisario Domínguez rooftop studio.[27]

While in New York, Pablo produced four sketches for the *Daily Worker*, the newspaper of the American Communist Party. He drew simple, cartoonlike renderings of Latino workers showing their solidarity for their American comrades and carrying signs, in both English and Spanish, with party slogans such as, "the wedge that does the trick," the curious "work or wages" (you'd think they'd want work and wages) and "Down with Yankee Imperialism."[28] Pablo signed the sketches "by Paul." (Some *Daily Worker* artists used only their first names; others used first and last.)

The "work or wages" sketches later were republished in *El Machete*, with the slogans (now all in Spanish) denouncing capitalism, defending the Soviet Union, and seeking support for the Communist Party.

One of the drawings is cartoonlike figures in a crowd, apparently all men, wearing overalls and caps or hats, scowling or yelling. Two police officers stand in the background, with guns. The drawing is consistent with Pablo's lack of interest in the human figure at the time; the figures are crude, with little attempt at proportion.[29] This could also represent a deliberate intention to avoid an academic approach to art.

By 1931, Pablo was deeply committed to the Communist Party. Rosalio Negrete, a close friend of Anita Brenner who spent time with Pablo and Brenner's cousin, Abel

Plenn, in New York, called Pablo and Plenn "*más Stalinista que la Chingada, especialmente Plenn* [hard-core Stalinists, especially Plenn]."[30]

Pablo's work for the *Daily Worker* and his commitment to the party resulted in his receiving "the maximum honor for a Communist": an invitation to Moscow. Pablo was invited to study art for a year and was given a scholarship.[31] Most chronologies say he studied at the Academy of Art, but scholar Leonard Folgorait claims that this school did not exist in 1932 and suggests he might have studied at the Upper Artistic Technical Institute (VJUTEIN) from October 1931 to June 1932.[32]

As to the disposition of the painting Pablo made from the sketch of the New York melee that he said nearly caused him to miss the ship, the most common story is that he sold the painting to Rivera to help finance his trip to the USSR.[33] But in 1985, in an article for which María was interviewed, it was reported that Pablo sold the painting so he could attend a conference in the United States.[34]

Before leaving for the Soviet Union, Pablo began a collaboration with Leopoldo Méndez that would last for decades. Méndez, who is often called the Goya of Mexico or Posada's artistic heir, became a close friend of Pablo. Pablo and Leopoldo remained best friends until Méndez's death in 1969.

When Pablo left for the Soviet Union he left Charlot in charge of his studio, in the same building as that of another Rivera assistant, Emily Edwards. In mid-1931:

> Jean and Pablo lived in a room built on the flat top of an old disheveled house. You reach it from the central courtyard by first stepping up a series of stairs and then climbing up the last flight by ladder. A Mexican family also lived up there and they sometimes ate their dinners with him. The floors below were arranged into separate apartments.[35]

When Charlot went out of town in August 1931, Zohmah Day moved in with Edwards. She and Charlot were dating. With Jean away, Zohmah wrote in her diary, "I dreamed about Jean all night and awoke kissing Emily on the neck."[36]

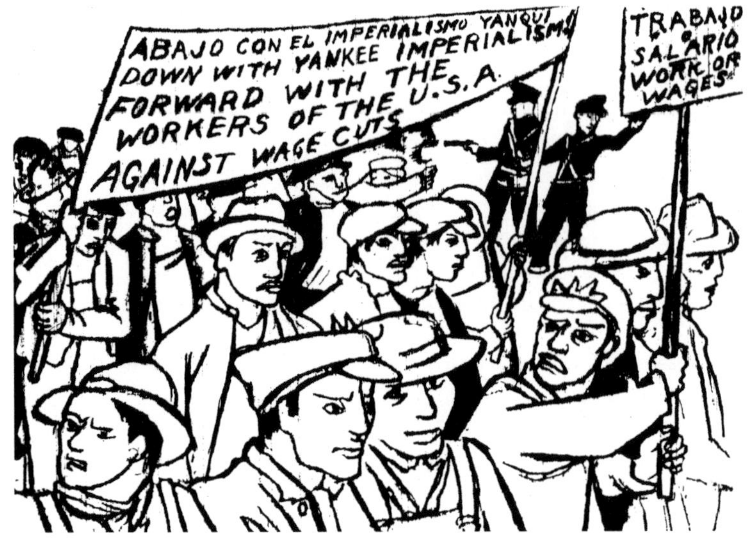

19

MOSCOW

After registering at the U.S. Embassy in 1931, on November 9, 1931, Paul Stevenson Higgins was issued a passport, which he needed in order to travel through Europe to the Soviet Union.[1] He stated that he intended to return within "an indefinite period" to the United States to reside there. To obtain the passport, he was required to take an oath, stating, "I do solemnly swear that I will support and defend the Constitution of the United States against all enemies, foreign and domestic; that I will bear true faith and allegiance to the same; and that I take this obligation freely, without mental reservation or purposes of evasion: So help me God." He listed the countries he planned to visit and gave the purpose of his trip as "France and Germany, studying." [2]

It is clear that by this time, Pablo completely subscribed to Communist doctrine, including the hard-line class-against-class stance of the Sixth International. Katherine Anne Porter sent a letter to him in Moscow referring to the Soviet government as "your" government and admonishing him to respect the art of czarist Russia while performing his revolutionary duties. She wrote:

> So I hope your government (Soviet), while it is melting down the silver from the churches, is at the same time preserving carefully the true works of art, quite as we preserve the archaic Greeks and the ancient Egyptian things, all made in honor of gods that no one any longer believes in; but their value is no less for all that.[3]

Porter's sarcasm reflected her growing cynicism with the idea that art must be a social tool. She was skeptical of Pablo's view that "all art was mere childishness in the face of the great oncoming world change."[4]

Being chosen to study in Moscow was a high honor. David Jenkins, a member of the Communist Party in the United States, said he had never been invited to Moscow to study as had others because he was not seen as a "future proletarian leader of the American Revolution."[5] Based on Pablo's work at the *Daily Worker* in New York, Pablo was handpicked as someone who had promise in the party. The party would not be disappointed. He became, in Híjar's words, "an exemplary Communist."

On his way to Moscow, Pablo met up with Katherine Anne Porter in Berlin.[6] Porter said she had witnessed huge political rallies of both Nazis and Communists and remarked at how controlled the Nazi rallies were.[7]

In Moscow, Pablo saw new, modern apartment buildings for workers, hospitals with the most advanced medical equipment, schools orderly and well equipped.[8] All of the effort of the new Soviet Union seemed directed toward improving the lives of the workers, no matter their ethnicity or economic position. The main square was filled with children playing, lovers promenading, and grandparents gossiping. People were lined up in front of a theater at the edge of the square.

Everything Pablo had seen in his first few days in the Soviet Union reinforced his feelings about Communism as being the fairest, most humane political system. He and other visitors to the country had been shown new cities created just for workers, new public facilities, gymnasiums, and nurseries. They saw a country making remarkable progress toward fulfilling the aims of the Soviet Revolution. Martha Dodd, an accused Soviet agent whom Pablo would befriend in Mexico, visited Russia in 1934 when her father was U.S. ambassador to Germany. She described an idyllic place:

> Milk factories, a workers' city growing up at the edge of the old city, hospitals, theaters, parks where people promenade, flirt, sing, and drink until late at night. I inspected everything, remembered the cleanliness of the workers, the medical and educational care taken of them, and couldn't help marveling over the fact that everything good in life was being supplied for the vast majority of the population. There was no race hatred, no class antagonism, no grinding down of individuality under the brutal economic laws that kept, in other countries, the poor always poorer, the rich always richer.[9]

Pablo sent Katherine Anne Porter "glowing reports from Moscow on Soviet progress toward a classless society and a "truly humane world."[10] Porter was not completely convinced. She was questioning whether the revolution in Mexico had helped the poor Indians "in whose hearts foreign intruders raise 'false hopes' of prosperity."[11]

The revolution may have changed the USSR but it hadn't changed the academic system in Moscow. Pablo's art classes were a duplication of the classes he had hated in San Diego—hours of sitting in stuffy classrooms copying the art of old masters. Stalin did not mandate what came to be known as socialist realism until 1932. Until then, film, not visual art, was the medium the new Soviet Union had chosen to communicate the revolution to the masses.

Pablo's plea to his drawing instructor was accepted: he was allowed to draw from Russian rather than Greek statues and permitted to go to the railroad station to sketch.[12] There, Pablo was able to observe a side of life in the Soviet Union apart from the officially sanctioned tourist sites. He learned of the real lives of the workers, the hardships they suffered—food shortages, high prices, and long lines for the simplest food such as potatoes and beets. This dark side of the new socialist experiment would not be fully known until after World War II, when the world learned that Stalin, in 1932, had intentionally created a famine that killed millions in the Ukraine.[13] According to María O'Higgins, the sketches Pablo made became important historical documents of a time when few Soviet artists were depicting the common worker.[14]

It is not clear why Pablo accepted an art school scholarship to the Soviet Union when he had no interest in the formal study of art. Rivera, during his seven months in the USSR in 1927, had become very critical of the government's approach to art. The Soviet government had asked him to paint murals in the "Empire" style, and, at art lectures he gave, the students defended easel painting and criticized him for admiring "backward peasant handcrafts." [15] Diego was always very vocal in sharing his opinions: upon his return to Mexico, he wrote an article, "The Position of the Artists in Russia Today." [16]

Pablo surely knew that the Soviets still taught traditional methods, but he would not have turned down the great honor of being invited to the Soviet Union. It placed him in the same category as Rivera and Xavier Guerrero, both of whom had been guests of the Soviet government.[17] Living in the Soviet Union would allow him to see for himself the system he believed in and give him credibility when people like Porter questioned his knowledge of it.

Pablo may have had another motive for accepting the scholarship to Moscow. Pablo told Byron Randall that he went to Moscow because he was in love with a woman there who had been a model for Rivera's murals at the agricultural college at Chapingo.[18] This may have been true, or Pablo may have been posturing for Randall, a painter of voluptuous nudes. If it were true that Pablo went to the USSR because Modotti was there and he was in love with her, he would have suffered greatly as he once again saw yet another older, more sophisticated, more intellectually powerful, more radical man than himself, Vittorio Vidali, come to Modotti's rescue.

Had Pablo found Modotti as Elena Poniatowska described her in her novel, *Tinisima*, he may not have recognized her, concealed in a dark gray coat and hat, looking identical to all the other women on the streets.[19] But her walk, which had bewitched every man in Mexico, identified her.

Modotti located Xavier Guerrero as soon as she arrived in Moscow but he insisted their relationship was over. She went to work for the Communist International's Red Aid, which was helping refugees entering the Soviet Union from other countries.[20] Modotti felt she had wasted her life until then, that all the art she had done solely for beauty really helped no one, and she was glad to have found her calling.

Modotti chain-smoked Russian cigarettes, which were turning her fingers and teeth yellow. She told Pablo of her struggle to find milk for refugee children and how difficult it was to move things through the bureaucracy, of the food shortages that hampered her work. None of the problems she spoke of diminished her utter faith in the Soviet system—they were merely the challenges she faced as a servant of the party.

As soon as Pablo saw Modotti and Vidali together, he knew they were a couple. During her last few months in Mexico, Modotti's social world seemed to have shifted to her brother's Italian radical friends. Vidali turned up on the ship Modotti took when she left Mexico.[21]

Vidali, an agent of the Comintern, was proud of the successes of the party. He told Pablo how the Soviet Union had moved from the last in the world to one of the first in terms of production of electricity, petroleum, and coal and how the party had transformed the country into the largest agricultural producer in the world. He spoke of how workers in the USSR suffered less unemployment than those in the United States. Modotti and Pablo both were mesmerized by Vidali's intellectual power and his commitment to the party.[22]

Modotti had left Mexico with an Italian passport and knowledge that it would be disastrous to set foot in Mussolini's Italy. When she arrived in Holland, Italian authorities attempted to extradite her. Workers' organizations in Holland convinced their government to allow her to pass through Holland the same day. Before moving to Moscow, Modotti spent six months in Germany, where the Nazis were accumulating power. She became depressed and paranoid. Anita Brenner said that when she saw Modotti in Hamburg in 1930, Modotti gave her "the willies." [23]

Moscow, in contrast, energized Modotti. When she arrived in 1930, she set aside her photography and dedicated herself to her political work.[24] She described herself as "living a completely new life, so much that I almost feel like a different person."[25]

Pablo kept Katherine Anne Porter informed of his experiences in Moscow. He expected her and Presley, who were living in Europe, to come to Moscow and advised them to bring plenty of grammar books "for morale [sic] support." [26] Demonstrating his commitment to the Sixth International, he wrote "glowingly" about the country's "advances toward a classless society." [27] Pablo found Russia beautiful, but his living situation was not to his liking. He slept in a room with six other "comrades," and so could not paint. (After he returned to Mexico, he recounted this to Jean Charlot, adding that he was glad to be back in Mexico—"who would not.")[28]

Modotti helped Pablo become accustomed to the way of life in Moscow. At times, they would visit famed Soviet filmmaker Sergei Eisenstein. Eisenstein was in despair after spending a year in Mexico filming *Que Viva Mexico!* When he finished, his backer, author Upton Sinclair, asked the producer of the Tarzan movies to discard controversial footage showing the tyranny of the Catholic Church and satirizing Mexican bureaucrats and politicians and to edit the footage into an innocuous work that would assuage the Mexican government and sell. The pallid result was released as an Eisenstein film called *Thunder Over Mexico*.[29] Pablo said that Eisenstein was suicidal over the fiasco and that he and Modotti tried to comfort him.[30] Fifty years later, the footage was edited by the late Eisenstein's colleagues into what they believe he intended: a slow-moving paean to the Mexican Indian that romanticizes their lives, showing them as healthy and beautiful, living tranquil, carefree lives in a lush tropical setting until things change. Hacienda owners, fat, and drunk on pulque, rape one of the Indian women. When the Indians try to rescue the woman, the hacienda owners brutally kill them.[31]

Pablo wrote to Katherine Anne Porter that Moscow was a "wonderful new world," and that Modotti was "well and cheerful" but no longer doing photography because there was not enough light.[32]

Pablo must have gotten a new sense of Modotti, who to his dismay, called him "mi'jito," or "my dear son." He knew her work in Moscow was more important than photographing flowers, that the chain-smoking Modotti with graying hair and deep-set eyes was doing more for the world than the sensuous Modotti sitting on the lap of Edward Weston. Pablo was always drawn to radical "Kollontai types." [33] But a part of him may have missed the old Tina.

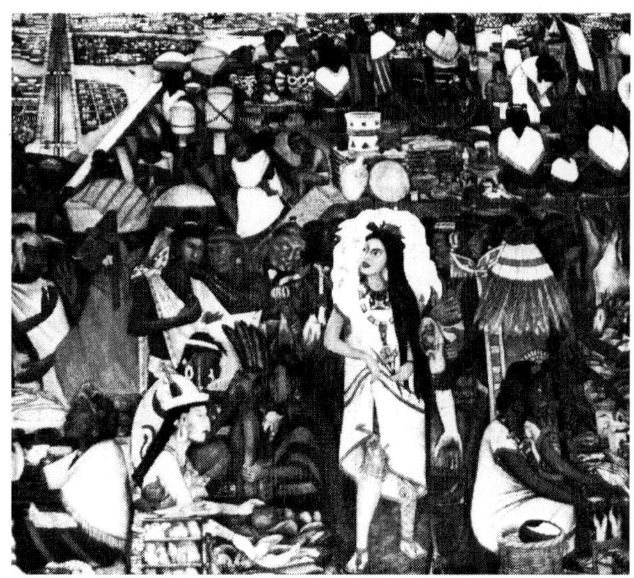

20

A HORNET'S NEST

While Pablo was in Moscow, a scathing, fifty-five-hundred-word article on Rivera appeared in the February 1932 edition of *New Masses*, the magazine cofounded by Joseph Freeman, Ione Robinson's now ex-husband. "Painting and Politics, the Art of Diego Rivera" was a long, sustained assault on Rivera Freeman wrote under the pseudonym Robert Evans. When Robinson read the article, she "realized at once that this was the answer to Pablo O'Higgins' letter, written so long ago . . . ." [1] Pablo's letter, written just after Modotti's final exhibition, had notified Joe and TASS, the Soviet news agency for which he wrote, about the oppression of Communists and Siqueiros's criticism of Rivera. Robinson concluded, "as Communists are supposed to follow orders, this article against Rivera was just a job to be done in Joe's life," suggesting that Joe, in writing it, was following orders from the party conveyed through Pablo.[2]

Freeman called Rivera's art awkward, lacking in imagination, and boring, and said it stole meaning from its subjects—the workers and *campesinos*. He accused Rivera of only "flirting with Communism" because he liked the color red. Freeman said that Rivera, while a member of the central committee of the party and head of the Workers' and Peasants' Bloc, had ignored the government's "campaign of terror" against Communists in 1929 because of his relationship with the government, including painting the National Palace and becoming head of its fine arts school. Freeman said Rivera had abandoned the revolution in favor of the U.S. (which was holding U.S. labor leaders in prison), as he had accepted a commission to paint for U.S. Ambassador Dwight Morrow, the "representative of American imperialism," and was painting bourgeois easel paintings for millionaire Americans.[3]

In the same issue of *New Masses*, the John Reed Club called Rivera a "renegade and a counter-revolutionist," and called upon "writers, artists, and other cultural workers to repudiate this unprincipled demagogue and to expose him at every opportunity."

Freeman's article did stir up a hornets' nest, setting off a series of attacks on Rivera that escalated into what he called the "Battle of the Century" over his murals at Rockefeller Center in 1934 to 1935.[4] Rivera's main critic was Siqueiros. Pablo corresponded with Siqueiros in 1934, and they jointly lobbied the University of Michoacán to give a mural commission to two young American artists, one of whom had worked as Siqueiros's assistant in Los Angeles.[5] Pablo expressed his preference for Siqueiros over Rivera in a letter to Marion Greenwood that James Oles believes Pablo wrote in May 1934, in which Pablo hoped that Rivera would not be involved in a mural project Pablo was working on (at the Mercado Abelardo Rodríguez), saying, "it will seem we are a group working under Rivera and Rivera has lately come out openly for Trotsky . . . . It would be much better if we had Siqueiros in Rivera's place." [6] The letters Pablo sent to Marion Greenwood in 1934 reflect that he was fed up with Rivera, his politics, his bullying, and his hypocrisy. In one letter, he calls Rivera "as magnanimous as Henry Ford," and says, "He's hypocritically trying to get your stairway and loves us as much as poison." [7]

Freeman later explained the basis for publishing his attack on Rivera:

> In the summer of 1929, painters who were Communists or who, and [sic] students of Diego, and under his influence were committed to the art of 'social conscience' and said that he had abandoned the line upon which he had developed his career; instead of painting the workers and peasants revolution, as he had done in the murals at Chapingo and at the Secretariat, he had turned to 'national' art. For the original design in the central pane of the National Palace mural, he had transformed the woman with the workers and peasant in her arms to the woman with the mangos.[8]

Letters and notes Freeman wrote over many years explain the events leading to his 1932 article. In several, Freeman refers to the painters who were upset with the subject matter of Rivera's National Palace murals as "Americans." Other letters indicate that the Americans included Pablo. In a letter written in 1933, he mentions the change to the National Palace mural that brought his attention to Rivera's shift in artistic subject matter and said, "You may remember of course that this change caused some indignation not only among Communists but also among the young artists (Pablo Higgins, Louis Bunin, etc.)." [9] Abel Plenn, Anita Brenner's cousin, told Freeman that Pablo "really knows more about it than anyone." [10] Indeed, Pablo wrote to Freeman, "I separated from Rivera before and during the preparation of [National] palace walls painting . . . ." [11]

Was it Pablo's intention to have Freeman skewer Rivera? Since Pablo and Freeman were not close friends, and since Pablo wrote to "Joe and TASS," according to Robinson, his letter appears to be a news tip, suggesting that Beals was not properly reporting the events in Mexico and letting him know that an ardent member of the PCM, Siqueiros, believed Rivera was acting contrary to party interests. Pablo did not write to Robinson, a friend and Rivera apprentice; he wrote to her reporter husband, a Communist hard-liner who had supported the party's decision to expel Rivera. Pablo would have known that Freeman, like most other hard-core party members in Mexico City, was not sympathetic to Rivera and did not consider him a "'pure' Communist." [12] In addition, Pablo may have known that Freeman held a personal grudge against Rivera. Just months before Pablo wrote the letter to Freeman in 1929, Robinson had been modeling nude for Rivera in his studio when Kahlo flew into the room warning that Joe was downstairs with a pistol. Freeman grabbed Robinson and hauled her to the Soviet Embassy, where she was lectured on the disgrace she brought to Freeman by posing nude for Rivera.[13] Pablo would have been certain that Freeman was against Rivera on a political and possibly a personal level.

Pablo also likely knew that Freeman shared his own concerns regarding Beals's reporting for TASS: Freeman considered Beals unable to cover the news in Mexico properly because of his "bourgeois background." [14] Beals's background included a father who was a lawyer and education at University of California at Berkeley and Columbia University. (Freeman himself was a Columbia University graduate.)[15] Pablo had told Freeman that Beals was "lukewarm" and had "shown reactionary tendencies as of late." [16]

Pablo, like Freeman, was a devout party member who saw things in black-and-white, a trait that in Pablo would annoy some friends and in Freeman would cost him his marriage to Robinson.[17] Pablo was a militant and a Stalinist and would have seen Freeman and himself (and Modotti, who sold photographs to *New Masses*) as solid party soldiers and Rivera, a Trotskyite, as an enemy of the people.[18] In Mexico, many party members at this time, including Modotti, considered Rivera a traitor.[19] Pablo's esteem for Rivera was at a low point. The hard-line Sixth International approach, which included reporting on members who were out of line, would, in the party mind-set, justify the tip.

But Pablo's friends repeatedly said that he was "politically naïve." Pablo, at the age of twenty-four, may not have known what trouble would result from his letter to Freeman but might have learned some lessons from what transpired.[20]

Pablo learned of the aftermath of his letter to Freeman when he returned from the Soviet Union in the fall of 1933. Had Pablo been naively unaware that writing a letter to a journalist might result in a news article, he might have learned a lesson the hard way about talking to the press—for the rest of his life, he tended to avoid intentionally putting himself in the middle of political and artistic disputes. After Pablo's death, Alberto Híjar described him as able to avoid controversy by focusing on the long term:

> He doesn't lose the Communist line. In the middle of this he stays on the same path and at the same time he has the long view that is typical of a Communist, not looking at tomorrow but at what will happen in the long run. I think it extraordinary that in spite all of this Pablo wasn't a person of controversy, disputes or confrontation.[21]

Letters between Pablo and Freeman indicate that Pablo was not happy being in the middle of the dispute, and they also show that Pablo's break with Rivera was based on politics. Freeman, in 1933, wrote just about everyone he knew in Mexico asking them for pictures of the National Palace mural, before and after Rivera's alleged change in the mural's subject matter, making it less political. Pablo wrote back to Freeman, describing his recollection (that Rivera removed the female figure because it was potentially "chauvinistic") and defended Rivera's actions as those of a middle-class artist. He wrote:

> I remember your article in the *New Masses* on Rivera, which traced political history as such accurately enough but I think you made a mistake in pointing out supposed plastic decadence in his work, a sudden esthetic deflation as it were, as a result of his expulsion from the P[arty], and his open serving the P.N.R. and imperialists, it's about time people interested realized that Rivera always has been a *genial* [brilliant] middle class painter. As such, he has produced his finest work and still continues to. He was admitted to the Party together with many middle class elements who were later expelled or left, on the grounds of

> his anti-imperialist activity, which was sincere and at that time useful to the P[arty].[22]

Pablo seems, in this letter, to be defending Rivera's middle-class background and perhaps the party's pre-Sixth International admission of people like Pablo, who were from middle-class backgrounds. By now, 1933, having seen the brouhaha that resulted, Pablo might have had regrets about complaining to Freeman about Rivera.

When Freeman's scathing article was published, Rivera was in the United States, which was three years into the Great Depression. David Jenkins, who would later direct the California Labor School, recalled New York City in the early 1930s:

> There was such mass unemployment. People were sleeping all over Central Park. . . . I deeply believed at that point in social change. My generation was unemployed. The hope seemed to be lying in a changed society. We were endlessly furious at the signs of great wealth and terrible poverty. . . . Sixth Avenue, where all the employment agencies were, was flooded with seemingly a million unemployed people.[23]

The popularity of Communism was growing. The party gave regular workers the opportunity to feel they were involved in something bigger than just trying to make a living. Regarding seamen, those who worked on ships, Jenkins said:

> [T]hese were men whose lives were lived in terribly deprived circumstances, boarding houses, missions, isolated from mainstream American life, and they were suddenly regarded by the [Communist Party] as proletarians leading a revolution and changing the nature of the world. They were given a whole new dignity and stature, and they responded to it with enormous enthusiasm. They flocked into the Party. [24]

In addition, the United States was now discussing recognition of the USSR and was sympathetic to its Popular Front approach.[25] In the 1932 U.S. presidential election, the Communist Party candidate got more than one hundred thousand votes, the most a Communist Party presidential candidate has ever received.[26] In 1933, membership in the U.S. Communist Party jumped from eighteen thousand to twenty-six thousand.[27] Increasing membership was also attributed to a "makeover" of the U.S. party by its head, Earl Browder, who began changing the party from one headed by foreigners with a mostly immigrant membership to a party of "old-fashioned Americanism updated for the modern era." In 1941, Browder changed the name of the U.S. Communist Party to the Communist Political Association.[28] Browder, like Pablo, was from "English stock that could be traced back to Revolutionary times." [29]

Rivera, who had a commission to paint a mural at Rockefeller Center, had arrived in New York to great interest. While the majority of the population of New York City struggled to make ends meet, Rivera, now a former Communist, and Kahlo received celebrity treatment and were surrounded by New York society. The Freeman letter cycled into more controversy and culminated in a radio broadcast with Rivera defending himself. Perhaps in an attempt to redeem himself in the eyes of the party he painted figures of Communism into the Rockefeller Center mural. But he could not help but include a portrait of Trotsky, further distancing him from the party.

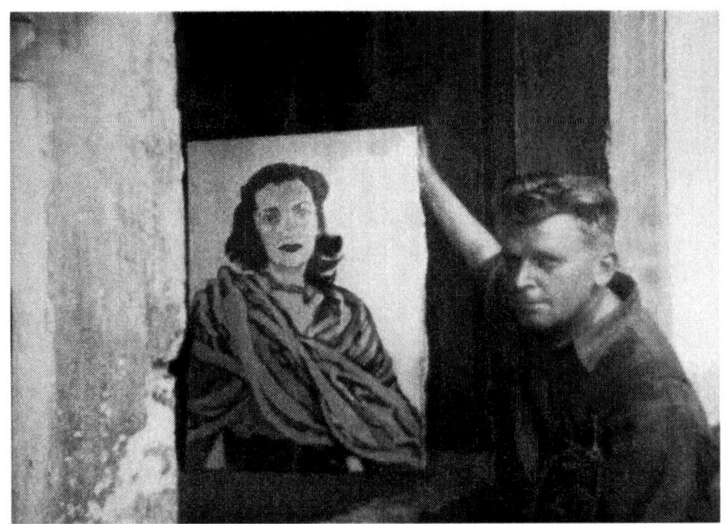

21

RETURN TO MEXICO

Pablo's month-long homeward journey by sea in 1932 gave him the opportunity to reflect on his visit to the USSR and Europe. Pablo's experiences abroad had cemented his commitment to Communism; in the 1930s he was calling his friends "comrades." [1]

When the ship made a three-hour stop in Havana, Cuba, Pablo went ashore to deliver a letter to the family of Cuban poet and lawyer Ruben Martínez Villena, whom he had met in the USSR in a park near a sanatorium where Villena was recuperating from a disease. Villena, in 1923, had led a group of thirteen people protesting the corruption of the government of Cuban President Alfredo Zayas. In Moscow, Pablo and Villena had spent hours talking of the common problems of Mexicans and Cubans.[2]

Pablo returned to Mexico deeply concerned about the spread of fascism in Europe. European industrialists had watched as the USSR expropriated privately-owned railroads and factories, and many began supporting Hitler, Mussolini, and the Spanish Falangists who promised to protect private property.

The Communist Party in Mexico, while concerned about fascism, was still illegal and struggling to simply exist. Those involved in it, especially those who distributed *El Machete* throughout Mexico City, did so at great risk. Benita Galeana, a poor, uneducated peasant, the very person the revolution was trying to help, reportedly was arrested and held fifty-eight times between 1929 and 1934 for her activities on behalf of the party, including distributing *El Machete*. She was on the front lines of the fight between the PCM and both the government and the fascist groups.

Galeana's memoir, in which she vividly describes these years in Mexico City, sheds light on the challenges Pablo faced seeking to be accepted as a Communist artist/activist among Communist "street fighters" like her. Galeana made it clear she had little tolerance for gringos (she assumed their businesses stole from Mexicans), Mexicans who spoke English (such as Dolores del Río), and the bourgeois. When an admirer would take her to a "bourgeois" restaurant, she would pretend not to know what the eating utensils were and ask for tortillas with which to scoop up her food, Indian-style.[3] Galeana condemned Frida Kahlo for being on the sidelines of the fight, along "with the artists." [4]

Pablo therefore inherently had disadvantages in wanting to be accepted as a Mexican Communist: he was a gringo, he spoke English, he was a U.S. citizen, and he was from a bourgeois background. He was on the sidelines with the artists, not in the middle of the brawl with the police and fascist groups. With his artist friends who tended to be part European, or educated in Europe, or at least well educated and from the middle class, he could feel he was an activist in spite of these limitations. But with people like Benita Galeana, who could easily detect artifice, Pablo faced a higher standard of authenticity.

In interviews, people who knew Pablo often talk of the people in his social circle: Rivera, Siqueiros, Modotti—people who put themselves in the spotlight, making noise, and some getting arrested. Pablo could not be in the spotlight nor was it his nature to draw attention to himself. And he could not be a street fighter (of the artists, only Siqueiros was). As a U.S. citizen and a Communist Party member, Pablo likely would have been deported if he had been arrested during the years that the PCM was illegal. Bertram Wolfe, one of the founders of the PCM, was deported in 1925 for his activities in the party; he returned only later when the liberal Cárdenas took office. Charles Phillips, a member of the PCM, was deported by Obregón.[5] Pablo had to become working class and non-bourgeois in order to avoid being one of the opportunistic gringos against whom the revolution was in part fought, and in order to avoid his own criticism of Rivera—that he was "middle class." He had to work to be accepted as Mexican, rather than as "another suspect gringo, throwing his weight around, south of the border." [6]

In this setting it is no wonder that Pablo did not mention his family's source of livelihood—private mining interests—or his father's involvement in the execution of labor martyr Joe Hill. The door was closing very quickly on his past. That he would later meet Galeana and make a lithograph of her for her autobiography adds a fascinating layer to his story: he was accepted as authentic by a hard-core Communist and peasant-born agitator. [7]

Bertram Wolfe commented on this dynamic in his second biography of Rivera, referring to "the thin layer of urban politicians and artists living at the narrow top of a pyramid, the foundation of which is the nameless mass of Indian peasants and peons." [8] Galeana complained, "[I]t's unbelievable, in all these years of the struggle, I have not had so much as a 'Good morning, Benita,' from [Hernan] Laborde," the head of the PCM.[9]

In spite of the repression of Communists, during the last years of Calles's power, there were certain pockets of liberalism and openness to public art projects. In 1931, Marxist Narciso Bassols, founder of the National University's School of Economics, took over as minister of education and designed a plan to improve the public schools of Mexico. In light of the worldwide depression, and with the belief that a hungry student cannot learn, Bassols implemented a program to bring food, knowledge, and skills to the poor to help them advance economically. He strictly enforced the prohibition against religion in the schools.[10]

Bassols hired architect Juan O'Gorman as chief of school construction. O'Gorman, who later created the famous mosaic mural on the library at the National University, hired artists to decorate the schools.[11] Pablo was hired to teach drawing in elementary schools and he was awarded his first mural commission, for an elementary school, Escuela Emiliano Zapata, in the Zona Industrial of Mexico City.[12] He painted murals showing the exploitation of children in factories and the need for children to be educated to escape the oppression of employers and the clergy.[13] This would counter the Catholic Church's teachings of the moral superiority of poverty.

Rivera's influence can be seen in Pablo's use of solid, well-rounded figures, a tendency that later disappeared from his work, and in his use of Rivera's standard symbols of wealth—monocles and money bags.

Pablo's receipt of the commission was reported in June 1933 in the *San Francisco Chronicle*, which stated that he was a native of San Francisco.[14]

Pablo's unenthusiastic attitude toward teaching, which he demonstrated in Seattle in 1975, may have begun in 1933. James Oles says that Pablo was hired by the Ministry of Public Education in January 1933 as a *profesor de dibujo* (drawing professor), to work twelve-hour days for eighty-six pesos a month.[15] It was the sort of job obtained "through friends and contacts." [16] He took off the first two weeks of February to travel to Veracruz with Méndez to explore a mural project, which never materialized (Tamayo, the head of the Plastic Arts Section of the ministry, granted him leave), and was later admonished to try to be more punctual. In July, he missed two classes, and finally resigned. His attendance record actually may have been worse, since he spent March of 1933 in Taxco helping Marion Greenwood with her mural. When he resigned his position he did so "*en virtud de tener asuntos particulares que reclaman toda mi atención* [because of private matters that demand all my attention]." [17] Later that year, in October 1933, he assisted Greenwood with another mural, at the University of Michoacán in Morelia.[18]

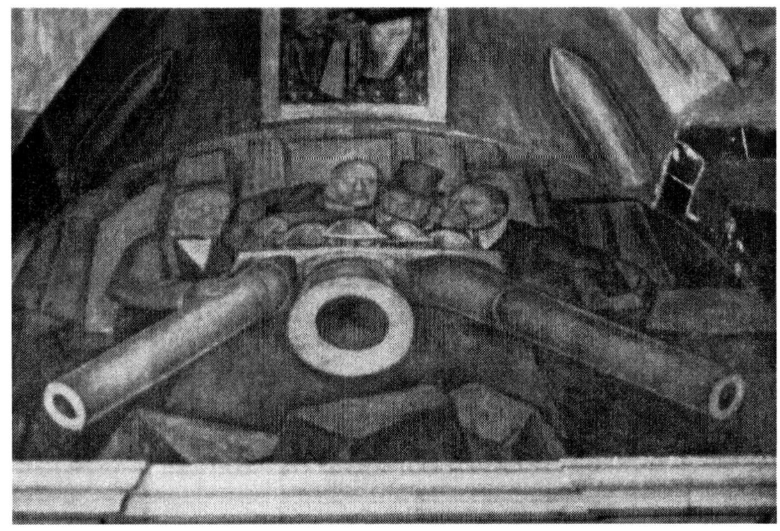

22

THE LEAR

In 1934, Pablo, along with Leopoldo Méndez, Siqueiros, Juan de la Cabada, and Luis Arenal, cofounded the Liga de Escritores y Artistas Revolucionarios (League of Revolutionary Writers and Artists, or LEAR), to fight against imperialism, fascism, and war.[1] The LEAR sought "to unite all the liberal anti-Fascist painters, writers, musicians, photographers, architects, dancers, teachers, men of science and in general just about anyone" in the fight against fascism.[2] Pablo would devote the next four years to this organization, which Mexican art critic Raquel Tibol called the "institution that opened the second great chapter of public contemporary art."[3] Its membership grew to more than five hundred and included many artists, writers, and musicians who were or would become well known in Mexico.[4]

The LEAR was formed under the directives of the party's Sixth International and it mandated that the working classes rise against the ruling classes and thus against the Mexican government. The group's most active section was the Plastic Arts Section; Pablo was the head of its mural subsection.[5] LEAR disseminated its messages through the magazine *Frente a Frente* (*Head to Head*, indicating confrontation) as well as prints and broadsides it posted around Mexico City and distributed to workers.[6] *Frente a Frente* followed closely the ideals of socialist realism established at the 1934 First Congress of Soviet Writers in Moscow and was closer to the party than *El Machete*.[7]

The principles of the LEAR were fiercely pro-Soviet, antibourgeois, and anticlerical. LEAR's mission was "to restore diplomatic relations between Mexico and Soviet Russia . . . the international bastion of true culture for the productive masses" and "to legalize the Communist Party and raise the class consciousness of the revolutionary proletariat." [8] More militant than the Sindicato of the 1920s, the LEAR accused the government of repressing the *campesinos*, being indifferent to attacks on Communists, and sending cultural missionaries into increasingly dangerous situations (twenty-five teachers would be murdered in the first eight months of 1938; others lost ears. All carried guns).[9] The LEAR, says Noah Bardach, had "a sense of the *obreros* and *campesinos* threatened by absolutely everyone, with the support of the Soviets as only a distant glimmer in the background." [10] Members of the LEAR were to adhere to the strict class-against-class party dictates and to work to "[unmask] the bourgeois' intentions for capitalist domination." [11]

The first issue of *Frente a Frente* praised Oregon-born Russian revolutionary John Reed and his book *Ten Days that Shook the World*. It must have inspired other American Communists that a U.S. citizen from a bourgeois background—Reed's mother was an heir to an industrialist's fortune—could become a hero of Communism.

With its antigovernmental stance, LEAR had to be against Rivera, who still was closely tied to the government. (In May 1934, *New Masses* published Siqueiros's four-page attack on Rivera, calling him an opportunist, a saboteur, technically backward, and an agent of the government.)[12] The LEAR chose to announce its displeasure with Rivera and the government on the cover of the first edition of *Frente a Frente* through a lithograph by Méndez depicting Rivera as a key celebrant in the opening in 1934 of the opulent Palacio de Bellas Artes, the Beaux Arts marble monolith under construction since the Porfirio Díaz administration.[13] The opening of this relic of the Europhile period dramatized the conflict developing in the Mexican art scene: the music performed at the high-society opening gala was the *Sinfónia proletaria* (*Proletariat Symphony*) composed by Carlos Chávez.[14] The price to hear the *Proletariat Symphony* was twenty-five pesos, nearly ten days' salary for an art teacher in the public schools. Rivera's activities in the United States, where he had been in the eyes of the Communist Party a "painter for millionaires" (ironically, getting in trouble for painting Communist themes), further distanced him from the party and LEAR.[15] Had Pablo believed his letter to Freeman had set off the firestorm against Rivera, he may, at this point, have felt justified, with the party so firmly set against Rivera.[16]

Over the next decade in Mexico, prints (many incorporating the calavera) would take the place of murals to a great degree. Prints had many advantages over murals: they didn't require government involvement or buildings, and they were easy and cheap to reproduce and distribute.

By 1935, Mexico's new president, Lázaro Cárdenas (who took office at the end of 1934), was proving to be an aggressive supporter of revolutionary ideals. His main accomplishment while in office was regaining and redistributing the natural resources of Mexico. He did this through two drastic steps: taking possession of hacienda land and dividing it up for the *campesinos*, and nationalizing the oil industry by expropriating the oil fields owned by Americans and other foreigners.

The party, at the Seventh International in Moscow the same year, abruptly changed its class-against-class approach and ordered its international organizations to fight the spread of fascism. Híjar said the party recognized the necessity of creating a united front, with Communists leading other organizations, including the progressive middle class, to fight fascism.[17] Thus parties around the world formed alliances—sometimes uncomfortable ones—with socialists, Leninists, Trotskyists, IWW members, and even capitalists.[18]

For the next ten years, the Communist parties of Mexico and the United States would begin emphasizing their commonalities with other groups, including mainstream political parties, opening their arms to a broader membership, recharacterizing themselves as less exclusionary and foreign and more consistent with national historical roots, and therefore attracting far more members. This "Popular Front" period would reach its pinnacle in 1944 to 1945, when Pablo was involved in—and captured in his art—a virtual lovefest between the Communist Party of the United States and the Democratic administration of United States President Franklin D. Roosevelt, only to see the party and its members fall from grace in the United States faster than Icarus.

In May 1935, the party ordered the PCM to support Cárdenas and Mexico's Regional Confederation of Mexican Workers (CROM). LEAR gave up its antigovernmental stance and embraced Cárdenas's efforts. Artists whose political expression in Mexico had been held in check under Calles burst forth with projects to publicize the danger of the situation in Europe and to support Cárdenas's commitment to return dignity to the Mexican worker, beginning with restoring rights guaranteed workers under the 1910 Constitution.[19] Pablo said:

> Believe me, none of us took these cultural mandates lightly. We sweated to produce leaflets with a message and with a purpose. Our 'employers'—the unionists, the peasants, the people—didn't want shoddy work any more than we intended to give it to them. And the writers felt the same way. Maybe the throwaways they wrote and we illustrated won't be in the American Historical Society, but here's another kind of history that does not gather dust and we played our little part in making it.[20]

Cárdenas reestablished the mural program. LEAR members received a commission to paint the walls of a huge enclosed market spanning blocks, the Mercado Abelardo Rodríguez, with several artists creating their own mural panels. The artists were happy to paint murals in a very public space—a new market in an old colonial-era school that the average person in the neighborhood would visit on nearly a daily basis. Past murals had been in office buildings not always open to the public, such as the Secretaría.

The Abelardo Rodríguez murals were to be painted by Pablo, Antonio Pujol, Pedro Rendón, Ramon Alva Guadarrama, and, from the United States, Grace and Marion Greenwood (who gave up some of their space for Japanese-American sculptor Isamu Noguchi).[21] Rivera had the role of approving the artists' proposed designs but did little else. He marked Pablo's "Vo. Bo. Muy buena composición." (*Vo. Bo.* slang for *visto bueno*, meaning that he had a good look at it, then "very good composition.")[22] Pablo played a very active role in the project, including assigning walls to other artists.[23] The artists were paid "rather well for those days," according to Marion Greenwood, thirteen pesos per square meter. On payday, they would "stand on line with all the workers, and we'd be given great bags of pesos," she said, adding, "We all felt very rich on payday in Mexico City." [24]

The murals turned the corner in terms of themes: rather than depicting historical events, such as the conquest or the revolution, they addressed the current issues in the lives of marketgoers.[25]

The section Pablo designed and painted is a commentary on the production of food, involving science (a doctor examining a patient as if he were a specimen), middlemen, and sinister U.S industrialists with their war machine. Pablo included the standard symbols of the bourgeoisie (a corset, high-heeled shoe, and shoehorn) and depicted the plight of unemployment, an anti-fascist brawl, and the oppression of the worker. Pablo's work reflects Rivera's influence with angular lines and geometry that dominated Rivera's work because of his training in cubism. Compared to Pablo's later work, the murals seem flat and restrained, though his color is vibrant. Art historian David Craven believes that Pablo's work stands out from the other seven painters who worked on the murals. He calls Pablo the "one major artist of the group," and "one of the finest of the Popular Front artists." Pablo, says Craven, was "adept at brooding color interaction, oscillating draftsmanship, and especially at foreshortening for dramatic effect." [26]

Alberto Híjar points to Pablo's including a call to arms in the murals as evidence that he is "the most radical of the Communists." On a vaulted ceiling, Pablo portrayed arms along with the language, "*armas para los trabajadores para aplastar a la reacción* [arms for the workers to quash the reactionaries]." [27]

The Greenwood sisters, Brooklynites who had studied at the Art Students League, were the first women to design and paint their own murals during the Mexican mural movement. Between 1933 and 1936, they painted five murals in Mexico.[28] In 1964, Marion Greenwood spoke of how beautifully the collaborative process worked on the Abelardo Rodríquez project, perhaps because Pablo, rather than Rivera, oversaw it.

> [W]e'd take old master's reproductions of Giotto and all the wonderful mural paintings of the Renaissance, and Piero della Francesca, and we'd analyze this according to the golden mean. . . . I learned so much about geometrical and architectural composition. It was wonderful and will be with me [for] the rest of my life. . . . I learned so much more than from any of the art schools back home, or for that matter, when I studied in Paris. It was a marvelous experience. It was a time that is finished and will never happen again.[29]

The project was not without politics or struggle, however. James Oles recounts in great detail the project's bureaucratic and administrative difficulties, most of which Pablo worked through. The correspondence relating to the project reflects Pablo's increasing friendship with Siqueiros and his continuing resentment of Rivera, both on political grounds and in terms of how Rivera threw his weight around.[30]

Despite these challenges, Greenwood said she had more freedom to paint whatever she wanted in Mexico than she ever had in the U.S. Work Project Administration (WPA), which she said was burdened with bureaucracy. She did acknowledge that the murals in Mexico were "propaganda" and that LEAR was a "group of what you call Stalinists at the time." She later wished she had concentrated on her own easel painting.[31]

Sculptor Isamu Noguchi, who created a twenty-meter-long relief mural of concrete for the market, also found Mexico liberating as an artist. He said, "How different was Mexico! Here I suddenly no longer felt estranged as an artist; artists were useful people, a part of the community." [32] Noguchi was in Mexico for eight months to work on the mural. According to Frida Kahlo biographer Hayden Herrera, he and Kahlo had an affair during this time.[33]

Time magazine seemed amused that "Ringleaders of the little group were not Mexicans but two sisters from Brooklyn . . . and a young man from California named Paul Esteban O'Higgins." The magazine described the work of the U.S. painters, depicting swindlers, moneybags, and "porcine bureaucrats," and Pablo's cry, "Against Imperialistic War!!" "embattled" compared to the work of their Mexican counterparts who painted "simple, Maya-like designs." [34]

Greenwood had warm recollections of Pablo. He had directed her to Taxco when she first came to Mexico, and helped her with her first mural there, giving her the formula for the plaster and training the plasterer. After the Mercado Abelardo Rodríguez project, she got a commission for a mural at the University of Michoacán of San Nicolás de Hidalgo in Morelia.

> Pablo came with all the wood for the scaffolding, and great crowds gathered and I got up there in my blue jeans and started painting away. They used to call me la *gringuita*, the little gringo, who was there working all through the siesta hour. They didn't realize that I had to keep on working because the plaster was drying. Sometimes I'd work for eight, nine and ten hours a day on the scaffolding. [35]

Marion Greenwood mentioned that in Mexico the peasants were used to art and had a better sense of it than the inhabitants of the low-income housing projects in the United States, who asked her why everyone in the paintings wasn't smiling. She told them, "You've only seen toothpaste and magazine advertisements, you've never seen real painting." In contrast, in Mexico the poor "were used to art around them all the time, and so it wasn't in any sense a happy experience."

Oles calls the Mercado Abelardo Rodríguez murals "among the greatest murals executed by Americans anywhere in the 1930s in terms of the formal resolution of their complex subject matter with their architectural spaces, and also in terms of their clear political statements." [36]

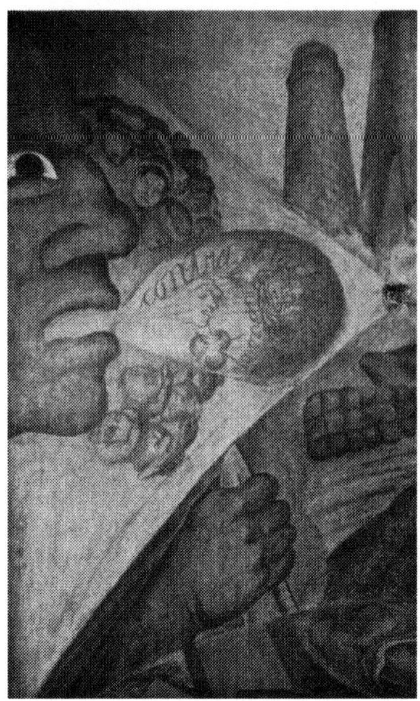

23

THE SPANISH CIVIL WAR

The Spanish Civil War, beginning in 1936, united many of the leftists in Mexico City. The years leading up to it, however, were tumultuous. Though happy with Cárdenas, the leftist art community in Mexico City was divided on issues of art and politics. Upon his return to Mexico from the United States in late 1934, and likely still stinging from the "Battle of the Century" in the United States, Diego immediately revived his debate with Siqueiros regarding the proper role of art and whether Stalin or Trotsky was the rightful heir to Lenin. Diego continued to be criticized for having been the "painter for millionaires" in the United States.[1]

The discussions were often heated; at least once Diego pulled a gun to make a point.[2] In fall 1934, a public debate between Diego and Siqueiros took place before a crowd that included the future founders of the Taller de Gráfica Popular: Juan de la Cabada, Leopoldo Méndez, Pablo O'Higgins, Antonio Pujol, Ángel Bracho, Luis Arenal, and Ignacio Aguirre.[3] Diego and Siqueiros hammered out an agreement conceding that the art movement that began in the 1920s had become romanticized, and had resulted in works ending up in the hands of European collectors and murals mainly hidden from the public. They advocated for art more accessible to the masses, namely, publicly visible art, prints, portable art, and art of service to the worker and *campesino*, not the government.

Based on these goals, the LEAR, in October 1935, formed a night school for workers, called the Taller–Escuela de Artes Plásticas, offering free art classes for workers, as well as classes in the history of art through Marxism, taught by LEAR members, including Pablo.[4] Pablo's experience with this school would later open doors for him in the United States when the Communist Party would seek art teachers to instruct the flood of workers joining the war effort in World War II.

The LEAR envisioned itself as an international organization and participated in meetings of other writers' and artists' organizations. In 1935, it sent Antonio Pujol as its representative to the American Writers Congress in New York organized by *New Masses* and attended by more than four hundred writers and critics, including John Dos Passos, Theodore Dreiser, and Lewis Mumford. LEAR artists' work was shown. The following year it sent representatives, including Pujol, Siqueiros, and Orozco, to the first American Artists' Congress Against War and Fascism, in New York. LEAR members brought art to the United States for an exhibition and may have submitted pieces to a juried exhibit of the congress that would be duplicated in several cities in the United States. Hundreds of artists submitted prints and one hundred were chosen. The pieces selected for the exhibits were included in a book, *America Today: A Book of One Hundred Prints*, which lauded the artist as worker rather than as an "ornament of the pink-tea, a playboy companion of the dilettante patron, a remote hero with a famous name." These artists were, in contrast, "[workmen] among workers." [5] Pablo's work was not included, but works by Miguel Covarrubias, Max Weber, Ione Robinson, Anton Refregier, George Biddle, and Lucienne Bloch were.[6]

While the government did not interfere with the activities of the PCM, Cárdenas's liberalism created a resurgence of fascist groups, including Catholic groups angry about the government's mandate to teach hygiene (which the Catholic groups called sex education) in the public schools.[7] These right-wing groups attacked both Communist Party members and the government. The Goldshirts aligned with other fascist groups around the world, such as Italy's Blackshirts and the Nazis' Brownshirts, and targeted the LEAR, the PCM, the anti-Calles Comité de Defensa Proletaria (Committee for the Defense of the Proletariat), other leftist groups, and unions.

On March 2, 1935, at a rally at the Plaza Santo Domingo commemorating the anniversary of the death of Karl Marx and the opening of new PCM headquarters, the Camisas Doradas attacked.[8] While the crowd was listening to a speaker, the assailants surprised the group, assaulting them with pistols, sticks, clubs, stones, and knives. The speaker, as well as many others, was wounded. Benita Galeana spent the night under a doctor's care for the injuries she received.[9] The LEAR publicized this attack in a flyer that included a woodcut by Méndez showing men attacking workers with clubs, knives, and guns and warning of their intent to create fascist terror in Mexico.

Six months later, at a celebration of the Mexican Revolution at Mexico City's Zocalo on November 20, 1935, as many as five thousand Camisas Doradas, including some on horseback, attacked a group of approximately three hundred Communist students, workers, and *campesinos*, killing several. Cabdrivers used their cars as tanks to block the attackers.[10] LEAR member José Chávez Morado documented the assault in a print showing the attackers on horseback. It was published in the April 1936 issue of *Frente a Frente*. Feeling threatened, some LEAR members, not including Pablo, took up arms to guard their own offices, near the Plaza Santo Domingo.[11]

Calles, although out of office, was still trying to stir things up in Mexico. His days were numbered and LEAR members in the art school produced prints for a supplement to *El Machete* using calaveras to depict "tumult in the Calles pantheon." These, like many other prints produced by LEAR members, were unsigned. Since LEAR had a strong belief in the collective process and did not value individual artistic expression, artwork often was published without credit to the artist.

There was also tumult in the Rivera pantheon. Rivera had not wanted to leave the United States after his and Frida's three-year stay there. But in Detroit, Frida had suffered a miscarriage, and after several months in New York she desperately wanted to go home. Diego conceded but was not happy. Shortly after their return to Mexico, he began an affair with her younger sister, Cristina. Frida had trusted her sister so much that she had arranged for Cristina to pose nude for Rivera.[12]

The paintings Frida created in the aftermath of the affair are some of her most painful. The tiny *A Few Small Nips* shows a murdered woman whose blood extends onto the rough wood frame around it (the title is from a newspaper article in which a murderer said he'd given his victim just a few nips). *Self-portrait With Curly Hair* shows Frida's long, sensual hair cropped boyishly short and her flamboyant feminine Indian clothing and adornments replaced by a common shirt and simple jewelry.

Frida engaged in payback in several forms over the next few years. One was her affair with Isumu Noguchi while he worked on the Abelardo Rodríguez murals. According to Noguchi, he and Frida had "assignations" at Cristina Kahlo's house in Coyoacán.[13] Legend is that Diego found the two in flagrante delicto and chased Noguchi out of the house, sending him up a tree, where he confronted Noguchi with a gun.[14]

By April 1935, Frida had moved into an apartment at 432 Insurgentes owned by Alberto Misrachi, who the same year had become Diego's art dealer and the couple's accountant.[15] Misrachi was an attractive, French-speaking Sephardic Jewish immigrant from Macedonia who owned Central de Publicaciones, a bookstore and art gallery on Avenida Juárez No. 4, across from Bellas Artes. When Frida lacked household funds, she would write pleading letters to "Albertito," asking him to front them money.

The Spanish Civil War, dramatically documented in the poetry of Pablo Neruda, the art of Pablo Picasso, and Ernest Hemingway's *For Whom the Bell Tolls*, killed a half-million soldiers and civilians over three and one-half years. It was especially felt in Mexico because of the country's historic ties to Spain. Many refugees fled to Mexico, where the peasants' struggle against wealthy landowners and the Catholic Church echoed the war in Spain.

Spain's situation in the 1930s was not too different from Mexico's before the revolution: the majority of its population was rural and illiterate and scraping out a living working the land of wealthy owners. In 1936, liberal groups united as the Popular Front and seeking a democratic Spanish republic won the presidential election. (Confusingly, the Popular Front side was also called Republicans and Loyalists.) Just months into office, General Francisco Franco, the army, and the Church joined conservatives to form the Nationalists. In July 1936, they invaded Spain from the nearby Spanish Morocco colony. Mussolini and Hitler assisted them in their infamous bombing campaign of Madrid in August 1936 and, in April 1937, of Guernica, immortalized in Picasso's famous painting, *Guernica.*

The Spanish Republicans' struggle became a popular cause of the left, including Americans suffering in the Depression. Refugees arrived in the United States and Mexico telling of the horrors of the war, demanding that democratic governments intervene. Preoccupied with their own economic woes and not seeing the threat of another world war (having recently ended the "war to end all wars"), France and Britain decided not to intervene and persuaded twenty-five other countries to sign a nonintervention pact. The only countries to support the Spanish Republicans were the USSR and Mexico, under Cárdenas. The Soviet Union ordered Communist parties throughout the world to form volunteer brigades and forty thousand men and women fought in them, including twenty-eight hundred from the United States in the Abraham Lincoln Brigade. A third of the U.S. volunteers died and most of those who lived suffered war injuries.[16] Many who survived were later accused by the U.S. government of being "premature anti-fascists," including when they would try to serve the United States in World War II.[17]

Tina Modotti, whose family had suffered under fascism in Italy, threw herself into Spain's struggle. Working for the Party's International Red Aid, Modotti nursed wounded soldiers and scrubbed floors at Madrid's Workers Hospital, which lacked both medical staff and supplies.[18] For five days she guarded Dolores Ibarruri, the charismatic political activist nicknamed *La Pasionaria* (the Passionate), whose moving radio broadcasts rallied the Spanish to fight for the republic.[19]

Vidali, as a member of the Soviet secret police, now presided over execution squads.[20] Modotti and Vidali worked together to evacuate the hospital to Valencia when Madrid was attacked and taken by the Nationalists in November 1936.

As the atrocities in Spain escalated, the Cárdenas government asked the LEAR to paint, on the walls of the Talleres Gráficas de la Nación (National Print Shop), a mural addressing the situation in Spain and emphasizing workers' right to strike. Painted in January and February of 1936 by Pablo, Méndez, Zalce, and Fernando Gamboa, it was the LEAR's last mural.[21]

Using the print-shop workers as models, Pablo painted panels showing *La lucha sindical* (*The Struggle to Unionize*). He depicted a group of serious-looking men (the leader bearing a resemblance to Méndez) in suits viewing a drawing, blindfolded workers in overalls, and corrupt leaders. He included an image of Callista labor chief Luis Napoleón Morones, leader of CROM (Regional Confederation of Mexican Workers), next to an Italian flag (suggesting a tie to Mussolini) and, falling to the ground, booze, money, a Bible, and a rosary.

The inclusion of Morones in the mural did not please President Cárdenas, who was still in the process of cleaning house after the Calles years. Cárdenas had changed the name of the ruling party from the Partido Nacional Revolucionario (National Revolutionary Party, or PNR) to the Partido de la Revolución Mexicana (Mexican Revolutionary Party, or PRM) and had replaced Morones's corrupt CROM labor union with Vicente Lombardo Toledano's Confederación de Trabajadores de México (Confederation of Mexican Workers, or CTM), which represented three thousand labor unions and six hundred thousand workers.[22] The following year, Cárdenas would physically remove Calles and Morones from the country, dumping them in Texas. Cárdenas felt Pablo's satire would further stir things up and ordered Morones's face removed. Pablo complied by whiting out Morones's face, but he was still recognizable by his trademark huge rings.[23] The original painting was reproduced in the November 1936 issue of *Frente a Frente*.

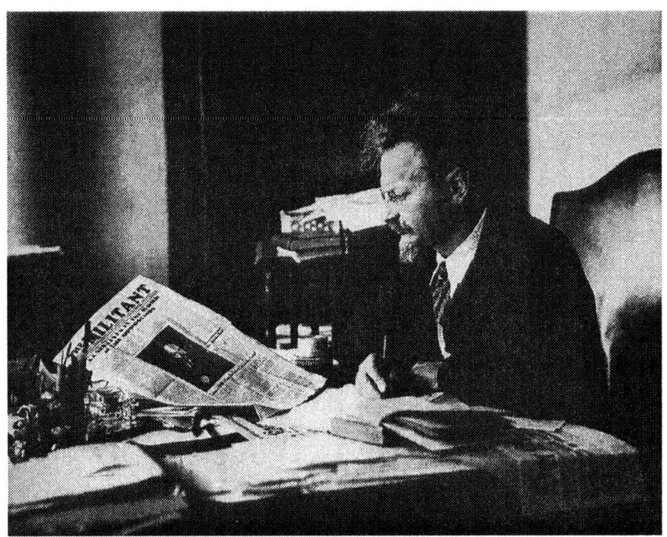

24

STALIN/TROTSKY SCHISM

Rivera began siding with Trotsky in the late 1920s, when he gave Pablo a book about him. He painted Trotsky's face into the ill-fated mural at Rockefeller Center in New York in 1934 and joined the Mexican section of Trotsky's party, the International Communist League, in 1936.[1] He was expelled from the PCM—for the second time—as a result.[2] Mexico's art community was deeply divided over the Trotsky-Stalin conflict.[3] Herrera writes:

> The conflict between Trotskyites and Stalinists in Mexico—as everywhere in the Western world—was virulent and violent. Battles between politicized artists were the talk of the town. Orthodox Communists not only reviled Rivera for his Trotskyism; since it was political, they stepped up their 'criticism' of his art as well. [4]

The battle escalated in late 1936 when Anita Brenner, who was in New York writing about the Spanish Civil War, made phone calls to Alberto Misrachi, Rivera's art dealer, and to Rivera himself, to see if President Cárdenas would allow Trotsky and his wife, Natalia, to live in exile in Mexico.[5]

Brenner had interviewed Trotsky in Paris and had written an article about him for *The New York Times Magazine*. She was a member of the American Committee for the Defense of Leon Trotsky although she never joined Trotsky's party.[6] Trotsky called Brenner a "nonpartisan radical." [7] Brenner contacted Misrachi, not because he was a Trotskyite, but because Brenner knew he could get a meeting with the president in an instant.[8]

Cárdenas approved Brenner's request and Trotsky and his wife arrived in Mexico City in January 1937.[9]

The Trotskys' arrival in Mexico was an historic event extensively covered by the international press.[10] Cárdenas sent his luxurious train car to Tampico to meet them. Rivera and Kahlo welcomed them to the Blue House, the Kahlo family home on Calle Londres in Coyoacán, not far from where Kahlo and Rivera lived in San Angel.

The moment Cárdenas granted asylum to Trotsky, the president became an enemy of the people in the eyes of the PCM. Moscow officials stated that they did not care that Trotsky was in Mexico so long as he did not plot against the Soviet Union, but the PCM was outraged. And the moment Rivera became Trotsky's host, "the Communist Party reopened its war on the painter." [11] *Time* reported that the Stalinist Mexican Communist Party gathered in Plaza Santo Domingo to listen to "Party chief Laborde as he roared: 'Down with Trotsky who is living in the home of the Capitalist Painter Rivera!'" and demanded Trotsky's immediate expulsion on the basis that he had broken his promise not to engage in politics.[12]

Lombardo Toledano echoed the call for Trotsky to leave.[13] Furthering the division between party members and those who were welcoming of Trotsky, within weeks of his arrival, Trotsky began criticizing the Soviet Union's actions in Spain.[14]

Trotsky demanded exoneration and for several months, beginning March 1937, the "Dewey Commission" convened in the Kahlo home and took testimony regarding Stalin's allegations against Trotsky. Trotsky was cleared of all charges in a 422-page report.

Meanwhile, Pablo and the LEAR were learning firsthand about what was happening in Spain. Refugees from Spain joined the LEAR, and in January 1937, Republican Spanish Ambassador to Mexico Felix Gordon Ordaz spoke at a conference organized by the LEAR, the Congreso Nacional de Escritores y Artistas (National Congress of Writers and Artists), to request support for Spain.[15] The event was accompanied by an art exhibit that included Pablo's work.[16]

Chilean poet and politician Pablo Neruda invited LEAR members to participate in the Second International Congress of Antifascist Writers for the Defense of Culture, in Valencia, Spain, in April 1937. Participating were Octavio Paz, W. H. Auden, Malcolm Cowley, André Malraux, Stephen Spender, and César Vallejo.[17] At least ten LEAR artists attended. Pablo's work was included in their exhibition, One Hundred Years of Revolutionary Mexican Art, which was displayed in Spain and later in Mexico.[18]

The LEAR artists who attended—Pablo did not— met up with Tina Modotti and Siqueiros. Siqueiros, upon learning of the trouble in Spain in 1936, when he was living in New York, had turned his apartment over to his students and traveled to Spain in January 1937 to join the war effort. He fought in an international brigade, serving under Modotti's lover, Vidali. Siqueiros saw action from the start and rose to become the highest ranking Mexican officer in the international brigades.

LEAR's congress had been such a success that the Mexican government was giving LEAR money and commissions. With LEAR in support of Cárdenas and Cárdenas in support of LEAR, the group changed dramatically from its original days. The group had attempted to be broad-based and had allowed not just artists as members but also like-minded intellectuals.[19] Membership, which had been around thirty when LEAR was a hard-core Stalinist, antigovernment group, jumped to several hundred artists who were seeking the benefits of belonging to a group that was tight with the government.[20] Craven says that during the 1920s and 1930s, "when there was no one ruling class" in Mexico, the government was so eager to unite the left that it supported art groups, such as the

LEAR, and allowed them to criticize "the very government that provided them with modest patronage." [21] This would draw together leftist groups (who were committed to the "promises of the [very radical] 1917 Constitution") to "fight off constant challenges from the right." [22]

Virtually every artist in Mexico City became a member of the LEAR, which opened the group up to political divides. The main division in the LEAR was between members such as Pablo and Méndez who supported labor leader Lombardo Toledano's politics and those who supported the more militant PCM.[23] Lombardo Toledano "criticized the PCM's uncompromising position that only a revolution could truly improve the condition of the working class. Instead, he advocated a more gradual transition to Communism, working from within the existing system to address the immediate practical needs of Mexican workers, such as education, housing, and a living wage." [24] Lombardo Toledano was a Marxist but never a Communist Party member. His "ideology was a synthesis of Marxism and nationalism." He believed that "supported by the progressive petty bourgeoisie," Mexico would gradually advance to socialism if it remained strongly anti-imperialist.[25]

Opening up the LEAR to a large membership also opened it up to the Trotsky-Stalin split not only in politics but in art. According to Alicia Azuela, of the Instituto de Investigaciónes Estéticas of UNAM, the PCM members who led the LEAR were rigid in insisting that LEAR members follow party directives. "The Stalinists maintained that representationalism was the only acceptable style and the worker the only subject of art," she said.[26]

The LEAR became dependent on the government, which provided it printing free of charge. When a government benefactor quit giving handouts, the group had no money to pay its bills. Faltering, the LEAR saw those who were in it for their own benefit quickly leave.[27] Méndez said the LEAR died because of opportunism; Pablo said that internal disagreements had made it unbearable. The final demise was the visual artists leaving.[28] Pablo concluded that the group would have survived had it remained a group of only painters.[29]

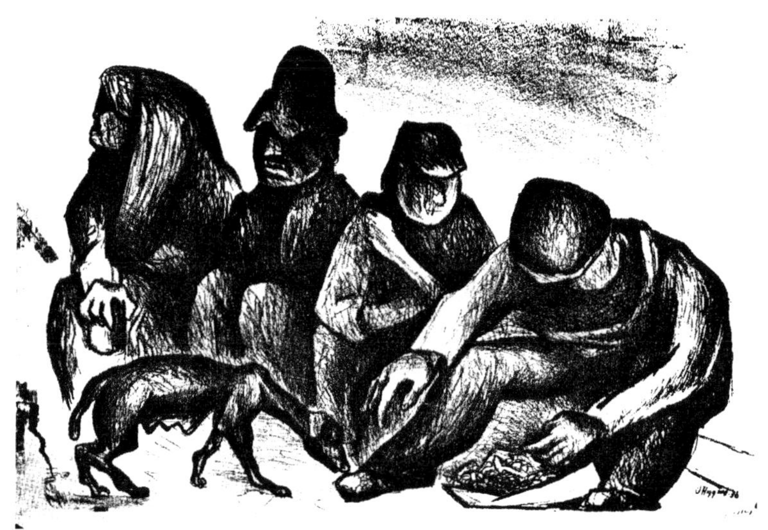

25

THE TGP

One day in 1937, Pablo and Méndez went out to get a cup of coffee. Méndez suggested to Pablo that they form a new workshop apart from the LEAR.[1] The two invited Alfredo Zalce and Luis Arenal, and together they formed the Taller de Gráfica Popular (People's Graphic Workshop, or TGP), whose goals, like those of the LEAR, were to support the popular struggle, to denounce fascism, and to encourage domestic reforms. The Taller de Gráfica Popular became internationally known and to this day is an inspiration to artists in the United States, Latin America, and beyond. Many printmakers, especially Latino and Chicano artists, cite the TGP as a model for creating socially-conscious and motivating artwork in a collaborative, community-based setting. Producing more than ten thousand works over the first quarter century of its existence, it has been called "arguably the single most significant graphics workshop in the Americas." [2] It has held exhibitions throughout the world.[3] Within ten years of the formation of the TGP, similar workshops sprang up in San Francisco, New York, Portland, and Los Angeles.[4]

Demonstrating its founders' close ties to Lombardo Toledano, its first location was Lombardo Toledano's Universidad Obrera de Mexico (Workers University of Mexico).[5] Throughout its existence, and eventually to its demise, the TGP's alignment with Lombardo Toledano would continue.[6]

The TGP became Pablo's home, artistically and emotionally, for twenty-three years. Daniel Lienau, a gallery owner who has sold TGP prints for many years, said that in his view it is "astounding" that this internationally known institution of Mexican political art was cofounded by an artist from the United States.[7]

The TGP carried forward some of the principles of the 1922 Sindicato to its own manifesto, which stated:

> The TGP is a center of collective work for functional production and the study of different branches of printmaking, painting, and the different media of production. The TGP is involved in a constant effort to insure that its production benefits the progressive and democratic interests of the Mexican people, primarily in its struggle for national independence and for peace. Considering that the social objective of plastic art is inseparable from its good artistic merits, the TGP stimulates the development of technical capacity in its members. The TGP will lend its professional cooperation to other workshops or cultural institutions and to progressive organizations in general. The TGP will defend the professional interests of all artists.[8]

The TGP required that the art be produced through the collective process and that members attend weekly meetings. This meant that TGP members collaborated on the initial design and provided criticism of the work of each member. Of the many artists who became involved in the TGP, most felt the process was very productive, especially for young artists.

Like members of the Sindicato, members of the TGP considered themselves "workers" in printmaking rather than artists.[9] The TGP's work had to have a progressive or democratic content and address matters of concern to all of Mexico, including the *campesinos*. The artists disseminated their work through pamphlets, posters, banners, and backdrops. Photographs of Mexico City street corners show their works plastered on the sides of buildings. The TGP's work includes fliers notifying farmers of the best types of corn to plant, posters encouraging support for striking workers, and prints reminding the people of the heroic acts of Mexico's revolutionaries. Their work was often done quickly and not always expected to last. Its purpose was to teach and inform the working class through easily understandable graphic images and simple words. Members of the TGP paid dues and gave the workshop 20 percent of their proceeds.

Artists were recommended for admission and the membership voted on them. The TGP members were mainly from the lower and working class, which its founders were proud of.[10] They did not always sign their prints (sometimes they included their initials, and sometimes the initials of two or three artists involved in creating a piece). In the beginning, they rarely numbered prints, as their objective was not to limit the number of prints to increase their market value, but to send out their political messages as widely as possible. As they saw a growing market for their prints as "fine art" pieces, however, some artists began to produce numbered prints on better paper, a practice anathema to the hard-core leftist artists.

The collaborative process also enabled artists to avoid aspects of printmaking they did not care for or did not feel accomplished in. Pablo did not like cutting into print blocks as one does to create linoleum or woodblock prints. He preferred lithography, in which the artist draws with a wax crayon on a stone. Méndez enjoyed the cutting. The result was often prints attributed to Pablo that carry very much of Méndez's distinctive cutting style.[11]

Pablo and Leopoldo Méndez complemented each other. Art critic and former PCM Secretary-General Rafael Carrillo described them as Siamese twins—"Leopoldo was the mischievous Mexican, [Pablo], the soul of God." [12] Until Méndez's death in 1969, he was Pablo's closest friend. Méndez named his son after Pablo.

The two pillars of the TGP, Elena Poniatowska said, were two men: one dark and very handsome, and the other light and very handsome—Méndez and O'Higgins, and they loved each other as brothers.[13] Mariana Yampolsky, the TGP's first female member, called them *café con leche* (coffee with cream). She described them as the core of the TGP.[14]

Both were very popular with women.[15] Mexican poet Germán List Arzubide called Méndez "a dandy in overalls." [16] Both Pablo and Méndez enjoyed "the adoration of younger artists, young women." [17] Bardach says that the two handsome men were "dreamy, with their overalls and their murals." [18] He says the first thing that Yampolsky said when he sat down to interview her was, "I didn't sleep with Leopoldo." [19]

Méndez, said to be "the literal embodiment of the TGP," was born in Mexico City in 1902 into a working-class family.[20] His father raised Leopoldo and his six siblings after their mother died. Méndez showed artistic talent at a young age, enrolled in the Academy of San Carlos, and after graduating, studied in the plein air schools and worked in public education.[21] He became involved in a group in Mexico called the Estridentistas (Stridents), whose graphic images clearly reflect the influence of Russian futurists. Like Pablo, his commitment to Communism was based on his love of *el pueblo* (the people). Méndez was considered to be the leader, or the most important member, of the TGP.[22]

The TGP first set up shop in the studio space of the LEAR's art school. It eventually acquired a printing press from a friend of Pablo in Chicago and rented a studio at Belisario Domínguez 60, near Pablo's studio. The beloved printing press carried the mark "Paris 1871" and was thought to have belonged to the Paris Commune.[23] From the beginning, the TGP, in the new Popular Front period, sought interaction with U.S. artists. Two besides Pablo would become Mexican citizens, Mariana Yampolsky, in 1954, and Elizabeth Catlett, in 1962. Many European and U.S. artists visited as "guest members" and played important roles in the organization.

The TGP had its first exhibit at the Artists' Union of Chicago in 1938. Five exhibits of works of TGP artists followed in New York in 1939 and 1940, including one of Pablo's works. They also exhibited in Russia to unenthusiastic reviews. The Soviets never cared for the TGP's work because it didn't show *campesinos* and workers as heroes. From the time of its founding until 1965 the TGP had seventy-three exhibits in the United States.[24]

Pablo spent a great deal of his time, including evenings, at the TGP. He was tour guide for many visitors from the United States. In fact, when artists from the United States talked about their time in Mexico, they often mentioned that it was Pablo who found them an apartment or otherwise helped them negotiate the big city. One visitor, writer MacKinley Helm, vividly recalled finding the TGP on a "shabby street" in "the dingy quarters of the old city" through the "patio of an ancient palace" in a "dreary tenement" with an open-air toilet serving "a couple hundred tenants." There, he said, they produced "the most glamorous prints" in the Western Hemisphere.[25]

Members of the TGP would have felt trivialized by Helm's description of their prints as "glamorous." Surely that was not their intention. The TGP artists did not value art that lacked social utility. Pablo was adamant about this—he believed that art had to serve a social purpose.

Pablo strongly believed that the worker was the artist's boss. He never considered himself better than any common worker, even as an artist. He had no tolerance for the glamorization of art or artists, nor for excuses for not working. Echoing the Protestant work ethic he grew up with, he once said, "Muse? Inspiration? This is something invented by critics or lazy people who don't feel like working. A painter should work every day like a bricklayer, like a manual laborer. Inspiration is sweat—*la gota gorda*." [26]

Zalce said, about the TGP, "The nice part was the connection with the people. Anyone makes good engravings, but we did what the people liked and needed. The workers asked for something and we did it." [27]

To Pablo, the worker, with his untrained eye and outwardly unsophisticated approach, was the best teacher and the final judge of a work of art. In 1939, he described how a worker helped him complete a portion of a mural:

> I was in one of those jams all artists run into at one time or another. The mural had been going along fine and then suddenly the color on one of the themes began to get weak and the more I mixed and experimented, the weaker it got. I beat retreat after retreat to the other side of the room to squint at the mess, and then I bumped into him. 'Sorry,' I said, and looked around.
>
> He was standing with his broom under his arm, his brown eyes half closed as he sized up the mural.
>
> "It is very good," he said in a quiet and excellent Spanish.
>
> "But I think you need a stronger brown in that larger figure. And perhaps bolder lines which would give a sharper sense of movement."
>
> I went back to the mural without saying a word and for an hour carried out his advice. And he was right. There may be a few artists in America who would be shocked at the idea of a porter in the Graphic Workers Hall giving a mural painter ideas of color and line. But I wasn't and I knew before I started that his judgment was correct. You see, Mexico is like that.[28]

Here, Pablo goes a step further than Marion Greenwood when she said that Mexican Indians had a better aesthetic in terms of subject matter—they didn't expect to be surrounded by smiling, toothpaste-advertising faces. Pablo, who would allow a porter to tell him how to execute his work, lacked the egomaniacal attitude of Rivera, who enjoyed being *el maestro* (the teacher). He may have lacked confidence. Pablo lacked the formal art training of many of his contemporaries and had not yet developed a strong style of his own.

Pablo's job in painting a mural in a public place was to produce something that an uneducated person could understand and appreciate. He strongly believed in the magic of the revolutionary art movement, which taught that the Mexican peasant had a more authentically Mexican sense of aesthetics than an urban, educated Mexican, and certainly a European-American.

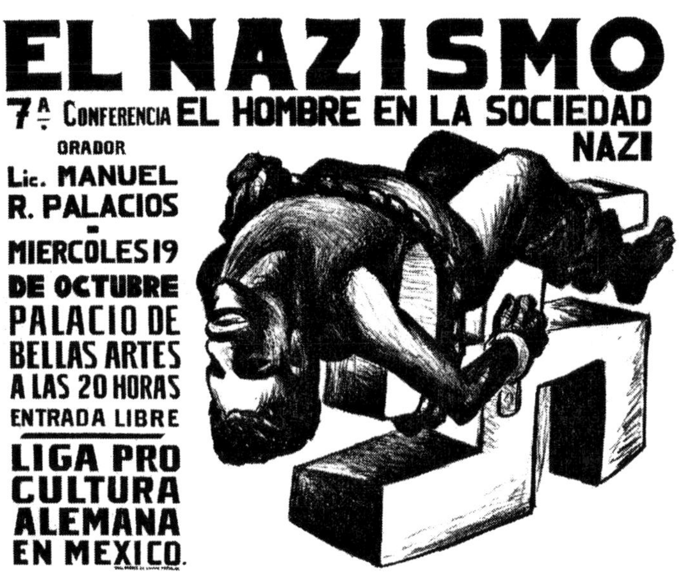

26

THE FIGHT AGAINST FASCISM

"Pablo, come to my performance tonight!"

Lilyan Tregob, a slight, redheaded young actress from Cleveland, Ohio, was in Pablo's studio again. She had heard about him and had wandered over several weeks ago and now considered him her best friend. She bragged about him to her girlfriends every morning at Sanborns, where they sat in a back booth and chatted while waiting for their mail to arrive at the American Express office.

Pablo's studio in the center of Mexico City had always attracted visitors. But now a constant stream of artists, actors, and writers from the United States marched through it. Some were fascinating, others were annoying.

Pablo turned to Tregob. He had almost forgotten she was there, he was so involved in sketching a clenched fist for a lithograph. Tregob had no real interest in the cold black fist of fascism, but wanted to chat about her work selling ads for *Esta semana* and to get Pablo to commit to seeing her in a theater performance that evening.

"Pablo," she pleaded in her high-pitched voice. He knew she would not leave until he agreed to have coffee with her or promised to go to the theater.

Pablo guided Tregob to a stool and picked up a sketch pad. From then on, any time she visited, he quieted her down by making her sit for him. Over time, he produced a lovely oil portrait, which he gave to her.

Later, Tregob would visit him at a mural project, trailing her friends behind her, telling them how wonderful Pablo was and that he was her best friend. She was disappointed that he didn't recognize her even after she told him her name.[1]

Pablo had little time to attend the theater. The war in Spain and fear of a fascist Europe (and of a fascist Mexico) dominated the early work of the TGP, as it had the LEAR. Jean Charlot said, "When World War II loomed imminent, it added as targets three puppet-figures, international dictators that no image maker could resist: Mussolini, Hitler, Franco." [2] In the first year of the TGP, Pablo produced art that slammed this trio.

One year after founding the TGP, Pablo produced one of his strongest political pieces in terms of subject matter, a lithograph of a man lying with his back chained to a massive swastika. It was used to promote a seminar, "Man in Nazi Society," part of a series of anti-fascist lectures at Bellas Artes sponsored by the Liga Pro Cultura Alemána, a "Comintern-affiliated" organization of Jewish and Communist German immigrants who fought openly against Nazism through posters and conferences.[3] This series of posters "greatly expanded the T.G.P.'s portfolio and significantly raised their visibility," according to Noah Bardach.[4]

Another lithograph Pablo created that year, *Franco*, denounces the Spanish immigrants living in Mexico who supported Franco. It depicts a pair of vultures—one a calavera vulture—lording over poor people and hoarding the food the poor cannot afford to buy. It condemns Spanish merchant-middlemen for jacking up prices and depicts them as supporting the bombing of Spain and the killing of women and children.

Oddly, in the words *frijol* (beans), and *mujeres y niños muertos* (women and children dead), the *j*'s, the *y*, and an *n* are backward. (The artist has to write and draw in mirror image for a lithograph or block print, which takes some practice.) Pablo was a beginner in printmaking.

Two other lithographs by Pablo, *Waiting for the Sign Up*, and *Veracruz, 1938*, depict crudely drawn, chunky workers with out-of-proportion bodies. Similar in style to the *Daily Worker* pieces he did in New York, they show Pablo's lack of comfort drawing in black wax crayon on stones, lack of interest in spending time perfecting the human form, as he had been expected to do in art school, or a desire to eschew art school teaching in favor of a more common-man approach. Art critic Margarita Nelken once commented that she had wished Pablo had "taken better advantage of his stay in Europe to study the art of Paris." [5]

In 1938, Pablo created a lithograph, *Paz fascista* (Fascist Peace), showing a tank rolling into Czechoslovakia, and on top of it, the four principals at the September 1938 Munich conference that led to the dismemberment of Czechoslovakia: Benito Mussolini of Italy, Neville Chamberlain of Great Britain, Adolf Hitler of Germany, and Édouard Daladier of France. This print was included in a supplement to *El Machete* titled *Spanish Fascist Fair.* [6]

The first joint project of the TGP was a calendar for Lombardo Toledano's Workers University. Pablo contributed three prints for the calendar, two addressing the situation in Spain and one the oppression of Mexico's indigenous population.[7] The TGP, determined to be self-sufficient and escape the fate of the LEAR, paid its bills by selling "portfolios"—collections of their artwork accompanied by text that espoused its own views—but it nonetheless depended upon commissions to pay its rent.[8] It offered its "Graphic Propaganda" services, as it called it, to the government, and to rural schoolteachers.[9] The TGP's subject matter included domestic issues and increasingly, the war in Spain.

In February 1938, fascist forces attacked Málaga, on the southeast coast of Spain, forcing the evacuation of tens of thousands of civilians. As evacuees poured out of the city, Franco's planes strafed them and his tanks barreled toward them. Modotti was there, delivering blood. She called it a "massacre of women, children, and old people." [10]

The Cárdenas government's support of Spain was causing tension at home. Trotsky was still in Mexico and he and Rivera criticized Stalin's handling of the war. Mexico's powerful foreign oil companies also began criticizing Cárdenas's alliance with the Soviet Union. A right-wing pro-Catholic group called the Sinarquistas—literally "without anarchy"—similar to the Cristeros, formed in 1937 in opposition to Cárdenas's policies, and drew as many as eight hundred thousand members with its antigovernment views.

Against this backdrop, President Cárdenas in 1938 took one of the boldest moves of a Mexican president—the expropriation of foreign oil companies. This move had its beginnings in Mexico's deep-seated resentment of the foreign oil companies' exploitation of Mexican workers. In 1936, oil workers demanded that their employers grant wage increases and allow Mexicans to become executives. The oil companies refused and a strike broke out. A government mediating board decided in favor of the workers and Mexico's Supreme Court confirmed the decision.

After the foreign oil companies questioned Cárdenas's personal promise that the wage increases would not exceed $7.2 million, Cárdenas issued a warrant on March 18, 1938, for the seizure of seventeen oil companies.

The oil companies expected the United States to come to their aid; it did not. President Roosevelt, dealing with the extreme poverty of the Depression, stood by his nonintervention policy and issued a statement that "the United States would show no sympathy to rich individual Americans who obtained large land holdings in Mexico for virtually nothing . . . and claimed damages for seized property." [11] The Mexican government eventually paid twenty-four million dollars for the property seized.[12]

While the United States didn't object to the expropriation, the move did strain relations between the countries. The United States was not comfortable with Communist concepts such as the expropriation of private companies and was wary of Communism in general. Roosevelt kept a friendly demeanor with the USSR while the country was its ally but the friendship would stop abruptly at war's end.

The Mexican government was still negotiating with the oil companies when, through the TGP, Pablo received a commission to create a mural in the auditorium of a technical high school in Mexico City named after the state of Michoacán, where Cárdenas was born. The mural, which Pablo painted in 1938 to 1939, depicts the struggle of oil workers against their American bosses, and the benefits received by the people of Michoacán through the Cárdenas government, shown as the building of a community and the introduction of education and sports.

In the fall of 1938, Pablo's mother, Alice Higgins, then seventy-four years old, spent several months visiting Pablo. In a letter to her niece, with the return address Belisario Domínguez 43, Alice wrote that she and Pablo were looked after by a "nice, clean Mexican woman," Nieves, who did the marketing and cooking. After serving food prepared the way Alice liked it, Nieves would cook "firerey [sic] Mexican messes" for herself. "They smell appetizing," Alice wrote, "but when you swallow a spoonful it leaves a red hot streak that calls for ice water."

Alice enjoyed meeting friends of Pablo, traveling, learning Spanish, and seeing "old acquaintances," an indication that she had visited Pablo in Mexico before. She delighted in the tropical fruit—the *zapotes*, chirimoyas, and especially the bananas, "with their golden, honey-sweet pulp."

By then, she saw her son as "Pablo." She wrote, "Everyone here calls him Pablo (I rarely hear the name Paul) and I find myself calling him that—it comes so easy."

Alice, in her letter, said nothing of Pablo's art or politics. She mentioned that the altitude in Mexico City was very troubling to her, and alluded to a fainting spell on a previous trip. She mentioned that Pablo was talking about driving with friends to New Orleans and then New York and that she was thinking about meeting him in New York. Although her son was now thirty-four years old she worried about his health and raised her eyebrows over the home remedies he was using for a cold: "foot baths and garlic tea." Alice talked about returning to Los Angeles and staying with her sister-in-law, Will's wife, Eva, then visiting her daughter, Gladys—Pablo's half sister and cousin—and her granddaughter Marjorie, in the Bay Area. While Alice remained loving and loyal to Pablo until her death, other family members did not. Gladys, a few years later, would slam the door in his face.

In late 1938, Pablo traveled to New York for an exhibit of his work at Blanche Bonestell Gallery in February 1939. It appears from the letter his mother wrote that year that Pablo might have planned to accompany Méndez on his Guggenheim-sponsored study in the United States, with an itinerary that took him through New Orleans (to meet an anthropologist at Tulane) and to New York. Pablo did not go with Méndez, but they may have met in New York for the opening of Pablo's one-person exhibit of lithographs and paintings on February 16, 1939, the opening of which was listed in *The New York Times*.[13] Jean Charlot wrote, "Paul Higgins is having a show at Blanche's. It looks nice, all sorts of workers, all in overalls." The twelve paintings he sent for the show were never returned or paid for.[14]

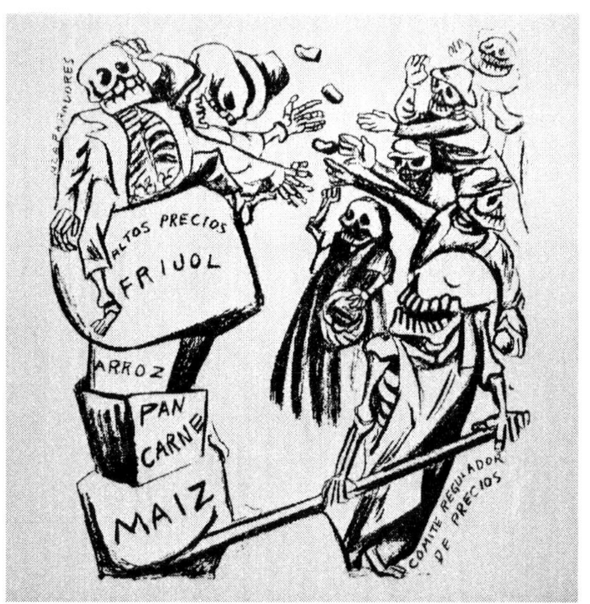

27

SEEDS OF DOUBT

In 1939, artist and Communist Party member Pele deLappe created a lithograph titled *1939*, which shows people listening with extreme concentration to a radio broadcast. California printmaker Mark Vallen, in his blog, asked:

> What terrible news might they have been listening to? In 1939 the Nazis invaded Czechoslovakia in March, and the Italian fascists occupied Albania in April, the same month the Spanish Republic fell to fascists under General Franco. Joseph Stalin and Adolf Hitler would sign a Non-Aggression Pact in August, and the Nazis would invade Poland in September. There was plenty of bad news to be heard—and the gloomy looks on the faces of the characters drawn by deLappe seem to tell us that they've heard it all.[1]

Communism, which in the 1920s had offered simple, black-and-white solutions to complex problems, took on shades of gray in the late 1930s and early 1940s through the Party's Non-Aggression Pact with Germany and the assassination of Leon Trotsky. These were the two events that shook Pablo's commitment to Communism.[2]

For five years, Pablo, Méndez, and the other TGP members involved in the LEAR had devoted themselves to fighting fascism and the Nazi threat through their art and activism. On August 23, 1939, they were told to stop. It was not the fascist Sinarquistas telling them to stop, nor the government, nor any of their other traditional enemies. It was their own Communist Party.

Until August 1939, the Communist Party had had a friendly attitude toward Roosevelt and the New Deal and had cooperated in the "Democratic Front." Members of the TGP were producing Mexico's strongest anti-Nazi messages, which were plastered on the walls of Mexico City. However, even as the Nazi buildup and aggression in Europe increased, Pablo's anti-Nazi images, as well as those of other TGP members, disappeared in late 1939.

Pablo and his colleagues were silent when Germany invaded Poland on September 1, 1939. They did nothing when the USSR failed to join the Allies in the fight against fascism after Britain and France declared war on Germany on September 3, 1939.

They did nothing because, to the shock of the world, on August 23, 1939, the USSR entered into a friendly agreement with Nazi Germany to give it economic support, to permit its aggression in Europe, and, in a secret side agreement, to divide up Europe. Party members were told the enemy was no longer the Nazis and fascism, but imperialism, including the United States.

Germany sought the Non-Aggression Pact so it would not have to fight on both a western front with western Europe and an eastern front with the Soviet Union, as it had during World War I. In a secret agreement denied by the Soviet Union until 1989, Germany offered the USSR the Baltic States of Lithuania, Latvia, and Estonia, as well as eastern Poland and parts of Romania in return for the USSR agreeing not to intervene if Germany invaded western Europe. Germany also extracted food and supplies from the USSR in exchange for machinery and other German-made products.

Two weeks after it entered the Non-Aggression Pact, Germany invaded Poland from the west, and, pursuant to the pact, the USSR invaded Poland from the east a few weeks later. Britain and France declared war on Germany two days later, marking the beginning of World War II. The Soviet Union did not join the Allies to fight against Germany, but continued to give economic support to Germany, thus helping Germany circumvent Britain's blockade.

This situation shocked many Communist Party members.[3] U.S. party member David Jenkins described learning of the pact while at sea.

> The ship's delegate was a guy named Campbell [who] was a reactionary and right-winger, sort of pro-Fascist. We had been fighting all trip and after the pact he came to me, shook my hand, and said, 'We're comrades together.' I thought, Jesus Christ! . . . I guess I waited until I was at shore to find out what it all meant.[4]

The U.S. Communist Party told members that they should oppose the United States joining in the fight against the Nazis, since, pursuant to the Non-Aggression Pact, it would also be a fight against the USSR. During the two years of the pact, PCM membership dropped from thirty-five thousand to fourteen thousand.[5] Communists in the United States also, especially Jews, were horrified that they were expected to be supportive of Nazi Germany.

But loyal party members, including David Jenkins, who was Jewish, found a justification for the pact.

> [A]t that time I accepted the rationalization that the Pact was a good thing. The Soviets had to move in some direction to protect themselves. [We] felt legitimately, [that] the German-Soviet pact grew out of the attempt by the Western powers to pit Germany and the Soviet Union against each other.[6]

The party's rally cries became "Keep America Out" and "The Yanks Are Not Coming."

Although many members left the party after the pact, Pablo, like Jenkins, and tens of thousands of other party members, dutifully complied. In Mexico, the pact "intensified the internal conflict in the PCM." [7] Party members who did not accept the party's change in position, including party chief Hernan Laborde, were expelled.[8] The PCM lost many members and supporters in Mexico because of the pact. [9]

The TGP, according to James M. Wechsler, adopted "the Comintern view that the Non-Aggression Pact was not destructive . . . ." [10] Demonstrating their alignment with the party, Pablo and other TGP members dropped anti-fascist messages from their art for the nearly two years of the pact.

Pablo was not the only one uncomfortable with this situation. Modotti arrived back in Mexico the same day the pact was announced. Modotti and Vidali had returned to Mexico after the defeat of the Republicans in the Spanish Civil War. She was sick with congestive heart disease and appeared tired, her skin yellowish, and her ankles swollen. She looked "horribly worn out." [11] In addition, Vidali's affairs with women during their years away had defeated her.[12] Vidali's young (and married) lover called her "the old lady." [13]

Modotti had entered Mexico as Carmen Ruiz Sánchez, a teacher. She was edgy, worried that people would recognize her and she would again be deported. She did not need to worry. People acted with disbelief when told the thin, tired woman was the legendary Tina Modotti. One writer described has as "looking as if she wanted to disappear into the sofa on which she was sitting." [14] Word was out that she was back, and friends sought her out and tried to encourage her to take photographs. She never again picked up a camera for artistic purposes.

Having lived the horror of fascism in Spain, Modotti refused to accept the Nazis as allies of the USSR. Vidali, the ultimate Communist Party man, tried to explain to her that it was just a "clever play for time" by Stalin, but Modotti remained firm that she would never side with Hitler.[15]

But Modotti, like Pablo, remained in the party. Because of that she found herself unwelcome by friends such as Frances Toor, who had come to detest Stalin and the positions the party was taking.[16]

Modotti and Vidali were still together, living as a married couple, though Vidali was having an affair with one of Modotti's friends—a situation that Modotti did not seem to mind.[17] She threw herself into party activity to the detriment of her health. Vidali led his life separate from hers, and likely was involved in planning and carrying out with Siqueiros an attack on the Trotsky home.

The Non-Aggression Pact raised suspicions that party members were collaborating with Nazis. It was instrumental in hardening the U.S. government's attitude toward Communists, which would be fully realized during the McCarthy era, drastically affecting the lives of U.S. citizens in Mexico. The House Un-American Activities Committee (HUAC) had been formed in 1938 and, in 1940, after the Non-Aggression Pact, Congress passed the Smith Act, making it a crime to "knowingly or willfully advocate, abet, advise or teach the duty, necessity, desirability or propriety of overthrowing the Government of the United States or of any State by force or violence, or for anyone to organize any association which teaches, advises or encourages such an overthrow, or for anyone to become a member of or to affiliate with any such association." [18] Next came the Hatch Act, outlawing the hiring or retention of federal employees who advocated the overthrow of the government. Then came Public Law 135, requiring that the FBI investigate any employee who is a member of a subversive organization.[19] Communists in the United States immediately felt "the cold breath of the informer." [20]

During the Non-Aggression Pact, the U.S. government prosecuted and convicted Earl Browder, the head of the U.S. Communist Party, for passport fraud, sentencing him to five years in a federal penitentiary.[21] Pablo, who in his 1931 application for a passport to travel to the USSR, had sworn allegiance to the United States, could have been similarly charged. He commented on the political situation in a February 1939 interview with Howard Rushmore of *People's World*, a publication of the U.S. Communist Party.

> We have a new Valley Forge. The United States has its conservatives, people who want to return to the times of Hoover, who pretend to defeat the culture of a country through expulsion of artists, writers and actors. In Mexico also there are those who would return to the days of Calles and we know that if this were to occur, a Taller de Gráfica Popular would not be allowed to exist, and the murals that speak the truth would disappear, as well as any other type of culture.[22]

Pablo's use of the word pretend indicates that after fifteen years in Mexico he was thinking in Spanish, as pretender means to try, which seems to be the English verb he was meaning to use.[23] In this 1939 interview, Pablo likely believed he could speak freely to Rushmore, a fellow Communist. Yet that same year, Rushmore left the party and began a career as an informant. He ultimately became one of Senator Joseph McCarthy's most important sources: he testified at the HUAC hearings in Hollywood in 1957, identifying Charlie Chaplin and others as Communists.

From 1934 to 1941, the years of the Non-Aggression Pact, domestic issues were of more concern to the TGP than the spread of fascism. Pablo produced prints on domestic issues such as the fight for Mexico's oil resources, *Guerra petrolera* (*Oil War*) and on the price of food, *Guerra de los frijoles* (*Bean War*) (see p. 129). These were included in a TGP portfolio, *Calavera extra, guerra extra* (*Skeleton Extra, War Extra*). He did a lithograph of bricklayers at work and other works depicting equally nonpolitical subjects. Méndez produced a portfolio, *En nombre de Cristo* (*In the Name of Christ*), consisting of seven lithographs showing the Cristeros' assassination of rural teachers. Other TGP Non-Aggression Pact art depicted Mexican folklore, such as Angel Bracho's four lithographs showing the rituals of the Huichol people, and exalted Cárdenas, such as Méndez's 1940 *Con una piedra se matan muchos pájaros. . . . ¡Viva Lázaro Cárdenas!* (*With One Stone You Can Kill Many Birds . . . Long Live Lázaro Cárdenas!*). Raúl Anguiano turned his concerns to milk, producing a print asking, "Why the High Cost of Milk?"

The TGP published a portfolio, *El pueblo de México y sus enemigos de 1935–39* (*The Mexican People and their Enemies from 1935–39*), which, consistent with the Non-Aggression Pact, attacked not their fascist enemies, but trusts, the press, the inadequacy of Mexico's water supply, and the bureaucracy that was managing the expropriated resources.[24]

THE SECOND EVENT THAT SHOOK Pablo's faith in the party involved Trotsky. Siqueiros had returned to Mexico after valiantly serving the party in the Spanish Civil War, only to find Trotsky, an enemy of the party, enjoying exile in his country and criticizing Stalin's efforts to fight fascism in Spain. He vowed to get Trotsky out of the country and chose to lay blame on the TGP.

On May Day 1940, thousands of workers took to the streets of Mexico City carrying signs with Communist slogans to protest Trotsky's presence in Mexico.

The Trotsky compound, now a museum, is a verdant patch of gardens and buildings surrounded by a high wall in Coyoacán. On the night of May 24, 1940, a group of men dressed as police officers, including Siqueiros, entered the compound and fired two hundred machine gun bullets through the windows of the house. Trotsky and Natalia escaped by (accounts differ) rolling onto the floor between the bed and the bedroom wall or huddling in a corner. Their fifteen-year-old grandson, Seva, asleep in a different room, was wounded in the toe (or the face) when a bullet ricocheted.[25] News of the assassination attempt sent Mexican leftist artists fleeing. Rivera was suspected because of his involvement in Trotsky's exile in Mexico and his later falling-out with him. Rivera's house was staked out. He went into hiding for a few weeks and then left for the United States, where he would secure mural commissions in the San Francisco Bay Area.[26] Members of the TGP were suspected because the police uniforms the attackers wore were found later in the TGP studio. Méndez, the president of the TGP at the time, was arrested and jailed. José Chávez Morado said he was jailed as well.[27] Pablo, alerted by the TGP's printer José Sánchez, hid out in the state of Mexico at the home of Chucho Díaz, who had worked as a laborer on the Mercado Abelardo Rodríguez mural and whose image Pablo had painted into various murals.[28] Pablo told a friend that he was out of town when the attempt occurred, a fact that he was able to prove, exonerating himself.[29]

The TGP was also ultimately exonerated and Siqueiros, who admitted involvement, was implicated.[30] Rafael Carrillo explained, "Before the assault on Trotsky's house, they changed their clothes in the TGP taking advantage of the fact that Pujol had the keys. They changed clothes and put on the uniforms and then the police intervened and put Leopoldo [Méndez] in jail thinking that he was Siqueiros's accomplice, which wasn't true." Carrillo said that the Soviet government "instigated" the assassination attempt, "used [Siqueiros]," and Siqueiros, who "didn't think of anyone but himself . . . got a lot of people involved." [31] Pablo said that he himself was suspected because Siqueiros had left behind a bandana that Pablo often wore around his neck, in an attempt to implicate him, "to blame it on the gringo." [32]

According to Mexican sources, this was the full extent of any TGP involvement in the attack, though scholars have suggested Antonio Pujol was involved in getting the key from Méndez, under the ruse of making prints, and giving it to Siqueiros. Under the new conservative government of Ávila Camacho, the full extent of Siqueiros's punishment for the attempted murder and the wounding of the child was a four-year exile in Chile, paid for by the Mexican government, during which the government procured a mural commission for him.[33]

One authority on Trotsky, however, states that TGP member Luis Arenal and his brother, Leopoldo, whose sister was married to Siqueiros, were involved in the assassination attempt and killed a guard in the course of it.[34] The details of the attack are gruesome. Following the assassination attempt, the guard, Robert Sheldon Harte, a twenty-five-year-old from New York, who had opened the compound's gate to the would-be assassins, was taken to a farmhouse, where he was kept for several days, until:

> [o]n the night of May 29 [Leopoldo and Luis Arenal] had a pleasant conversation with him before he went to sleep. Later in the night they crept into his bedroom and shot him twice, once in the neck, in the approved G.P.U. [Soviet secret police, eventually the KGB] manner. Then they carried the body into the kitchen in the basement where a grave had already been dug. Quicklime was poured over the body, the grave was filled, and a day or two later the Arenal brothers fled to New York.[35]

The authors of a recent book on the KGB conclude that Harte was complicit with the assassins but was killed because he expressed regret after learning that the Trotskys' grandson had been injured. [36]

It is certain that Pablo was in no way involved in the assassination attempt carried out by Siqueiros.[37] Yet it seems that what drew the TGP into question was not just the uniforms left behind but also the fact that one of its members, Arenal, was related by marriage to Siqueiros and had fled, as did TGP member Antonio Pujol.

Three months later, a more sinister plot developed. An agent of Stalin's secret police, Spaniard Ramon Mercader, had a girlfriend, Sylvia, who spoke fluent Russian. She got a job as Trotsky's secretary and Mercader gained the trust of the Trotsky family by treating the rather homely girlfriend like a princess in their presence. On August 24, 1940, Mercader came to pick up Sylvia, and asked if Trotsky might read a pro-Trotsky article he was writing. He was permitted to go alone upstairs to Trotsky's office (as he had a week earlier on a test run). Under a raincoat draped over his arm (the staff later realized there was no threat of rain that day), Mercader had an ice ax, which he pulled out and plunged into Trotsky's head. Trotsky died the following day.[38] The United States assumed that the assassination was the work of Stalin's agents working in conjunction with their new Non-Aggression Pact friends, German Nazis, in Mexico.[39] Mexican researcher Juan Alberto Cedillo, in his book *Los Nazis en México*, drew the same conclusion.[40]

Méndez was livid with Siqueiros for staging his attack at the TGP and causing himself to be jailed. Méndez felt that the party had chosen to "sacrifice" him by pinning the attack on him.[41] Siqueiros said that they were not trying to kill Trotsky, just to show that he was in danger in Mexico.[42] Pablo and Méndez both suspected that the party ordered the assassination of Trotsky.[43] Méndez and Siqueiros butted heads for years over this, even though Siqueiros was allowed to be a "guest artist" of the TGP after his four-year exile in Chile.[44]

Besides the Trotsky assassination, a difference in what TGP members should charge for their work caused a rift between members. Helga Prignitz says that TGP members Chávez Morado, Raúl Anguiano, Francisco Dosamantes, Jesús Escobedo, and Everardo Ramírez thought that the poor should not be charged for prints. They thought the fine art prints should be sold to tourists and the Mexican middle class for thirty pesos. Méndez, Pablo, Zalce, Bracho, Aguirre, and Mora wanted to keep the prints cheap, at eight pesos for all. The matter was resolved by a party mediator.[45] The Méndez group prevailed and the others left the TGP.[46]

For Pablo, the Non-Aggression Pact and the assassination attempt marked the beginning of a decade of soul-searching regarding his own identity: politically, nationalistically, and personally.[47]

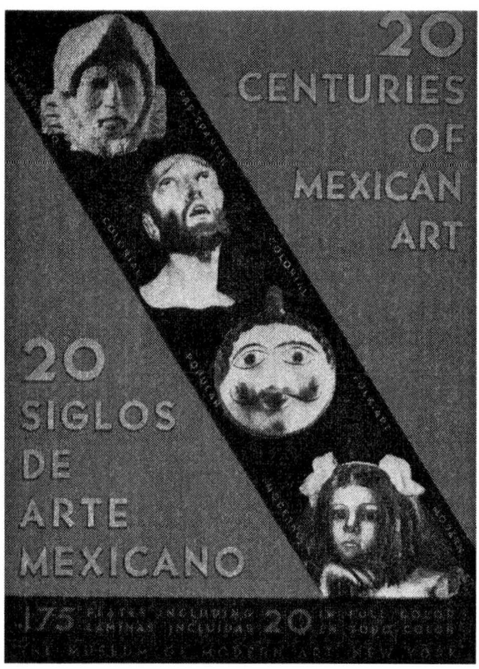

28

A MEXICAN ARTIST

Despite the turmoil of the Trotsky assassination and the discomfort created by the Non-Aggression Pact, the decade of the 1940s began on a high note for Pablo with an event that confirmed that, despite having U.S. citizenship, he was Mexican.

An often repeated story in books and chronologies about Pablo is that, in 1940, he was the only artist born in the United States to be included in a major exhibit of Mexican art at the New York Museum of Modern Art (MOMA), Twenty Centuries of Mexican Art.[1] There was, however, according to the exhibit catalog, another United States-born artist included—Miguel Covarrubias's wife, Rosa Rolanda, born Rosemond Cowan in Los Angeles to an American-born father of Scottish descent and an American-born mother of Mexican descent.[2] Rolanda, like Pablo, was a U.S. citizen, but she is never mentioned in these publications.[3]

Other artists not born in Mexico but included in the exhibit were natives of Spain, Guatemala (Carlos Mérida), France (Charlot), and Japan (Tamiji Kitagawa). The show, which opened the summer of 1940, included more than three thousand works of art. Pablo's work was displayed among works by Rivera, Orozco, Siqueiros, Tamayo, Chávez Morado, and many others. In biographies contained in the catalog's appendix, Pablo is listed as, "Painter, fresco and graphic artist. Born San Francisco, California, 1905. To Mexico, 1927." (Charlot was listed as, "Born Paris of partly Mexican parents.")[4]

For Pablo, his inclusion in the exhibit was a very public, very official confirmation that he was indeed a Mexican artist. Pablo's art had been selected by the Mexican government and Miguel Covarrubias, who was in charge of selecting the modern works of art. The exhibit received high praise from the press.[5] Mexican art would not again receive such attention in the United States for many years. With the war in Europe, refugees were arriving in the United States, bringing with them the abstract expressionism popular in Europe. This was the beginning of the end for social realism.

Perhaps taking advantage of the good reputation Mexican artists enjoyed in the United States, the TGP began advertising art classes in English-language publications.[6] In 1940, it offered a six-week summer school costing fifty dollars. Pablo created a promotional piece that included a linoleum print and text inviting students to the "Workshop School of Painting and the Graphic Arts. Summer 1940, July–August. Mexico City." [7] At the TGP school, Pablo taught mural painting, Méndez, woodcuts, and Gabriel Fernández Ledesma, "Review of Folklore." Bardach notes the irony of an anti-imperialist group with strong ties to Communism offering classes to U.S. students:

> It is interesting to note that the classes were advertised in English, only in American newspapers, and that the T.G.P. billed itself as the 'Workshop School of Painting and the Graphic Art [sic].' The 'Popular' component of the Taller's name seems to have been carefully excised and, apparently, the ad mentioned nothing of the group's politics. It seems the T.G.P.'s policy was 'come one, come all.' Even experience with art was not a requirement; 'previous study in art is helpful but not compulsory,' the ad read. This is another example of the T.G.P.'s ability to bend and morph when necessary to achieve its ends and ensure its financial survival.[8]

These classes, says Prignitz, saved the TGP financially and established friendships with U.S. artists.[9] Bardach notes that friendship with the United States is "not necessarily an agenda that one would expect of a Mexican leftist group that in recent years had denounced Yankee imperialism." Bardach views this as "very calculating." He describes the TGP as an organization with a "fluid identity" that was "self-defining," "as it saw most convenient," and willing to revise its own history.[10]

With the war in Europe escalating, and with a new, more conservative president, Manuel Ávila Camacho, Mexico was standing side by side with the United States in the war. Pablo and other TGP members, however, maintained their moratorium on anti-fascist art, as the Non-Aggression Pact required they view the Nazis as friends. Thus, when Pablo, Méndez, Zalce, and Chávez Morado obtained a commission for murals at the National Teachers School they planned a mural showing how the Catholic Church kept people in a backward existence and how this could be remedied through the free socialist education guaranteed by Article Three of the Mexican Constitution. The project was cancelled when payment fell through. One wonders, however, if it had to do with President Camacho's 1940 repeal of Article Three.[11]

It was becoming increasingly risky in Mexico to follow the Communist Party line. Camacho was a Catholic "believer," a former army general, less a revolutionary and more a modern bureaucrat. His focus was on governing Mexico in a conventional way (no more pistols and bandoliers), with an emphasis on economic development rather than "revolution for revolution's sake." [12] His biggest conflict was with unions, especially Vicente Lombardo Toledano's powerful Confederation of Mexican Workers (CTM), which had predominated throughout the Cárdenas term after Cárdenas had booted the Morones-run Regional Confederation of Mexican Workers (CROM). During the Non-Aggression Pact, the CTM, like the party, fought against Camacho's anti-Nazi, anti-fascist, pro-Ally efforts.

On June 22, 1941, Communists throughout the world heard in horror that Hitler had launched a surprise attack on the Soviet Union, sending three million troops over its border. The results were devastating: three hundred thousand Soviet soldiers killed in three days. Stalin, an expert in treachery and lies, not to mention mass murders, had not seen Hitler's backstabbing coming.

Consistent with their Communist loyalties, Pablo and TGP members, as well as party members in the United States, immediately reverted to anti-fascist art with a vengeance, as if to make up for lost time. U.S. Communists ditched the slogan the "The Yankees Are Not Coming" and advocated for the United States to join the war. Pele deLappe, a writer for the *People's Daily World*, wrote:

> We were finally at war, the 'Good War,' against fascism. Our left-wing slogan, 'The Yanks are not coming,' was shelved when Hitler invaded the Soviet Union. We hung blackout curtains on our windows and supported Russian War Relief.[13]

Members of the TGP produced some of their most forceful pieces upon the end of the Non-Aggression Pact. Zalce produced *La URSS defiende las libertades del mundo. ¡Ayudémosla!* (*The USSR Defends the World's Liberties—Let's Help it!*)[14] Méndez created an enormous poster, *Luchamos en la misma frente. ¡Unidos venceremos!* (*We are Fighting on the Same Front. United We Will Conquer!*), for the first convention of the Friends of the USSR, held June 22–25, 1941, in the theater of the Mexican Union of Electricians.[15] Francisco Mora made a heroic portrait of Stalin, *Bajo la bandera de 'Lenin' adelante hacia la Victoria* (*Under the Flag of 'Lenin' Will Come Victory*), for a November 22 celebration in honor of "Comrade José Stalin on his 63rd birthday," produced for the Mexican Union of Electricians, Hidalgo Cell of the Communist Party.[16] Admission to José Stalin's birthday celebration was free and the movie *Lenin in October* was screened.

The TGP's support for the war was not the support of all the Allies, but of the Soviet Union. Mexico's unions took the same position. In doing so, they lost credibility with the new government of Camacho, and Toledano Lombardo was removed as secretary-general of the CTM and lost his influence in the ruling party, the Partido de la Revolución Mexicana (Party of the Mexican Revolution, PRM), which later became the Partido Revolucionario Institucional (Institutional Revolutionary Party, PRI).[17] The TGP's emphasis during World War II on support of the Soviets would later be used as evidence against its members during the McCarthy era, when, just after the end of the war, the United States began seeking out and harassing Communists.

On December 7, 1941, Japan bombed Pearl Harbor and the United States entered the war. This event inspired many U.S. citizens living in Mexico to take action. Artist Emmy Lou Packard, who had been living with Rivera and Kahlo in Mexico, immediately took a job in the shipyards of California, first in Southern California and then in Oakland.[18] Art teacher Stirling Dickinson, a Republican and longtime resident of San Miguel de Allende, returned to the United States and registered for the draft.[19] Pablo chose to stay in Mexico; eight days later, he signed an application to register as a U.S. citizen in Mexico. U.S. citizens living abroad were not, at that time, required to register for the draft.

On January 5, 1942, Tina Modotti attended a party with friends. Vidali left before her. Modotti left at midnight but didn't return home. At one o'clock in the morning, word arrived that she had died in the backseat of the taxi taking her home from the party. The official cause was a heart attack. She was forty-five. Though Modotti worked tirelessly for what she believed in, she did not live to see the defeat of fascism.

Pablo was devastated by her death. He wrote that Modotti had created the "strongest and most fertile photographic expression Mexico has ever had," offering "the reality of the people, their beauty, their struggle." [20]

Mexico joined the Allies on May 14, 1942, after German torpedoes sank two Mexican tankers. Until then Mexico was ambivalent about going to war. Its Communists had been muzzled by the Non-Aggression Pact, and its right wing, including five hundred thousand Sinarquistas and Italian expatriates, clearly didn't want Mexico to oppose the Axis. Ultimately, however, thousands of Mexicans served in World War II, both in Mexico and in the U.S. armed forces.[21]

Mexico's entry into the war was celebrated at a large gathering at the Zocalo, for which the TGP created posters. The TGP's enthusiasm for the war generally focused on the Soviet Union. In December 1941, when the Soviet Union launched a successful counterattack on German forces approaching Moscow, Méndez responded with a delicate lithograph of Field Marshall Timoshenko of the USSR Red Army, *Mariscal S. Timoshenko sus triunfos son los nuestros* (*Mariscal S. Timoshenko, Your Triumphs are Ours*), published in June 1942.[22] That same year, word of Hitler's concentration camps began arriving in the Americas. Perhaps embarrassed by two years of "sitting on their hands" as friends of the Nazis, the TGP responded with forceful art depicting Nazi horrors.

The most significant anti-Nazi work of the TGP was the idea of Hannes Meyer, a Swiss architect who was director of the Bauhaus between the tenures of Walter Gropius and Ludwig Mies van der Rohe.[23] Meyer arrived in Mexico in 1938 after six years in the USSR and travels in the United States, and became the TGP's business director in 1942. Under his direction, the TGP produced a unique book commissioned by the Camacho government, *El libro negro del terror Nazi en Europa* (*The Black Book of Nazi Terror in Europe*).[24] This four-hundred-page book included photographs of the Nazi atrocities never before viewed in the West, including those of massacres about to take place and the aftermath, and mass graves, prisoners in concentration camps, and decomposing civilian bodies, as well as essays describing the horrors.[25] Eleven members of the TGP contributed twenty-two graphic images. Three works of Pablo's were included, most notably a lithograph of barefoot men paraded down a street with signs on them reading "Jude." The book is considered one of the most powerful anti-Nazi publications made during World War II.[26]

Meyer was also involved in the creation of a printing house, La Estampa Mexicana, to print the TGP's work. The printing shop was created to address what Méndez called human nature: rivalry and envy that had developed because of the TGP work displayed and sold in its small art gallery next door.[27] The first work published was a collection of prints by Posada.[28] Meyer and Georg Stibi, who also served as director in the 1940s, took on the roles of promoting TGP artists' work by, among other ways, getting the attention of galleries and labor unions in the United States.[29] Pablo also played a key role.

While Stalin waited for the help that the United States had promised in the form of attacking the Nazis in continental Europe, the Germans blasted through the Soviet Union. The Soviets suffered devastating casualties. When the Germans approached Stalingrad on July, 17, 1942, Stalin ordered his officers not to surrender. They repelled the Germans over the next six and a half months but at a cost of nearly one-half million lives and the near total destruction of the city. During the siege, Pablo created his poster *The Soviet Front is our first line of defense—let's keep it up!* for the first national convention of Friends of the USSR.[30]

With the Soviet's success keeping Stalingrad out of the hands of the Nazis, President Roosevelt's administration relaxed their disapproval of U.S. Communists and released CPUSA president Earl Browder from prison. U.S. labor unions, including the AFL, CIO, and ILWU, agreed to a "no strike pledge" and received some concessions from the government in return. The Communist Party, ordinarily never willing to compromise workers' rights to strike, supported this pledge.

On June 6, 1944, D-day, the United States finally fulfilled its promise to Stalin and launched an invasion of Nazi-occupied France on the beaches of Normandy. Commemorating this opening of a second front, Pablo created a print, *Segundo frente, ya mero . . .* (*Second Front, Almost . . .*), which was included in the TGP's annual calavera issue, *Calaveras estranguladoras* (*Strangling Skeletons*).[31]

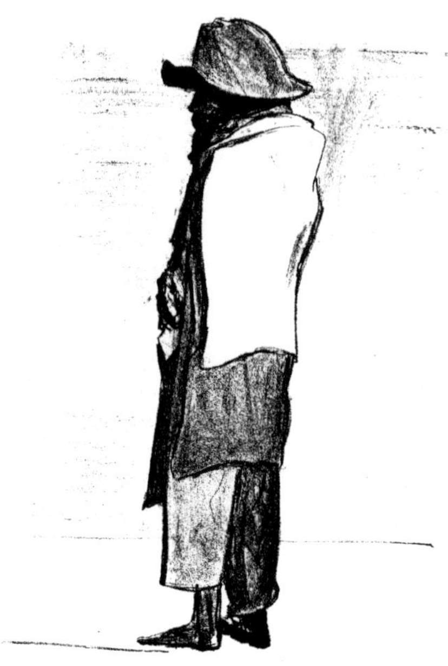

29

NOT MEXICAN ENOUGH

A lithograph Pablo produced in 1943 depicts a man suspended between two cultures. *El hombre del Siglo XX* (*Man of the Twentieth Century*) shows a shoeless *campesino* against a background of nothing more than a few soft lines.[1] The man is turned so that only his back, side, and a rough profile can be seen. Most of his face is covered by a beard—unusual for a *campesino* but echoing his Spanish forefathers. His hat is in the shape of the helmets of Cortes's army. One pant leg is rolled up as a *campesino* would wear it, the other is straight. Rather than being in motion, at work, as are most of Pablo's workers, he is still, as though suspended between movements, just as he is between cultures. Pablo made several versions of this piece.

Pablo said that he spotted the man, a *cargador* (someone who moves heavy loads), as Pablo was leaving the National Palace, where he had gone to look at Rivera's murals while the TGP was grappling with the political aspects of muralism. Pablo concluded that Rivera's National Palace murals were decadent in comparison to those of Chapingo. He had left the National Palace worrying about where one could encounter muralism. He saw the man, "*con la preocupación de aquél que no tiene a dónde ir* [looking like he didn't know where to go]." [2] After this, Pablo returned to his studio and created the lithograph in one sitting, unusual for him.

It is interesting that when Pablo was contemplating the political aspects of muralism he turned to Rivera's National Palace murals, the murals Pablo had complained about to Joseph Freeman in 1929, calling them, in Freeman's words, "decadent" (and later explaining to Freeman that they were simply the result of Rivera being "middle-class").

Perhaps Pablo in 1943 was revisiting his actions in 1929 and confirming to himself that he had then drawn the right conclusion.

The lithograph says visually what Mexican writer Octavio Paz would say a year later, in his book *The Labyrinth of Solitude*. "The Mexican does not want to be either an Indian or a Spaniard. Nor does he want to be descended from them. He denies them. And he does not affirm himself as a mixture, but rather as an abstraction: he is a man. He becomes the son of Nothingness." [3]

At the time Pablo created this lithograph, he too was a man suspended between cultures. He was a U.S. citizen residing in Mexico. Had he been living in the United States he likely would have already been drafted into the U.S. military (absent any medical condition). He considered himself Mexican, but he apparently was not, at least during wartime, Mexican enough. A year earlier, in 1942, he had suffered a devastating blow when the Mexican government awarded him a commission to paint a mural at the Ticomitl School in Mexico City, only to revoke it on the ground that he was a foreigner.[4] This was startling to Pablo, who had lived and worked in Mexico for eighteen years and had been included in the MOMA exhibit only two years earlier as a Mexican artist. Some say the grounds for the revocation was a "pretense," but do not specify what the real reason was. Mural contracts historically favored Mexican citizens, and noncitizens did not have the same rights under them, according to Oles.[5] Murals were very political; if it was not revoked for Pablo's status as a foreigner, it was likely revoked because the proposed content did not meet the approval of the politician granting the commission.

The government's action was met with disapproval from both the artistic and diplomatic communities. Méndez and other artists issued statements of protest. Former U.S. Ambassador Dwight Morrow said that Pablo was "the best unofficial diplomat the United States has had in Mexico." [6] The magazine *Tiempo* called Pablo "more Mexican than Teotihuacan," referring to the indigenous temples near Mexico City.[7] His inclusion in the Twenty Centuries of Mexican Art exhibit at MOMA was cited as additional proof of his Mexicanness.

In the 1920s, when Pablo arrived in Mexico, artists of the mural movement who were of at least half Latin American descent were generally Mexican enough to be "Mexican artists." Thus Frida Kahlo (half German, half Mexican), Juan O'Gorman (half Irish, half Mexican), and Jean Charlot (maternal grandparents born in Mexico; maternal grandmother half Aztec) qualified as Mexican artists.[8] The Mexican mural movement drew people from all over the world and its members were liberals, in the words of TGP member Alfredo Zalce, "without prejudices in terms of race or nationality." [9]

In the 1930s artists from the United States nearly flooded Mexico.[10] Yet none purported to become a Mexican artist. But in nationalistic times, even artists who were born in Mexico and of Mexican heritage were subject to scrutiny. MacKinley Helm, writing in 1941 about the TGP, said of Miguel Covarrubias, "when he turned up in Mexico City early in 1940 to assemble some pictures for the modern section of the Twenty Centuries of Mexican Art exhibition at the Museum of Modern Art in New York, many of the Mexican painters were resentful. 'What,' they asked, 'does Covarrubias know about Mexican art today?' He is never here and besides he isn't Mexican.' " Helms noted that Covarrubias was born in Mexico City, "and keeps a delightful house in suburban Coyoacán, but it is perfectly true that he has lived outside of Mexico for the greater part of his adult life." [11]

Pablo, at the time the commission was revoked, had lived in Mexico for eighteen years. He was accepted by those who mattered to him, the Mexican workers and *campesinos.*

He was passionate about his adopted country, sincere, and devoted. He was humble, respectful, and giving. For most of his life, he turned his back on the materialistic values of the United States and lived a simple life as a poor artist. Rafael Carrillo said Pablo "had a very attractive personality when he came to Mexico, very nice, for his generosity and kindness. All the money he earned didn't last too long because he distributed it to everybody who needed it."[12] He did not have the arrogance that characterized some members of the expatriate community.

Besides being accepted for his personality and his sincerity, Pablo was likely appreciated as someone who gave credibility to the political movement. People who "come over" to another political party or the other side of a divisive movement give it credibility. The mural movement criticized "Yanquis" and U.S. imperialism, so to have a Yankee join the movement both confirmed its rightness and the strength of its messages.

That Pablo fell in love with Mexico is also understandable. Mexico is an inviting, accepting country. One reason people from the United States are drawn to it is the warmth and openness of Mexicans. It is a country that does not have to make excuses for enjoying life. Its *si Dios quiere* (God willing) attitude is welcoming to people from countries like the United States who are taught to make use of every minute and who believe they have, or should have, control over all outcomes.

Comments in letters between Pablo and his mother, Alice, indicate that Pablo was from a family with the values of practicality and hard work. Alice chides Pablo for daydreaming as a child. While she was a lover of the arts, she mentions in a letter that artists are not "realistic."[13] Alice's exposure to the arts would have been through women's clubs and cultural events. During Pablo's last year of high school, local artist Alice Merrill Horne held art exhibits in the Tiffin Room, a restaurant in Salt Lake City's first department store, Mormon Church-owned ZCMI (Zion's Cooperative Mercantile Association), and at the Hotel Newhouse.[14]

Certainly Pablo's parents would have thought his choice of a career as an artist was "unrealistic." Utah culture, too, would have enforced both the work ethic (its state symbol is a beehive) and the idea that art is an impractical career.[15] But in Mexico, artists were highly valued and at the center of community life. The artists of Pablo's time were far more famous than the politicians, lawyers, doctors, or judges.

By 1942, Pablo had devoted many years to improving the lives of the Mexican people. Alfredo Zalce, when asked in 1971 whether Paris-born Jean Charlot was Mexican, said:

> In some ways. He was like me. He didn't look Mexican, but there was something in his character. We're both mestizo, mixed. In those days, people used more the racial (Tamayo was a pure Indian, and so on). But I was completely out because I looked like a Spaniard. Jean had an accent. But it's difficult to say what's Mexican. . . . Between artists, nationality doesn't mean anything. The important thing is what the people do. Higgins did a lot for Mexico.[16]

Having his Mexicanidad judged on what he did for Mexico forced Pablo continually to have to prove himself. Throughout his life, his main topic of conversation was his concern for Mexico. Close friends often said he didn't speak much about personal matters, only about Mexico. Rafael Carrillo said, "Pablo never talked to me about personal problems as a painter but the country's problems, problems he saw happening in different parts of the republic. His worries were about the people, their problems, the peasants in particular."[17] Near death, Pablo shared his concerns about what he would leave behind for Mexico.[18] His deep and sincere concern for Mexico can't be disputed, but he also must have felt a need to continually demonstrate it, simply to be accepted as a Mexican, which he already felt he was.

Joel Hancock, professor emeritus of the Spanish Department at the University of Utah, who now lives in Mexico, suggested that blond-haired, blue-eyed Pablo may have felt he needed to prove his Mexicanidad. Hancock, who has the same coloring and height as Pablo, lived in Mexico City from the time he was an infant until he went to college. He says that he was offered a job in Chicano studies at a U.S. university, based on his writings about Chicano poetry. "I turned it down," he says, "because with my coloring and my last name, I would constantly be having to prove myself." [19]

The overall picture one gets from the biographical information on Pablo published mainly in Mexico is that Pablo cared only about Mexico, never about himself. A recent book published in Mexico recounts that one night Pablo couldn't sleep because it was raining. The next day, his friend asked if the rain kept him from sleeping, but Pablo said, no, it was his worry that the rain would harm the paintings in the Templo Mayor of Tenochtitlán, the Aztec temple discovered in Mexico City during the late 1970s during excavations for a subway line.[20]

Yet in 1942 Pablo, who held U.S. citizenship, was not Mexican enough. "So many years of intense work, painting and living like a Mexican, weren't sufficient," María said.[21] Pablo was upset when he was treated like a gringo, yet for most of his life, he held on to his U.S. citizenship. He told people he kept his U.S. citizenship so he could visit his mother in the United States because she could not tolerate the altitude of Mexico City. But Pablo, had he really wanted to become a Mexican citizen, could have done so and met his mother in a city with a lower elevation, such as Guadalajara, or in Northern Mexico, near Los Angeles, where she lived from the 1930s until the time of her death.[22]

In 1942, Pablo's keeping his U.S. citizenship while insisting he was a Mexican could be seen as wanting to have it both ways.[23] He insisted that he was Mexican but was not willing to place his destiny in the hands of Mexico, its unpredictable political situation, and its difficult economy. If things got tough, Pablo could return to the United States, to enjoy the privileges of citizenship, as he did in 1944 or 1945 when he reportedly worked a paying job in the shipyards and painted a mural in Seattle, and in 1952, when he painted a mural in Hawai'i and showed his art in San Francisco. Had he moved back to the United States in the early 1940s, however, he would have had to register for the draft. Men in his age group living in the United States were required to register by February 16, 1942.[24]

The argument that eighteen years of living in Mexico should provide him with the benefits of citizenship is valid: Mexico likely would have been happy to give him citizenship. But it would have asked that he do the same as the United States asked of Mexican immigrants who had lived long term in the United States and sought citizenship: to renounce their citizenship in their country of origin. Pablo was not willing to do that.

After having lost the mural commission in Mexico, Pablo likely focused on creating works for his show, Mexico and Its People, February 1 to 15, 1943, at the Associated American Artists Gallery at 711 Fifth Avenue in New York. Perhaps still smarting from the loss of the mural commission, feeling his last name too un-Mexican, he signed his name only "Pablo." The exhibit featured eighteen paintings, including two on loan from collections of Mr. and Mrs. Alfred K. Stern (*Three Peasants*) and John O. Crane (*Refreshment*). (Pablo would reputedly have an affair ten years later with Mrs. Stern.)

On January 2, Pablo wrote to Jean Charlot saying the gallery director, "Sr. Lewenthal," was very excited about the pieces he had already sent, but, "you know I have never had much confidence in galleries." [25] Pablo still had not received back from Blanche Bonestell or been paid for the twelve paintings that she had exhibited in 1939; he had written asking her to send them to the AAA gallery but she had not responded.[26]

The New York Times' Edward Alden Jewell reviewed Pablo's exhibit along with five other solo exhibits, including those of Stuart Davis and Marsden Hartley. He said Pablo's easel paintings showed that he is "essentially a mural painter," in that he simplified his subjects, which were portrayed with "a keen awareness of what is native to them, of what in them is essential." He called Pablo's forms "flatly and decoratively handled, emphasis being placed on the elimination of all unneeded detail." Although he called the works "sometimes clumsy and in a degree inchoate," he said that the paintings "convey their message with a refreshing candor," demonstrating the artist's "real understanding of a country, of a people and of a people's environment." [27]

The comments of the critics, underscoring Pablo's Mexicanidad, somewhat eased the sting of the year before. If Mexico did not consider Pablo Mexican, the U.S. art critics certainly did. *Art News* reported, "O'Higgins . . . has integrated himself so entirely with the Mexican revolutionary traditions that only the amputation of O'Higgins remained to make the transition complete. This he has recently done by signing himself simply as Pablo." [28]

Besides preparing for the AAA exhibit, Pablo, according to his letter to Jean Charlot, spent a lot of time trying to get an exhibit in Mexico for Charlot by talking to people, having José Clemente Orozco talk to the director of Bellas Artes, and searching for other venues. He said he was spending time with Orozco, who was working on his *Four Riders of the Apocalypse* mural in Guadalajara. Pablo said he was also working at the TGP with Méndez and Zalce on anti-fascist posters. His only mention of the World War, now in its second year, is that it was an excuse for Bellas Artes to turn down an exhibit of Charlot's work.

Two months after the exhibition in New York, Pablo found himself "imprisoned" in a clinic suffering from malaria. On April 27, 1943, he wrote to Charlot, saying he would be in Mexico for ten to fifteen more days, but that the doctor had said he would be cured. Charlot and Zohmah had married in 1939 after an eight-year courtship characterized by long, dramatic letters to each other, Charlot's filled with drawings of crocodiles, often eating little girls.

The Charlots had lived in New York and Iowa. In 1943, they were in Athens, Georgia, where Charlot was teaching. In April, Pablo wrote to Jean Charlot that his February exhibition at the American Artists Gallery had been a success. He had sold several paintings and received "*mucha gritería de publicidad* [a lot of loud publicity]." The gallery, he said, may become his dealer. He discussed the possibility of an exhibit of Charlot's work in Mexico and noted that the TGP was looking for a new space.[29]

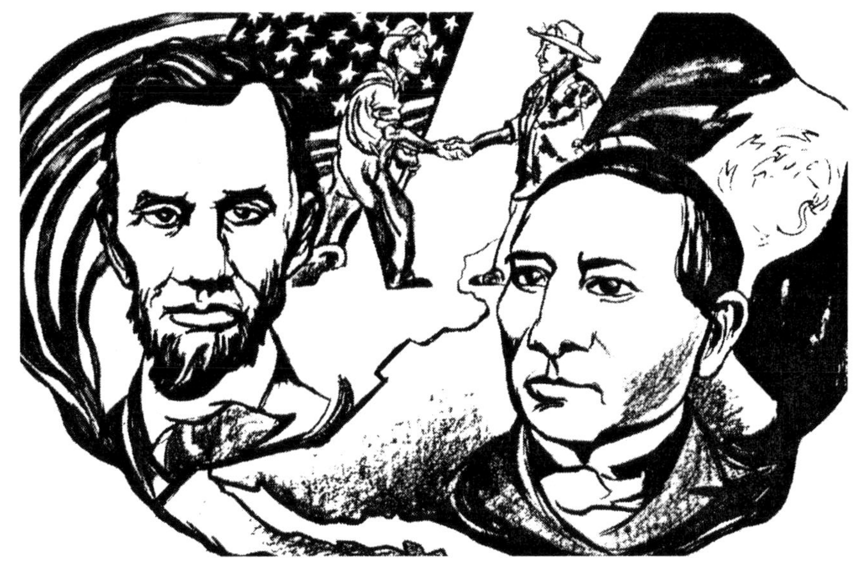

30

TEHRAN ACCORD

Pablo remained in Mexico for most of the war years. In his dozen pages of letters to Jean Charlot during 1943, he mentions the war only twice. He talks about the TGP creating anti-fascist posters and about Bellas Artes not wanting to host an exhibit of Charlot's work because of the war.[1]

In 1944, however, Pablo came to the United States "to spend a year working in the San Francisco shipyards," according to an interview he gave in 1949.[2] Some accounts give the year as 1945 and some state that in doing so, Pablo was fulfilling a duty he felt as a U.S. citizen to serve his country.[3] Poniatowska says, "*Durante la guerra, Pablo viajó especialmente a Estados Unidos a cumplir con su ciudadanía y fue soldador en un barco en San Francisco* [During the war, Pablo traveled to the United States to fulfill his duties as a citizen and worked as a welder on a ship in San Francisco]." [4] Other publications report that Pablo felt a "moral duty to go to the U.S. to fight fascism from his country of origin." [5] There is no mention, however, whether he registered for the draft, was drafted, or enlisted in the military, though as a male U.S. citizen living abroad, he would have been required to register for the draft by December 31, 1943.[6]

Any sense of moral or civic duty as a U.S. citizen arose late in the war (the United States entered the war in 1941 and the war in Europe ended in May 1945), but corresponded with the January, 7, 1944, announcement by Earl Browder, head of the Communist Party in the United States, that based on meetings in Tehran, Iran, between Joseph Stalin, Winston Churchill, and Franklin Delano Roosevelt in late 1943, "Capitalism and socialism have begun to find their way to peaceful coexistence and collaboration in the same world." [7] Suddenly party members believed there was a way to reconcile their belief in Communism with American values. [8]

The shroud of suspicion regarding Communists was lifted and they felt welcomed and a part of the mainstream United States. With this promise of coexistence, membership in the U.S. Communist Party reached an all-time high.

Browder saw an extremely important role for Latin America in this new world vision. He promised more equalized relations between the United States and Latin America based on the modernization and industrialization of Latin America. He said that at war's end, "Latin Americans would 'collaborate with our new capitalists in finding the markets they must have' and thereby inaugurate an extension of the Good Neighbor Policy." [9] In May 1944, the Mexican Communist Party, at its ninth congress, embraced "Browderism" and made peace with the CTM (Confederation of Mexican Workers). The PCM "declared an indefinite postponement of the struggle to implant socialism in Mexico," in favor of maintaining "national unity" to further "industrial development, independence and progress." [10]

Carol Cuenod, a former party member and a librarian for the labor history archives at San Francisco State University, knew a couple who named their child Persia, as the child was conceived "during the time in 1944–45 when there was going to be a great period of peace between the Soviet Union and the United States," she said. Cuenod attended the California Labor School in 1945 when Pablo taught there, and got to know him in Mexico City in 1949. She suggested that the Tehran accord was what brought Pablo to the United States in 1944. [11] This seems consistent with Pablo's description of the time he was in the United States during the war, "when the allies were together—the U.S., France, England, the Soviet Union. That's when there was a unity with the Soviet Union. The war was against Fascism. Then during the McCarthy era they changed." [12]

People in the United States who knew Pablo at the time said he would not have come to the United States to collaborate with it in the fight against fascism—that his support of the war was support of the Soviet Union.[13] He had proved this during the Soviet–Nazi Non-Aggression Pact, when, contrary to the interests of the United States, he had dropped his criticism of the Nazis—until they invaded the Soviet Union. In addition, he came to the United States "feeling Mexican," though he still held his U.S. citizenship.[14] A year after the war ended he wrote a letter to a friend describing himself as "a Mexican." [15]

The Tehran accord gave Pablo a way to reconcile his Communism with his U.S. citizenship, allowing him to believe that there was nothing inconsistent between Communism and U.S. patriotism. The Tehran era was characterized, in San Francisco longshoreman David Jenkins's words, by the "Americanization of the Party, the reliance on its own historical sources, relying on a new literature which would identify the Party with its American beginnings, getting away from a kind of control by the International Communist movement." [16] Pablo, in a 1939 interview with a Communist newspaper, drew a parallel between his own political activities and those of his English ancestor (whom he erroneously called O'Higgins) who fought in the U.S. Revolution of 1776.[17]

Before coming to the United States, Pablo received a commission that exemplifies the spirit of the Tehran period. In 1944, he created a color lithograph poster titled *Buenos vecinos, buenos amigos* (*Good Neighbors, Good Friends*), depicting Abraham Lincoln and Benito Juárez. (Pablo had done color lithography as early as 1938.[18]) It was commissioned by Herbert Cerwin of the Office of Inter-American Affairs, established pursuant to Roosevelt's Good Neighbors Policy, which sought to reverse U.S. interventionist policies in Latin America.[19]

Directed by Nelson Rockefeller, the Office of Inter-American Affairs was a massive U.S. government program designed to replace Axis propaganda and European influence in Latin America with U.S. culture. It was interested in economic and commercial activities and sought to "gradually expose Mexicans to values and rhetoric that fostered the American ideals of freedom and democracy." [20] It did this through the largest advertising campaign in U.S. history—one hundred forty million dollars spent between 1940 and 1945 to bring U.S. culture and values to Latin America through radio programs such as *Viva America*, newsreels, theater, and cultural activities, all focused on locations where the Rockefellers had substantial investments.[21] Artists from the United States who were involved included Walt Disney, who created a 1942 film, *Saludos Amigos*, for the program.[22] The office commissioned six thousand prints of Pablo's poster.[23]

With the TGP dedicated to combating the threat of "economic and cultural invasion from their 'good neighbor' to the north," it is ironic that Pablo and the TGP would accept a commission from a Nelson Rockefeller-run organization in the biggest-ever campaign to get U.S. culture, including Mickey Mouse, to Mexico. Pablo and the Mexican left had protested Rivera's cozying up to Rockefeller in the early 1930s, but now they had an opportunity to make some much needed money.[24]

That the TGP was willing to do so demonstrates how flexible the TGP—and Pablo —were in speaking the revolutionary line while taking money from the "imperialist enemy" when necessary. But perhaps in the spirit of earning a living and of the Tehran accord, they were able to overlook these inconsistencies: Prignitz said that Pablo's poster, "though not a masterpiece," saved the TGP from eviction and bankruptcy. She added that his lithograph "indicated a clear tendency towards the simplification of history." [25]

Pablo was in Mexico for at least part of 1944. Mariana Yampolsky said that her first impression of the TGP when she arrived there in 1944 after graduating from the University of Chicago was meeting Méndez and Pablo.[26] A recent book on Pablo said that in 1944 he went to Los Angeles to be close to workers of his country during the war and that he worked in the port.[27]

Books and chronologies on Pablo often say that while working in the shipyards, he hid his identity as an artist but was discovered to be Pablo O'Higgins, the muralist, when someone came to give him his paycheck.[28] This would indicate that he had joined a union, since during the war, union membership was required to get a job. David Jenkins, who worked in the San Francisco shipyards in World War II (but did not recall Pablo having worked there), said of the war years, "These unions suddenly had huge treasuries. The initiation fees were enormous. You had to be a member of the union in order to work." [29]

This information might indicate that Pablo had come to the U.S. intending to spend a year working in the shipyards but that his plans were cut short when he was discovered to be the famous artist Pablo O'Higgins and sent to Seattle to paint a mural. But those involved in the mural recall that the commission was arranged while Pablo was in Mexico and that he came to the United States from Mexico in order to paint the mural, not to work in the shipyards. (See Chapter 32, n.3.)

The letters Pablo wrote in 1945 and the following year discussing his activities in the United States during the last years of the war do not mention his coming to the United States to fight the war against fascism or to work in a shipyard as a welder. In a May 28, 1945, letter to Jean Charlot, he wrote that he left Mexico City on April 2, 1945, and went to Los Angeles to visit his mother. He traveled in California all of April and part of May, before going to Seattle. He says he brought art to San Francisco to show at the "Gump Gallery," the gallery connected to Gump's, an exclusive shop near Union Square.

He was then invited to Seattle for three weeks to give a class. He planned to return to San Francisco to teach a class (likely the one he gave at the California Labor School in the summer of 1945), and in August, return to Mexico. He gave Charlot tips on where and how to find an apartment for his family in Mexico City, and asked his friend to write him before leaving for Mexico. (Charlot and his family were returning to Mexico in June 1945 on a Guggenheim Fellowship that financed his writing of the book, *The Mexican Mural Renaissance, 1920–1925*.)[30] Pablo said nothing to Charlot about working as a welder, working in shipyards, or fighting the war against fascism from U.S. soil.

On October 8, 1945, Pablo wrote Charlot expressing regret that he had not been in Mexico when Charlot and his family had arrived there that summer.[31] He said he had to come to California to visit his mother and ended up with a lot of things keeping him from leaving for a month and a half. He talked about the mural for the Ship Scalers Union and said he planned to finish it by around October 15, spend two to three weeks in Los Angeles with his mother, and be back in Mexico at the end of November.

Pablo also wrote a letter to "Ballad of Joe Hill" composer Earl Robinson describing his time in the United States in 1945, again mentioning nothing about working in a shipyard or feeling compelled to join in the war efforts. His letters to both friends are filled with talk of art (music in the case of Robinson) and friends.

Other sources corroborate Pablo's busy schedule during 1945. One source said that Pablo was painting the Seattle Ship Scalers mural when President Roosevelt died and that he had to paint and repaint FDR's portrait eleven times before the union members were satisfied.[32] President Roosevelt died on April 12, 1945. The Ship Scalers' files indicate that Pablo was in Seattle in June 1945, and the *Oakland Tribune* reported he was "in town" on July 1, 1945.[33] The California Labor School records indicate he taught a class there in the summer of 1945. Thus, if he worked a year in the shipyards of San Francisco, as he stated in his interview, it must have been in 1944 (though he was in Mexico when Yampolsky arrived, so it might have been less than a year).

Since Pablo's death, his travel to the United States during the war has been used as an example of his substantial sacrifice for the war against fascism. María said that in coming to the United States Pablo had to leave behind everything that tied him to Mexico: his possessions, his friends, and his job at La Esmeralda (where, actually, he would not teach until five years later), and suggested that in taking a job as a welder in San Francisco he was willing potentially to sacrifice his vision.[34] She has used his trip to the United States to illustrate Pablo's commitment to just causes, his "elevated sense of civic duty," and, oddly, as an example of his life as a "revolutionary."[35]

Pablo, however, never mentioned making these or other sacrifices when he said he came to the United States to work in the shipyards for a year. Indeed, most friends in the United States did not know of him spending a year during the war working in the San Francisco shipyards or working in the shipyards at all. He did not share this information with his many friends from the United States who served in the war, including David Thompson, his future mural assistant, who sacrificed his leg.[36]

According to Thompson's widow, Pablo never told them that he worked in the shipyards as a welder.[37] He never told his postwar veteran friend Steve Murin that he had worked in the shipyards as a welder or otherwise sacrificed during the war.[38] Nor did he share this information with his friends who worked in the Bay Area shipyards as civilians, such as Emmy Lou Packard, Byron Randall, or George Gutekunst.

During his time in the United States during the war years, Pablo would have been paid well for his work as a union welder, paid for teaching at the California Labor School, and he was paid two thousand dollars for his work painting the mural in Seattle. He must have known that having a well-paying job and being able to come and go as he pleased was not nearly the sacrifice others had made.[39] Perhaps this is why he never mentioned to his friends in the United States any sacrifices he made during the war.

Nor did Pablo mention to friends in the United States that he was fulfilling a moral duty by coming to the United States during the war years.[40] From 1939 to 1941, Pablo had faithfully followed the mandate of the Communist Party to accept the Soviet Union's two-year friendship with the Nazis, even when it was clearly not in the interest of the United States to do so. And, as demonstrated by his art, including his 1941 piece *The Soviet Front is our Best Defense—Let's Maintain it!,* his support for the war primarily was support of the Soviet Union. Pablo's friends in the United States who knew him at the time said that any feeling of moral duty to fight for the United States would have been inconsistent with his pro-Soviet beliefs.[41] Perhaps it was later, during the McCarthy era, that his wartime travel to the United States came to be characterized as evidence of a moral duty, "elevated" civic duty, or patriotism toward the United States.

The "war efforts" of the TGP artists consisted of doing what they loved to do: producing political art. Bardach has questioned why they mobilized and even went to Spain to fight fascism but they did not fight in World War II: "By WWII, global fascism was an infinitely greater threat than when Franco's forces overran Spain. Why, then did none of the artists sign up to fight in this conflict?" [42]

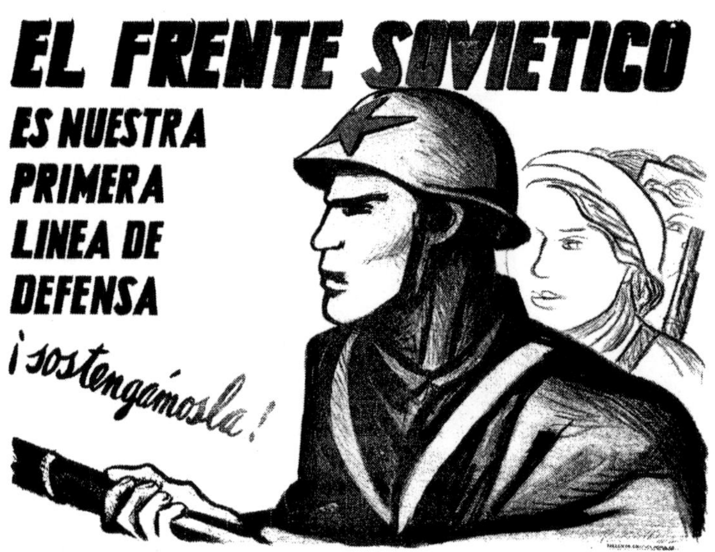

31

THE LAST HURRAH OF COMMUNISM

Three years into the war, San Francisco had doubled in size. The war transformed it into a diverse, labor-union city. In March 1945, when, according to Pablo's letter to Earl Robinson, he arrived from Mexico, the city was preparing for ten thousand visitors from fifty countries coming to celebrate a month of festivities, culminating with the June 26 opening of the first meeting of the allied countries joining together as the United Nations.

During his time in San Francisco, before heading to Seattle to paint the Ship Scalers mural, Pablo forged relationships with members of the powerful International Longshoremen's and Warehousemen's Union (ILWU). These relationships would last many years and secure him teaching opportunities and a major mural commission in Hawai'i. During his months in the United States, Pablo helped create connections between U.S. artists interested in political graphic art and the TGP—connections that exist to this day.

The ILWU viewed the influx of workers to the city as a great opportunity for labor to educate a workforce for the future—one knowledgeable about workers' rights and committed to unionism.[1] This union, which essentially controlled the waterfront of the western United States, set up a school for the mostly uneducated and minority workers who came to the port cities of Seattle, San Francisco, and San Diego to join the war effort.[2]

A workers' school was consistent with the Communist Party's goal of making itself more attractive to a broad base of Americans, pursuant to the Comintern's mandate of a Popular Front at its seventh congress. Pablo's party membership, his experience teaching art and Marxism to workers—both at the LEAR's art school and the TGP's school advertised to English speakers—his work in the Soviet Union, and his connection to Latinos, made him an asset to the party.

The California Labor School, directed by longshoreman David Jenkins, was originally called the Tom Mooney School, after the eponymous militant who had been convicted (and later pardoned) of the 1916 bombing of a Preparedness Day parade in San Francisco that killed ten. But by 1943, that name did not properly reflect the Popular Front, "post-Tehran" image the party wanted to convey in its attempts to increase its membership, including from the American Federation of Labor (AFL). Jenkins said:

> [Mooney] was too Left really for the established AFL. We were trying very hard to get AFL unions into the Labor School with some success, so we at that point took the Tehran line of the Party, enunciated by Earl Browder and adopted by the Party. We felt that greater unity was important. . . . In our publications, we changed the name of the school to the California Labor School.[3]

The school did not have to worry much about hiding its party ties. The House Un-American Activities Committee (HUAC) had suspended its operation during the war years.[4] Membership in the party swelled enormously after the United States entered the war.[5] The party had bookstores in every city in California and more than a hundred full-time employees.[6] "[T]he Party, which had 3,000-4,000 members in the Bay Area alone, during the Browder period of leadership was an enormous force in California," said Jenkins. Jenkins recalled how easy it was to recruit party members at the California Labor School during the U.S. alliance with the USSR:

> [A]t one point in the Labor School, I recruited 160 people into the Party in one three-month period. Just through normal social and political intercourse—and talking about philosophy and ideas. After all, we as a nation were backed by a great Red Army who was out fighting in Stalingrad. The Soviets were part of our allied campaign against fascism.[7]

The school became enormous. "Overnight the union movement in California and around northern California quadrupled. . . . [E]very union just exploded with new members. . . . [T]he school announced classes in parliamentary procedure, how to run a union meeting, how to build a steward system." [8] By May 1944, it had served more than six thousand students, forty percent of whom were African-American.[9]

Art, said Jenkins, was taught as "a weapon in the struggle for socialism, for education as well as for self-expression." [10] During its peak, from 1944 to 1948, the Labor School's art department was bigger than that of the San Francisco Art Institute.[11]

The art department attracted some of the most talented artists in America to its faculty. It would influence the Actors Workshop, the San Francisco Mime Troupe, and the Teatro Campesino.[12] It had a famous chorus. Equally famous was its annual Halloween Ball, sometimes a raunchy affair.[13]

Anton Refregier, who painted murals at San Francisco's Rincon Annex, was head of the art department. Art teachers included sculptor Robert Stackpole, painter Victor Arnautoff, Pele deLappe, and guest teacher and former Rivera assistant Emmy Lou Packard. Pele deLappe taught life drawing to retired longshoremen. The class was held at the beach with a live model. DeLappe said, "I suspect they attended mostly to ogle the model." [14] In June 1944, the party moved the school from Turk and Van Ness to a six-story building at 216 Market Street in the Financial District, bringing it into San Francisco mainstream.[15] The "Tehran line" allowed the school to expand its curriculum into areas that the party had previously made off limits, such as psychiatry.[16]

The Labor School struck a coup when it became accredited and therefore able to enroll returning service people on the GI Bill. At the Labor School's height, in 1945, the State Department, through Library of Congress Librarian Archibald MacLeish, asked it to sponsor labor delegates from the Soviet Union coming to San Francisco to participate in the opening of the first session of the United Nations. It was a huge event in San Francisco and included a cocktail party for the Communists at the Fairmont Hotel on Nob Hill. According to Jenkins, "All of society was vying for one of the Russians." [17]

The unions, with their ability to break or maintain labor's wartime "no strike" promise, had considerable power during the war years, and industry, which relied on union workers, was raking in money on government contracts. This made it easy for the most powerful union on the West Coast to raise money: Jenkins, a Communist with an eighth-grade education, was easily able to schmooze donations from captains of industry ("imperialists" in pre-Tehran terms), including executives and lawyers for Crocker Bank, Bank of America, Levi Strauss, and even Gump's, because industry was anxious to keep labor happy. The school, said Jenkins, "was probably the best expression nationally of Tehranism that the [Communist Party] had . . . ." [18]

A history of the art of California labor says, "The celebrated American/Mexican muralist and printmaker Pablo O'Higgins taught several influential classes in lithography, first in 1945 and again in 1949, and his students remember carrying heavy litho stones home on the streetcar to work on so they would have something ready to print the next day." [19]

After several months in the Bay Area, Pablo left for Seattle to paint the mural for the Ship Scalers Union—but not before stopping by the ILWU and suggesting they remodel. California Labor School student Carol Cuenod remembers him walking by the union's conference room and saying, "How can they ever come to a positive decision in such an oppressive room?" He suggested they "change the lighting, paint the ceiling blue, and get rid of the paneling." [20]

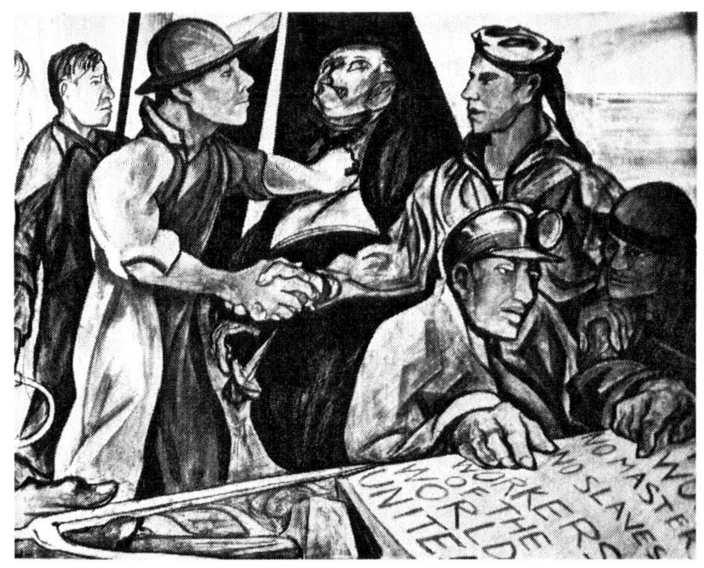

32

SEATTLE, 1945

It was still the war period, and the fight was still against fascism, but the union that commissioned Pablo to paint the Seattle mural was already fighting the next great battle of the left, the battle for civil rights. The mural Pablo painted for the Ship Scalers echoed the theme of the *Good Neighbors, Good Friends* poster he had created the year before: that the future held friendship between the United States and Mexico, Communists, socialists, and capitalists.

Seattle's Ship Scalers, Drydock and Miscellaneous Boatyard Workers Union, Local 541, was comprised of men and women who did some of the dirtiest, nastiest work on the docks: they cleaned the barnacles, scales, and muck off and out of ships, crawling through their oily gallows. The majority of its members were African-Americans drawn to Seattle by wartime jobs. Its head, Don Del Castle, and other key leaders were Communists looking forward to a world absent class struggles and social injustices.[1] The union's first battle was being fought within labor itself. Del Castle told a reporter that in 1940, "labor was so short that the King County Labor Council finally agreed that it was their patriotic duty to accept black workers into their ranks." [2]

The union's headquarters was the site of civil rights efforts during the war years. W. E. B. DuBois spoke there and the union organized lunch-counter sit-ins protesting racial discrimination. John Caughlan and Del Castle, in June 1945, were working to create a state-based antidiscrimination law along the lines of the federal Fair Employment Practices Act (FEPA), which prevented discrimination against blacks during the war, but was expected to expire at war's end. The union's coffers were full and the union was looking for a way to honor the civilian workers who contributed to the war efforts. Hallie Donaldson, who had been a visiting artist at the TGP and knew Pablo, recommended that he be commissioned to paint a mural. The union chose as a theme the struggle against racial discrimination with the mural to be dedicated to the people of the United Nations.[3]

The mural consists of three panels showing the principles of the union, the racial discrimination and poverty of the worker before unionization, and the better life offered through unionization. It shows Lincoln and Roosevelt standing above a document listing four freedoms: freedom to worship, freedom of speech, freedom from fear, and freedom from want. The mural also includes a reference to the FEPA antidiscrimination legislation.

Pablo's mural was very significant for the union. The *Seattle Times* reported:

> The heady sense of mission within the ship scaler ranks climaxed in 1945 when Pablo O'Higgins, the Mexican muralist and dedicated leftist, came to Seattle. He had agreed to paint a mural for the union . . . . The O'Higgins mural was sort of a high-water mark for the progress of American socialism at mid-century.[4]

Containing the portraits of Mao and Lenin, as well as Del Castle with a hammer and sickle on his lapel, the mural continues to be controversial. In 2002, it was attacked in the University of Washington student newspaper as anticapitalist.[5]

Perhaps it was during the Tehran period that Pablo knocked on his sister's door in Palo Alto, hoping she would have the same "Good Neighbors, Good Friends" spirit as the union members in Seattle. Gladys's son, Edward N. Glaeser, said that he heard a knock on the door one day and opened it.[6] A tall man was standing there who said he was the boy's uncle. Edward had heard of his uncle Paul, and wanted to meet him. But Gladys came to the door and slammed the door and locked it. A few hours later, the doorbell rang again. Another person handed Gladys a cardboard tube. The next day, Edward found it in the garbage, unopened. He took the tube but oddly didn't open it for many years. It contained lithographs by Pablo.

Gladys, as well as some other family members, would have nothing to do with Pablo once they learned of his Communist activities. When Gladys's son wanted to visit his famous artist uncle in Mexico City, Gladys said he couldn't because Pablo lived in the ghetto.[7] Gerda Katz, whose knew Pablo in Mexico, said, "I knew his family didn't agree with him." [8] Gladys wouldn't talk to him after he went to the Soviet Union.[9]

Two half siblings couldn't have been less alike. While Pablo was spending May Days watching, attending, and painting workers' rallies, Gladys, who was a registered Republican married to an accountant and the deputy grand matron of the Masonic Order of the Eastern Star, was spending her May Day decked out in a lace gown having ribbons wrapped around her as she stood holding a maypole. The *San Mateo Times* reported Gladys's activities of the previous May Day.

> The Laurel chapter of the OES threw the deputy grand matron [Gladys Glaeser] a May Day Fete. The chapter room was beautifully decorated with an abundance of iris and baby roses adding a touch of spring. Officers wore white while the deputy was gowned in rose lace. The deputy held the May pole in the center as the officers wound the colored ribbons around her.[10]

When Gladys closed the door on him, Pablo closed the door on her as well, never mentioning to his future wife that he had a sister.

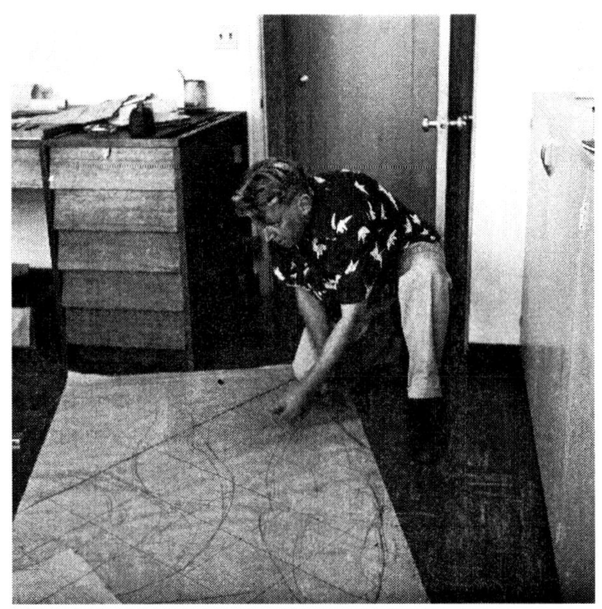

33

EARL ROBINSON

In 1945, Pablo met his counterpart in the creative field that had dominated the first eighteen years of his life: music.

Earl Robinson was the United States' first widely successful political songwriter. With a career spanning decades, a Guggenheim Fellowship, and music credits for the Academy Award-winning film *The House I Live In*, he is best known today for the "Ballad of Joe Hill," famously sung by Joan Baez at Woodstock in 1969. Pablo and Robinson become close friends: over a twenty-month period in 1946 and 1947, Pablo sent him thirteen pages of letters in his large, slanted handwriting.

Robinson, in 1945, was the most famous leftist songwriter in Hollywood. In 1936, he put the "Ballad of Joe Hill," a poem by Alfred Hayes, to music. The song turned the name Joe Hill into a household word, especially in labor circles.[1] It has been performed for generations by well-known singers, including Paul Robeson, Pete Seeger, Joan Baez, and The Dubliners.[2]

In 1939 Robinson had composed the "Ballad for Americans." Made famous by African-American singer Paul Robeson, it became the "unofficial anthem of the [Popular Front]." [3] Like Pablo's Seattle mural, it drew parallels between liberal values and U.S. history. Both the Republican and Democratic parties chose the "Ballad for Americans" as the theme song for their 1940 national conventions.[4]

In 1945, on his way back to Mexico from Seattle, Pablo stayed with Earl Robinson and his wife and son, Perry, as their houseguest in Los Angeles. By then, Robinson, "thanks to 'Ballad for Americans' and *The House I Live In* . . . was one of the American left's most renowned creative figures, and doubly so as one who had, to some extent, made it in Hollywood and contributed to mainstream entertainment." [5] Hollywood's welcome would soon end: Robinson would spend twenty years on the Hollywood blacklist.

Pablo found a kindred spirit in Robinson. Both he and Robinson were talented musicians at a young age. They shared a zeal for reconciling Communism with U.S. values, especially drawing parallels between the 1775 U.S. Revolution and modern struggles of "the people": the "Ballad for Americans" references the American Revolution and Lincoln's Gettysburg Address. Robinson was from Seattle, and Pablo had just painted the mural there. Both were committed to ending racism. But there was something that Pablo did not share with Robinson: his father's involvement in the Joe Hill case.

Pablo was then forty-one years old. He had spent twenty years on the left and the past seven months with the most radical labor union in the country. Even under María's scenario—that Pablo, as a child, never knew about his father's work on the Joe Hill case—he would have known by then that Hill had been executed in Salt Lake City, since the third stanza of the song refers to Salt Lake City, and that both his father and his brother had worked at the Utah attorney general's office.[6]

Had Robinson known that Pablo was from Utah (and anyone meeting a blond-haired, blue-eyed man with a U.S. accent who called himself a Mexican would ask where he was from), he most certainly would have asked what he remembered of the Joe Hill case. Seattle Centro de La Raza founder Roberto Maestas, upon learning that Pablo had grown up in Utah, immediately asked, "What year was Joe Hill executed there?" [7] Earl Robinson, in his autobiography, said that Pablo was from Wisconsin.[8] Robinson's son was certain his father didn't know of the connection of Pablo's father to the case.[9]

Pablo must have resolved to keep his father's involvement in the Joe Hill case a secret, even when friends gathered around the piano with Earl Robinson and sang the "Ballad of Joe Hill." María recalled friends around the piano singing the song and "everyone knew the words."

It was wise of Pablo to keep this secret. When Maestas learned that Pablo's father had been an attorney for the prosecution in the Joe Hill case, he shook his head in disbelief. So did Goldie Caughlan. Earl Robinson's son, who was eight or nine years old when Pablo stayed with the Robinson family and remembered him vividly sixty years later, said, "Oh my God!" when told of Pablo's father's work on the case.[10] Both Maestas and Goldie Caughlan asked the same question: Was his activism an attempt to atone for his father's involvement in Hill's execution? Or an attempt to rebel against his father? John Caughlan said that if he'd known of Edward Higgins's role in the Joe Hill case, "It wouldn't have endeared me" to Pablo.[11] Perhaps this was one of the reasons that Pablo separated himself from his life in Utah.

A series of letters Pablo wrote to Robinson after staying in his home reveal that Pablo, in the mid-1940s, fresh off a war victory and a successful mural project in the United States, enthusiastically was expanding his circle of friends in labor to the benefit of the TGP, himself, and the leftist cause. His correspondence shows the extent of his contacts and influence and his desire to use them to bring together like-minded artists for artistic collaborations.

U.S. artists were hungry for this. In an article a few years later about Pablo, Pele deLappe mentioned that artists in the United States "pine to do collective work for trade unions as part of the labor movement." [12]

A few weeks after returning to Mexico, on January 13, 1946, Pablo wrote to Robinson. He described how, after his ten months in the United States, he returned to find Mexico had changed.

> First of all, I was to find an extremely different character and life of Mexico—now, than when I left 10 months ago. What you and Helen and our other friends were seeing—the changes & struggles—in the States—are now appearing here—more openly—and, of course, based on a different social structure than ours—using very openly pro-fascist methods. What will really happen soon will depend on the possible unity of the progressive organizations—which, now, I'm sorry to say, are split and divided. Anyhow I'm not losing confidence, because even in its most precarious moments the Mexican people have been able to give a powerful answer to reaction. I'm sending you, for example, several of the last magazines that Siqueiros and Toledano are getting out—and soon will send some of the popular leaflets from the Taller.[13]

The letters Pablo wrote to Robinson show his dual allegiances. In this letter, Pablo noted that Mexico has "a different social structure than *ours*." In a letter to Robinson he wrote two months later, Pablo referred to himself as "a Mexican." [14]

The "changes and struggles" in the United States were those brought on by the end of Roosevelt's Good Neighbors policy. While President Harry S. Truman continued to give it lip service, the end of the war brought, almost immediately, the revival of the government's suspicions regarding Communism.[15] At war's end, the parallels between the U.S. Revolution of 1776 and the Soviet or Mexican revolution were increasingly met with skepticism—the Sons of the American Revolution, an organization of which Pablo's father was a proud member, soon began "Red-baiting." One of its targets was the California Labor School in which Pablo had just taught.[16]

The struggles Pablo referred to in Mexico at the end of the war were an upsurge of conservativism and a fragmentation of the left. The "boys of the Taller" (as Pablo referred to them earlier in his letter to Robinson) had celebrated the end of the war with a poster, created by Angel Bracho, featuring a large flag with the star of Stalin's Red Army, and behind it, the flags of the United States and Great Britain. It shows the decaying face of Hitler stabbed in the eye by a bayonet, surrounded by detritus of the Nazis and Italian fascists going up in flames. At the bottom it says, "Victory! The artists of the Taller de Gráfica Popular have joined to celebrate all of the workers and progressive men of Mexico and of the world for the triumph of the Red Army and the arms of all of the nations united against the German Nazi, as the most significant step for the total destruction of fascism." [17]

The TGP's celebration of the end of the war as a victory for the USSR is one of the factors that would cause it to be labeled a Communist front by the United States, resulting in serious problems for some TGP members and visitors over the next twenty years.

War's end had reignited the pro-fascist elements in Mexico. A Sinarquista demonstration ended in the government killing and wounding a number of the attackers. To placate them, the government allowed a Sinarquista candidate to win the governorship in Guanajuato. The conservative Partido Acción Nacional (National Action Party, PAN) had been founded in September 1939 by Sinarquistas.

Pablo, however, still was optimistic about the left and about collaborating with labor in the United States. He suggested to Robinson that he meet José Revueltas, "the revolutionary novelist," and Juan de la Cabada, who was in New York, to collaborate on a piece, the "Ballad of Latin America." [18] Pablo also recounted a meeting he had in Beverly

Hills with Mexican composer Carlos Chávez. Pablo wrote about a possible collaboration with John Cohee, from the American Newspaper Guild and a member of the Citizens' Committee for the Defense of Mexican-American Youth (later Sleepy Lagoon Defense Committee), defending Mexican and Mexican-American teens in the "Zoot Suit" case, which had ignited racial tensions in Los Angeles in the mid-1940s.[19]

At the end of his letter to Robinson, Pablo writes, "Please write, and I'll do the same. Greetings to our friends, and please tell Martha to write to me." [20]

Martha was Martha Dodd, an infamous alleged Soviet spy who lived a high-flying life of wealth and political risk and became a close patron and friend, if not lover, of Pablo.

Dodd was barely out of college when her father was appointed U. S. ambassador to Germany. First, she was enthralled with the Nazis; later, after a visit to the Soviet Union in 1934, she changed her allegiances to that country. Gorgeous and adventurous, she was also, like Tina Modotti and Alexandra Kollontai—other radical women Pablo had admired—scandalous. Nearly every mention of her refers to her sexual attitudes. A longtime friend said, "We called her the anti-Fascist nymphomaniac—a wonderful woman. She should have written her memoirs. She once said to me 'Jurgen, you're the only resistance fighter I haven't slept with.' " [21] A recent book, *Spies*, refers to an extended conversation Dodd had with her KGB contact in 1941 that left him exasperated. "Seemingly she spent most of her time in bed. . . . In addition to the Russian or Russians, she slept with a full-blown fascist, General Ernest Utet. . . . She asked me if it was now a rule that people in our work were not to have a sexual life." [22]

On her return to the United States from Germany, Dodd married Alfred Stern, from Fargo, North Dakota, a "handsome and charming fellow" with no career goals, who had been married to Marion Rosenwald, the daughter of Sears Roebuck magnate Julius Rosenwald, and inherited a fortune upon Marion's death.[23] Dodd and Stern lived in Manhattan and Connecticut and had a busy social life with many Soviet and Eastern bloc diplomats.[24] Dodd had many friends who were from Eastern Europe in New York, where "people would drop off a package and they would give it to someone else." [25] She collected the work of Pablo and other Mexican artists and helped him sell his work in New York.[26] She was "extremely interested" in his work, according to a friend of Pablo.[27]

Dodd and her husband, in 1942, moved to Los Angeles, where Dodd hoped to get a film made about her experiences in Germany. By 1946, when Pablo was trying to reconnect with her, Dodd was entering a business partnership in Los Angeles with Borris Morros, a Russian spy, and unknown to her, a double agent.[28] Pablo would reunite with Dodd in Mexico before she went into hiding in Prague.

At the same time, Hollywood was embroiled in its own drama. The motion picture studios of the 1930s and 1940s were fighting for the attention of theatergoers. A strike of the progressive Conference of Studio Unions in 1945 brought out the underside of Hollywood high-stakes politics, including charges of Communism in the union. The offspring of this struggle were censorship, the conviction of the Hollywood Ten, and the Hollywood blacklist.

This is likely the strike that Pablo referred to in his November 15, 1946, letter to Robinson: "I realize that, even though some of the important strikes during last spring and summer are over, for the moment—there will be future struggles of great importance and art, as our friends must know by now is an important weapon." [29] It resulted in the first Hollywood exiles finding their way to Mexico, one of just two countries U.S. citizens could travel to without a passport, the other being Canada.[30] The U.S. government denied passports to applicants it deemed members of the Communist Party on the grounds that their travel abroad was "contrary to the best interests of the United States." [31] Scenic artist Philip Stein, a member of the union who had gone to jail during the strikes, and his wife, Gertrude (not the writer Gertrude Stein), were among the first to arrive in Mexico in 1948.[32]

In spite of these challenges in Mexico and the United States, Pablo, in his letters to Robinson, seemed certain that he would continue to be able to work freely in both countries. In his November 1946 letter he said he hoped he could return to the United States, "and see, again, the possibilities of the mural work in the unions."

McCarthyism, however, soon would thwart Pablo's plans of great collaborations between leftist artists in the United States and Mexico, at least in the long term. Pablo mentions to Robinson that he had written to Phil Connolly, head of the California Congress of Industrial Organizations (CIO), with whom he and Robinson had met and discussed "working together—a Mexican, a Negro, and a white American—for a very telling result in the work." Connelly, who was also on the Sleepy Lagoon Defense Committee for the Zoot Suit case, must have been the "Negro" Pablo referred to, Robinson the "white American," and Pablo the "Mexican." [33]

III

THE CULTURAL YEARS

"He'd become pretty much part of the establishment, I'd say."
—Viola Patterson[1]

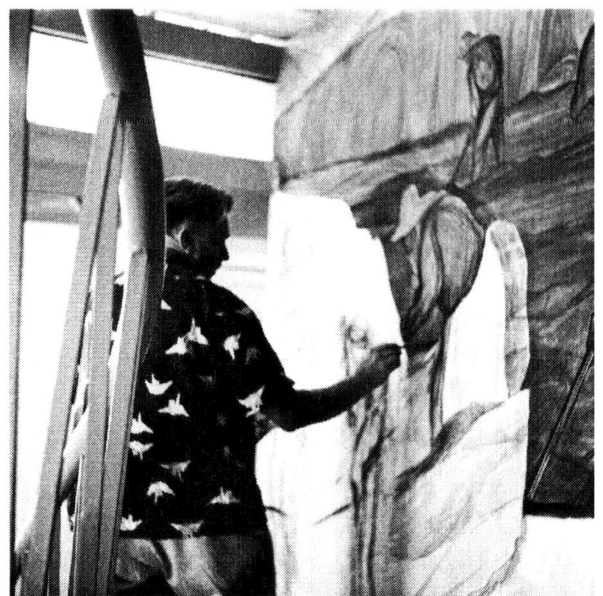

34

A NEW REVOLUTION

Pablo obtained a mural commission from the Mexican government upon his return to Mexico after the war. In 1946, he was commissioned by architect Ricardo Rivas to paint a fresco mural in a maternity hospital. Pablo asked Méndez to assist him, even though Méndez was a printmaker, not a painter. Méndez said Pablo "did not hesitate to sacrifice his prestige as an experienced painter in order to inspire me to paint." [1] Pablo told Earl Robinson, "The walls are beautifully proportioned and the theme is revolutionary in its content." [2] The mural, called *Maternity*, showed the contrast between women giving birth in modern hospitals with trained doctors and modern equipment and giving birth in poor villages with the midwife and "magic doctor" attending.[3]

Pablo's description of this mural as "revolutionary" in theme reflects a new definition of *revolution* that would be used after World War II by the TGP and the government of Miguel Alemán Valdés, whom the TGP supported in his successful 1945 bid for the presidency.

Revolution in Mexico had previously referred to efforts to eradicate the privileges of the rich, foreign investors, and the Catholic Church and to give land back to the poor. But under President Alemán, *revolution* came to mean building modern hospitals, bridges, and highways, and the twenty-five-million-dollar Ciudad Universitaria (University City, the campus of the National University).[4] President Alemán aptly changed the name of his party from the Partido de la Revolución Mexicana (Party of the Mexican Revolution, or PRM) to the Partido Revolucionario Institucional (Institutional Revolutionary Party, or PRI). Mexican historian Enrique Krauze wrote, "The truth is the revolution has died but the reality is that it cannot die." [5] In other words, the revolution, and its emphasis on bettering the lives of the poor, was over, but this could not be admitted, so whatever the government chose to do had to be called revolutionary.

Octavio Paz observed in 1975 that the "turn taken by the social programs of the revolutionaries . . . degenerated into a policy of 'development'" that would benefit "only a small minority" of the population. [6] He said:

> Our poor revolution [was a] victim of a two-fold takeover: it had been co-opted politically by the official government [p]arty, a bureaucracy that is similar in more than one respect to the Communist bureaucracies of Eastern Europe, and it had been co-opted economically and socially by a financial oligarchy that had intimate ties to huge American corporations.[7]

For the TGP, a group, in Méndez's words, *animados por un verdadero romanticismo revolucionario* (driven by true romantic revolutionary ideals), the subject of their work had to be revolutionary.[8] Thus, whatever subject matter it was hired to depict it called revolutionary. Like Pablo, the TGP was protean when it came to adapting itself to the political situation of the times and doing what was needed to survive. The TGP began walking down a path toward alignment with the ruling party, the PRI, which would cause it to be scorned by younger generations of artists. Pablo's closeness to the PRI would peak in 1976, when Pablo and María and their fourteen-year-old guest Kathryn McCormick, decked out in tuxedo and ball gowns, attended the inauguration of Mexico's President José López Portillo of the PRI.

This transformation began when, after the war and in financial straits over rising rent, the TGP offered to create campaign materials for Alemán's presidential campaign. [9] The TGP earned six hundred pesos a month from its involvement, a little more than half its rent.[10] The TGP's support of Alemán, who, according to Mexican poet and scholar Carmen Boullosa, "had no revolutionary instincts," caused its credibility to suffer (as did the return of would-be assassin Siqueiros to the group). Boullosa, a former fellow at New York Public Library and a Guggenheim recipient who now teaches at City University of New York (CUNY), says, "It was not only the TGP's support of Miguel Alemán and its affiliation with Siqueiros that cast a shadow over the TGP. If their goal was to be 'revolutionary,' their link to the PRI was a colossal ball and chain." [11]

Pablo's letter to Robinson indicates how, in the postwar spirit, he put a "revolutionary" twist on modernization: Pablo explained that Mexico's challenge was to modernize the country without the influence of the United States and other "imperialist monopolies." [12] Pablo also expresses hope for Alemán. He compares the industrialization of Mexico to Cárdenas's expropriation of Mexican oil—the last revolutionary act of a Mexican president in the previous sense of the revolution.

> [T]he elections came through in a very well organized way, for Mexico, and Alemán, so far, is appearing to be a progressive president. It will be interesting to see if he will carry through the basic program, of Mexico industrializing its own country for its own people—combating the Imperialist monopolies. It would be a second step ahead—after the expropriation of the . . . oil companies and would keep on with the road ahead that Cárdenas started—confronting our own new elections—with the reactionary Republicans grabbing important positions.[13]

Ironically, with the United States a source of imperialistic capital and a historical enemy of the Communist Party, Pablo and the TGP spent substantial time in the postwar years building connections with the United States. In this same letter to Robinson in which Pablo called the U.S. elections *our* own new elections, he also referred to himself as a Mexican. Clearly, Communism, with its emphasis on avoiding U.S. imperialism, and the Good Neighbor idea, with Rockefeller promoting U.S. culture in areas of Latin America where his family had oil interests, were contradictory. But the Tehran accords obscured these conflicts and gave people like Pablo false hope for what the future would hold.

The TGP was modernizing and changing as well. Its high-rent, larger space had areas for artists to work, for printing, exhibiting work, and sales.[14] In 1946 it had its most successful year to date financially, earning a profit of fourteen thousand pesos.[15] It had gained "international fame and influence" through its interactions prior to and during World War II. By 1949, half its members were "guest artists" from other countries.[16] It attracted attention in the United States, and as a result had many visitors: Elizabeth Catlett and husband Charles White had heard about the TGP in Chicago and had traveled to Mexico in 1946 to take part in it.[17] Los Angeles artist Seymour Kaplan described working for almost two years at the TGP after the war.

> We usually would go on an outing to the villages on the weekend and during the week would develop sketches. We would work on the stones. José Sánchez did the printing. And we had meetings with collective criticism. Artists would put their work down and had discussions on how to best express what they had in mind. Discussions were in English and Spanish (some people wanted to practice their English and others their Spanish). Everyone was accepting. You didn't have to agree with them. We spent time every day socializing and had special meetings in the evenings. During the day, when you worked on the stones, you had to be there. Students who worked for Rivera and Frida would come and join us. You had to leave a copy of any print you made in the file.[18]

Between 1945 and 1946, the TGP had exhibits in Seattle, Boston, San Francisco, and Chicago.[19] But this was not enough to keep the TGP afloat. With postwar inflation in Mexico at around 200 percent, the TGP remained in a precarious financial situation and made it a habit of turning to the government of Alemán for help. Miguel Alemán would not, however, be the "progressive president" Pablo had hoped for. Alemán turned out to be disastrous for the left. To the chagrin of leftists, Alemán caused a shift in Mexico from an agricultural economy to an industrial one, resulting in an economic inequality of peasants that had not been seen since the age of Porfirio Díaz, and prompting writer Daniel Cosío Villegas to call the Alemán era the "Neoporfiriato" (referring to a new dictatorship, similar to that of Porfirio Díaz).[20] Enrique Krauze writes, "The official propaganda, which painted [Alemán's opponent Ezequiel Padilla] as an ally of the United States, had its effect." [21] Lombardo Toledano, Mexico's most powerful leftist labor leader, "repented a thousand times that he helped launch" Alemán on his way to the presidency. [22] The PCM called Alemán's administration a "government of national betrayal." [23]

In 1946, Méndez was expelled from the PCM. Pablo left the same year, likely out of solidarity with Méndez and other TGP members.[24] Leaving the party, for both of these inseparable men, was a major shakeup in their lives and in the TGP, which, for the rest of the time Méndez and Pablo were involved in it, would be divided "between moderate socialists and hard-line Communists." [25] Noah Bardach says, "There were many divides in the TGP but this one was the one that cleaved the deepest." [26]

Both Pablo and Méndez had been members of the party for nearly twenty years. Both had paid for their party affiliation: for Pablo it was his family's rejection of him; for Méndez, it was his arrest and imprisonment after Trotsky's murder.

In early 1947, Méndez sat on a Mesa Redonda de los Marxistas Mexicanos (Round Table of Mexican Marxists) that Vicente Lombardo Toledano called to make plans for a new party.[27] The result was the Partido Popular (Popular Party), which in 1960 became the Partido Popular Socialista (People's Socialist Party).[28] Lombardo Toledano had a long history in Mexico City. He had served as rector of the National Preparatory School when he was a new law school graduate, and later taught at the law school of the National University. He founded the Workers University, the Latin American Confederation of Labor (CTAL), and the Confederation of Mexican Workers (CTM).[29]

The Partido Popular was made up of working professionals rather than the working class, which allowed it to have a better relationship with the more conservative government of the PRI.[30] (Its members are said to have looked down on the more working-class members of the PCM.) The Partido Popular sought to reunify the Mexican left, which had begun to fragment after Cárdenas left office. It attracted many students, teachers, intellectuals, and artists.[31] The Partido Popular was not able to take the CTM under its umbrella, however, as the CTM, though founded by Lombardo Toledano, had become firmly lodged with the PRI.[32]

Méndez and Carrillo both influenced Pablo and most of the other members of the TGP to switch to the Partido Popular.[33] Says Bardach, "For many members of the T.G.P., most importantly Méndez, Lombardo was the guiding intellectual and ideological voice for the dark decades between 1940 and 1960." [34] By the end of 1947, Méndez, the de facto leader of the TGP, had made membership in the Partido Popular pretty much essential for TGP membership.[35] The handsome and charismatic Méndez personified the TGP. Its members were "starry eyed" over him.[36] But the sway he held over the group would also be a factor in its demise.

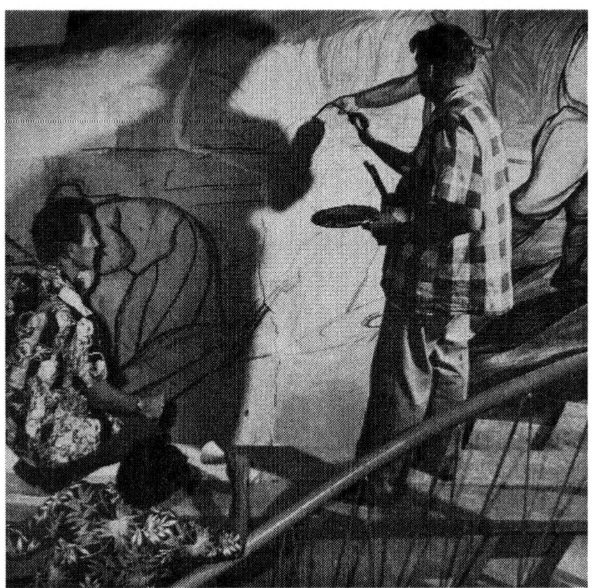

35

TGP SHAKEUP

Carmen Boullosa spoke to an audience at Yale about how, as a young poet in Mexico City in the 1970s, she wanted to stay as far from the TGP as possible. "They were dinosaurs! . . . To my generation, they were no different from the hideous PRI," she said.[1]

The TGP had been relying more and more on the Mexican government's help since moving into a bigger space in 1945. The CTM workers' union, which Boullosa calls "one of the most corrupt institutions to ever exist in Mexico," also sidled up to the government, adopting anti-Communist rhetoric, and becoming, in Enrique Krauze's words, "the spinal column of the PRI." [2] As a result, it lost the support of the left.

The TGP, however, did what it had to do to survive; the compromises it made in doing so would be its ultimate downfall. It began receiving commissions from the union, causing conflict with TGP members who were Communist Party members and who, now in the post-Tehran period, saw the government of Alemán as an enemy of the people.[3] Perhaps this is what Pablo referred to in a letter when he wrote, "I've been try [sic] to start and plan new work in the Taller—which, with the facing of new problems—needs a real shake up—and we are hoping to resolve some of them soon." [4]

Pablo and Méndez stayed close to the PRI during the late 1940s and 1950s in order to get work, and, in Pablo's case, this strategy appears to have helped him avoid harassment and potential deportation during the McCarthy era.

Alemán had expressed his support of the U.S. cold war efforts when President Truman visited Mexico in March 1947, the one-hundred-year anniversary of the U.S. invasion of Mexico at Veracruz.[5] Two months later, Alemán became the first president to visit the United States in more than one hundred years.[6] During his administration, the U.S. FBI helped Alemán set up Mexico's secret police, the Mexican Dirección Federal de Seguridad (DFS, or Federal Security Agency), and invited members of Mexico's petroleum industry to the United States to learn how to avoid Communist influences.[7]

The relationship between the Alemán administration and the U.S. government "took on the hues of a honeymoon," according to Krauze.[8] At the same time that Alemán was drawing closer to the United States, he was tossing bones to members of the PCM, promising them political patronage, according to Bardach.[9] "[T]he Alemán administration had the non-trivial task of juggling its Revolutionary credentials, simultaneously catering to the Left and industry, while being an active partner in Washington's war against Communism," he says.[10] The TGP, which once considered the government its enemy, was now beholden to it: two years after it assisted Alemán with his successful presidential bid, when it had financial troubles, the group "accepted . . . a 4,500 peso contribution from President Alemán himself, in recognition of the Taller's support for his campaign." [11]

Perhaps in an attempt to redirect itself and the public to the principles of the Mexican Revolution, in 1947 the TGP produced a portfolio of iconic images of the revolution, *Estampas de la Revolución Mexicana* (*Prints of the Mexican Revolution*), a collection of eighty-five graphics by sixteen TGP artists. The work glorifies the country's revolutionary heroes, from Madero to Cárdenas, and seeks to identify any shortcomings of the revolution as the fault of Nazis, Sinarquistas, and other fascist enemies of the revolution.[12] Pablo's contribution was a linocut addressing the struggles of miners: *La huelga de Cananea: Los obreros mexicanos reclaman igualidad de derechos frente a los obreros yanquis* (*The Strike of Cananea: Mexican Workers Claim Rights Equal to Those of the American Workers*). The images in this portfolio, says Bardach, "have come to characterize the historical events [of the revolution] for a generation of Mexicans." [13]

But the revolution was no longer compelling for younger artists, as noted by Boullosa. Seymour Kaplan, who worked at the TGP for two years in the late 1940s, said the political climate in Mexico City was changing. "Younger artists were coming in, like Tamayo. They felt that color and abstraction was selling now. The war was over and politics had changed." [14]

Another graphic workshop was formed in 1947—the Sociedad Mexicana de Grabadores (Society of Mexican Engravers), founded as an "intellectual" counter group to the TGP.[15] Unlike the TGP, which the new group felt was stultified, these artists worked independently and were committed to experimentation and modern printmaking methods. This group was considered more artistic and less doctrinal than the TGP.[16] They produced fewer prints per run than the TGP and sold them for more money; the TGP made hundreds of copies and sold them very cheaply.[17]

The same year that abstractionist José Luis Cuevas was making his first print, Pablo created one of his most powerful posters, a large piece for the PRI-pleasing CTM carrying the words, "Only a worker's movement conscientious, united, and honest can successfully defend the interests of the workers and help the betterment of Mexico." [18]

Many of the artists of Pablo's circle had received Guggenheim Fellowships to finance their studies and work in Mexico and beyond: Anita Brenner, Hart Crane, Katherine Anne Porter, Leopoldo Méndez, Ione Robinson, and Jean Charlot. Charlot's return to Mexico in 1945 was financed by a Guggenheim, and it was likely at his urging that Pablo, in 1947, applied for one. In a letter to Charlot dated November 3, 1947, he tells Charlot of his work on a portfolio and the TGP's work on *Calaveras aftosas con medias naylon* (*Skeletons with Hoof and Mouth Disease in Nylons*). He reported that "regarding my own work, I'm dissatisfied—I've painted little here in the studio and I haven't been able to organize the necessary rhythm of work. The little work I've done, I'm not happy with." [19]

He hoped to accomplish something in November, after which he would visit his mother in Los Angeles. Pablo told Jean that he had sent in the Guggenheim application, presenting the plan that Jean recommended. He expected to hear back in February. Pablo included as sponsors Charlot, Covarrubias, Rivera, and Norman Pearson. Pablo said he hoped being a sponsor wouldn't interrupt Charlot's work, which was more important. Pablo mentioned he didn't send photos of his work along with the application because they weren't requested, but asked Charlot if he thought he should.[20]

Pablo was having equally bad luck getting inspired in his easel painting. "In easel painting I haven't been able to begin any new work that excites me," he wrote. [21]

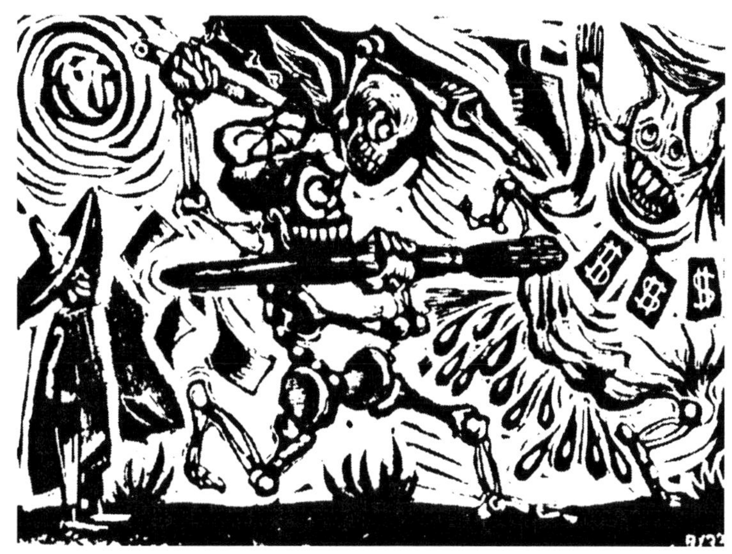

36

THE TGP IN CALIFORNIA

The arrival of printmaker Jules Heller at the Taller de Gráfica Popular in the spring of 1947 helped Pablo and the TGP strengthen their relations with artists in the United States, especially in Los Angeles. Heller, a printmaker who later taught at the University of Southern California, arrived at the TGP with a "letter of presentation" from muralist Edward Biberman, who had known Rivera in Los Angeles.[1] Heller joined the TGP and lived with Méndez during his months in Mexico.[2] He became a great fan of Méndez's work. In 1999, he co-curated and wrote an exhibition catalog for *Codex Méndez*, an exhibit of Méndez's work in Phoenix, Arizona.

Pablo wrote to Robinson about Heller with enthusiasm, not so much for his art as for his interest in setting up a graphic art workshop in Los Angeles. "He's done some fine work with us—and I think of importance for he's returning to Los Angeles with the plan of organizing a group for the possibility of a Taller, like ours down here—in Los Angeles. If that can be realized, it would be an important contact between the Mexican artists." Pablo told Robinson that he wanted the two of them to meet.[3]

That same year, 1947, Heller, his wife, Gloria, along with Arnold Mesches, and Pablo, who was in Los Angeles at the time and a houseguest of the Hellers, founded the Graphic Arts Workshop in Los Angeles. The Bryant Foundation in Los Angeles financed an English-language filmstrip (high technology at the time) called "Mexico City's Famous Taller de Gráfica Popular," showing one hundred works of the TGP. The strip sold for four dollars.

The medium had been popularized in the United States, says Prignitz, as a way for unions and workers' parties to provide appealing visuals for their gatherings.[4] This effort began a new phase of popularity for the TGP's work in the United States.[5]

The Los Angeles Workshop held an exhibit of its members' works on September 17 to 19, 1948. It was sponsored by the Los Angeles Council of the Congress of Industrial Organizations (CIO), which had been involved in the Sleepy Lagoon Defense, and featured the works of "16 Mexican artists" as well as Mexican food, entertainment, folk dances, and refreshments. It was held at the CIO building at 5851 Avalon Boulevard.[6] The workshop also supported the U.S. presidential campaign of Henry Wallace, the candidate of the U.S. Progressive Party, the new third party in the United States similar to the Popular Party in Mexico.[7]

The fifteen members of the workshop met once a week, just as the TGP did, on Hollywood Boulevard to discuss their work.[8] Mesches recounted that "Since Pablo's visit marvelous things have happened." The group had reached out to the United Auto Workers of the CIO to discuss how best to use graphics in a strike. They had plans to make signs weekly as well as to produce audiovisuals to raise the morale of the strikers and inform the public.[9]

Yet artists were becoming reluctant to produce political art, reflecting the growing tensions in Los Angeles at the time. Los Angeles County began firing employees who refused to sign loyalty oaths, relying on a list of 145 organizations in the area that were "suspect," including the Motion Picture Cooperative Buyers Guild and the Anti-ROTC (Reserve Officers' Training Corps) Committee.[10] That fall, the House Un-American Activities Committee began subpoenaing film industry people to testify about their Communist activities and to name people who had attended Communist meetings as far back as the early 1930s. The HUAC, says historian Rebecca Schreiber, was "infatuated with entertainers and artists." [11] Former Communists, Communist sympathizers, and people who were simply against loyalty oaths eventually changed their art as well as their lives, refraining from creating political works and opting for landscapes and flowers.

Pablo, however, was eager to jump into the fray: "I know that it's certainly a changed world in the States than when I left," he wrote to Robinson in September, 1947, "but I want to go up and get into it all—and confront the possibilities of a useful answer." [12] He said he was going to have Heller bring Robinson "a small and unknown work of Silvestre Revueltas—written as a homage to his friend, [Federico] García Lorca—There you'll really see the character of the work of the best Mexico composer!"

Pablo's letters to Robinson belie the characterization of Pablo as someone who did not promote his own work. He clearly is "wheeling and dealing" to make connections, connect others, and obtain commissions through his many friends in the labor movements of the United States and Mexico.

Having lived in Russia, Mexico, and the United States, Pablo had great credibility during the Popular Front period. With his de facto dual citizenship and bilingualism, he moved easily between the United States and Mexico. He became friends with powerful people in the labor unions of the United States and Latin America, such as Toledano and Louis Goldblatt, secretary-treasurer of the ILWU, the second "best-known labor figure on the West Coast," after Harry Bridges. When a Soviet delegation came to Mexico in 1943, "Pablo knew all those guys," says George Gutekunst, at the time a member of the Marine Cooks and Stewards Union, who also attended.[13]

Pablo truly was in his element. Having U.S. citizenship and having avoided problems with the Mexican government, Pablo could come and go in and out of the United States as he pleased, acting as an art ambassador between the two countries and using his connections, his political beliefs, his generosity, and his likable personality to bring people together. Pablo's travel perhaps reflects an idealism that the arbitrariness of borders might someday disappear. He was multicultural, multilingual, a citizen of the world—an advanced idea at the time.

Pablo was no longer the quiet young man who sat alone at parties observing. He was at the forefront of the artistic sector of the labor movement of two countries, a leader, a mentor, even if quiet and unassuming. He may not have had money (though his two thousand dollars from the 1945 mural would have gone a long way in Mexico), but he had prestige and, with his ability to move between these cultures, advantages. With the Tehran promise of peaceful coexistence between capitalism and Communism, Pablo must have seen his future as offering a reconciliation between his "Sons of the American Revolution" heritage and the Marxist revolution he believed in.

This period of promise, however, was short-lived; by 1946 it began eroding and by 1951 the remains of hope came crashing down. The battle of McCarthyism would be one that few U.S. artists would dare take on. The TGP spoke out only on what it considered the most outrageous act of the U.S. government—the 1953 death sentence of the Rosenbergs—with a poster illustrated by Angel Bracho, in 1953, titled *Help Stop This Crime.* But beyond that and an ill-fated print created by Méndez in 1953, the TGP, as well as Pablo, appears to have been mostly silent on the injustices of the McCarthy era.[14]

When Pablo returned to the United States after finishing the *Maternity* mural in late 1947, the spirit of cooperation that had characterized the Tehran period quickly ended. Artists, however, freed from war activities, were motivated to set up cooperatives modeled after the TGP, such as the one in Los Angeles. Their success would vary, but their associations with the Mexican TGP would follow them, in both positive and negative ways.

"Browderism," the term for the "lite" Communism that prevailed during the 1940s under the leadership of Earl Browder, ended in 1946 with his expulsion from the party. In 1946, the Tehran era ended with the so-called Duclos letter: In 1946 Jacques Duclos, head of the party in France, criticized Browder in a letter backed by the USSR, saying that his Tehran position was a capitulation to imperialism.[15] The U.S. party head, William Z. Foster, agreed with Duclos and a power struggle began in the CPUSA. Browder left the party.[16] Foster, soon to be the new head of the CPUSA, admitted that Browderism had weakened the guard of Latin American countries against U.S. imperialism.[17] The cold war began on March 5, 1946, when Churchill, at Fulton, Missouri, gave his famous speech on the "iron curtain" that had descended across Europe, from the Baltic Sea to the Adriatic Sea.

The suspicions of the U.S. government were confirmed. It had been uncomfortable with its allegiance with Stalin. In 1941, the Germans discovered the bodies of twenty thousand Polish military officers Stalin had massacred after his invasion of Poland in 1939. Though Stalin blamed the killings on the Germans, the age of the corpses made it clear that Stalin was responsible. Roosevelt and Churchill had looked the other way while "Uncle Joe" was their ally and taking the brunt of the war. (Nearly twenty million Soviet troops and civilians died in World War II, compared with eight hundred thousand U.S. and British troops and civilians.)

At war's end, the backlash against Communists, ex-Communists, friends of Communists, family members, and "fellow travelers" (meaning sympathizers)—even those who had left Communism in horror after the Non-Aggression Pact—hit hard, and many, like Earl Robinson, and Paul Robeson would pay for decades.[18]

McCarthyism hit the unions hardest. According to T. Michael Holmes, author of *The Specter of Communism in Hawai'i*, where the ILWU was the strongest union:

> No sector of the population was more subject to virulent antiCommunism in the United States during the years immediately after WWII than organized labor. And no labor leader was hounded with such determination as was Harry Bridges, the Australian born president of the [ILWU].[19]

Indications of whether one was or had been a Communist could include the people one associated with, the meetings one attended, and the books one read. David Jenkins described how he could tell that Harry Bridges was a Communist: he picked his nose (evidence of his non-bourgeoisness), and he advocated that people read the *Daily Worker*. The U.S. government looked at whether a person had supported the war during the Non-Aggression Pact and whether, when the United States entered the war, the person supported mainly the United States or the USSR.[20] They also looked at the books people had on their shelves and what bookstores they patronized. In New York, people began turning the jackets of their books inside out.[21] One person simply dumped all of her books into a canal.[22]

On his 1947 trip to the United States, Pablo first visited his mother in Los Angeles. The city had been hit hard by racial tensions, including the Zoot Suit aftermath, and the Hollywood blacklist. Emil Freed was driving his station wagon around Los Angeles collecting incriminating books from people on the left. He later would use these to build the Southern California Library for Social Research.[23] Martha Dodd and Alfred Stern were under constant surveillance.[24] Paul Robeson, Earl Robinson's friend and the singer of his songs, was finding his concerts canceled. Anybody "contemplating the rental of a facility to Robeson was immediately visited by the FBI, and their livelihood was threatened." His passport was revoked two years later on the basis that "it was not in the best interest of the United States to have Robeson travel abroad" because "he has been for years extremely active politically [on] behalf of the independence of the colonial peoples of Africa." [25]

While in Los Angeles during December and January, Pablo learned about color lithography from printer Lynton R. Kistler, a friend of Charlot, who had printed Charlot's book, *Picture Book*, in 1933.[26] At the end of December, Pablo wrote to Charlot that he was still waiting to hear about the Guggenheim. He remarked that his work with Kistler had inspired him.[27]

Pablo was disheartened about the Guggenheim and doubted his decision not to send photos of his work because the application said not to send anything unless asked. He asked Charlot whether he should send them nonetheless. "*Favor avísame, antes de que pase mucho tiempo!* [Please advise me before much longer!]," he wrote.[28]

In San Francisco, Pablo reunited with Byron Randall, who had worked in the TGP in 1940 and had formed the Artists' Guild in San Francisco.[29] Pablo and Randall worked with Victor Arnautoff and Adelyne Cross Erikson of the California Labor School to set up a center for graphic production modeled after the TGP. Randall created a humorous calavera linocut for the opening, showing an artist calavera attacking a grimacing balloonlike figure with dollar signs on the front of it (see page 169). Its weapons are a paintbrush used as a battering ram, a pencil, and a pen. In the corner is a dark-skinned Mexican peasant with a satisfied grin. The image appeared on a poster promoting the "First West Coast

Showing of Graphic Work by Members of the Taller de Gráfica Popular of Mexico City, on January 20 from 8 p.m. to midnight at 173 Jackson Street." Pablo gave the opening talk for the exhibition.[30] The exhibit included the work of Pablo, Catlett, White, Méndez, Zalce, Bustos, and others.[31]

Prignitz says the San Francisco workshop did not have the same success as the Los Angeles workshop and Randall's image may have been the only one produced.[32]

A New York workshop had more success, according to Prignitz. Founded in 1948, its members included Stan Kaplan (Seymour Kaplan's brother), Jay Landay, Charles Heller, and Charles White.[33]

Prignitz suggests that the lack of success and longevity of the U.S. workshops had to do with Americans' focus on individualism over collective work. She quotes TGP member Mariana Yampolsky's experience with a presumably American young man who rejected the group's criticism, insisting that his work was his own manner of self-expression. Never, she said, had that occurred in Mexico's TGP.[34]

According to Seymour Kaplan, a TGP alumnus who was involved in the Los Angeles workshop, the workshop was short-lived because "we got a few artists together but they couldn't buy the idea of working for free. The artists were also interested in the salability of their work. They felt that the TGP approach was outdated. People didn't want to get involved in political art." [35] Once McCarthyism set in, the U.S. government began promoting abstraction as a preferred alternative to political art.[36] In addition, said Kaplan, "the galleries didn't like black and white." [37]

In April of 1948 Pablo received news that he had been turned down for the Guggenheim. He wrote to Charlot, "As I anticipated, I didn't receive the Guggenheim, and Jean, I appreciate greatly your help—I'm sorry to have bothered my friends—wasting their time on a useless thing—and I'm not going to do it again." [38]

Pablo said he met "Sra. Chouinard," Nelbert Murphy Chouinard, who suggested he teach classes at her art school, which she had established in 1921 as the Chouinard School of Art in the Westlake area near downtown L.A.[39] He said this would work well, as it would allow him to see and stay with his mother.[40] He asked Charlot, who taught there in the summer of 1947, to put in a good word as Pablo was unable to show her any of his paintings.[41]

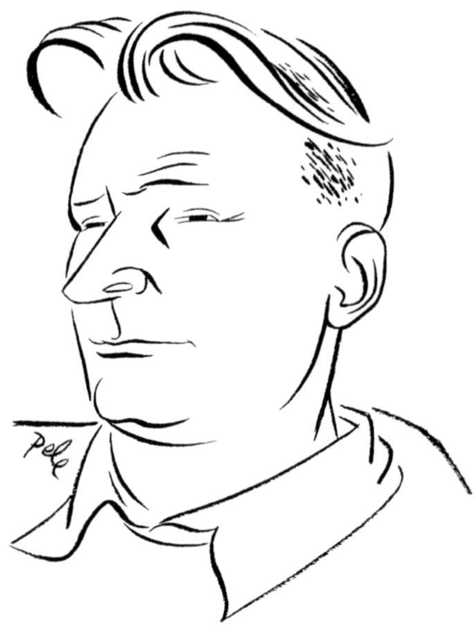

Pablo O'Higgins

37

CALIFORNIA LABOR SCHOOL

Carol Cuenod, a student at the California Labor School in 1949, recalls Pele deLappe lugging her heavy lithography stone around the school on her way to one of Pablo's classes, saying, "Everyone who is anyone is carrying a litho stone." [1] Pablo taught lithography at the California Labor School in 1949—one course in January and another at the end of the year. Although they were short, two-week intensive courses, they had an impact. John Skovgaad, in his thesis on the California Labor School, wrote:

> Pablo O'Higgins returned to the school in 1949, teaching drawing and lithography during the winter term. The contribution to the school's art program of such nationally known artists cemented its connection with the rest of the country's art scene, while at the same time creating a regionally significant style, wedded to the Bay Area's leftist community.[2]

Pablo's course, costing twenty dollars, consisted of ten afternoon sessions on lithography technique and six evening sessions on "composition for the graphic media." Pablo asked that the class be limited to "twelve advanced students or practicing artists who wish to learn lithography." [3] The head of the art department described Pablo's January 1949 class.

> As you may know, PABLO O'HIGGINS, the distinguished American-Mexican muralist and graphic artist, will be a guest of the Labor School for the two weeks from January 31 thru February 12. Mr. O'Higgins is coming here from Mexico City where he has recently completed a series of murals on commission

from the Mexican government. He is also well known to American artists as one of the founding members of the Taller de Gráfica Popular and as a leading practitioner in the fields of lithography and linoleum cuts.[4]

Two days after the course ended, deLappe's interview and sketch of Pablo appeared in the *People's Daily World.* DeLappe described him as a "quiet, sandy-colored man in his mid-forties," and an "esteemed member of the great team of 18 Mexican artists known at [sic] Taller de Gráfica Popular, or People's Graphic Workshop." She wrote:

> TGP has long been looked to wistfully by artists here who pine to do collective work for trade unions as part of the labor movement. Up till now, it's been a pretty haphazard business—certainly not the sort of dependable employment you can feed the wife and kids on. Well, the artists who constitute TGP, while not wallowing in wealth, are sufficiently employed to live reasonably well and keep on painting. More important, they are a vital and recognized force in the whole working class movement." [5]

DeLappe reported that Pablo was born in Salt Lake City, and had first come into contact with the paintings of Rivera and Orozco while he was studying at the San Diego Academy of Art, adding that Pablo had commented, "what I had been doing was very academic, no?" He told her he did not return to the United States until 1931, when he had the show in New York (this was not true, as he returned in 1926). Pele deLappe wrote that Pablo returned to the United States in "1944 . . . to spend a year working in the San Francisco shipyards." When I interviewed her, together with Byron Randall in Tomales Bay, California, in 1992, however, neither of them had any knowledge of Pablo working in a shipyard—other than Pablo telling Pele deLappe that he had.[6]

This appears to be the first time that Pablo's working in the shipyards is referenced—in the context of an interview with a Communist newspaper. Ten years earlier, in another interview with a Communist newspaper, he said he worked as a longshoreman in San Diego—although there is no evidence of this.

DeLappe concluded that Pablo, "no question about it, IS a Mexican artist, with none of the derivative quality frequently seen in the work of expatriates. But like his fellow artists in the TGP, his work also has a universality which transcends national traits." She suggested that Pablo's presence in the United States might "spur an integrated vigorous collective art, a Taller de Gráfica Popular, California style, in San Francisco." (Randall had set up such a workshop two years earlier; deLappe and Randall were to spend the last years of their lives together.)

The situation in California for leftists worsened. California State Senator Jack Tenney, advocate of a loyalty oath for state employees, including all teachers, was at the peak of his power. By June, University of California professors and employees were required to swear they were not Communists.[7] Pele deLappe wrote in her biography:

> [T]he secluded Berkeley hills were no escape from the ugliness that pervaded our lives. Bert was harassed for his work as a left-wing lawyer; we were looked on in the neighborhood as dangerous reds. My seven-year-old Nina was hit with a hammer for being a 'Commie,' by a boy from a supposedly liberal family down the block.[8]

When they moved to Oakland, word spread that they were a "Commie family with Negro friends!" [9] The FBI rented the front room of the house across the street to take down the license plates of her visitors, and report on her son's Boy Scout activities.[10]

The California Labor School, too, was suffering. While it had reached peak enrollment in 1945, received the honor of GI Bill enrollment, and had hosted the United Nation's Soviet delegation, its decline was equally precipitous, brought on in part by the war's end. With the need for war materials gone, thousands of industries closed their doors, and unemployment rose.[11] Another factor was the party's new post-Browder hard line: the party dropped courses on psychology and would not allow psychiatrists or anyone in therapy to join.[12]

The FBI had its eye on the school. In fall 1946, Jenkins and art department head Holland Roberts were subpoenaed by California's Un-American Affairs Committee.[13] Veterans tried to revoke the school's GI Bill funding. Some of its art teachers left the country—Arnautoff and Refregier moved back to the Soviet Union, and Robert Stackpole returned to France.[14] Jenkins said, "The progressive and Left unions were expelled from the CIO, the veterans' program at the school started to be attacked; the Tenney Committee was starting to subpoena me and others, Bridges was starting to get re-indicted." [15] Jenkins left the school to head the Bridges-Robertson-Schmidt Defense Committee, to defeat efforts by the U.S. government to deport ILWU head Harry Bridges.[16]

Perhaps flirting with danger, or feeling that harassment was inevitable, members of the California Labor School faculty provided illustrations for a publication of the *Communist Manifesto*.[17]

Pablo's last involvement with the Labor School was another two-week lithography class he taught in late 1949. Although the school closed, its influence, especially in its connection with the TGP, remains: the San Francisco Graphic Arts Workshop continues to produce prints in a studio on Third Street and 23rd.

Pablo's friends from the California Labor School were with him in Mexico City later that year for a peace conference that would land a number of them on the State Department's report of subversive organizations.

The left's focus, worldwide, after World War II, was on peace in a new and unfamiliar atomic age. But the United States didn't buy it. It considered the postwar "'peace' offensive," "[t]he most dangerous hoax ever devised by the international Communist conspiracy . . . ." [18] Pablo's involvement in a peace conference would place the TGP on a blacklist lasting, for some TGP members, as long as twenty years.

In August 1949, U.S. Ambassador to Mexico Walter Thurston "summoned the publishers of the top five daily newspapers in Mexico City—*Excelsior*, *El Universal*, *Novedades*, *El Nacional* (the government newspaper), and *La Prensa*—to denounce what he called "a scandalous Communist 'peace campaign' being carried out in Mexico and other countries." [19]

The FBI "opened files on many American citizens, including most of the art school teachers it viewed as Communists or Communist sympathizers." [20] The San Miguel de Allende school of Stirling Dickinson, where Pablo had taught and Siqueiros had painted a mural, was deemed Communist. Signs began appearing on the doors of nearby homes reading, "Catholic yes, Communist, no." [21]

The TGP's reputation as a Communist front group was cemented, in the eyes of the United States, through an event in the fall of 1949. In early September, Pablo welcomed to Mexico City four women he knew from the California Labor School: Carol Cuenod and three female friends, including her fellow Labor School classmates Lilli Ann Killen Rosenberg and Ruth Rodríguez. The women came to Mexico City to attend the American Continental Congress for Peace. Pablo had a role in the conference, Cuenod recalls.[22]

Rivera spoke, she said, and in attendance were Lombardo Toledano, Chilean poet Pablo Neruda, and former Mexican president Lázaro Cárdenas. Siqueiros was in jail at the time.

Pablo took the students to a European-style restaurant he liked and immediately after the conference ended he spent a day taking them to see murals, mostly Orozco's. Orozco had died during the conference and even waitresses were crying, Cuenod recalled. The women stayed in a tiny hotel in an alley. They saw a major retrospective of Rivera's work.

The U.S. government was very interested in the conference and took careful note of the proceedings, especially the role of Pablo, whom they called the "Chief Organizer" of the conference. The U.S. State Department reported that it was in Pablo's studio, nine years earlier, that "the artist Alfaro Siqueiros disguised himself to prepare the first attempt to assassinate Leon Trotsky." [23]

The government reported on the TGP, including its efforts to establish workshops in Los Angeles, Chicago, New York, and San Francisco. It mentioned Carol Cuenod's friend, Lilli Anne Killen Rosenberg, and listed Hollywood writer Albert Maltz and Pablo's friend and patron Martha Dodd as supporters of the peace congress.[24]

The U.S. government observed that Lombardo Toledano charged the United States "with seeking to make an 'economic colony' of all Latin-American countries." It noted that when one speaker offered "mild criticism of the Soviet Union," the next speaker denounced such talk as "outrageous slander of the Soviet Union," which "was received with an ovation."

One month later, the United States denied Lombardo Toledano a visa to enter the United States to attend an October National Labor Conference for Peace in Chicago that featured singer Paul Robeson. According to the State Department, "Toledano was prevented from attending . . . when he was denied a visa by the State Department because of his pro-Communist record." [25]

The United States could prevent Mexicans, like Lombardo Toledano, from entering, but at the time, it could not prevent U.S. citizens from coming in. Pablo was able to return to the United States in late 1949 to visit his mother in Los Angeles and to teach his last two-week course at the California Labor School.

In Los Angeles, U.S. artists who had been guest artists at the TGP were being followed by the FBI, whose Red-stalking efforts were buoyed by the conviction of eleven leaders of the CPUSA for violating the Smith Act, which made it a crime to conspire to overthrow the U.S. government.[26] Seymour Kaplan, the Los Angeles artist who worked at the TGP in 1948 and 1949, found he was tailed by FBI agents when he returned home to Los Angeles. They would call his house and, using one of their intimidation tactics, ask to speak to his wife. "[Because of] the fact that I had spent time in Mexico and at the Taller, my record was tainted," he said.[27] Bay Area artist Frank Rowe, too, was suspected because of the time he spent working with the TGP in 1946. His daughter said, "He quickly learned not to discuss publicly his association with the TGP." [28]

During Pablo's visit to Los Angeles, he taught a two-week course in lithography and exhibited his work at the Freymart Gallery on La Brea Avenue.[29] The exhibition was arranged by Yvonne Templin, whose husband, Ernest, was a Spanish professor at UCLA. Templin became a friend of Pablo and assisted him in selling his art in Los Angeles.[30]

When Pablo returned to Mexico, he received the honor of being asked to teach art at La Esmeralda, where faculty had included Rivera, Kahlo, Orozco, and Francisco Zúñiga.[31] Although he had previously rejected the formal study of art and had had an unsuccessful teaching experience in 1933, Pablo accepted the position.

A student of Pablo's at La Esmeralda, Daniel Gómez, recalls him as a demanding, forceful teacher. He insisted on honesty and integrity in painting. He implored his students to paint Mexico and its people exactly as they were—not to sentimentalize, glorify, or soften the harshness of the Mexican landscape or of life. Pablo's influence on his students' work was seen in their paintings of workers engaged in common activities, according to Gómez.[32] Pablo considered his students' failures his own. If a student did not seem to be incorporating his teachings, Pablo would threaten to leave the class, believing he was not being effective.[33] He taught his students the "golden section," the concept used in visual art and architecture in which a rectangle or line is divided into unequal parts with the smaller part bearing the same ratio to the larger part as the larger part bears to the whole.[34] Pablo felt the golden section was the "bones" that held a painting together.[35] He was normally a patient teacher, but he had no tolerance for tentativeness and indecision in his pupils. He told his students, "Paint like a man, not like a girl." [36]

As the United States became less friendly to the TGP in the late 1940s, Mexican galleries as well as those in Europe and Eastern Europe were becoming more important to the group. Rather than give a portion of their sales income to gallery owners, Pablo, along with other TGP members, including Elizabeth Catlett and Francisco Mora, founded the Salón de la Plástica Mexicana (Salon of Mexican Visual Art) in 1949. A nonprofit gallery funded by the government, it permitted independent artists to exhibit and sell their work without having to pay a gallery commission.[37] This strengthened their ties with the Alemán government, something that eventually brought them criticism. The majority of Pablo's exhibits in Mexico over the next decades would be in this gallery.

Artists of the TGP found themselves in write-ups in the cultural pages of art magazines and in "Sunday supplements," presaging their drift from being "revolutionary" artists to being cultural brokers.[38] This change, says Bardach, is reflected in one of the TGP's most important works, published in 1949: *El Taller de Gráfica Popular—Doce años de obra artística colectiva* (The People's Graphic Art Workshop—Twelve Years of Collective Artistic Works), a 196-page book with 450 illustrations and five original engravings by fifty artists.[39]

The introduction to the book states that the TGP's future is "identical with that of the Mexican nation and of the revolutionary forces within . . . ." [40] "Unfortunately," says Bardach, "for both political art and the Mexican Revolution, [this] insightful prediction was correct." The demise of the TGP was its complete alignment with the government and the government's co-opting of the revolution.[41]

After the war, the TGP became less political and acted more as a promoter of culture; in the mid-1950s it actually would change its mission statement to reflect this switch. Presaging it, in 1949, Pablo created two prints as homage to one of his favorite composers, Chopin.[42] The works were commissioned by Gita Sten, cultural envoy of the Polish embassy, in celebration of Chopin's birthday.[43]

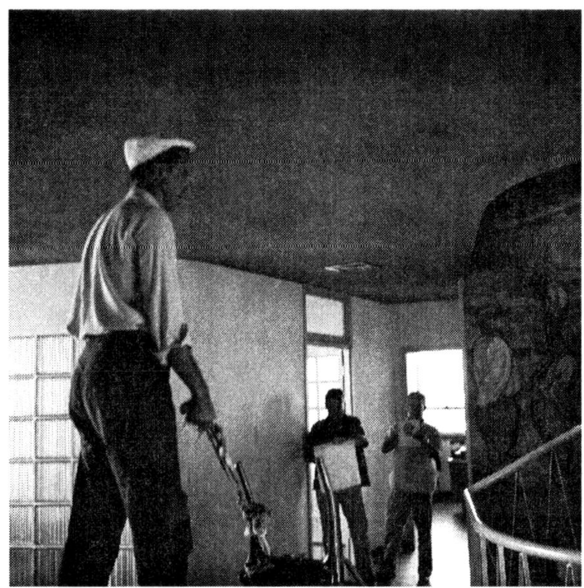

38

AN EXPATRIATE COLONY

In Mexico, the U.S. government's monitoring of foreigners turned into a formal anti-Communist campaign.[1] In January 1950, the U.S. National Security Council created the "NCS 68," a "top secret report on national security policy" that expanded the cold war to include not just the USSR and its satellites but Third World countries that might be influenced by the Soviet Union.[2]

U.S. expatriates began arriving in Mexico. The first large wave came in 1950, after the U.S. Supreme Court upheld the Hollywood Ten's convictions for contempt of Congress, sending them to jail for refusing to give testimony to the House Un-American Activities Committee. This terrified many leftists in the United States, who decided they had more to risk from staying in the United States than fleeing to a new country whose language most did not speak and that likely offered little in terms of employment.

The TGP and La Esmeralda, according to Schreiber, nurtured the artists who fled cold war oppression in the United States.[3]

Pablo became a resource for the new arrivals. He met many of the expatriates, especially those from Los Angeles involved in the creative arts. Diana Anhalt, whose family fled the United States for Mexico in 1950, listed Pablo, as well as Rivera, Siqueiros, Covarrubias, and Francisco Zúñiga, as "Mexican intellectuals sympathetic to [the expatriates'] politics and cognizant of the events responsible for their leaving the U.S." Anhalt said these artists sought out the expatriates.[4]

U.S. citizens living in Mexico, including Pablo, had three ways of being in the country legally: they could get a tourist visa, which had to be renewed every six months in the

United States; a "capitalist investors" visa if they were setting up a business in Mexico; or an "*inmigrante*" visa, meaning they were seeking either a work permit, *inmigrado* status (like a green card, which they would get after five years of *inmigrante* status), or citizenship. Tourists and *inmigrantes* couldn't work, but capitalists and *inmigrados* could. Still, if noncitizens of Mexico engaged in political activities, they could be "33'd"—deported without any notice under Article 33 of the Mexican Constitution.[5]

Mexico, under Alemán, cooperated with the United States in its attempts to ferret out Communists. Mexico extradited to the United States citizens who had fled to Mexico, and it deported U.S. citizens whom the United States believed were involved in Communism.[6]

The knowledge that "the FBI, DFS, Gobernacíon, and the media could act with impunity," coupled with abductions and deportations, put the "fear of death" into the community of U.S. citizens living in Mexico.[7] During the Alemán years, the exile community understood that the government "would not countenance" any involvement with the PCM.[8] For the foreign community, says Anhalt, participation "in an event supported by the PCM and other left-wing organizations received widespread press coverage in both Mexico and the United States." [9]

On August 12, 1950, seven art teachers at the Escuela de Bellas Artes in San Miguel de Allende and its head, U.S. citizen Stirling Dickinson, the Republican Princeton graduate who had registered for the draft after the bombing of Pearl Harbor, were arrested by Mexican authorities in the middle of the night and deported by train to Texas—likely because of a dispute between Dickinson and a former director of the school.[10] (Pablo had taught there in 1940 and had lived with Dickinson.)[11]

According to Dickinson biographer John Virtue, Dickinson and the teachers found themselves in the same hotel in Laredo, Texas, as Helen Sobell. Sobell and husband Morton were friends of alleged Soviet spies Jules and Ethel Rosenberg. Morton was in jail and Helen was being guarded in the hotel by federal agents.[12]

The conservative newspaper *Novedades*, on August 15, 1950, fully supported the deportation of the "San Miguel Eight," reporting correctly that the U.S. citizens were working illegally in Mexico on tourist visas.[13] The August 18 edition of *Excelsior* reported "*Entraron como turistas y violaron la ley* [They entered as tourists and broke the law]." The media's eagerness to jump on stories of alleged U.S. Communists in Mexico and to give their stamp of approval to the deportations was characteristic of the 1950s. Anhalt says that "During Alemán's term in office, the media regularly stirred up public opinion in an attempt to create a climate favorable to Cold War policy." [14] Some media reports seemed oddly timed with deportation proceedings: just twelve hours after the headline, "*Cuernavaca, convertido en nido de rojos prófugos de eeuu* [Cuernavaca becomes nest for Red refugees from the United States]," appeared in the October 8 edition of *Excelsior*, Gus Hall, former secretary-general of CPUSA, was deported back to the United States.[15]

The Sobells were extradited to New York, where Morton Sobell would be convicted of espionage and sentenced to thirty years in prison (he would serve nineteen).[16] Dickinson used his extensive connections to get his group released back to Mexico.

The same day that *Excelsior* reported on the San Miguel de Allende deportations, the magazine *Tiempo* (whose founder was allied with the government) published a review of Pablo's individual exhibition at the TGP-founded and government-funded Salón de la Plástica Mexicana. *Tiempo* called it "*Una exposición muy Mexicana* [A very Mexican exhibit]." [17] It mentioned the depth of Pablo's understanding of the Mexican people and the absence of "false folklorism" in his work. Two political pieces were mentioned, the portable mural *Veracruz* and *Los Lobos*, both expressing political themes of the Mexican people coming together to defend their country, but Pablo's political activities and affiliations were not mentioned. The *Veracruz* mural condemned the 1914 U.S. invasion of Mexico, but the article did not specifically describe that. The piece gave biographical details, among them that Pablo was born in San Francisco, California, but says nothing of his study in Moscow or his former Communist Party membership, even though involvement with the party was clearly the hottest newspaper topic of the day.

The article quoted Méndez explaining that Pablo had an extreme lack of interest in money, that he would take bread from his own mouth to give to a hungry person, and would take off his shirt for another. Méndez spoke of Pablo's devotion to the common man, workers, and *campesinos* who engaged in the arduous daily struggle for the common good. Méndez mentioned that Pablo's work shows an inquietude, not because he is vacillating about anything but because his work is reaching to find the complete expression of his impressions of reality, alive and changing. Pablo, he says, has lived in Mexico, painting for the people of Mexico. Mexico, Méndez says, owes him a great debt.[18]

This type of article would be the dream of a public relations agency hired to keep Pablo out of trouble, if he had had one. It contrasts him with the new U.S. arrivals, who had little connection with Mexico and basically chose the country because they could enter without a passport, which would have been denied to suspected Communists. The newcomers sent their children to American schools and socialized primarily with Americans.[19] The media liked to depict them as lolling on verandas drinking margaritas. The *Tiempo* piece describes Pablo as humble and content to be poor, sacrificing for the Mexican people. It describes his art as innocuous and free from anything but the most prescribed "revolutionary" themes, such as the Mexicans standing together to protect their *patria* (homeland). Mexico, Méndez seems to suggest, could repay Pablo for his loyalty by passing him over in the deportation sweeps.

Pablo's exhibit also was reviewed in the August 27, 1950, issue of *Excelsior*, the same publication that two months later would describe Cuernavaca as a "nest of Reds." In *Excelsior*, Mauricio Devaux called Pablo "a Mexican artist," and a distinguished member of the national plastic movement, again mentioning nothing of his past Communist Party membership or his study in the Soviet Union. It concedes that he was born in North America but does not mention his U.S. citizenship.[20] The review lauded Pablo's work as showing a deep understanding of the most humble of the Mexican people, without aesthetic or intellectual "poses." It notes that the stamp of Pablo's art is his ability to delve into the spirit and psychology of the humble Mexican of the city or country. His art, the reviewer says, has the great purity of his own personality.

With Pablo and the TGP so close to the Alemán administration, having worked on his presidential campaign, and the Partido Popular a supporter of Alemán, it is likely that Pablo got "a pass" from the government-controlled press. A former U.S. embassy official, who worked in Mexico in the 1950s, said that positive articles in the Mexican press were gotten through payoffs.[21] Indeed, the government controlled the press by giving journalists, at the beginning of each month, a sealed envelope containing cash.[22]

Krauze says the true client of the press was the government and that no newspaper publisher at the time would criticize the government. "It could boldly attack Communism (which in fact was one of its favorite targets during the 1950s) but it never mentioned—or even hinted—at the paradox of its own situation, which was that in Mexico, freedom of the press was more theoretical than real" and its mandate under Alemán was "with the President, always." [23] With the president behind the TGP, Pablo was protected, for the time being, although his fellow TGP member, U.S. citizen Elizabeth Catlett, was not.

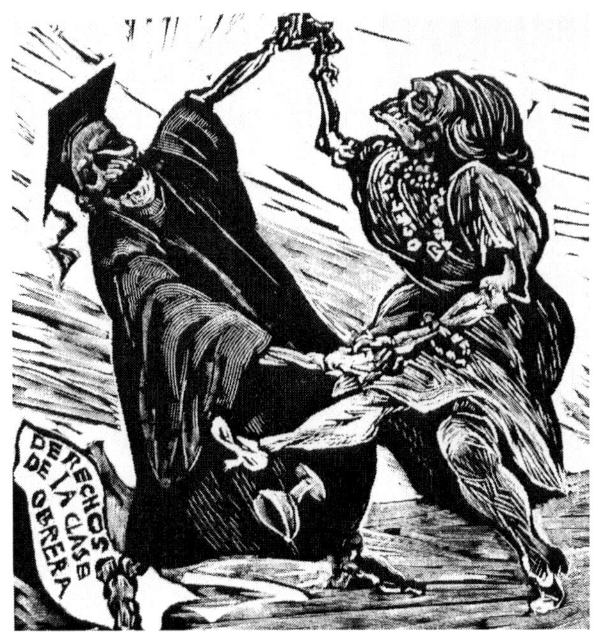

39

A "SUBVERSIVE ORGANIZATION"

On April Fool's Day, 1951, the U.S. State Department published the report of the 1949 peace conference and labeled the TGP a subversive "Communist Front" organization.[1] Based on 1977 conversations with Pablo, Ignacio Aguirre, and Francisco Mora, Prignitz says that after 1951, TGP members were prohibited from entering the United States.[2]

It does not appear, however, that Pablo or Elizabeth Catlett, another U.S. citizen member of the TGP, were "blacklisted" by the United States at this time. Both Catlett and Pablo were allowed to enter the United States. Pablo visited the San Francisco Bay Area in 1952 on his way to and from painting a mural in Hawai'i (which was then a territory), and Elizabeth Catlett returned to the United States in 1954 and in 1961, while she was still a U.S. citizen.[3] It should be noted that a person did not have to be on any specific list to be blacklisted. To be blacklisted could mean your file was flagged by the State Department or the attorney general's office.[4]

The United States had the power to punish U.S. citizens living in Mexico for their leftist activities by denying them passports, which beginning in June 1952 were required to enter and exit the United States.[5] Until 1958, the U.S. State Department could deny U.S. passports to U.S. citizens based on suspected Communist activities, and could deny U.S. citizens travel out of and into the United States unless they possessed a valid U.S. passport, thereby restricting the travel of U.S. expatriates in Mexico "largely to Mexico itself," where they were under "continuing surveillance" by the "Mexican Foreign Office and secret police." [6]

Catlett suffered more harassment than other TGP members in Mexico during the McCarthy era—perhaps because she was an African-American woman married to a Mexican man in an era rife with racism and intolerance for "miscegenation." [7] Catlett, however, told Bardach, "I never had an issue in Mexico because of race." [8] Schreiber says that in the "early 60s" (after Catlett had become a Mexican citizen) the "American Embassy in Mexico refused to grant [Catlett] a visa (because the staff believed that the Taller de Gráfica Popular was a 'front' for the Communist Party)." [9]

It is unclear if any TGP members who were Mexican citizens were actually prevented from entering the United States between 1951 and 1971 or were just fearful.[10] If Mexican members of the TGP were indeed barred from entering the United States but U.S. citizens were not, Pablo had a good incentive to keep his U.S. citizenship, which he claimed he kept in order to be able to visit his mother in Southern California.

By 1951, any surge of loyalty to the United States Pablo may have felt during World War II was quelled by the rise of McCarthyism. Daniel Gómez, a student of his in the 1950s, said Pablo criticized the United States to his students.[11] In 1951, the same year the TGP landed on the State Department's report, Pablo produced the lithograph of a skeleton judge dancing with a skeleton prostitute—whose title comments that justice is a farce of the gringos and the rich. The work was for the newspaper *A La Cargada, Calaveras*.[12] A year earlier, he painted the portable mural condemning the U.S. invasion of Veracruz, Mexico, in 1914, and confirming Mexico's resistance to U.S. interference.[13]

The door to Pablo's seeking Mexican citizenship opened in 1951. In June, Pablo lost his mother, a great source of love, encouragement, and support. Alice Higgins died at the age of eighty-four while visiting her niece, Marjorie Ireland (Will and Isabel's daughter), in San Jose, California. Alice enjoyed traveling and kept up with her relatives through frequent visits and long letters. Ten days into her visit, she became ill. Two weeks later she died of congestive heart failure in the Santa Clara County Hospital in San Jose, California.[14]

Pablo could now pursue his dream of becoming a Mexican citizen. But he didn't. Some have suggested that his application to become a Mexican citizen would have been denied by the Mexican government because of his membership in the Communist Party, but Pablo was close enough to the Alemán government that he very likely easily would have cleared the application process. Three years later, in 1954, his TGP colleague, U.S. citizen Mariana Yampolsky, was granted Mexican citizenship.[15]

It is more likely that Pablo kept his U.S. citizenship because he knew the value of it. Art dealer Daniel Lienau said, "a lot of what the TGP wanted to do was to make their views known to a greater population, so access to the U.S. would have been valuable." In addition, the art market in the United States was lucrative. "Siqueiros did prints on ends of fruit boxes in prison and brought them to Los Angeles to sell," Lienau said.[16]

Through his involvement with the ILWU Pablo knew of the struggle of the union's founder, Harry Bridges, to get and keep a U.S. passport in light of his alleged Communist activities. Bridges, born in Australia, fought deportation proceedings in 1939 and was officially absolved of Communist affiliation. A year later, the U.S. Congress passed a bill to deport him, but it was struck down by the Supreme Court and he was given citizenship in 1945. But five years later, in 1950, he was charged with falsely swearing that he had never been a member of the Communist Party and convicted to five years in prison.[17]

If Pablo were to give up his U.S. citizenship, as a former Mexican Communist Party member, he could be denied entry to the United States. Pablo was not ready to put aside the friendships and opportunities in the United States that he had nurtured during the war years. Mexico was treating him as a citizen, as was the United States.

With the TGP declared subversive in the United States, TGP artists who had previously enjoyed close connections with the United States and had had exhibits in galleries across the country now sought to establish connections with other countries. During the 1950s, Pablo's art was included in exhibitions in Great Britain, Japan, Czechoslovakia, Italy, China, and France. Photographs in Prignitz's book show crowds packed shoulder-to-shoulder to see an exhibit of TGP art in La Paz, Bolivia, in 1952.[18] Based on records from the Organization of American States, from 1924 to 1950, all eleven of Pablo's individual exhibitions were in the United States; from 1950 to 1983, all but two of his twenty-two individual exhibits were in Mexico.[19]

Still, some Mexican art was subject to censorship in the 1950s. Works that were too political would not be accepted during the cold war in exhibits in Western Europe and the United States because of a belief, since the time of the Mexican Revolution, that Mexico was "infiltrated with Communists." [20] A mural Rivera painted in 1952 for a Paris exhibition called *Nightmare of War, Dreams of Peace*, including depictions of Stalin and Mao Ze-dong, disappeared one night from Bellas Artes before it was to be shipped to Europe. It showed the leaders of France, the United States, and England as promoting war and those of the USSR and China as advocating peace.[21]

For conservatives in Mexico, these were good times. In September, *Time* magazine reported that Mexico's new middle class, who "make money fast and like to spend it," had "done a far better job than either the Reds or the Rockefellers in taming that old radical, Diego Rivera, by keeping him busy painting the portraits of their daughters." [22]

The "revolution" had been transformed by Alemán and his successor Adolfo Ruiz Cortines (in office December 1952 to November 1958) into a *lucha* (struggle) for roads and bridges, dams, and schools to accommodate the country's ever-growing and increasingly industrial population. And the revolutionary artists were transformed as well.

The art market in Mexico was thriving. The postrevolutionary generation of Mexican artists enjoyed, for the first time, a strong domestic market for their works. The emergence of a moneyed middle class led to private art galleries and created a buying public for the easel painter.[23] Former revolutionary artists who had condemned easel painting now had an opportunity to make a living from it. The left had been almost thoroughly tamed by Alemán. Krauze says that in six years, Alemán did what had taken Porfirio Díaz thirty years: he made intellectuals in Mexico indirectly dependent on the government, with the government "'gripp[ing their] guts.' . . . [S]upport from the state permitted them to continue doing what was most important to them—their personal creative work." [24]

Under Alemán, the "national icons" Rivera and Siqueiros "continued to rely on generous state patronage while they painted the walls of public and private buildings, hotels, theaters, the homes of artists and high society." [25] Alemán gave positions in government agencies to favored artists, even if they were Communist.

The Partido Popular was taking money from the government, says Krauze, and "became the loyal opposition on the left. . . . It would selectively oppose actions by the PRI that it considered retrograde or support actions that it considered progressive." [26]

The TGP, too, became the "loyal opposition." Scholar Carmen Boullosa says the TGP and the PRI "both claimed to be children of the same Mexican Revolution." [27] They criticized the government, but mildly. According to Bardach, they were easy on the government regarding its most heinous acts during the 1950s—the violence against and repression of striking workers. [28]

The decline of the strength of the left, including the TGP, can be seen in its responses to strikes. The strikes of the 1950s in Mexico should have been the fascism of the late 1930s and early 1940s for the TGP. In the first half of the twentieth century, the more democratic Mexico's government, the more strikes. Strikes were as few as seven a year during Calles's presidency and averaged around 428 per year during the presidency of Cárdenas.[29] In 1950, labor and the TGP put aside their growing external and, in the case of the TGP, internal differences, to protest the government's treatment of striking miners in Nueva Rosita and Cloete, in the northern border state of Coahuila. The government declared the strike illegal and imprisoned its leaders.[30] The miners marched twelve hundred kilometers to Mexico City. When the strikers arrived in Mexico City and camped out in the plazas of the city, the TGP created a visual diary, Diario de Campamento, documenting their struggle. Pablo, Méndez, and Catlett jointly produced four-color serigraph posters to raise awareness of the hunger and death that was occurring as a result of the strikers losing their jobs.[31]

Four years later, however, the disintegration of these alliances of the left and inside the TGP would silence the group during the strikes of the late 1950s. These changes, along with political disputes, personality clashes, and the decline of social realism in general, led to the demise of the TGP: by 1959, Méndez said their work was worthy of a garbage can, and at the end of the decade he left the TGP and Pablo followed shortly after.[32]

The left overall was severely compromised: the same year, the leftist CTM union honored Alemán as "Worker-in-Chief of the Fatherland." [33]

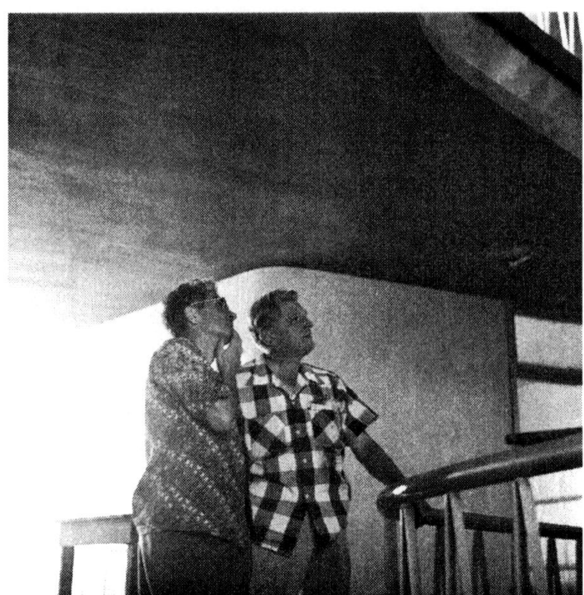

40

THE HAWAI'I MURALS

John Charlot remembers a strange visitor at his house in Honolulu, Hawai'i, during the 1950s when he was eleven years old, learning of the evils of Communism in Catholic school. This visitor was . . . a Communist. "But, Dad!" Don't worry, his father told him. He's a friend, a good person.[1]

Had Jean Charlot not vouched for him, it is not likely Pablo would have lasted long in Hawai'i. It was the spring of 1952. FBI agents were walking into college classrooms and escorting student leaders outside for questioning.[2] Jack Hall, president of the ILWU Local 142, had been arrested and indicted under the Smith Act the year before for associating with organizations the government considered subversive. For the next two years, until his conviction in 1953, and continuing until it was overturned by the U.S. Supreme Court in 1958, the ILWU would be anxious about this case and everything it stood for.

But the union also had a building project to tend to. Flush from the wartime boom, it had purchased land on Atkinson Drive, now prime real estate, but back then a semi-industrial area of Honolulu. As the building neared completion, Local 142 decided to commission a mural and solicited proposals from various artists, with the preference of having a local artist paint a mural about the significance of the union to the lives of the very diverse workforce in Hawai'i.[3] Pablo's relationship with Lou Goldblatt, developed during the postwar years, paid off. Pablo, along with Jean Charlot and another local artist, Wilson Y. Stamper, were contacted to see if they were interested in the project. At the beginning, the union's first choice was Charlot and second choice Pablo.[4]

Jean and Zohmah Charlot had moved to Hawai'i in 1949 and were raising their four children in Honolulu. Jean was teaching at the University of Hawai'i.

In mid-December, Pablo received a letter from Goldblatt suggesting the project. Goldblatt later said, "I got him to do the murals. Pablo had been a friend for a number of years. . . . I wrote to Pablo and convinced him he ought to go there." [5] On December 17, 1951, Pablo wrote to Charlot, "I've received a letter from Honolulu with the proposition of a mural job in the union hall of the ILWU," and asking Charlot to help him price it. Pablo's own estimate was five to six thousand dollars.[6]

The next day Pablo wrote to Goldblatt and mentioned the possibility of Méndez working on the mural with him. Pablo notes, however, that, "it may be difficult for Leopoldo to go and get there, not because of any personal problems, but to the present tensions in crossing the borders. You'll understand." [7] This indicates that Pablo believed that Méndez, a Mexican citizen, would not be permitted to enter the United States and supports the belief that Pablo kept his passport to enable himself to enter the United States to work or visit friends (now that he no longer needed his U.S. citizenship to visit his mother). In the same letter, he lets Goldblatt know that he is very flexible in terms of his price. Pablo mentions, regarding Jean Charlot, "as to the social theme, he's completely isolated . . . ."

In the meantime, Hawai'i ILWU boss Jack Hall, in a December 17 letter, with a copy to Goldblatt, wrote to Pablo saying there was no money for the project and it was to be put on hold. He mentions that Charlot was teaching at University of Hawai'i and painting a mural for a bank and had offered to do the project for six thousand dollars. Hall adds, "He of course, speaks highly of you as an artist, but not of your political views. We, of course, do not share his political views either." [8]

Hall had invited Charlot to talk about the potential project and the two of them—Hall and Charlot—did not hit it off. "They disliked each other the first time they met regarding the mural," John Charlot says. It was clear that if the mural was to have a political message, Pablo, not Charlot, was the right artist for it, says Steve Murin, who photographed Pablo painting the mural. Murin says that Charlot was not interested in painting the mural because the union did not want to allow him to control the project. For example, Charlot did not want to take up the entire ground-floor level with the union's constitution.[9]

Pablo wrote Goldblatt a letter on January 19, 1952, expressing his hopes that the project would go forward, and touting its value. "The mural could be of great help and importance for the ILWU if it's well done—based on present and future problems—which could be carefully planned and discussed." [10] Had Pablo actually worked as a longshoreman in San Diego before going to Mexico, now, clearly, would have been the time to mention it: when he was writing directly to Jack Hall's boss and trying to encourage him to go forward with the stalled project.[11] In the end, Goldblatt "bird-dogged the Hawai'i mural through," recalled George Gutekunst, a friend of the Goldblatts and of Pablo.[12]

By February, the union and Pablo had arrived at a figure of four thousand dollars for the mural, plus travel and living expenses and a plasterer. (Charlot's bid was still six thousand dollars).[13] Charlot may have set a high price because, not only did he not get along with Hall, but he also wanted Pablo to have the project, according to John Charlot.[14] Hall said that a local artist wanted the job, but he didn't have Pablo's "stature, recognition, or understanding," likely a reference to Pablo's political views.[15] Pablo was to arrive by early March.[16]

The union's newspaper called Pablo "an artist with great sensitivity and creative power, experienced in popular graphic art and with deep working class sympathies." [17]

Before Pablo arrived in Hawai'i, the *Honolulu Star-Bulletin* announced, "Left-Wing Artist Is Sought For ILWU Building's Mural." [18] It reported that Local 142 planned to use a local artist to paint the mural but, according to "unofficial reports," "the union's international officers in San Francisco stepped into the picture," saying, "Maybe you've got somebody in Hawai'i who can do a fresco, Jack, but we don't think he can get that good old ILWU fighting spirit into his work." Unlike the good press Pablo received in Mexico, with never a word of his involvement with the Communist Party, the *Honolulu Star-Bulletin* reported that "Paul Esteban O'Higgins" a "San Francisco born Irishman" "held a scholarship in Soviet Russia" and has been "listed as a member of the Legion of Revolutionary Artists of Mexico." The article indicated that Pablo had not yet been chosen to paint the mural and that the union was also considering Rockwell Kent, an "honorary member of the ILWU." In the end, however, Goldblatt prevailed and Pablo got the commission.[19]

Being "outed" in terms of his involvement with the party, Pablo could have been prevented from entering Hawai'i, according to Phil Meyer, a columnist for the *Honolulu Star-Bulletin*, who wrote a history of the mural in 1987. Although Pablo had beat out Charlot in getting the commission, Charlot supported Pablo, and that was invaluable. Meyer said, "Hawai'i's best known artist," Charlot, was asked to denounce Pablo, but he "refused to call him a Communist." Even though Charlot (who had "hoped to do the mural") could have prevented Pablo from entering the country, according to Meyer, instead he "told reporters 'he's very competent . . . a good choice.' " [20]

Charlot and Pablo had no hard feelings about Pablo getting the mural commission, Murin said. Pablo was the right artist for the job. The choice of Pablo, Murin said, was not about politics. He pointed out that Charlot later did a mural for the public workers' union that showed, like Pablo's mural, union members picketing.[21] But surely the union leadership would have seen Pablo's militant socialist views as more in line with their own politics; Charlot was a devout Catholic and had created art for the Catholic Church.[22]

Pablo arrived in Hawai'i by March.[23] He stayed in a dormitory on the top floor of the ILWU building and had dinner most nights with the family of the union's education director, artist David Thompson. A Marine Corps veteran of World War II who had lost a leg at Iwo Jima, Thompson was given a two-month leave to assist Pablo, including taking him to see the islands. Thompson's nickname became Diego, although it was Pablo who is credited with helping Thompson develop his many artistic talents.[24] Pablo also spent many evenings with the Murin family, and Charlot's diary shows at least five occasions over the six months Pablo was in Hawai'i that they got together as well.[25] Murin says, of Jean Charlot and Pablo, "They got along beautifully. They had a very fraternal relationship. They were like brothers." Charlot, he said, "was an intellectual, he could converse. Pablo was not an intellectual, he was a down to earth man, more proletarian."

Pablo spent the first three months of his stay traveling around the islands, learning Hawai'i's history and culture and talking to members of the union about their histories and their work. On June 25, Pablo and "Diego" got to work on the mural, assisted by a plasterer, Fred Tanimoto. They began working on the mural in a circular staircase, with Pablo ultimately painting about five feet a day of wet plaster.[26]

Both the union and Pablo insisted that the mural represent the experience of workers in Hawai'i, which centered around the racial problems of the islands' many ethnicities: Japanese, Chinese, Filipino, Portuguese. What resulted was a three-story fresco mural describing the principles of the union, depicting the racial discrimination and poverty of the workers before unionization, and showing the successes of the union.

The mural is lush in deep blues and greens, colors rarely seen in Pablo's Mexican murals of this time. Entering the staircase visitors experience the sensation of being deep under water, looking up and seeing sunlight flooding in three stories above. The ground-floor mural depicts sea level. Painted in deep azures and turquoise, it shows the dock workers of Hawai'i's islands and those of the mainland linked together. The many shades of blue seem almost impossible to land-locked visitors until they look out at the ocean from Sandy Beach and see Oahu's infinite range of blues. This ground level also includes images of the iron-rich orange soil of Hawai'i (the same color as pottery that Murin made when he was not doing photography), as well as calligraphy of the preamble to the union's constitution.

Entering the second level, one reaches the higher land of the sugar plantations, where Japanese and Filipino workers before unionization cut sugar cane. They look with fear and pain as burly bosses beat workers and a Japanese foreman admonishes them to keep working. At the second-floor landing, a defeated looking Portuguese-Hawai'ian family hands in their statement of living expenses, which will reduce their pay to nothing.

The top panel presents workers post-unionization, stepping on the local newspapers that celebrate the victories of union busters and Red-baiters, carrying banners with union slogans (An Injury to One Is an Injury to All), joined in unity and walking toward the light, which, on a typically perfect Honolulu day, streams in a window at the top of the staircase. Pablo recreated several images from the mural in lithographs, a habit he learned from Rivera.[27]

Today the mural is the focal point of a newly remodeled building that has been restored to its 1952 design.

The mural presented an unusual technical and artistic challenge. Mitsue Thompson, wife of David Thompson, recalls that Pablo "had a fit" when he saw that the wall was circular.[28] He had to allow for the distortion caused by the curve and the fact that the mural would be seen from both ground level and above. A study for the mural shows complex perspective lines that Pablo used to plan the mural, which not only sweeps up three flights of stairs, but curves around the circular staircase.

Pablo may have underestimated the intensity and complexity of the blues and greens in the Hawai'i landscape. Near the end of the job, on September 15, he sent an RCA Radiogram to Flax, an art supply store in San Francisco, to rush order four additional jars of "cerulian [sic]" (cerulean, a deep blue), four of cobalt (a deeper blue), and two of "veridian [sic]" (viridian, dark green). (His bookkeeping was not precise; after returning to Mexico, the union got a bill for these materials and asked him to settle up personally with Flax for the $13.20, the cost of the four jars of cobalt and two of viridian, since he had not provided invoices for them.)[29]

The mural shows a change in Pablo's work in the late 1940s and 1950s. His lines became the force of the work, sweeping and curving with boldness and confidence to bring life, movement, and energy to his work. Pablo "walked miles" while creating a painting—he would pace back and forth, thinking, and then boldly attack the surface with a dramatic stroke of his brush.[30]

Longshoremen and their family members modeled for the mural, the progress of which was about the only good news reported in the union newspaper. Its pages were dominated by updates on the Smith Act proceedings against Jack Hall and six others arrested on August 28, 1951, who came to be known as the Hawai'i Seven.[31]

That the union brought Pablo to Hawai'i to paint a mural that was political and showed workers denouncing Red-baiting was brave. Two years earlier, a HUAC hearing had been held in Hawai'i. Steve Murin was one of the "Reluctant 39" who refused to testify.[32] When Pablo was painting the mural, not only were the Hawai'i Seven on trial, but by 1952 the union's outspoken international leader, Harry Bridges, had been the subject of five federal proceedings seeking his deportation on the grounds that he was a Communist.[33]

According to Mitsue Thompson, there was some apprehension about attending the October dedication of the mural. "People were nervous to come because of Pablo's politics," she noted.[34] Murin said, "Just the fact that the ILWU had done it was enough to outrage the right-wing." [35] "*The Honolulu Advertiser* at the time was very reactionary," Murin recalled. "They had daily editorials against the ILWU, Hall, Harry Bridges, Goldblatt, as well as front-page propaganda, 'Dear Joe' letters to Stalin." [36]

The mural was "denounced by some as Communist and anti-American," according to a story about the mural many years later.[37] The hysteria of the times prevented Pablo from showing his work publicly during the time he was in Hawai'i. "Politically it was an uneasy period, so there were no shows of his work," Mitsue Thompson said.[38]

The articles and promotional pieces for the mural list Pablo as born in Salt Lake City, Utah, in 1904, raised on his father's ranch in El Cajon, and studying for one year at the San Diego Academy of Art.[39] Had he revealed that he grew up in Salt Lake City, he likely would have encountered questions about Joe Hill. Hill was never far from Pablo: in 1911, four years before his execution, Hill had lived in a shack on a black sand beach in Hilo, Hawai'i, and worked as a longshoreman loading sugar onto ships.

In 1979, when the Hawai'i union staged a play about Hill, it petitioned Utah Governor Scott Matheson to pardon Hill posthumously on the grounds that he had not had the money at the beginning of his ordeal for a lawyer, that prejudices had run high against him because of his involvement with the IWW, and that the three judges who heard the appeal were also on the Board of Pardon.[40] Matheson, a Democrat, declined, saying that he did not have the power to do so, but expressed his "intention to refer this request to that Board in the near future." [41] Hill, to this day, remains a convicted murder.

ON THE WAY BACK TO MEXICO from Hawai'i, Pablo stopped to visit the Goldblatts in the Bay Area, where anti-Communist activities were very intense. The Goldblatts had a cocktail reception for Pablo on Sunday, October 19, 1952, at their home on Ashbury Terrace, "hosted by the officers of the ILWU and the San Francisco Council of the Arts, Sciences and Professions." [42] David Jenkins, formerly of the California Labor School, bought several lithographs.[43]

Nancy Rowe, whose father, Frank, was fired from San Francisco State University for refusing to sign a loyalty oath, described what life was like during these years.

> Most distressing and alienating was the fear of expressing ideas. The political forces encouraged friends to turn in friends, name names, suspect even the slightest allusion to co-op buying or love of Russian ballet. I remember taking ballet lessons at the S.F. School of Ballet, and being afraid to mention the name of my favorite Russian ballerina. The word 'Communism' was everywhere. Red Scare. We were afraid of the people on the street . . . they, of the 'reds' hiding under every bed; we, of those neighbors who might hear our words, learn of my father's stand and turn us in. It seems an exaggeration now, but it was like swimming in a pot of tea where the poisonous tea bag steeped the water into a darker and more acidic brew the longer it sat. Soon all life was tainted.[44]

Former Communist Party member Carol Cuenod said, "You wouldn't tell people where you worked, for fear that they would tell your employer of your political views and you would be fired." [45]

The Hawai'i mural was Pablo's last mural in the United States. After completing it and visiting California, he would not return to the United States for another twenty three years. On September 9, 1952, the governor of the Territory of Hawai'i, Oren E. Long, wrote a letter to Mr. Willis H. Young, acting chief of the State Department Passport Division, assuring him that if Mr. Paul Stevenson Higgins applied for a passport, such application would be referred "directly to the [State] Department in Washington." [46] Had the 1951 State Department report not "blacklisted" him, this letter may have. Pablo already may have had a passport, however, since he was allowed to enter the United States after leaving Hawai'i, a U.S. territory at the time.

In the library of the ILWU in Honolulu is a print that appears never to have been published. Before leaving Hawai'i, Pablo had asked Leopoldo Méndez to create a print for the union's use in its efforts to defend Jack Hall. On December 3, 1952, Thompson sent Pablo a letter urging Méndez to send the lithograph, as the Hall trial was already in its fifth week.[47] (See page 192.) Eventually, the union received, folded up in a manila envelope, a striking linocut of Méndez's, postmarked April 18, 1953, showing a judge accusing Jack Hall.[48] The judge's bench sits on moneybags and behind him is the now rather archaic symbol of a capitalist in a top hat restraining an ILWU worker. The print arrived months after Pablo had left Hawai'i but while the seven-month Hall trial was still ongoing. Still in its envelope, it was placed in a filing cabinet where it remained for decades.

That Méndez, who did not need to travel to the United States during the McCarthy era, created such a powerful piece of art denouncing the United States government's actions, and Pablo did not, raises the question whether Pablo was laying low in terms of political art condemning the United States in order to be able to travel to and from the United States during these perilous times.

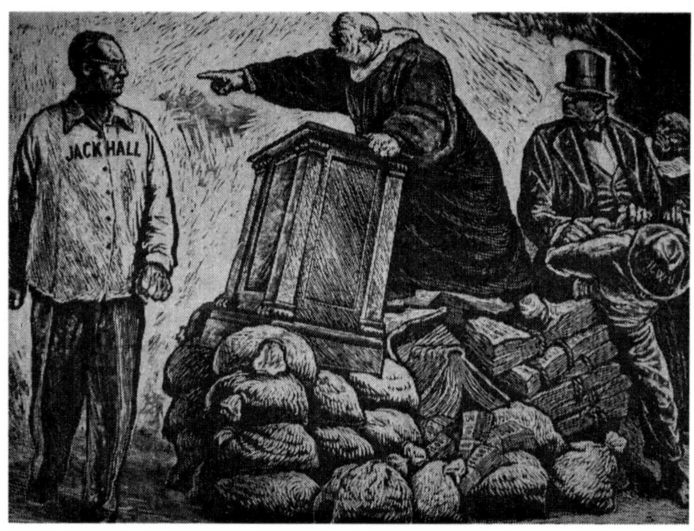

41

EXECUTIONS AND EXILES

The situation was equally bad for U.S. citizens on the left in Mexico. In December 1952, over President Truman's veto, the McCarran-Walter Act went into effect, banning admission to the United States to anyone declared a subversive by the U.S. attorney general. Members of Communist and "Communist-front" organizations were subject to deportation.[1] The act "vastly simplified" the U.S.'s ability to deport non-U.S. citizens suspected of being Communists or Communist sympathizers.[2] It increased the number of expatriates in Mexico. Many British and Canadian citizens working and living in the United States were harassed by the U.S. government every six months when they had to reapply for a visa, and faced questioning about which books they read and who their friends were.[3]

The new administration of Adolfo Ruiz Cortines, installed December 1, 1952, defined itself as different from Alemán. But Ruiz Cortines did not attempt to make over the government created by Alemán, only to run it better. While Alemán had been interested in Cadillacs, speed boats, and acquiring new real estate, Ruiz Cortines's passion was numbers.[4] A statistician, he devalued the peso and shored up financial checks and balances, creating greater efficiency.[5]

For U.S. citizens living in Mexico, the first four years of Ruiz Cortines's presidency were relatively calm, thanks to his clear message that he would be independent in his foreign relations.[6] This changed, however, due to three events in the early 1950s that upped the stakes for expatriates.

The first was the execution of Julius and Ethel Rosenberg at New York's Sing Sing Prison on June 19, 1953. The executions increased people's fear of associating with suspected Communists and made life extremely difficult for Communists and former Communists, both in the United States and in Mexico. After the executions, when Frank Rowe sought work as an art teacher, he was told, even by private schools, that it would be easier to hire a convicted felon than a person who had been fired for refusing to sign a loyalty oath.[7]

The second event, which would come to a head in 1957, began with the arrival of Martha Dodd and Alfred Stern in Mexico City in 1953. They were ducking subpoenas to testify before the House Un-American Activities Committee. Their alleged crime involved passing secrets to the Soviets. The federal government felt the couple was "possibly more important than either [Alger] Hiss or the Rosenbergs." [8] Friends believed that if the Sterns were guilty, it was through naive, unwitting involvement, such as complying with friends' requests to pass on packages to others. The authors of a recent book on Soviet espionage, however, assert that Dodd and Stern were KGB agents who sought out serious work only to be treated as dillitantes by the Soviets.[9]

Dodd and Stern, along with their son, Robert, stayed in Mexico until 1957, when the couple was indicted for espionage, including for financing Soviet spying activities. Diana Anhalt, in her book about the McCarthy era in Mexico, recalled that Dodd "thought nothing of inviting many of [Mexico's leftists artists, including Pablo] to her celebrated affairs along with ex-Ambassador Bill O'Dwyer, a couple of second tier Mexican politicians, and a large sprinkling of American leftists. Those parties were famous." [10]

Dodd created quite a storm. The Sterns, said Anhalt, "were [the expatriate community's] 'big fish.' "

> [T]hey were known . . . for their considerable wealth, ostentatious life-style and unorthodox marriage. (When it came to sex, most of the self-exiled, their political tolerance notwithstanding, were downright prudish. One woman told me Martha had scandalized the community when she sunbathed bare-breasted in mixed company.)[11]

Dodd reportedly had affairs in Mexico with Rivera, Siqueiros, and Pablo.[12]

Although Dodd has been described as someone who "just liked sleeping with attractive men," Randall says that Pablo's relationship with Dodd was different. According to Randall, who spent a great deal of time with Pablo in 1956 to 1958, Pablo was deeply in love with Dodd and she cared greatly for him. Randall says that Pablo began suffering grand mal seizures in 1954 and that Dodd paid for him to have the best doctors.[13]

Yvonne Templin, who arranged exhibits for Pablo in Los Angeles and became a friend, said that Dodd set up a trust fund for Pablo with the intention that he would never have to worry about money.[14]

Like Tina Modotti, Martha Dodd was a beautiful, intelligent, radical, and risk-taking woman. Like Modotti, she rejected the conventional expectations of how a woman should behave sexually, and did what she felt like doing. Sadly, she, like Modotti, died an unhappy woman. In 1986, she said, "I couldn't bear to talk about my life to anyone now. . . . It is too painful. We've both [Dodd and her husband] had tragic experiences which predominate over the happy or productive ones." [15] These included, likely, their son's diagnosis of schizophrenia, their conviction for treason, and their perceived inability to return the United States.

The third event in Mexico that increased the risk of U.S. citizens being deported was Mexico's opposition to a CIA-sponsored coup in Guatemala in 1954, which gave the United States additional reason to suspect Mexico of being friendly to Communists. Bay Area artist and blogger Mark Vallen describes a mural Rivera painted in Russia in 1954.

> [T]he mockingly titled *Glorious Victory* has as its subject the infamous CIA coup of the same year that overthrew Guatemala's democratically elected government. At the center of the mural, CIA Director John Foster Dulles can be seen shaking hands with the leader of the coup d'état, Colonel [Carlos] Castillo Armas. Sitting at their feet is an anthropomorphized bomb bearing the smiling face of U.S. President Dwight D. Eisenhower—who gave orders to launch the military coup. In the background, a priest can be seen officiating over the massacre of workers, many of which can be seen lying slaughtered in the painting's foreground.

The head of the Central Intelligence Agency at the time of the coup, Allen Dulles, and the U.S. ambassador to Guatemala during the coup, John Peurify, are depicted handing out money to various Guatemalan military commanders and fascist junta officials, as Mexican Indian workers slave away at loading bananas onto a United Fruit Company ship. Allen Dulles was on the board of directors of the United Fruit Company when the United States overthrew the government of Guatemala.[16]

Thousands of people, including the dying Frida Kahlo, flooded the streets of Mexico City to denounce the coup and support ousted President Jacobo Arbenz, who had been inspired by Cárdenas. On June 10, 1954, during the coup, artists of the TGP wrote a letter to Arbenz, expressing their solidarity.[17] Pablo and Ignacio Aguirre also created a poster based on a lithograph, *La amistad México-Guatemala* (*Mexico-Guatemala Friendship*).

In response, the FBI stepped up its surveillance of U.S. citizens living in Latin America. In Mexico City, it reported on people attending picnics and softball games.[18] It arrested "nine Communist leaders in Puerto Rico and one Puerto Rican Red in New York," bringing "the number of Communist leaders seized under the Smith Act since 1948 to 132." [19]

The Mexican government of Ruiz Cortines, by midyear, was cleaning Communists out of its own agencies. In mid-July, Dr. Andrés Duarte was dismissed as head of Bellas Artes for allowing a Communist flag to be draped over the coffin of Frida Kahlo. *The New York Times* reported this on July 20, 1954, in an article titled, "Mexico is prodded to clean up Reds." The *Times* reported that the firing of Duarte "provoked a comparatively light outcry from the left." [20]

By the mid-1950s, Elizabeth Catlett, according to biographer Melanie Herzog, "as a foreigner living in Mexico, could not even think of becoming a member of any political organization because this would be grounds for deportation." [21] In addition, "as a foreigner she had to refrain from making political imagery for which she could be deported." [22] Catlett said she ultimately became a Mexican citizen so that she could engage in political activities.[23] Until then, Catlett provided covers and layout for the newsletter of the Mexican organization Paz (Peace). She told Herzog that she felt it "was the only political activity she could engage in without fear of deportation." [24]

Catlett, who increased the TGP's awareness of issues of racism, arranged for the TGP to create of a series of prints, Against Discrimination in the U.S., to be reproduced in *Freedom*, a newspaper that Paul Robeson published in Harlem.[25] She hoped they would also be included in a magazine sent to rural Mexican schools. The TGP produced the prints in late 1952 and early 1953 and sent them to the newspaper. The editors of

Freedom, however, decided that Pablo's lithograph of abolitionist Frederick Douglass was "weak." [26] They asked that it be redone as a linocut.[27] Rather than pull Pablo's print and have someone redo it, the group withdrew the entire sixteen prints, according to Catlett; the series went unpublished in *Freedom*. Prignitz quotes Catlett as telling the magazine to "take it or leave it" in terms of the whole series of prints.[28] It is unknown if Pablo had asked that he, or someone else, be permitted to redo the print so that the series could be printed, therefore raising awareness of racism and of African-American heroes.[29]

Catlett was summoned to the U.S. Embassy in Mexico City in 1955. She was told that a requirement of keeping her U.S. citizenship was providing the U.S. government a list of all the Communists in Mexico City. Testing them, she asked if her three sons—who were also U.S. citizens—would have to do the same. She was told yes, that the oldest, age eight, could write the statement for himself and his two brothers.[30] It would be interesting to know if Pablo was asked to produce such a list as well.

As in 1950, when other U.S. citizen artists and art teachers were deported from Mexico but Pablo was given glowing reviews in the newspapers, he once again was able to avoid harassment. On January 23, 1955, an article, "*El muralismo Mexicano, bajo el pincel de Pablo O'Higgins* [Mexican Muralism under the brush of Pablo O'Higgins]," appeared in *Novedades* along with a picture of his painting, *Mujer del valle de Toluca* (*Woman of the Valley of Toluca*), an oil he painted in 1954.[31] The painting was labeled "owned by Señor Maltz," blacklisted Hollywood writer Albert Maltz. The review mentioned that Pablo had attended art school for *unos meses* (a few months), but did not mention that he studied art for a year in the Soviet Union. Nothing was mentioned of his U.S. citizenship or his former Communist Party membership. The reference to Alfred Maltz as being the owner of the painting reproduced in the article, however, may have been an intentionally placed clue that Pablo associated with this suspect expatriate community.

With U.S. citizens suffering in Mexico, Pablo could have become a Mexican citizen, but doing so might have prevented him from visiting the United States. According to Schreiber, "individuals who either had never been American citizens or who had become Mexican citizens experienced the most obstacles entering the United States." [32] Pablo may have believed that as a U.S. citizen he would continue to be able to travel to the United States, or that the McCarthy era would be over soon and he would have his de facto dual citizenship restored, thanks to the TGP's close relationship with the Mexican government. It appears that he was not ready to give up the possibility of once again being able to move freely between the countries, as he had in the war years.

Pablo did pay a price: the TGP, says Bardach, made no criticism of the governments of Camacho, Alemán, Ruiz Cortines, or López Mateos, who took office in 1958.[33] But how great was this price? Pablo was on his way to becoming a "revolutionary" artist in name only.

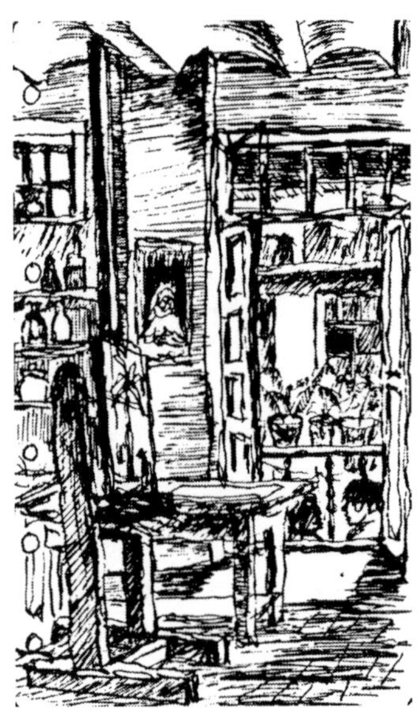

42

INTERNAL CONFLICTS

Shaken by external criticism, internal problems, including disagreement over how to spend some prize money, and the reality that its members were of an older generation in a changing Mexico, the Taller de Gráfica Popular began crumbling in the 1950s.

Catlett said when she joined the TGP in 1946, the members were "all friends" and simply happy to be with each other. They were all poor and would eat out together; on weekends, she and her husband, Francisco "Pancho" Mora, would join Pablo, Mariana Yampolsky, Alberto Beltrán, Méndez and his wife and kids on weekend trips to places like Veracruz.[1] Arturo García Bustos, too, who joined the TGP in 1945, said it was less a political organization and more a group of idealistic friends who believed that socialism could change the world, and relatively quickly.[2] They were motivated by the idea that they could play a part in that.

Catlett said that by the 1950s, however, new people joined the TGP who were more conservative and cared more about their own art, and "the whole revolutionary thing was dissipated." They simply did not get along.[3]

The tension between moderate socialists, such as Méndez and Pablo, who supported Lombardo Toledano and were members of his Partido Popular, and the Communists, including Catlett and Mora, would cause the most damaging divide in the TGP's existence.[4]

Méndez was the TGP member closest to Toledano, and according to Bardach, he expected TGP members to support the Partido Popular, specifically the branch of it led by TGP member Enrique Ramírez y Ramírez.[5] Pablo sided with Méndez politically, but, says Bardach, echoing others, was simply "in favor of *el pueblo* [the people]." [6]

When the Partido Popular supported Lombardo Toledano's campaign for president of Mexico in 1952, TGP members were expected to do so as well. The Mexican Communist Party also supported Toledano, so there was no conflict. But when Toledano lost to PRI candidate Ruiz Cortines, Toledano and Partido Popular members, to the fury of the Communist Party, began supporting the PRI victor.

In December 1952, Siqueiros harshly criticized the TGP for having lost its collective spirit, and Méndez for being undemocratic.[7] The role of the TGP by the 1950s, according to Prignitz, devolved to participating in "innumerable national celebrations, including conferences, books, and expositions" of things like the anniversary of Benito Juárez's birthday, which produced portraits of Juárez from every possible angle and incurred the criticism of Siqueiros, who called them religious icons.[8] The TGP produced more than fifty prints on these themes.[9] Siqueiros "called it the 'Taller Católico de Gráfica Popular' [People's Catholic Graphic Arts Workshop] and accused it of inundating the country with religious estampillas [in this context, cheap throwaways]." [10]

Méndez was demoted to manager of the Estampa press in January 1953.[11]

In addition to suffering from internal struggles, the TGP was becoming less relevant in Mexico. It had won its battle against fascism. The masses were increasingly literate. It was, in the words of curator Lyle Williams, "a victim of its own and the revolutionary movement's success." Also, it was "less socially relevant," especially since it would not budge from its "steadfast adherence to social realism." [12]

The year 1953 was a low point in artistic production by the TGP, but a high point in terms of exhibits outside Mexico and the receipt of prizes "based more on its prestige than on the quality of its work," in Prignitz's words.[13] Its highest honor was receiving the International Peace Prize of six thousand pesos from the Soviet World Peace Council, in recognition of its artistic works in service of peace.[14] This sparked another internal conflict that would last nearly a decade.[15] Méndez felt the prize money was his; others felt it was meant for the group.[16] Both Méndez and Luis Arenal, the latter as a representative of the TGP, went to Vienna to accept the prize, but it was given to Méndez.[17]

In December, Méndez gave half of the prize money to the TGP.[18] With the prize, "the TGP gained fame instantly." [19] Randall said, "the Taller was very important in the new democracies in Europe. They were having a lot of shows in Eastern Europe. They won the Stalin prize and gained international recognition as the most important graphic workshop in the world." [20] Although it was suffering internally, the TGP had unending requests to contribute to efforts to denounce the U.S presidency and to support workers' strikes. TGP members' work increasingly appeared in magazines.[21] Rivera, in 1954, told Emmy Lou Packard that the TGP was the "most significant manifestation" in Mexico.[22] Prignitz says that "from 1954 to 1956, the museums of Mexico were empty" because of so many exhibits of Mexican art in Europe, Eastern Europe, Japan, London, and Paris.[23] Fewer TGP prints were being seen in Mexico in general: in 1955, a new law made it illegal to post on the walls of Mexico City.[24]

In 1956, the TGP underwent a change to a civil association to reduce taxes and ease customs issues. The majority also wanted to make changes in its charter to make the group more democratic.[25] They successfully moved to change the "declaration of principles" from the *lucha en contra de la reacción fascista* (fight against reactionary fascism) to a program of "defense and enrichment of national culture." [26] These concepts were in line with the goals of the Continental Congress of Culture, held in 1952 in Santiago, Chile, poets Pablo Neruda and Gabriela Mistral presiding, which sought to promote culture and cultural exchange and defend free expression.[27]

This new direction changed the TGP dramatically from its origins; it became a cultural center, inviting "bourgeois" writers and historians, and occasionally a union representative, to participate in cultural conferences at the TGP every few months.[28]

A tribute to the TGP's status in the Mexican art world, a twentieth-anniversary retrospective exhibition of its work called A Great Showing of the Work of the People's Graphic Workshop, was held in Mexico City in 1956 at Bellas Artes.

Also in 1956, Pablo had an exhibit in the Salón de la Plástica Mexicana for which Rivera wrote the preface to the catalog, saying that one day Pablo would be considered to be in the same realm as Vincent van Gogh. While some, aware of Rivera's hyperbole, have taken this statement with a grain of salt, it is quoted in almost every promotional piece and publication regarding Pablo. Tamayo believed Rivera said such things "to prove he was the nation's greatest *maestro* [teacher]." [29]

Divisions between Communists and those who left the party became wider with the revelation, three years after his death in 1956, of the genocide committed by Stalin. On the last day of the Twentieth Congress of the Communist Party in Moscow in February 1956, in a closed-door speech to his confidants, Nikita Khrushchev revealed Stalin's atrocities, including the Great Terror of the 1930s, and decried the cult of personality that had grown around him. The information was leaked and soon reported all over the world.

These revelations were devastating to many party members. David Jenkins said it was "like a rape, a mental and emotional rape because we were involved with hundreds of non-Party people to whom we had denied the possibility of these 'slave labor' camps, the murder of honorable and fine people." [30] For some, it confirmed suspicions. Cuenod said, "It was almost a validation of my quiet unease [with the Party]. The Party always had to be right. It was like an absolute religion. You had to have faith—blind faith. The principles were great, but how they carried them out were very disturbing." The twentieth congress, she said, "was the end of the Communist Party in San Francisco." [31] Eighty percent of party members in California left.[32] Membership in the CPUSA dropped from approximately eighty thousand to ten thousand.[33] In the fall, "the Party suffered another severe jolt: the Hungarian uprising and its suppression by Soviet tanks." [34] Rowe said, "some people left the party by expulsion, and some left because of the incessant persecution of the party . . . but many left, I believe, because they became disillusioned." [35]

Other Communists, like Caughlan, took it in stride, at least outwardly. "Many people," said Rowe, used the cliché, "You can't make an omelet without breaking eggs, or some other rationalization to excuse tyranny." [36] Octavio Paz saw the horrors of Stalin as a condemnation of his regime only, and not of socialism or Communism in general.[37] Jenkins said, "[W]e in the mass movement, would have had to defend the Party and reject the Red baiting, although it was made terribly difficult. We had already gone through the catharsis of expelling Browder and rejecting the Tehran period and going back to the hard anti-imperialist line . . . ." [38]

Even those who remained defenders of Stalin and the party may have had reservations. Goldie Caughlan says her husband, "a Stalin apologist until his death in 1999," may have had unexpressed doubts. "I think that's perhaps why he never wrote his memoirs," she said.

The TGP never expressed outrage regarding the murders perpetrated by Stalin. Bardach interviewed numerous members of the TGP and asked each about this. Catlett told Bardach, "I don't think we ever had any discussions about Stalin. It never came up. We were very busy with other things." [39]

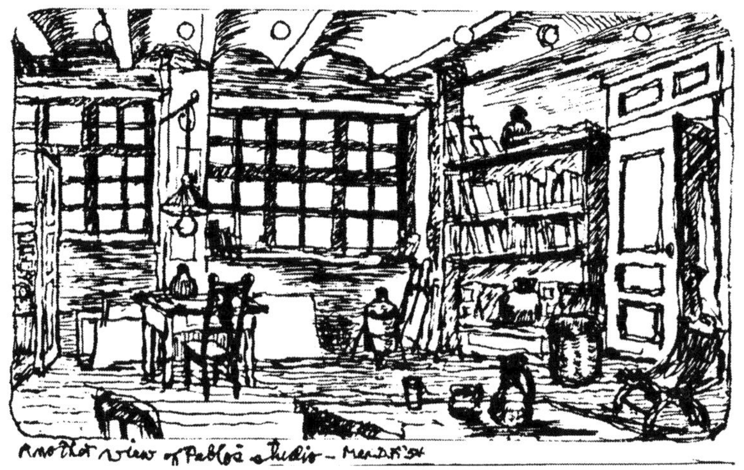

43

DEPORTATIONS

In 1957, after four years in Mexico, Pablo's friend, patron, and possible lover, Martha Dodd, and her husband, Alfred Stern, were indicted in absentia for espionage, the same crime that sent the Rosenbergs to the electric chair. The United States asked Mexico to extradite the Sterns to the United States for trial, but Mexico sat on its hands, allowing them and their son to flee to Prague on Paraguayan passports. Elizabeth Catlett said TGP members planning to travel to Prague gave up their spots on the airplane so the Sterns could take them.[1] The Sterns lived in Prague and in Cuba from 1963 to 1968.[2] The espionage charges were dropped in 1979, but they remained in Prague for the rest of their lives.[3]

In Mexico, the harassment of Communists and former Communists turned from bad to worse after the Sterns' departure. Angry that Mexico allowed the Sterns to get away, the United States kicked off a period of terror for U.S. expatriates in Mexico, and Mexico's government cooperated. It was in this context that Pablo's sister, Gladys, the same sister who had slammed her door in Pablo's face years earlier, and their cousin W. C. Higgins and his wife paid Pablo a visit.[4] Given the tension at the time and Gladys's aversion to Pablo's politics and living conditions, it is unlikely this was a pleasure trip. Gladys was then sixty-eight and a widow. It was likely a trip to check up on him.

But they need not have worried. Pablo seems again to have been immune from threats of deportation, although Elizabeth Catlett was not.

The TGP was in the good graces of the government and regarded "as a guardian and promoter of 'national culture.'" [5] The TGP and the Frente Nacional de Artes Plásticas

(National Front for Visual Arts), founded by TGP members, continued to produce for the government flyers and banners and prints for national celebrations, including the 1956 celebration of the birth of Benito Juárez, Mexico's first president of Mexican indigenous heritage.[6]

On September 9, 1957, *Time* announced, "Mexico is a thriving colony of wealthy expatriates representing every shade in the Communist spectrum, from parlor pink to Moscow Red." It described Stirling Dickinson's home as a gathering place for "Communists and fellow travelers," who would "idle away the hours in avant-garde jazz cellars, drink tequila and loaf," and reported that a few were "engaged in genuine cloak-and-dagger plotting" following orders of the "suspiciously oversized (200 staff members) Soviet embassy in Mexico City." [7]

Embarrassed that the Sterns escaped, Gobernacíon (the Mexican Secretary of the Interior) with President Ruiz Cortines's tacit approval, ordered raids on the leftist expatriate community. Beginning in 1957, the raids peaked in September 1958, the same time that labor unrest in Mexico was peaking.[8] Mexico's press happily reported the events.[9] *Excelsior*, on August 24, 1957, ran the headline, "Undesirable Foreigners," and reported, "58 expelled from Mexico in 2 months—yesterday Article 3 was applied to 3 more undesirables." On August 31, 1957, "Red counterspies at large at the border—500 men on duty to prevent them from escaping from Mexico." [10] At the same time, many articles appeared in the Mexican, U.S. and international press describing Mexico as a haven for Communists.[11]

A description of San Miguel de Allende's Stirling Dickinson as the ringleader proliferated through the international media, including in the *New York Herald Tribune*.[12] Dickinson's wealthy family pursued a libel action and soon won a settlement from *Time* and a glowing piece about him in the *Herald Tribune*, calling his school the "Sorbonne of Mexico." [13] Dickinson realized that if he had not had relatives in a high-powered law firm, he never would have come out of the situation unscathed.[14]

In April 1958, after Labor Secretary Adolfo López Mateos had been chosen as Cortines's PRI successor, weakening Cortines's power, labor strikes, mainly of teachers and railroad workers demanding higher salaries and revamped union leadership, broke out in Mexico City after five years of relative calm. The government, including its FBI-trained federal security police, harassed the head of the teachers union, detaining him six times, arrested union leaders, and countered workers' demands with clubs and teargas.[15] During the two-year battle, teachers and railway workers went to prison.[16] The usual suspects, alleged Communist leftists from the United States, including blacklisted Hollywood writer Albert Maltz, were accused of fomenting the student strikes.[17]

Krauze says, regarding the strikes of 1958 to 1959, "The system had responded ferociously against the real or supposed beneficiaries of the Revolution—against the workers. From that moment, any rebellious unions who wanted to 'try out' the government knew what they could expect to face." [18]

Although the Partido Popular, which Krauze called a "weak party of opposition," attacked the government's actions, the TGP's inertia prevented it from effectively condemning the government.[19] On September 6, 1958, the government broke up the railroad strike, and conducted the largest detention and deportation project ever: a week-long sweep of "international agitators" accused of having supported or financed the strikes or student protests.[20]

On a night of the roundups, TGP member Elizabeth Catlett, who was home alone with her three young children, heard a knock on her door. She opened it and three men who said they were from Gobernacíon demanded to see her papers. She tried to close the door, but one grabbed her by the arm, twisted her around and, with his arm under her chin, pulled her off her feet. When her oldest son, eleven-year-old Pancho, tried to stop him, he was knocked down. As Catlett was dragged out of the house, she told her son, "Call!" Pancho phoned Pablo, who set off to get Catlett's husband and take him to look for a lawyer. At the detention center, says Catlett, they checked her name off what looked like an embassy alphabetical list of all of the leftists in Mexico. The list included *inmigrados*, living and working in Mexico legally.[21] The same night, three names Catlett had seen checked off the list were also apprehended—John Bright, Bernard Blasenheim, and Allen Lane Lewis (possibly alphabetized under *A*).[22]

Catlett argued that her children were Mexican, and Catlett and Mora and their friends appealed to "prominent figures on the left," including Lombardo Toledano and the secretary of education, who arranged for her release Monday evening after she had spent the weekend in jail.[23]

The three men imprisoned the same night as Catlett were "summarily deported" within a few days and would never return to Mexico.[24] "The community was thrown into a panic," says Diane Anhalt, "taken off guard by the intensity and suddenness of the attacks." [25]

Following the weeklong raids in September 1958, articles appeared in *Excelsior* (September 11, October 1, 2, 3, 1958), *Novedades* (September 9), and in *Ultimas Noticias de Novedades* (September 10, 11, and 27, 1958) speculating on the other names on the list.[26] The September 10 *Ultimas Noticias de Novedades* article named Pablo, along with Albert Maltz, Catlett, Charles Small, interpreter Asa Zatz, and others.[27] Pablo, "Paul Higgins," was listed as "part of the group of North Americans who, with other European and North American Communist agitators, were in charge of the infiltration and other activities of agents working for the Kremlin." [28]

During the next few weeks, as the government worked its way down the list, "Americans with a history of left-wing politics made themselves scarce." [29] Once the strike was broken through the detention of labor members, the harassment of the "network of foreign agitators" quieted down and people returned to their lives.[30] Still, many suffered in the aftermath. Some were deported; some left voluntarily. One couple, Harvard- and Sorbonne-educated Maurice Halperin, and his wife, Edith, left for the Soviet Union.[31]

The idea that the government was not at fault in repressing the strikers, but that all wrongs were the fault of "Communist infiltrators," was consistent with the government's approach since the time of Alemán—claiming to be "revolutionary" and blaming outside forces if the goals of the revolution were not met.[32] During the McCarthy era, foreigners and Communists were the scapegoats.

When López Mateos took office in December 1958, nothing improved. Méndez and likely Pablo, who followed Méndez politically, supported his candidacy. López Mateos showed his colors in his repressive response to railroad strikes in early 1959.[33] On March 28, 1959, more than nine thousand people in Mexico were detained, suspected of supporting the strikes. A Soviet embassy group was expelled and some "North American political expatriates" were deported.[34]

The TGP was unable to respond with any force to the atrocities of the strikes and oppression. Bardach says that because of the divisions within the group, "the Taller ceased to exist as a functional collective organization. By July of 1959, collective activity in the Taller has more or less ceased." This was when Méndez, "complaining of the works' quality, wrote that much of it was fit to be thrown away." [35]

Catlett had to decide what to do about her status as a U.S. citizen. According to Schreiber, to get *inmigrante* status (allowing her to live but not work in Mexico), the first step toward *inmigrado* status (allowing her to work), she would need the U.S. government to provide her a certificate of citizenship, which it likely would not do.[36] The U.S. embassy had denied it to Maltz, saying they would not help facilitate his foreign residency.[37]

But why was Pablo immune from this harsh treatment? Even Ralph Roeder, who had arrived in Mexico in 1943 and been awarded the highest honor Mexico bestows upon foreigners, the Aztec Eagle award, for his biography of Benito Juárez, was detained for ten days.[38]

One's fate as a U.S. citizen in Mexico depended greatly on whom one knew. Accounts of people who escaped deportation or worked their way out of ongoing deportation proceedings usually conclude with, "they contacted [Siqueiros, Rivera, Toledano, or a Mexican general] and were returned to Mexico." No wonder Hollywood writer Dalton Trumbo began hosting parties for government officials.[39] Anhalt recounts the U.S. citizens living in Mexico who were subject to threats of deportation. All of them who avoided deportation did so by calling on their powerful friends:

• Stirling Dickinson and his art teachers were permitted to return from Texas, "thanks to powerful friends: Siqueiros, a handful of Mexican generals, and several highly placed governmental officials intervened on their behalf." [40]

• Albert Maltz, seeking to get *inmigrante* status in Mexico was advised by his lawyer to go around to "big shots" and present each with a translated, autographed copy of his novel. It worked.[41] When he feared deportation, Maltz wrote a letter to the incoming president, López Mateos, and included with it a letter from the president's cousin.[42]

• John Menz was picked up and taken to Gobernacíon for deportation, but phoned an economic adviser to the president, then Alemán. The advisor rushed "from the Presidential Palace to Gobernacíon waving his Presidential badge . . . ," and Menz was let go.[43]

• Rivera and Pablo helped artist John Wilson stay in Mexico by providing letters of recommendation for a grant.[44]

• Luis Buñuel was helped with his immigration problems by a friend who introduced him to the interior minister, Hector Peréz Martínez. Buñuel, who had quit the Inter-American Agency because of an attack on him as a Marxist, became a Mexican citizen.[45]

• Alleged "Cuernavaca Red" Gordon Kahn had a friend "with political connections in Mexico" get his residency papers from Gobernacíon after a former business partner had had Gobernacíon "misplace" them.[46]

Maltz summed it up: "We might get deported in the middle of the night; we might get our papers of . . . permission and remain here unmolested for quite some time; or we might get our papers and three weeks later a reversal of policy would see us deported; or we might be refused our papers, go to the border and also be refused a return tourist visa card; or we might get another tourist card." [47]

It is interesting that when Catlett was in trouble and had just enough time to yell to her son, "Call!" before being dragged out the door by the DFS, her son called Pablo. This indicates that Pablo was very well connected, and perceived as someone with power to remedy the situation.

Good news could not come too soon. With the U.S. Supreme Court overturning the Rockwell Kent case, by 1958, U.S. expatriates in Mexico could get U.S. passports and thereby travel.[48]

Still, the government of López Mateos, installed in late 1958, gave the United States full cooperation regarding the political expatriate community, keeping it in a state of uncertainty.[49] López Mateos maintained close ties to the CIA: he attended the wedding of CIA Chief Winston Scott in 1962. The CIA had an extensive network in Latin America.[50] Suspicious activities of U.S. citizens, such as attending a Communist-sponsored conference, were reported by the FBI to the international press, who described conference attendees as "American traitors." [51] Anhalt says, "virtually all those in Mexico, with few exceptions, ended up leaving the party." [52]

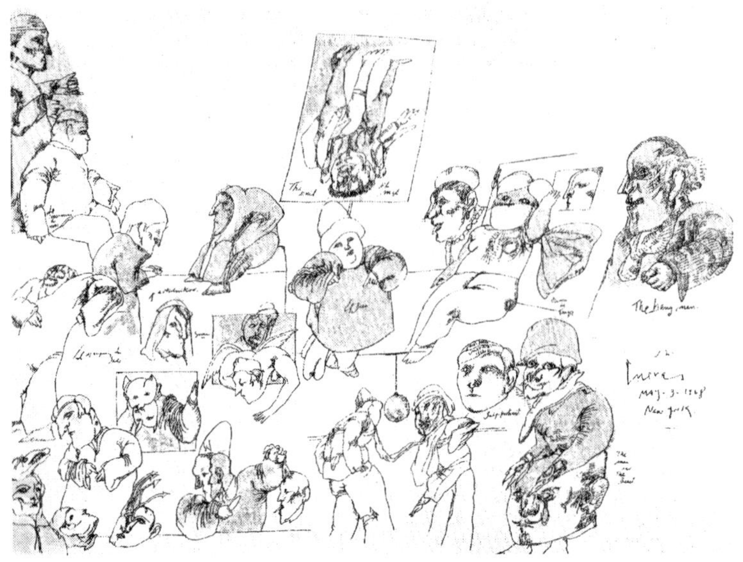

44

LA RUPTURA

By the late 1950s Bellas Artes, the massive marble art palace whose walls were covered with murals by Rivera, Orozco, and Siqueiros, had sunk another few feet into Mexico City's soft, former lake-bed ground. Bellas Artes had been the center of the art world for the Mexican School, but now it was the site of protests—young artists carrying posters on sticks, the kind the TGP had once produced for demonstrations, showing imperialists stomping on the rights of workers.

The comfort Mexican School artists enjoyed in the early 1950s in the form of gallery exhibits and a buying public was short-lived. Soon they were the targets of attack—not by their old enemies, the government and the conservatives—but by their own would-be protégés, the younger generation of artists, who, like a rowdy bunch of adolescents, found fault with their teachers' fundamental values.[1] They attacked everything, even the formerly sacred *tres grandes*. They caricatured Rivera, the master of caricature, as an oaf who was out of touch and incomprehensible to the people.[2] Siqueiros was portrayed as an idiot.

"La Ruptura," the rejection of social realism and communal art in favor of individual expression and abstract art, "arrived in force and, like a tidal wave, swept clean the face of Mexican culture, making way for the next generation of artists to build their own foundations," says Bardach.[3]

"[P]olitical art, which had been the darling of those in power for generations, suddenly found itself down-and-out. Artists who had previously been able to count on teaching positions or exhibitions suddenly met with suggestions that they retire or move 'a provincia,' something akin to disappearing in highly centralized Mexico . . . ." [4]

Nearly fifty years later, artists who were in the TGP at the time were still expressing pain and frustration about La Ruptura, says Bardach.[5] The book, *La Ruptura,* was on Pablo's bookshelf.[6]

Young artists no longer wanted to paint magueys and workers in sombreros. They had not lived through the revolution or its aftermath, nor did they see the need to perpetuate it through art. They believed the Mexican School artists no longer knew what the people wanted, had been co-opted by the government, were stagnant, had stifled individuality, and were ignorant of new technologies.[7] They advocated for new media, such as photography, and questioned the value placed on collective work. They disputed what Siqueiros said in 1958: "*No hay mas ruta que la nuestra* [There is no way but ours]."[8] To get their point across they carried a coffin with one word painted on the side—"*realismo* [realism]."[9]

The attack on social realism pierced the soul of the TGP. Its members strongly believed in the collective process and were convinced that nonrepresentational art would be "incomprehensible for the masses."[10] And the TGP's commitment to collective work seemed irreconcilable with abstract expressionism's emphasis on the individual.[11]

Throughout the storm, Pablo remained faithful to Méndez and to the TGP principles. To him and to Méndez, an artist could not work apart from the people. Pablo rejected the internationalization of Mexican art, believing it must reflect Mexican life.[12] He described the close tie between the artist and the pueblo that his generation of artists committed to in the 1930s.

> Most of the artists in Mexico today are teachers. They may be in the city schools or in the peasant country where new clean adobe houses serve as a simple classroom. There the artist paints his murals on the walls, does his posters for distribution over the countryside. And always at his elbow are the people of the community, listening, asking, advising. He is their artist, he is one of them.[13c]

The criticism of the work of the TGP and their beliefs had to be hard on Pablo. Pablo himself, during his life and to this day, has been practically immune from any criticism. Nor had his art been the subject of much criticism, beyond early comments that it was too influenced by Rivera and the criticism of social realism in general.[14] The few art critics in Mexico who have called his art simplistic or romantic are dismissed by Bellas Artes as being "foreigners" (Margarita Nelken, Antonio Rodríguez, and Raquel Tibol) or "Communists"—(Nelken)—odd grounds for challenging their credibility, since Pablo was both.[15]

Prignitz considered Pablo the best lithographer of the twentieth century.[16] His style has been described as having a "Daumier-like line," referring to nineteenth-century French printmaker and satirist Honoré Daumier; it can also be described as curvilinear and flame-like.[17]

The external and internal criticisms of the TGP were insurmountable. Méndez drifted away from the TGP: by late 1959, he had shifted his energies to his new art book publishing company. With the crumbling of the inner core of the TGP, Pablo was unmoored. But Pablo's world would change when someone would come into his life and offer him a dream proposition: I'll take care of everything, you just do your art.

IV

THE SOLITARY YEARS

The light in the window symbolizes the presence of man in the painting.
—María de Jesús de la Fuente de O'Higgins[1]

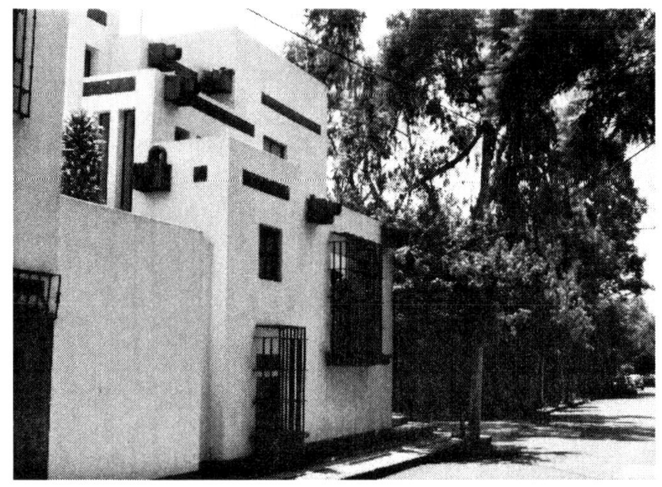

45

MARÍA DE JESÚS

Gilberto Bosques, Mexican ambassador to France, exalted Pablo and María, "*su musa companera* [his muse/companion]," writing, "*Pablo y María, María y Pablo. Transfusion de dos almas, en la Vida, en el Amor y en el Arte, a la luz de Mexico* [Pablo and María, María and Pablo. Transfusion of two souls, in life, in love, and in art, shining brightly in Mexico]." [1]

Pablo, at age fifty-five, after thirty-five years in Mexico as an adored bachelor, did something no one expected him ever to do: he married. Most of Pablo's friends say he was never looking. Some said it was generally assumed Pablo was gay because he didn't seem interested in women.[2] Several said he was asexual.[3] Seymour Kaplan, who knew Pablo when he was single, said that women had to work hard to get his attention.[4]

While visiting a ceramic factory in Monterrey in early 1959 in preparation for a mural he was to create in Poza Rica, Veracruz, he met María de Jesús de la Fuente, who was assisting Leopoldo Méndez with a printmaking class in an art school she had attended.[5] María, who was thirty-eight when they met, says that when Pablo saw her, he said to himself, "If that woman is single or widowed or divorced, I'm going to marry her." [6]

After a short courtship, the couple married, in May, 1959, in Monterrey, Mexico, and sent an announcement to friends reading, "La Srita. Ma. de Jesús de la Fuente y el Sr. Pintor Pablo O'Higgins le participan su Matrimonio Civil y Religioso [Señorita María de Jesús de la Fuente and Señor Painter Pablo O'Higgins were Married Civilly and Religiously]," and invited friends to attend a lunch on May 23 in Monterrey.[7] (Randall was surprised that Pablo, a Marxist, would marry in a religious ceremony.)[8]

María, who was from the town of Rayones in the state of Nuevo León, was a lawyer. When she met Pablo, she was working in Monterrey at a legal clinic she had established to defend the rights of women in domestic cases. Earlier, she had worked as a criminal defense attorney, but, she said the work was too depressing, since it seemed the poor people went to jail and the rich went free. In an interview in 2008, María said that before marrying Pablo in early 1959, she also established a school for social work in Monterrey, where she taught law, and an art school for children.[9]

María may have appeared to Pablo to be a dedicated political activist, like the other women to whom he had been attracted, including Tina Modotti and Martha Dodd. María was passionate about the Cuban Revolution.[10] She suggested that social and political issues brought them together.[11]

María offered something that may have appealed greatly to Pablo at the time: the opportunity to focus entirely on his art and not to have to worry about anything else in life. A recent book of Pablo's work published by María says that she "has dedicated her entire life to preserving the work and memory of Don Pablo, artist, humanist and creator." [12] While Pablo was living, she dedicated herself to helping him become a recognized and financially successful artist. In the decades since his death, she has continued to be a tireless promoter of his work and fierce defender of his legacy.

María also offered Pablo grounding and security at a time when he was unsure what the future would hold. Pablo's collective work had stalled almost completely. The TGP was barely functioning. In departing the TGP, Pablo had lost the constant presence of his best friend, Leopoldo Méndez. Pablo's name was on a deportation list and deportations continued.[13] Randall said, "She seemed to be what he needed for some security in his life."

María gave up her law career and what she believed was a promising art career of her own in order to manage his.[14] María said she continued to paint, although she said she was too busy running the household to spend much time at it.[15]

Pablo adored María and called her Querida (darling). Photographs of Pablo around this time show him smiling—rare for photographs of him in general—and content. By this time in life, Pablo had become broader and stockier. His blond hair had turned pure white and remained thick and bushy. (One friend compared him to a polar bear.)[16] Pablo's paintings of María show her as serene and sensuous, as do the photographs he would snap of her in the morning before she was fully awake, her long dark hair mussed and her eyes heavy. Photos of María and Pablo show them looking dreamy together. María is always solidly planted at his side, whether he was at an opening or painting a mural. María said Pablo teased her that when they were in a group of people, she would be holding his hand and talking to another man.[17]

María said Pablo was kind, thoughtful, and respectful. He brought her a flower from the garden every day and always thanked her for the meals she served him.[18]

The first thing people who knew the couple recount about María is that she improved Pablo's financial condition. Rafael Carrillo said that before Pablo married María, "All the money [Pablo] earned didn't last too long because he distributed it to everybody who needed it, then he met María de Jesús and she helped him organize his life a little bit and they got the big house and he had a permanent and organized place to work." [19] Poniatowska wrote, "Sometimes he didn't have money to eat. Then, with Mariá, his life became more secure." [20]

Terry Goldblatt observed that María "added structure or steadiness to his life, including economic stability. As a bachelor, he was poor. Very poor. He had not cared about material possessions. . . . He was happy to give away whatever he had and to live in his studio, where he hung his clothes on nails in the walls. He had absolutely no interest in money."[21]

María, however, was interested in establishing a comfortable home for them and the children she hoped they would have. (She and Pablo ultimately did not have children; María says she suffered a miscarriage in the early 1960s.)[22] María sought to achieve her goals by becoming his agent, his manager, and promoting his art. Pablo and María were able to reach a standard of living that was enviable, one closer to what both Pablo and María had experienced growing up. Méndez, in contrast, lived his entire life in poverty and spent the last years of his life in extreme poverty, "living with his lover in a cardboard shack."[23]

Pablo hated selling his works and had contempt for galleries. He claimed that he never had painted for money. In an interview, Pablo said, "Anything that is turned into business [has] something vacant about it. Empty, empty. Superficial, and superficial things are not healthy."[24] A capable businesswoman, María took over. She insisted Pablo be paid for his work, and she collected outstanding debts. She did not want Pablo to worry about money, and assured him they had money even when they did not.[25]

Over the next twenty-four years of his life, and for the many years since his death in 1983, María has successfully marketed the image of Pablo as a populist, an artist of the people, a "revolutionary" only in the most innocuous sense. Her example of his living the life of a revolutionary was working in the United States as a welder during World War II.[26] She has downplayed his past political involvement, denying that he ever was a member of the Communist Party.[27] These characterizations could reflect a very astute marketing strategy, beginning in the McCarthy period, of downplaying Pablo's Communist past. Maria would learn firsthand, in 1975, when she was detained by U.S. immigration officials, how damaging perceived past affiliations can be.

Oddly, for a man enamored with Tina Modotti and admiring of Alexandra Kollontai, the Soviet ambassador to Mexico who questioned marriage altogether, Pablo had traditional views about marriage, according to María. She said Pablo held the beliefs of nineteenth-century Mexican anticleric Melchor O'Campo, which are often read at civil marriage ceremonies in Mexico: "the man is to give his wife counsel, advice and support her financially, [and] she is to give him counsel and advice and respect him."[28]

Marrying Pablo placed María, an aspiring artist, in the center of the art world in Mexico. Instant inclusion in this very exclusive group would be a dream for any artist, person aspiring to be an artist, or person interested in the arts.

This art world was full of possibilities that Pablo had been oblivious to in terms of advancing his career and gaining recognition as an artist. Friendships could be developed and connections made, all to the end of selling Pablo's work and getting him recognition. María cultivated these connections, and their circle became the wealthy and famous of Mexico's art world.

Some people who had been friends with Pablo for years, even decades, found it difficult to accept María. In interviews, they often are effusive regarding Pablo, many calling him a "saint," then stop short and pause when María is mentioned.[29] The most common word used to describe María is manipulative. Others include materialistic ("bourgeois"), high class or aspiring to be high class, opportunistic, aristocratic, and prudish. Yvonne Templin said María was "more interested in living out her dream of being married to a famous artist than in accepting what was important to Pablo." María, according to Templin, "wanted Pablo to be great, but couldn't understand Pablo's greatness." Templin also said María was jealous and would probe Pablo's friends for information about his former romances. Templin said María was especially jealous of Pablo's relationship with Martha Dodd.[30] Byron Randall said,

"María undermined and sabotaged Pablo's work. She was always dragging him around to meet people, become known, in hopes of getting commissions." [31] Pablo's friends were also dismayed that María did not leave him alone to paint.[32]

Stories about María often end on a sour note or with a misunderstanding. One couple called her a *mujer de armas tomar*, literally a woman who would pick up arms, but meaning confrontational, tough, someone "you don't mess with." [33]

Pablo went from being "poor, very poor" and often not having money to buy food to living in a beautiful large home in the charming upper-middle-class colonial neighborhood of Coyoacán, where Rivera, Kahlo, and the Trotskys had lived, and having a second home near Cuernavaca, where wealthy Mexicans and expatriates have weekend homes. (See image of streetcorner in O'Higgins's Coyoacán neighborhood on p. 108.) His friends couldn't figure out how or why this came about, insisting that Pablo never cared about material things.

Modotti biographer Mildred Constantine met Pablo in 1936 and knew him "extremely well," she said. "María came from a wealthy, bourgeois family," Constantine said, adding, "Pablo lived in a way that was very different. It's not odd that Pablo married, but that he married María. María brought in her own friends and kept Pablo apart from his friends." [34]

Some of this criticism of María can be attributed to the mere existence of a wife in Pablo's life rather than to María specifically. Close friends of Pablo, particularly women, had enjoyed looking after Pablo. "He always had women taking care of him," Terry Goldblatt said.[35] The presence of a new person who claimed to have an equal or better understanding of Pablo's needs resulted in jealousy and resentment.

Yet friends acknowledged that Pablo was happy, saying he adored María. Still, Pablo did not reveal his entire self to María. She never knew about the involvement of Pablo's father in the Joe Hill case. She never knew he had a half sister. And he told her that his brother Roger had died during World War I rather than ten years later of a heart attack. Of many people interviewed for this book, some who had known Pablo since the 1920s, María was the only one who insisted that Pablo was never a member of the Communist Party.[36]

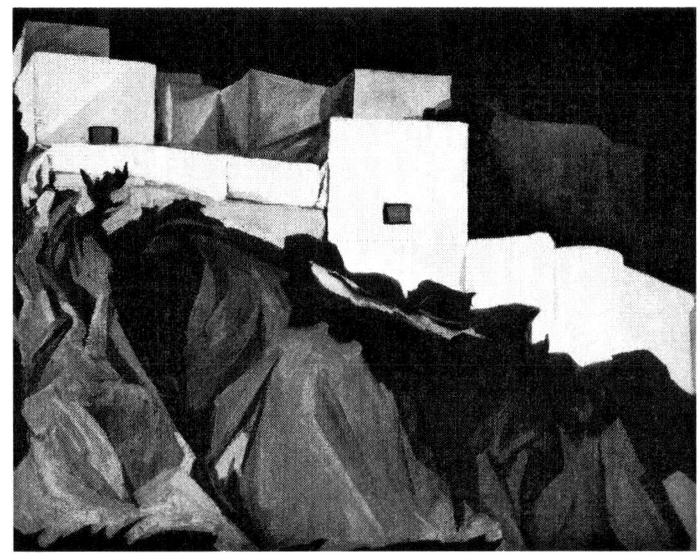

46

MEXICAN CITIZENSHIP

Bardach describes the demise of the original TGP as a "slow train wreck," but it also has all of the markings of a long, painful divorce followed by years of fighting over the boxes left in the storage unit.[1]

By 1960, the battle between the Mexican School and the younger generation had reached a peak. Two years earlier, the 1958 Biennial of Inter-American Painting and Printmaking in Mexico, sponsored by the government, had showcased the Mexican School, with homages to Rivera, Orozco, and Siqueiros.[2] An homage to Tamayo had been rejected.[3] But by 1960, everything had changed. The 1960 Biennial emphasized the abstractionists, giving Rufino Tamayo "singular attention" as well as the International Award of Painting.[4]

In the debates over abstraction and realism, the TGP was criticized. A particularly hostile discourse took place between José Luis Cuevas, the "symbol and spokesman against social realism," and Méndez, the "literal embodiment of the Taller." [5] Cuevas caricatured Méndez; Méndez disparaged Cuevas.[6] The tensions led Pablo to conclude about 1960, "I think this year is going to be like the temperature—of drought and dust storms, and no good harvest for the crops as well as for painting." [7]

The internal divisions in the TGP would prove fatal: its political divide between socialist and Communist members split wider over whether to support a boycott of the 1960 Biennial to protest the government's arrest of Siqueiros for disorderly conduct in connection with his speaking out against the policies of President López Mateos.[8] (He was actually arrested, according to Schreiber, for his support of the railroad strikes.)[9]

The TGP, along with the Frente Nacional de Artes Plásticas, founded by TGP members, officially refused to participate in the Biennial and published a statement to that effect.[10] Hundreds of Mexican artists ultimately boycotted the event to protest the actions of López Mateos's government.[11]

But Méndez, Pablo, Yampolsky, and Beltrán (the "Méndez faction" of the TGP) had supported the candidacy of López Mateos. They also chose to exhibit and accused the other TGP artists of not participating because they had no work to show.[12] Méndez was not about to criticize the government of López Mateos, who became the main backer of his publishing venture.[13] Moreover, Méndez was not going to help Siqueiros, whose actions against Trotsky had landed Méndez in jail twenty years earlier.

Méndez's refusal to join the boycott paid off. He was awarded the top prize in printmaking at the Biennial.[14] The Partido Popular also (Méndez had been kicked out in 1958) had refused to criticize the government's actions against Siqueiros.[15] Francisco Mora, Catlett's husband, left the Partido Popular because of this.[16] Mora said that Méndez, Pablo, Beltrán, and Yampolsky ultimately joined the "ruling party," meaning the PRI.[17] Catlett's explanation for the problems was simple, "Leopoldo was working with the PRI . . . ." [18] The division grew and it ultimately was the final nail in the coffin of the TGP of Méndez and Pablo. Méndez left the TGP and Pablo followed shortly thereafter, at the end of 1960.[19] The squabbling, however, would persist for decades, with demand letters flying back and forth regarding possession of the group's archives, and accusations that some members sold valuable prints created by others.[20]

Méndez was now close to López Mateos. Méndez "renounced the militancy of the TGP" and was able to get a meeting with López Mateos, resulting in his backing Méndez's new publishing company, El Fondo Editorial de la Plástica Mexicana, and its first book, the massive, bilingual *La pintura mural de la Revolución Mexicana* (*Mural Painting of the Mexican Revolution*).[21] Pablo, one year later, likely used these connections with the president to obtain Mexican citizenship.[22] In the meantime, these connections may have helped him avoid the harassment and threats of deportation that U.S.-citizen artists in Mexico were suffering.

Still, in the early 1960s, Mexico was deporting U.S. citizens thought to have Communist connections. In April 1960, sixteen residents of San Miguel de Allende were taken to the border—six wearing their nightclothes. This included U.S. citizens married to Mexicans. Only one was permitted back into Mexico (under Section 33 if a foreigner is deported from Mexico he or she can't return).[23]

Elizabeth Catlett, a U.S. citizen, had found that when she visited New York and Washington, D.C., in 1961, few of her friends from the 1940s were willing to be seen with her. They "maintained a careful distance from her." [24] In 1960, Catlett chose to become a Mexican citizen and filed the requisite papers. Two years later, she was granted citizenship on the basis of her marriage.[25]

Pablo did not have to jump through such hoops. He sought and was granted his Mexican citizenship in 1961 by presidential decree based on his service to Mexico.[26] This protected María from having her husband deported.

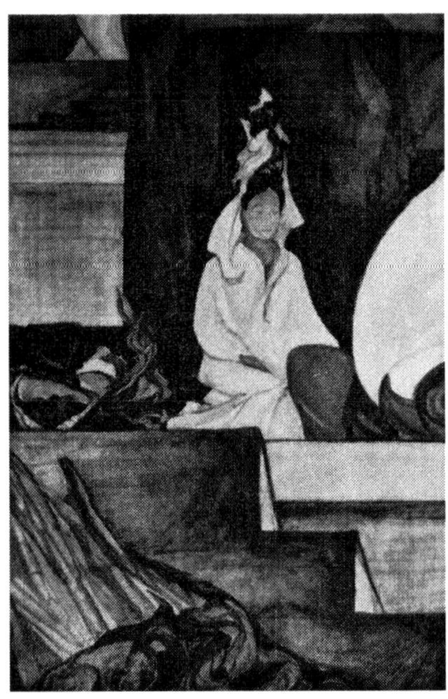

47

THE 1960s

Pablo's departure from the TGP and marriage to María marked a turning point in his art and his life. During the remaining years of his life, Mexico was ruled by very corrupt governments of the PRI—Díaz Ordaz, Luis Echeverría, José López Portillo, and Miguel de la Madrid, whose violence toward the left came to be called the PRI's "Dirty War." [1] But Pablo and Maria shrewdly (being very aware of the dynamics of Mexico's politics and its art world) put politics aside, leaving to the younger generation the formidable challenge of fighting political injustices, and instead focused on Pablo's art career.

Pablo had learned in the 1950s the benefits of staying away from all but the most tolerated political matters in Mexico, and María, who assumed responsibility for making Pablo's art profitable, likely concurred. Pablo was close to the PRI from the time President López Mateos of the PRI granted him his citizenship in 1961 until his death in 1983, when President Miguel de la Madrid's administration gave him a state funeral.

Had Pablo and Maria appeared to each other to be political activists when they met, they quickly set aside any such roles. Maria said that Pablo's "willingness to help around the house and to go over with her at the end of the day what had been done and what was left to do was more important than the social and political issues that had existed between them at the beginning." [2] Pablo, who had spent twenty-five years collaborating with other artists on a daily basis, became, according to María, "a very solitary person."

Pablo's TGP work continued to be displayed and met with criticism from younger artists who thought the TGP was living in the past. Bellas Artes included his work in an exhibit of prints sent to Brazil for the Sixth Biennial of Contemporary Painting.[3]

His work was also included in an October 1961 exhibit of Mexican lithographs of the TGP at La Galería de Arte Misrachi.[4]

But Pablo stepped aside in *la lucha*—the fight. Unlike Siqueiros, Pablo was not involved in the yearlong demonstrations preceding the 1968 Olympics, or the protests of the Tlatelolco massacre that occurred ten days before the Olympic opening ceremony. These events left hundreds of dead, the majority students, on the streets of Mexico City and the CIA swarming the capital.[5] He watched the unraveling of the dream of Communism, but, Byron Randall said, he was not devastated by it. Randall said that Pablo did not dedicate his life to the political struggle, to improving the lives of the poor: "Pablo dedicated his life to art," he said. Terry Goldblatt also said, "He dedicated his life to art, not to the cause of the worker." [6] This contradicts the image Pablo has in Mexico. Perhaps Pablo was more open with his friends from the United States. With them, he didn't have to constantly prove that he was Mexican or strive to be accepted by them through always being preoccupied about the fate of Mexico's workers, peasants, or archeological treasures. They would never believe he was Mexican and simply accepted him as an American, one who cared about the poor and oppressed, loved Mexico, and dedicated his life to art.

Pablo was now in his studio primarily creating art that María believed would sell, works that would appeal to collectors, art that did not contain angry faces, or ragged clothes or guns. Byron Randall said that María encouraged him to create work that was more saleable.[7] "There was a big change in him after his marriage," Terry Goldblatt said, "he became a part of the establishment." [8] Pablo's paintings began focusing more on historical events and romanticizing Mexico's landscape and Indian culture, and less on social realism and depicting the struggle of the worker or *campesino*. In the 1960s, "he began producing murals and prints more centered on historical and cultural themes, but without losing sight of the things that were happening in the country and the world." [9] Some friends and artists were happy with the turn his art took. Emily Edwards wrote to Jean and Zohmah Charlot about an exhibit of Pablo's work in Mexico in 1965, saying that Pablo's old friend Bodil [Christensen] "likes it VERY MUCH!" "She says that his color is wonderful, and that there is such force in his paintings; also, that he has gotten away from painting only workmen!" Edwards added that she was so "glad that he has the great honor of holding an exhibit in Bellas Artes," and hoped that Charlot would have one there too.[10]

Edwards's comments on her own Vietnam wartime political activity may have spoken for Pablo as well: she said, "I haven't stood in demonstrations in the body but my spirit is right there with those in the line." [11] Pablo too no longer fought *la lucha* in the outside world; he fought it in his heart.

Paintings Pablo did in the early 1960s, after he married María, show a bold, confident brushstroke and romantic themes. In 1962, he painted *El novio* (*The Boyfriend*), showing a man in the white clothes of a *campesino* leaning against a stucco wall patiently waiting. Overhead are the lush leaves of tropical trees whose white flowers contrast against a deep black sky. Everything about the piece is still and tranquil.

Pablo received a flurry of mural commissions and painted murals that were intense in color and line and exuberant in theme. In 1960, he painted a mural, *Tenochtitlán libre* (*A Free Tenochtitlán*) in the José Rubén Romero Theater at the University of Michoacán, in Morelia. And in 1961, he painted *Mercado interior indígena* (*Inside Indian Market*) in Mexico City's National Bank of Foreign Exterior. In 1963 and 1964, he painted three murals, *Paisaje tarahumara* and *Dios del fuego* (*Tarahumara Landscape* and *God of Fire*) and *Boda indígena en el pueblo de San Lorenzo* (*Indian Wedding in the Town of San Lorenzo*) in Mexico City's

National Museum of Anthropology. The *Dios del Fuego* mural depicts a Tarascan Indian wedding ceremony in which women display the typically Tarascan feather work in massive headdresses. Pablo uses sweeping brushstrokes to show the volume and movement of the women's colorful skirts as they arrange for the wedding. A sapphire blue sky covers over and seems to run into rich, turquoise mountains, giving a feeling of abundance.

For the first time since 1934, Pablo was working entirely on his own. He was faced with supporting himself and his wife through art independent from the TGP, in a market that was eager for portrait painting, landscapes, and other paintings of a nonpolitical nature—the types of paintings he and other artists had once condemned as bourgeois.

Pablo generally would paint all morning until María called him down to eat, and then paint all afternoon. María often would want him to go out to meet some of her friends. While he was out, he would be thinking about painting. And when he came home, he would try to paint some more.[12]

In 1968, Pablo and María met Luis and Lea Remba when they asked him to restore a 1928 painting of his that they had purchased. Pablo did, and when they tried to pay him, he said he should pay the Rembas for the pleasure of restoring it and asked if he could borrow it for an exhibit of his work at Bellas Artes. Luis Remba, who was trained as a mechanical engineer, had just taken over the print shop of his father in Mexico's City's Plaza Santo Domingo.

The Rembas printed a portfolio of Pablo's lithographs and Pablo was happy with the quality. They adapted their offset machines to better print lithographs, and developed a process whereby, rather than draw on a stone, the artist drew on a zinc or aluminum plate and then the work was printed on an offset press.

José Sánchez, the former TGP printer, came to work for the print shop, which was called the Taller de Gráfica Mexicana (Workshop of Mexican Prints). Pablo and María also brought Méndez and other TGP artists to the Rembas. "After work, the artists would come to the studio to print," Luis said. "We divided up the prints; we would sell ours in a gallery we set up." Unlike the TGP, this workshop was not political. Its name did not contain the word *popular* (people's). "Any artist could come; their political beliefs didn't matter. We invited everyone," Luis Remba said.

The operation grew over the years and the Rembas printed the work of many well-known artists. They eventually opened the Galería del Círculo (Circle Gallery) on Hamburgo Street in the Zona Rosa. In 1984, they were invited by the University of California at Los Angeles to open a print shop and give classes. Today, their company, Mixografía, occupies a two-story midcentury building in downtown Los Angeles, and includes a gallery and a voluminous and spotless print shop. They make a special paper used to print three-dimensional works of Donald Sultan, John Baldessari, Helen Frankenthaler, Ed Ruscha, and other internationally known artists, using a technique they developed for Rufino Tamayo. "Pablo and María helped us," Luis Remba says, sitting with his wife in a conference room surrounded by works of Tamayo, Sultan, Baldesarri, and Ruscha on the bright white walls. "They introduced us to artists. It was their idea to do the Taller. It changed our lives."

The Rembas and the O'Higginses became good friends and spent many weekends together, traveling all over Mexico.[13] "Mexico was Pablo's obsession," Lea Remba said.

This close friendship would come to an abrupt end seven years later.

The Rembas said that Pablo was never fully accepted in Mexico and suffered a lot because of it. Even after he had devoted all of his life to Mexico, "he could never be accepted totally, because he was a gringo. María complained a lot about this. He was respected, but there was always this barrier," Lea Remba said.[14]

In a way, Pablo took on an almost impossible challenge. The Mexican identity that the revolution and the revolutionary artists helped create was, to varying degrees, inherently anti-U.S. Thus, ironically, Pablo's role in perpetuating the leftist "revolutionary" movement was somewhat self-defeating.

In his study of identity, Nobel laureate Amartya Sen discusses how people choose their identity from the range of identities available to them based on where they come from (nationality, ethnicity, family, religion, profession).[15] Usually, there is a limit to the identities available. Sen, an East Indian man, says "I cannot readily choose the identity of a blue-eyed teenage girl from Lapland." [16] Pablo too had a variety of identities "available" to him, which he could have adopted with little difficulty: artist, Communist, activist, international traveler, teacher, lover of Mexican culture (like Frances Toor and Jean Charlot), and even a naturalized Mexican citizen like Catlett or Yampolsky. But he seemed to want to be accepted as a native Mexican. He set himself up for a major challenge, and at the same time, in working to keep the "revolutionary" flames burning, he undermined his ability to achieve this dream.

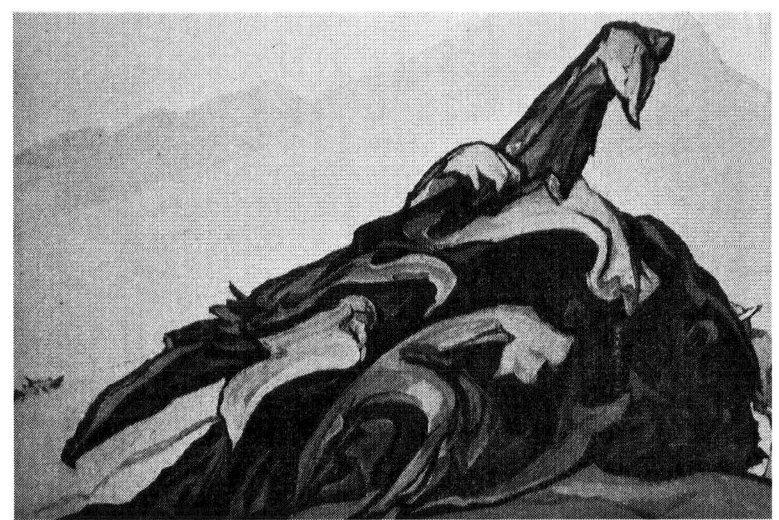

48

ANGUSTIA

By the 1970s Pablo's connection with the government and his isolation from the center of activism was sealed. The Taller de Gráfica Popular, as it had been originally envisioned, was distant history. Pablo was now very mainstream, very tied to the government's cultural machine. Boullosa says that for her, a young artist in the 1970s, "[The TGP's] art was supposed to be a tool to help society walk toward a fairer future, but they were tethered to the [PRI]—the perpetrators of the Tlatelolco murders, the architects of the disastrous Mexican government." [1]

In 1971, Pablo received from that government the Elias Sourasky prize in the arts, along with a fifty-thousand-peso award and a tribute in the opulent Palacio de Bellas Artes, Presencia de Pablo O'Higgins en la pintura Mexicana (The Presence of Pablo O'Higgins in Mexican Painting).[2] These honors were awarded by the government of Luis Echeverría, which, the same year, slaughtered between seventy and one hundred people, mainly students in Monterrey resisting conservative change at the Autonomous University of Nuevo León. The Mexico City students were attacked by Echeverría's "Falcons," "thugs-for-hire enlisted, trained, and armed by the Federal District government to carry out the dirty work of suppressing the student movement in Mexico City." [3] The slaughter is known as the Corpus Cristi Massacre.[4] Genocide charges were later brought against Echeverría but were ultimately dismissed. These atrocities did not appear in Pablo's work, nor does it appear that he or María, who was from near Monterrey, protested the violence.

The paintings Pablo produced in the post-TGP, María period of his life may not have been the paintings in his heart, but he put his heart into them, trying to remain true to his beliefs. He refused to call paintings of people portraits, instead calling them just paintings.[5] He continued to claim that he did not paint to sell. Perhaps against María's marketing recommendations, he often included the worker and *campesino* in his landscape paintings, which over time came to depict nature as overwhelming and hostile, and human figures as minute and transitory. Lines that once were calm and straight become undulating and diagonal. (See pages 215, 219, and 225.)

The change in Pablo's lines can best be seen in his depiction of the maguey plant. The maguey, to Pablo, was a symbol of the "harshness and toughness of life and the will of the people to survive." [6] It is a plant that provides *campesinos* with food, clothing (via its fibers), and refreshment, and also the potent death liquor, pulque. Pablo's personal style developed when his lines began following the sharp, undulating shape of the maguey. The closer Pablo came to the end of his life, the more his work reflected this symbol.[7]

In his early days in Mexico, when Pablo traveled the countryside with Charlot, he drew the maguey as a friendly bush with four or five little fingers of leaves reaching skyward. (See page 89.) Fifty years later his magueys were twisted, contorted, and threatening. Several of Pablo's maguey paintings and lithographs from the 1970s reflect that he was having thoughts about death. A 1971 painting titled *Quiero vivir* (*I Want to Live,* p. 219) shows a withered monster of a maguey leaning heavily to one side, as though it might collapse. A year later, in *Acarreando leña* (*Carrying Firewood,* p. 225), the heavy leaves of the maguey appear to pierce the body of the *campesina* and dwarf the mountains of the background.[8]

Pablo's work increasingly depicted the Mexican landscape as harsh and inhospitable and the *campesino*'s fate as bleak. A common remark about Pablo during the years following his marriage and his departure from the TGP is that he just wanted to be left alone to paint.[9] María described his response to art exhibits: "If he thought the exhibit was good, he'd say, 'I have to leave, I want to paint.' If he thought it was bad, he'd say, 'I have to leave, I want to paint.' " [10]

Yet it does not appear that Pablo found peace in the quiet of his perfect light-filled studio, in a comfortable home with a wife making sure he had nothing to worry about but his art. Gómez said, "One of the legacies that Pablo left to the artists was the idea that an artist does his work not for lucrative purposes but as a means to show through his art the reality of the country, the struggle of the peasants and workers. . . . [Pablo] told us that we had to show the worker dressed exactly how he is, not in very clean, neat clothing but with the real colors, dirty, doing his work, suffering, struggling." [11]

Pablo wanted his students to show the cruelty of the Mexican landscape. "But specially with landscapes, he wanted them to be not like French ones, refined, but with strong colors, but cruel, with more contrast. He succeeded in accomplishing that, because he could feel it."

With María at the helm, however, Pablo's workers were no longer living on the streets, as was his 1936 *Vida de perros* (*Life of Dogs*, page 125) or standing in ragged clothes, smoking, as in *El fumador* (*The Smoker*), 1940. His paintings from the period after he married María are primarily portraits and vivid, colorful landscapes that depict Mexico as stunningly beautiful, from its lush jungles to its harshest deserts. Human figures, which in earlier years had figured prominently, now appear, sometimes tiny, sometimes seemingly added in as an afterthought.

According to María, each of Pablo's beautiful landscape paintings, even those including not a single worker or *campesino* (see p. 231), were true to his ideals in that they were depicting the harsh lives of the workers. She said, of his dramatic oil, *Guanajuato at*

Night (p. 213), showing a neat white stucco house against a deep peaceful cobalt sky, that "the light in the window symbolizes the presence of man in the painting."[12] Of another striking landscape, María said it represented "the only beauty [the campesinos] have" in their lives, a comment that presumes a lot. Pablo, however, subscribed to social realism, in which the viewer did not have to engage in intellectual analysis to determine meaning. When he wanted to show a worker suffering, he showed a worker suffering, and did not use symbolism like a light in a window, or use beauty to demonstrate what they didn't have.

As the subject matter of Pablo's paintings changed, so did his style. Pablo's student Daniel Gómez observed changes in his work reflecting what he called an anguish or unrest (he used the word *angustia*, meaning anguish or despair). María, upon hearing Gómez say this, interjected adamantly, "*¡No tuvo!* [He didn't have it!]"[13]

Gómez said, "In his first paintings, in the 1920s, Pablo shows more calmness. Straight lines. Later his paintings show him as a man who suffered a lot. That is represented by his curvaceous lines. If he were calm his lines would have been straighter. The lines in zigzag show the anguish, unrest. The movement of lines express the agitation inside. Maybe personal worries besides of that of the country? At the end, his lines were very undulated, representing anxiety, worry." [14]

More than many of his oil paintings, Pablo's lithographs in the 1970s continue to reflect his love of Mexico and the Mexican worker and *campesino*. Just as LeConte Stewart had told his students to "paint what you love," Pablo chose as his subjects the people he saw and met in the countryside and villages, who, in his view, lived simple lives connected to nature. His depictions of *campesinos* show them increasingly a part of their natural environment and nearly integrated into its natural elements. In one he has drawn the trunk of an enormous tree. A woman in front of the tree is so much a part of it, she is barely distinguished from the tree itself.[15] Pablo, who never felt that he fit in growing up in Utah, may have been expressing an ideal of belonging, something he strove for his entire life.

During the last years of his life, Pablo appeared troubled and was preoccupied with dying.[16] At one point, he said, "I frequently ask myself how much life I have left at my age, and I worry about knowing what I am going to leave for Mexico." [17] Undoubtedly, he was concerned about his legacy, and personal troubles may have added to his preoccupation.

Pablo was also deeply affected by the death of Méndez in 1969, of cancer that had gone undiagnosed.[18] In addition, he may have felt apprehensive about the major retrospective of more than two thousand of his works in Mexico City in 1971 and his receipt of the Elías Sourasky prize. These tributes, like "lifetime achievement awards" may have marked that his career was nearing completion.

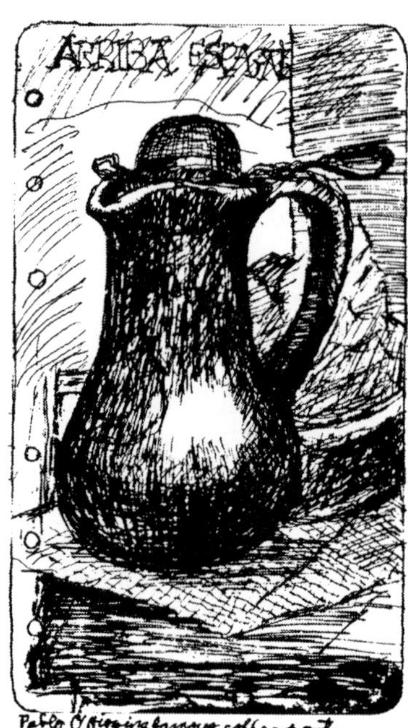
Pablo O'Higgins famous coffeepot.

49

MIGUEL

In 1971, María and Pablo invited a young Zapotec Indian from Oaxaca, Miguel Orozco, age sixteen, to live with them. Pablo needed help, and María and Pablo gave Miguel room and board and the opportunity to attend public high school (which didn't exist in his village), and then college at Instituto Politécnico Nacional (National Polytechnic Institute). In exchange, he was available to work, in his words, as a *mozo* (servant), from early morning until everyone in the household went to bed at night.[1] He lived and worked in the O'Higgins home for four years.

Thirty-three years later, Orozco, who has a degree in economics from the Politécnico, is a counselor in Seattle assisting Spanish-speaking clients with issues of addictions and domestic violence. He says he is grateful for Pablo and María giving him a roof over his head and food and, even more, for the opportunity to know Pablo and learn about art and literature, as well as the classical music that always played in their house. Living in the O'Higgins home for four years, he came to know Pablo and Maria very well.

Orozco said Pablo "had an *hermosura* [beauty]." "He had an *alma enorme* [a great soul], and you felt it in his handshake, his embrace. He was very innocent." Orozco says Pablo was "pure of heart," in his art. "He took out his heart" and put it in his depictions of Mexican people. He fell in love with the people of Mexico." Orozco said, "He was not only humble, but a simple person."

Orozco ground Pablo's colors, cleaned his brushes, picked up materials, delivered paintings, and modeled for Pablo. He accompanied Pablo to the countryside to take *apuntes* (notes). Pablo would see simple people and become interested in their expression,

Orozco said. "We'd stop and talk and get to know them. Pablo would write in his notebook, and later, in the studio, use the sketches for a painting. He would make them emotional, alive. He gave them life. I loved this about him. It was beautiful. He captured them eating, sleeping, standing. What interested him was what they were doing, what they were feeling."

Orozco observed Pablo making very extensive mathematical calculations for a painting. "*Era un genio* [He was a genius]," Orozco says. Pablo appeared to have extensive formal training in art.

Pablo wanted only to paint. "Drink coffee and paint," Orozco said. "He'd get up in the morning, put on his overalls, and go to his studio to paint. Come down for more coffee and paint. Sometimes he'd forget to eat. At the end of the day, he'd quit painting and go to bed. . . . He was always quiet, alone in his studio, immersed in his own world of painting." [2]

María was responsible for everything, Orozco said. Art people, agents, collectors, and dealers would come over and talk. "It was like a ritual. They would talk until dawn." This circle included wealthy collectors like Dolores Olmedo. "That was their circle," he said. María would insist Pablo attend functions, but Orozco did not know where they were going. "I never went. I didn't have shoes, and they weren't going to take me in my *huaraches*," he laughs.

María was very active in marketing Pablo. "There was always a lot of talk, writing articles, catalogs," says Orozco, "but nothing of substance." A German photographer who lived nearby produced the catalogs. María was in charge of all of this, and she wrote the introductions, Orozco said.

Orozco said that he never could see what attracted María and Pablo to each other, but that Pablo was happy simply for the opportunity to paint. "María took care of him. She allowed Pablo to dedicate all of his life to art. She controlled everything, including his diet. If he disagreed with her, he would say, 'But, Querida,' and that was all. María was in charge of everything involving the arts and administrated all of art and his daily life as well. . . . Pablo was *muy obediente* [very obedient], and humble. He was like a child in a man's body," said Orozco.

Echoing Rafael Carrillo, Orozco said Pablo was not a person of controversy. During four years of living with Pablo and María, Orozco got to know a man who was "apolitical." Orozco had a hard time believing that Pablo was ever a Communist Party member or involved in politics in any significant way. Pablo observed politics but did not participate, Orozco recalled. "As a person, he was not political," Orozco says. "His politics were in the human condition." [3] Orozco said Pablo came to Mexico "for the art" and by necessity—because art was so tied to politics—"he lived the politics but more as an observer." By the 1970s, Pablo "never spouted Communism—he saw it as a 'historical moment.' "

"His life was no social struggle, no political struggle. They were both from privileged worlds. Pablo had never suffered injustice. María had never suffered," Orozco said. "I never saw her at all political. She talked about social justice but did nothing. Pablo talked about injustices, but never about strategies for solutions. They were intellectuals who knew what was going on, but I didn't see them do anything about it. If they did I would have seen something." Like Randall and Terry Goldblatt, Orozco questioned Pablo's reputation as a political activist for social justice. "He was born to be an artist," Orozco says. In the four years Orozco lived with him, he never saw Pablo "lift a finger" to remedy social injustices.

The thought of Pablo working as an *obrero*—a longshoreman or a welder—struck Orozco as impossible. He didn't have the mental state, said Orozco. Pablo had never mentioned working in manual labor, and Orozco was surprised to hear that María characterized him as a worker. If Pablo revised his history, Orozco was certain that it was "unintentional." "He wasn't interested in the details," he said. He may have been exposed to longshoremen or welders, and therefore said he worked as one. "To him, it would have been irrelevant" whether he had or not. "He was always questioned, but these things weren't important to him."

From Orozco's observations, Pablo was "always an outsider." "He was never accepted one hundred percent. His politics were questioned because of his physical presence," in that he clearly was not a Mexican. "He was a *participante de afuera* [an outside participant]," Orozco said.

Orozco slept in Pablo's studio, often with other Indians whom Pablo allowed to sleep there. "When Pablo decided something, María couldn't stop him," Orozco said. "Pablo was the one who opened the door [to the Indians]."

Pablo did not express himself verbally, Orozco recalled. "Pablo was not a social animal. He was a man of few words. In a twelve-hour day, maybe two hours a day he would speak, the rest, he was silent as he painted." Orozco never heard him speak for more than five minutes. "He had to stop and think of words in English. He spoke very simply, in simple sentences, and he didn't speak much. A lot of that had to do with María. She talked and talked."

In groups, María would speak for him, and when Pablo tuned the conversation out, she would bring him back. But these social events were difficult for Pablo. "He was tortured," says Orozco, "if he couldn't get back to his studio to do his art."

Orozco said Pablo had health issues. "His spine was curved, maybe from standing for twelve hours a day," and he had constant headaches. When Pablo did eat, he ate well, said Orozco, but María was stingy with food. She controlled his diet." Pablo drank little alcohol. "I never saw him drunk," he said.

Orozco says that Pablo influenced him greatly. He "opened my eyes," says Orozco. "I returned many times to see Pablo."

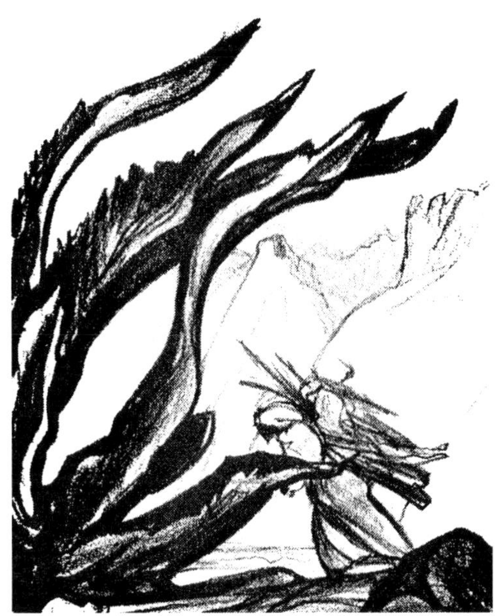

50

MUJER DE ARMAS TOMAR

By the mid-seventies, María and Pablo had developed a wide social circle that included the collectors María had cultivated from the art world, the family of the late Frida Kahlo, as well old friends of Pablo from the United States and from his Rivera days. One of them was Emmy Lou Packard, who had known Rivera as a young teen in the 1930s when her family lived in Mexico and her father, a socialist and agronomist, assisted the government with its *ejido* (cooperative) program. After the assassination attempt on Trotsky, Rivera had fled to the United States (fearing he would be arrested, or be the next target of Stalin), and stayed with Packard's family in Berkeley, California.[1]

After Packard's husband died in 1941, she came to Mexico and lived with Rivera and Kahlo for a year, a year that "saved her life," according to a friend.[2] In 1973, she returned to Mexico City and met María for the first time. Packard taped a conversation or interview with Pablo, in which he explained to her the golden section, something Rivera had once tried to teach her but she hadn't been listening.[3] Over the next ten years, until Pablo's death, Packard and Pablo and María would have a relationship that centered on Packard's time-consuming but ultimately futile efforts to write and get published her book about working with Rivera.

In a series of letters in early 1974, Packard asked Pablo to hire three California artists as assistants. She also suggested that Pablo come to the United States and paint a mural for the United Farm Workers, with the young artists serving as assistants. Packard had commented that Pablo and Juan O'Gorman were nearly the only painters getting mural commissions, and that younger artists had little interest in social realism. Packard maintained extensive correspondence with O'Gorman's wife, Helen, but said that Pablo and O'Gorman didn't get along, because of political differences.[4] María, at the end of a letter Pablo was writing to Packard, wrote a few lines in Spanish, suggesting that Packard organize a small exhibit of Pablo's work in the States.[5]

María, in correspondence with Packard around this time, seems gentle, but in her dealings in Mexico, she was forceful, a *mujer de armas tomar* (confrontational), in Lea Remba's words.[6] In 1973, Pablo and María cut the Rembas off almost instantly when they learned that the Rembas were printing the work of Rufino Tamayo. "The moment that we took on Tamayo, they quit speaking to us. They came and took all of Pablo's half-finished work. They took it all back and quit returning our phone calls," Luis Remba said.[7] "They also told José Sánchez [the former TGP printer] that he could no longer work for us."

The explanation that Pablo and María gave (María, Luis says, "was more angry than Pablo was") was that they didn't want the Rembas to work with an artist who was right-wing.[8] Tamayo, however, was not right-wing, just not political.[9] He had, however, years earlier, expressed anti-Communist views and had come to blows with Siqueiros over them.[10] But, María said, years after Pablo's death, that Pablo got along with everyone, regardless of their political beliefs.[11]

Lea Remba believes that politics was the pretense and that jealousy was the real reason that Pablo and María broke off their friendship. "Tamayo," she says, "was artistically, socially, and money-wise, on a different level." Tamayo, by then, had exhibited extensively internationally. His exhibit at the 1950 Venice Biennial had led to mural commissions and great honors.[12] "Tamayo had made a lot of money and had relationships with everyone," Lea Remba says. "Pablo and María were more isolated," Luis said, "part of a smaller group of artists who had been Communists." "If they had moved out of the circle of Communism, they would have sold more," Lea said. "*Artísticamente* [artistically]," Luis Remba said, "*no crecía* [he did not grow]." [13]

Lea said that María was bitter; she felt that Pablo never received the acclaim that he deserved. The Rembas realized that, though they spent much time with Pablo and María over five years, they learned little about Pablo. "They were very closed," Luis said, "very private, Pablo was mysterious. Like a wall." Like other people who considered themselves close friends of Pablo, such as Rafael Carrillo, the Rembas, too, realized they had never spoken of intimate things with him—nothing regarding his family, his childhood, his hopes, regrets, frustrations. Only of his love of Mexico, Luis Remba said, or "superficial things." Lea said, "He was very secretive."

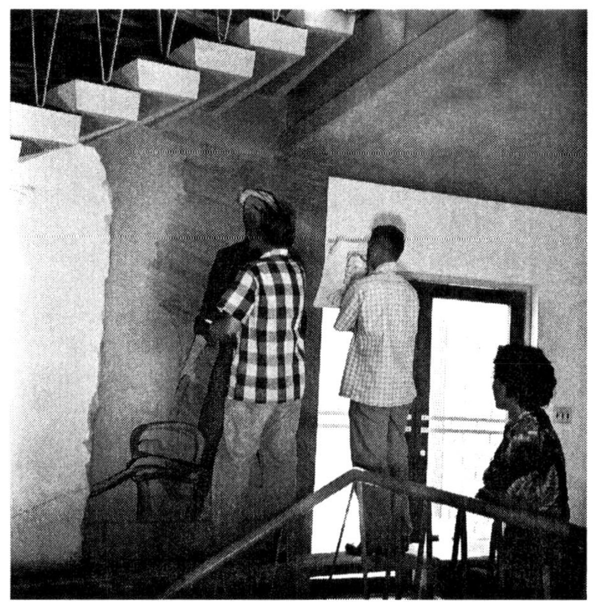

51

SEATTLE, 1975

In the first months of 1975, the war in Vietnam was still raging. The antiwar and civil rights movements of the 1970s, seeking equal rights not only for African-Americans but for Chicanos, were played out in part on college campuses, including the University of Washington.

This was the setting when Roberto Maestas, who was teaching a class at the university on community activism, learned about Pablo O'Higgins's Seattle Ship Scalers mural and turned tracking down the mural into a class project.

Roberto Maestas is a wiry, energetic man. He grew up in a small town in New Mexico with his grandparents, who supported seventeen family members. As a boy he was unsure whether he was Mexican, and he didn't feel like he was American. He described being Chicano as living "in limbo," not accepted by either Mexico or the United States, feeling caught between two cultures.

In 1972, he and a group of Chicano activists in Seattle, angry because of cuts to programs to teach English to immigrants, occupied an abandoned school building after the school district refused to sell the building to them to use as a community center. Soon the building was surrounded by police. The three-month occupation was the beginning of a thirty-year struggle that finally ended when the group was allowed to buy the building. When Pablo's mural surfaced in the spring of 1975, the group was just three years into this very public, controversial effort. Maestas said:

> We were strident, confident, gutsy. We'd occupied; we'd been to jail. We called a meeting with high-level administration—we had the momentum. The highest level was already very defensive because of the layoffs. Their attitude was 'another issue we don't need.' The university was scrambling. They had just hired their first administrator for minority affairs. The student organizations had the momentum. We dropped this bombshell on its lap. It was like stunned silence. We gave them the ultimatum—bring [Pablo] here. They went into motion. [The students] demanded O'Higgins be brought up to let Chicano students learn about art instead of working in the fields. It was a time-consuming negotiation. We didn't trust them one goddamn bit.[1]

The university said, "In no way did we have any intention of hiding" the mural, said Maestas, but to the activists that was an incredible statement. The House Un-American Activities Committee had held hearings in Seattle in 1948 and in 1955, during the same time that the mural entered the university's custody.

During the 1975 efforts, Pablo was referred to by the press as a Chicano artist. "If we contributed to the idea that Pablo O'Higgins was a Chicano," said Maestas, "it was because we were under siege." He recounted the tensions of the time. "We had come out of this occupation three years earlier. We were still having this building under twenty-four-hour security. People would throw Molotov cocktails and threaten us." Pablo, Maestas continued, "was 'Chicano *de corazón*.' He loved the Mexican culture. He was a Mexican citizen. He lived in Mexico. He spoke Spanish. We made him an honorary Chicano."

Emmanuel Montoya, an artist very involved in the Chicano movement in California, said that Pablo could not be Chicano as he was not of Latino ancestry, but agreed that he was "Chicano *de corazón*." [2]

Goldie Caughlan said that her late husband, leftist lawyer John Caughlan, who originally phoned Maestas to ask him what happened with the mural, would have supported calling Pablo a Chicano artist in order to further "the cause." The mural was, essentially, an ace in the hole for La Raza in their fight against the university.[3]

Considering the uncomfortable position the university was in, it is not surprising that the administration did not question La Raza calling Pablo a Chicano artist. But Pablo was not someone who, in 1975, was suspended between Mexican and U.S. cultures and in limbo because of his race or ethnicity. As a blond-haired blue-eyed U.S.-born man he was not subject to the discrimination sometimes suffered by Latinos in the United States.

Pablo came from what is now called a "privileged background" that offered him every possibility in the United States in terms of education and connections. He had excellent grades in high school and the opportunity to attend any number of colleges, should he have chosen to do so. He had enjoyed many opportunities in the United States, as seen by his work at the California Labor School and his mural commissions in Seattle and Hawai'i. Mexico too had offered him every opportunity it offered its own artists, with the exception of the one lost mural commission in 1942.

When Pablo, who was now seventy-five years old, arrived in Seattle, he was still shaken by the immigration authorities' treatment of María. He had told the Rembas a few years earlier that the U.S. government likely wouldn't give him a visa to enter the United States, but he hadn't expected María to have a problem.

Goldie Caughlan, however, said, "María was a Communist or had been a Communist. She was on some list even in those days. John had set up an immigration project in Seattle. He did immigration law. It was the kind of battle John loved." [4] John said that María likely would have a file with the U.S. government.[5]

Perhaps in denying Pablo's involvement with the Communist Party, in describing his trip to the United States in 1945 as fulfilling a "moral duty" to the United States, and possibly in saying he sold the May Day painting to Rivera to finance a trip to the United States to attend a conference rather than to pay for his travel to the Soviet Union, María was trying to protect them both from problems and from any taint of Communism affecting the market for his work. María persistently downplayed Pablo's involvement in Communism, wisely. As the Rembas observed, Pablo would have found a larger market for his work if he had moved out of his circle of Communists and former Communists.

Pablo had shipped to Seattle five paintings, which he said were "among the most important I've done." [6] They included *Watercolor of a Bird on Flower*. He was selling his lithographs for one hundred dollars, working drawings for murals for three hundred dollars, and an "introductory page for [a] suite of lithographs" for twenty-five dollars.

Goldie Caughlan said that during the month in Seattle, Pablo and John became close friends. Everywhere Pablo and María went they invited the Caughlans to join them. Goldie Caughlan said that shortly after they arrived in Seattle, "Pablo went shopping. He loved clothes. He went to the Yankee Peddler and bought a tweed suit. He came back and put it on and showed John." [7] John was polite and said it looked good. The next day Pablo went back out and bought an identical suit for John. He insisted they both wear the suits when they went places. John was uncomfortable with the gift of the suit—and wearing it with Pablo, like they were twins—but it turned out it was his favorite suit," Goldie said, "and he wore this suit for the rest of his life."

Pablo and John shared an interest in music, and both had "romantic notions about Marxism," Goldie said. "John defended Stalin to the end. When we visited Trotsky's house in Mexico City, John was climbing the walls. I'd never seen him like that." Pablo, Goldie said, was "warm, sweet, a bit of an airhead. And absentminded. When working on his paintings it was all encompassing. He was on another planet."

When remembering things, he would "glaze over" as he brought back his recollections. "He didn't need to understand the intellectual aspects of things," Goldie said. "Things were right or wrong."

Pablo taught a mural class through the art department of the university. He discussed the theory of fresco painting. John Caughlan said that Pablo seemed preoccupied and "didn't have his heart in his teaching. I didn't think Pablo took his teaching terribly seriously. It seemed like a budgetary [requirement] to justify the renovation job," Caughlan said.[8] What he seemed to say to his class was that "teaching without doing doesn't amount to much," John said. Pablo never mentioned to the Caughlans that he had grown up in Salt Lake City, and having done so would certainly have resulted in a question about Joe Hill, as Caughlan, who had an undergraduate degree from Yale and a law degree from Harvard, was well versed in labor history. Like Maestas, Goldie was stunned when she learned of the involvement of Pablo's father in the Joe Hill case.

Maestas described the October 24 unveiling of the newly restored mural:

> At the opening, the delegation arrives. There were *taquitos*, chiles, guacamole. I walk over—I will never forget. . . . I walk to the booze corner and the champagne is ready. It's Gallo champagne!"

Gallo was the target of a grape boycott for mistreatment of immigrant workers. An animated Maestas shows how he picked up the bottle and held it up to the crowd.

> 'Listen up!' I say, 'Listen up! Do not take a drink of this champagne!' The organizers and functionaries—maybe the president—they cannot believe the fuckup. We'd been kicking their ass, marching, we'd shut down the cafeteria. Probably some Republican bastard or functionary bought it.

University officials scurried to remove the bottles and fetch some appropriate champagne.[9]

On the way back to Mexico from Seattle, Pablo stopped in the Bay Area. The *San Francisco Chronicle*, on November 11, 1975, reported an interview with him in which he said that throughout his career he has been driven by José Clemente Orozco's admonition "that murals should 'teach those who cannot read,' " which he said was "not a formula for academic art." The article reported that Pablo was "born in Salt Lake City, grew up in El Cajon, and studied for two years at the San Diego Art Academy." [10]

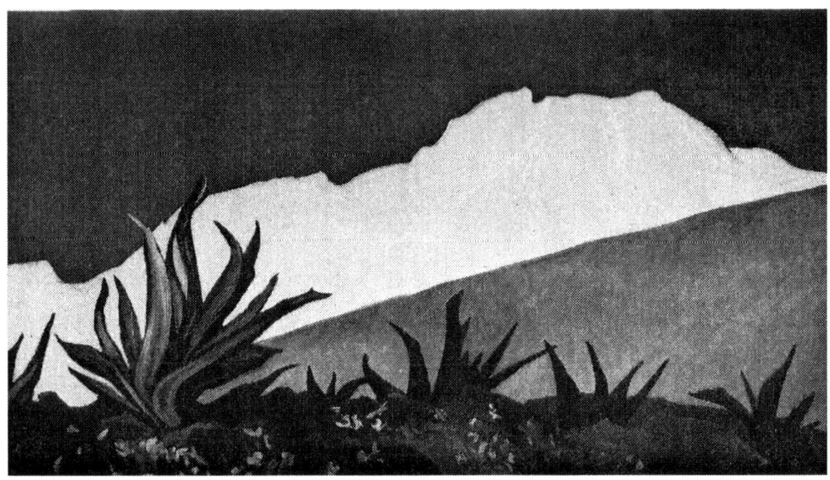

52

WUTHERING HEIGHTS

During their 1975 visit to Seattle, María was charmed by Goldie Caughlan's thirteen-year-old daughter, Kathryn McCormick, and insisted she come to Mexico to live with them.[1] The Caughlans were hesitant, but McCormick was strong willed and the two couples struck a deal that McCormick could go to Mexico in August 1976, and enroll in school so she could learn Spanish.

When the Caughlans sent Kathryn, at fourteen years old, to Mexico City in 1976 to live with Pablo and María, they thought she would have an experience consistent with the values that they believed Pablo and María shared with them. McCormick, however, ended up experiencing something unexpected—something involving high society, archaic courting rituals, an English finishing school, and a house servant—an experience straight out of *Wuthering Heights*.

McCormick had no sooner begun unpacking her suitcase in the guest room of the O'Higgins home in Coyoacán when a young man appeared and invited her out. María urged her to accept and she found herself in a VW Beetle driven (illegally) by the fourteen-year-old boy, and then in a booth at VIPs, a popular buffet restaurant, awkwardly sipping lemonade with Guillermo Kahlo, Frida Kahlo's nephew. "It was a rainy, gray day in August. I remember sitting there scared, with my knees shaking."

Thus began an uncomfortable five-month stay, McCormick says, during which María constantly took her around to show her off to her wealthy friends and enrolled her in a private "English finishing school" (in the words of her mother), where her schoolmates were relatives of the president and children of diplomats. Pilar Portillo, the niece of the president of Mexico, was in her class. McCormick, who had attended integrated, urban Seattle schools on the lower end of the socioeconomic scale, said, "The school was very rigid. I was required to learn to take shorthand in English. It was high school but they had spelling tests and you weren't allowed to erase even if you erased something perfectly and rewrote your answer."

María insisted McCormick abide by finishing school manners in her home as well. "I had to sit in their living room with my hands in my lap while they talked with their friends," she said.

Coming from a home of radicals, McCormick was uncomfortable in the wealthy milieu of the O'Higgins home and the school they enrolled her in, where "you would associate only with children of very exclusive families," she said.

Pablo and María were extremely well connected, McCormick said. John Caughlan said, "They were pretty close to the PRI and they knew everyone in the labor movement." [2] Pablo and María were invited to the inauguration of President López Portillo and took McCormick with them, after fitting her in a floor-length gown. (Prior to coming to Mexico she did not even own a dress; her mother had sewn her some for the trip.) Orozco backed the car out of the garage for María (Pablo didn't drive), and Kathryn wondered why Orozco wasn't invited. McCormick said Pablo and María knew many people at the inauguration and she shook hands with the new president.[3]

Governors would call the house, McCormick recalls. The ambassador to Czechoslovakia was a friend. McCormick remembered art collector Dolores Olmedo and her small dog making a grand entrance into the house with a toxic-smelling cloud of perfume preceding her and a trail of chiffon following her. McCormick went to parties in Las Lomas de Chapultepec, an elegant neighborhood of colonial homes where the president lived, in houses that had whole wings for the children, discothèques, and rolling, manicured lawns. Every Sunday the O'Higginses had *la comida* (the main meal of the day) with the relatives of Frida Kahlo.

It was not just in Mexico that labor and leftists had joined the establishment. In the United States as well labor radicals had gone mainstream. Unions were no longer run by the likes of Harry Bridges and Jack Hall, who kept a bottle of booze under his desk.[4] Holmes, who wrote about Communism in Hawai'i, said that by the 1960s:

> The ILWU had become part of the establishment. Its primary interest was in consolidating and protecting its considerable gains. As Jack Hall said in 1968, 'The radicals are no longer in the unions. They are on the campuses.' . . . When he died in 1971, he had become something of a labor statesman.[5]

McCormick, who was told that Pablo and María couldn't have children, eventually learned that María referred to her as her "granddaughter." But McCormick said she felt like she had been brought to Mexico as "a commodity." María took her around to the homes of her rich friends, introducing her to her friends' sons and daughters. McCormick felt that María was using her to achieve some social goal. Pablo was not involved in this, according to McCormick. "María was the one that seemed to want to show me off to her friends," she said.

An attractive woman with expressive brown eyes, McCormick drew her arms across her chest and shivered when remembering how terrified she was as a fourteen-year-old when María left her alone with men she didn't know in a country she didn't know. "I shake just thinking of it," she says. "It was almost an invitation for date rape."

McCormick was not interested in the rich families of María's friends. But María and Pablo had others in their home: poor Indians. During one of her first nights at the O'Higgins home, McCormick heard a rustle from the hall and opened her door to find an Indian sleeping on the floor of the hallway outside Pablo's studio. "They were the Indians who sold their handicrafts on the street, laying out the two or three items they had to sell on blankets. They were allowed to sleep on the floor of Pablo's studio at night, but never in the guest rooms, even if they were unoccupied," she said. "They were out of the house at the first light of dawn."

A Mixtec Indian girl from Oaxaca, Eugenia, who was McCormick's age, arrived about the same time McCormick did. Like McCormick, Eugenia was learning Spanish. It bothered McCormick to see that while she herself was treated as royalty and given a lovely guest room, Eugenia slept in a washroom behind the kitchen, waited on the family, and was not introduced to the O'Higginses' wealthy friends. Eugenia was not allowed to eat at the table with Pablo, María, and McCormick, but Orozco was, even though "María treated him as a servant," Goldie Caughlan said. "She would ration out food. Kathryn would save food for him."

McCormick was naturally drawn to Eugenia. But María reprimanded McCormick when she tried to lighten Eugenia's load by clearing her own plate from the table, as she did at home in Seattle, or helping with the dishes. McCormick also liked to join Eugenia in her tiny room and listen to ranchero music, which María also looked down upon. McCormick said, "It became clear to María that I was not clicking with her friends, but when Ana [Miguel Orozco's sister] arrived, I was out of there." McCormick knew from María's remarks that her disapproval of McCormick's socializing with Eugenia, Miguel Orozco, and his sister Ana, was a "class thing."

In terms of Pablo's involvement in the household matters, McCormick echoed many others who described Pablo after marrying María: he just wanted to he left alone to paint. He was, in McCormick's words, "disengaged" from the rest of the household and "sequestered in his studio." McCormick said she rarely even heard him speak.

McCormick said she did not herself observe the kind of adoring behavior that others said Pablo expressed toward María. "I didn't see that," she said. "Pablo called her Querida but I didn't hear her call him Querido. It seemed like there was tension in the house but maybe that was because I was there." She added, "He just tuned her out."

Kathryn said that María ran the household, but "I really don't know what she did because she had servants." María was, however, constantly "on the phone, an old black phone with a dial." She told McCormick that if you aren't constantly in touch with people they forget who you are. "She was his agent," McCormick said. Both Pablo and María took literally what Rivera had said, according to McCormick, and believed that Pablo was the rightful "heir of Rivera." [6]

Orozco attended school at night and McCormick during the day. On Saturdays, McCormick helped around the house and on Sundays they visited the villages where Pablo sketched. They would be back in time for *la comida* at the Kahlos' home.

McCormick, like Orozco, says she never saw Pablo or María engage in any activist activities. McCormick was surprised, since she herself had grown up "marching in protests and sending letters." But "María was an intellectual," she says. "I never saw her as a radical or involved in any activist activities. On Saturdays she would take me along with her women friends to Sanborns, VIPs, and on shopping trips. Her friends were in the arts, not activism. She was very aristocratic."

On a trip to the central Mexico city of Aguascalientes, they were all "treated like royalty," she says, "even by today's standards." They stayed in luxury hotels and had people scurrying around them.

Pablo, recalls McCormick, spoke of the United States only in generalities such as *imperialismo*.

Both Goldie and McCormick had the impression that Pablo was from a very wealthy family, and couldn't believe that he had worked for a year or six months as a welder, or as a longshoreman. "He had large, delicate hands," McCormick said. "I can't imagine him doing manual labor."

In December, Goldie and John came to visit McCormick and the O'Higginses. They were very disappointed to find out about the exclusive school McCormick was attending—it was contrary to what they had expected. McCormick was very unhappy and wanted to return home or change her situation. Orozco helped find her a language institute in Cuernavaca and drove her and her family there. For the trip, Pablo and María arranged for them to stay in the Kahlos' luxury guest home, where they felt awkward being waited on by servants.

This trip to visit her daughter was Goldie's first trip to Mexico. Although she grew up poor, on a farm in Idaho, she had never seen such poverty and suffering as she did in Mexico. "I remember being somewhere in Mexico City with María and walking outside and seeing an Indian woman, begging, surrounded by her maybe ten kids. I reached to give her some money, but María wouldn't let me, saying something about how they didn't need it. That was it for me," Goldie said.

To the chagrin of María, it was Orozco—the Indian servant—McCormick would fall in love with and marry, not any of the sons of her wealthy friends. When Orozco and McCormick got together several years later (they married six years later), "María was not happy," McCormick said. "She said something to me along the lines of me no longer being a girl of a certain class."

When McCormick was in college in Mexico City, she and Orozco began living together. They spent a year living in a rental house next door to Pablo and María, but they rarely saw them. "María was very disturbed I'd gotten together with Miguel. He was a peasant, indigenous, and we were living next door in sin. She was completely ashamed." Miguel Orozco too felt María's disapproval. "This is the whole contradiction of the intellectual world," he said. "They say things but then when it comes to their family or friends, they have different standards." He added, "I have no doubt that [María's disapproval] had to do with class." [7]

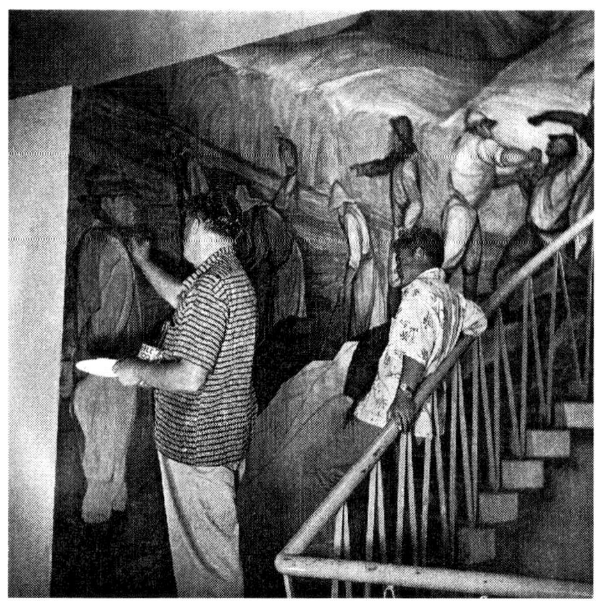

53

FRIENDS

In 1981, the Hawai'i ILWU building, now thirty years old, was in need of major renovations. It looked like Pablo's mural would be sacrificed: either destroyed altogether or chopped into pieces and reinstalled as panels, "preserved through photographic reproduction," or copied by another artist onto panels.[1] Although Pablo was told that "Protest letters and signatures do not help us at all," they did.[2] Mariano Flores Castro, director of Bellas Artes, sent a scathing letter saying that the destruction of the murals would be "an irreparable loss for the artistic heritage of humanity" and that the "suppression of the mural" would be considered "an act of hostility against the principles defended by all countries in forums such as UNESCO and other institutions conscious of preserving the artistic treasures of humanity." [3]

Artists in the United States and Mexico formed a "Committee of Concern [for] Pablo O'Higgins' Hawaiian Frescos." Emmy Lou Packard headed the "Letterhead committee," and created stationery for the group with a full fourteen inches of committee members listed down one side. It included fifty members of the Salón de la Plástica Mexicana, twenty-three high-profile members of the San Francisco arts community, and members of organized labor. The committee entreated the union to keep the murals in place and offered their technical assistance in how to renovate the building without moving them. They said the murals were very valuable, with Pablo's frescos now commanding twenty-five thousand pesos per square meter and his drawings selling for as much as sixteen thousand dollars.[4]

Demonstrating how labor and leftist art had become mainstream, powerful politicians and business leaders in Hawai'i came together to protect the mural. The "Big Five" in Hawai'i refers to the five powerful corporations that controlled the sugar and pineapple industries—the companies the unions were organized to fight.[5] John Charlot, who served on the committee to save the mural, said he was astonished to be in a room with these captains of industry—the very powers the mural railed against—defending and working to preserve the mural. "The whole congressional delegation was represented: House and Senate!" he said. The mural was saved.

Pablo and María returned the favor to Emmy Lou Packard in early 1982, when, although Pablo was in declining health, he and María opened their Mexico City home to Packard, installing her in their upstairs guest room. Packard planned to stay two weeks, but she stayed for more than six weeks, with María and Pablo helping her do things she said she "could never do alone" for her proposed book on Rivera's frescos in San Francisco and a documentary film project on Rivera.[6] Emmy Lou envisioned that Pablo would be on a committee to make the "VERY IMPORTANT" final decisions on her text.[7] Packard accompanied Pablo and María to Aguascalientes, where he had an exhibit. She wrote notes about the trip, including about how they were treated. "We are guests of the festival and we eat beautiful meals across from our hotel—fruit salads of papaya, watermelon, pineapple, cantaloupes, covered with lime juice . . . Filet of beef, many choices, and it's all free (for us)." [8]

Packard's long visit wore on María, with Packard asking for help in many things, including obtaining photographs for her book and filming Pablo at the Ministry of Education, as well as filming and interviewing others.[9] María and Packard began to clash. María said that Packard expected her to transcribe tapes for her.[10] A mutual friend said that Packard "ordered María around," after which María never liked Packard.[11] Packard, who had diabetes, offered her opinions about Pablo's health, which María didn't appreciate.

After she returned to the United States, Packard continued to write letters to Pablo and María peppered with words of warmth, love, and many hugs, along with requests that they run errands for her. She did not take the time to write in Spanish so that María could read the letters, although Packard's archives indicate that she spent hundreds of hours translating songs, letters, and magazine articles between English and Spanish. Eventually, Packard was put into contact with Martha Zamora, who was writing a book on Rivera, and Packard began corresponding with her and requesting her help obtaining photographs for her book.

On April 8, 1983, Packard sent a letter to Pablo and María asking them to call Rafael Carrillo for her and tell him that she wanted him to approve an introduction for the book on Rivera. She also sent a photograph to them that she had forgotten to send to Dolores Olmedo's son and asked if they could call him and tell him they had it.[12] On July 18, 1983, Emmy Lou Packard sent a telegram to Mrs. Pablo O'Higgins, saying in English, "Dearest Maria, Deepest Love, Sorrow for your loss of Pablo. Emmy Lou." Packard's archives at the Smithsonian, which include tens of thousands of pages of her notes, letters, receipts, drafts of articles, and scraps of paper, contain no further correspondence with María after Pablo's death.

Three years later, in a scheduled interview in San Francisco to talk about Pablo, Packard called Pablo a "sweet, kind person, somewhat lacking in a sense of humor." She said he had been "mad at me for pulling him off a mural." She added some off-the-record comments about María, and then made it clear she was interested only in talking about her book on Rivera.[13]

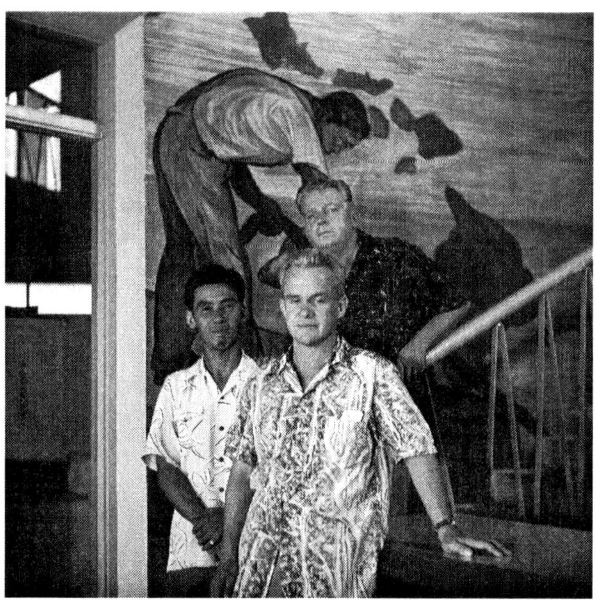

54

PABLO

Pablo never stopped working. He spent the last months of his life doing what he most enjoyed: visiting villages, exploring markets, sketching, taking notes, and painting. Terry and Lou Goldblatt spent his last Christmas with him and María in Mexico City and in Cuernavaca, "where Pablo and María had a lot of friends," she recalled.

Daniel Gómez, too, said Pablo worked very hard even in his last days. "He was a great painter and worker. He never liked to be called an artist." The last times he saw him, Pablo seemed "very distressed." [1] During the last year or two of his life, Pablo was preoccupied with dying. He was getting kidney dialysis, according to Miguel Orozco, at a prestigious medical center. Because of his contacts, he obtained whatever services he needed, said Orozco, services that would not have been available to the average person.[2] Pablo was troubled.[3] Nevertheless, when he was stricken ill and hospitalized in 1983 while preparing studies for a mural at the University of Colima, and the doctor asked him the date of his birth, Pablo engaged in a bit of American humor—which was lost on his Mexican doctor. A Marx Brothers routine from the movie *Duck Soup*, it appears in Mexican biographies of Pablo as if it were Pablo's original joke.

> "Date of birth?"
> "I don't remember, doctor."
> "You don't remember when you were born?"
> "No, doctor."
> "Really, you don't remember?"

"All right, my mother Alice McAfee told me I was born in Salt Lake City on the first of March in 1904 at such and such hours. . . . But tell me doctor, do you remember when you were born?" [4]

Pablo died on July 16, 1983, of kidney failure, the same disease that had claimed his father. President Miguel de la Madrid Hurtado's administration gave him a state funeral at Bellas Artes, but according to Martha Zamora very few people came, and "almost none of the big shots in the government." [5]

But what mattered most to Pablo was not his acceptance by government officials, museums, or rich collectors. Someone once asked Pablo what he needed to become famous, and Pablo answered, "Do you want to be famous like Coca-Cola?" [6] To Pablo, what mattered more than fame or public recognition was being accepted by the peasants who slept on his studio floor and by the common worker, those who had no idea he was a well-known artist, who would invite him into their modest homes, give him coffee, and call him Don Pablito.

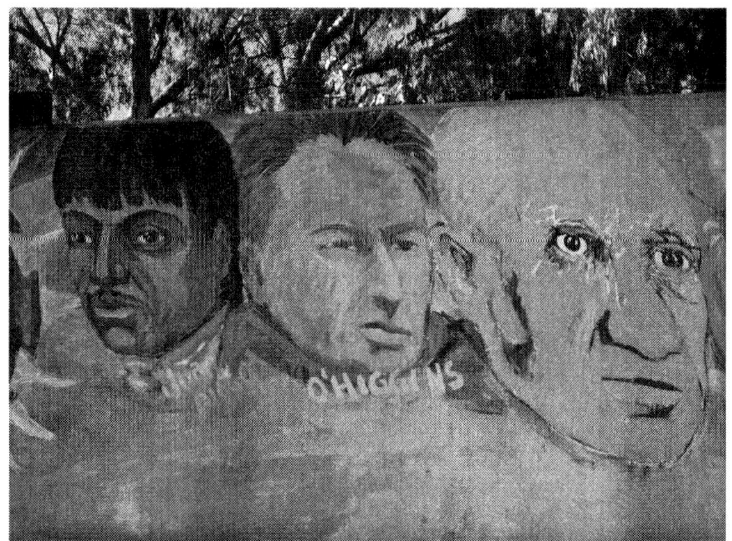

55

LEGACY

Pablo's face appears in a mural in Chicano Park in San Diego commemorating heroes of Mexico, including the Virgin of Guadalupe, Juan Diego (to whom the Virgin first appeared in 1531), Father Hidalgo, Morelos, Zapata, Che Guevara, César Chávez, Siqueiros, Diego Rivera, Kahlo, Orozco, and Picasso; the artists are included "for their roles in revolutionizing modern and contemporary art." [1] The mural, in a park under the freeway bridge linking the primarily Latino Logan Heights barrio to exclusive Coronado Island, has a history much like that of the Centro de la Raza in Seattle.

The area originally was home to Mexicans fleeing the revolution.[2] By 1940, 15 percent of San Diego's Spanish-speaking residents lived in Logan Heights. During the 1940s and 1950s, it was California's second largest Mexican-American community. The neighborhood changed, however, as junkyards moved in, and finally when the Coronado Bridge was built right on top of it.

The year the bridge was completed, 1969, a number of Chicano artists from Barrio Logan attended the first National Chicano Youth Conference in Denver. They returned committed to El Plan Espiritual de Aztlán (The Spiritual Plan of Aztlán), which included the mandate of community involvement. The neighborhood residents had already asked for a park under the bridge, winding around its massive concrete support columns, and they received promises from both the city and the state. The bulldozers that arrived on the morning of April 22, 1970, however, were not deployed to fulfill that promise but to build a parking lot and station for the California Highway Patrol. Residents instantly mobilized and within hours two hundred fifty demonstrators occupied the area. (Residents of the

Coronado Island side of the bridge were given a park.) The protestors occupied the site for twelve days, during which they began cultivating the land. Negotiations with the city began and would continue for years.

Salvador Torres, an artist who had studied at California College of Arts and Crafts and whose family home had been taken by eminent domain for the bridge construction, received permission to paint the pylons. Torres had traveled to Mexico City and studied the murals of Rivera, Orozco, and particularly those of Siqueiros at the Polyforum. Painting began on March 23, 1973. Chicano Park now is the site of the largest collection of Chicano murals in the United States. In 1980 it was designated a San Diego Historical Site.

Every year, the community gathers to celebrate the original occupation of the park. It stands as a "vindication for [residents'] Mexican ancestors of the nineteenth century," who lost California to the United States, "and for their indigenous ancestors of the sixteenth century as well," who were conquered by Europeans. It "reminds barrio residents of the struggles they have gone through, and continue to experience as a community and as a minority group." Pablo is a part of that reminder: his portrait appears between that of Picasso and Juan Diego.

Salvador Barajas, who painted the portraits of the revolutionary heroes around the artists, said, "We wanted to recognize the artists along with the revolutionary heroes because we see an obvious parallel between Diego Rivera and Pancho Villa, David Alfaro Siqueiros and Che Guevara, Pablo O'Higgins and Emiliano Zapata; they all fought for social and political justice. Therefore, they all are revolutionary heroes who belong together in a special place at Chicano Park." [3] Víctor Ochoa, one of the artists who painted the mural and who met Pablo in the early 1980s, said that when talking with Pablo, "I felt a Chicano solidarity with him. I believe he was exiled from the U.S. . . . Painting him at Chicano Park is the connection of the Mexican muralists to the movement here in San Diego . . . ." [4]

Bay Area artist Emmanuel Montoya says that Pablo, Méndez, and the TGP have greatly influenced Chicano artists. Montoya was one of the first Chicano artists to move from silk screens to relief prints. Inspired by pre-Hispanic clay stamps, he began experimenting with techniques used by Pablo and Méndez, and eventually traveled to Mexico to made acquaintance with TGP members.[5]

In Mexico, Pablo stands as an example not only to artists but to immigrants wishing to become Mexican citizens. In 2005, President Vicente Fox told a group of people becoming naturalized Mexican citizens to "Love Mexico always as before you Pablo O'Higgins and Luis Buñuel loved it with tenderness and passion . . . ."[6]

ILLUSTRATIONS

47. Mural detail, Pablo O'Higgins, *Mercado interior indígena* (*Inside Indian Market*), Banco Nacional de Comercio Exterior, Mexico City, 1961
48. *Quiero Vivir (I Want to Live)*, Pablo O'Higgins, oil on canvas, 1971
49. Pablo O'Higgins's coffee pot, Byron Randall, 1954
50. *Accareando leña (Carrying Firewood)*, Pablo O'Higgins lithograph, 1972
51. Pablo O'Higgins and David Thompson working on Hawai'i mural, 1952
52. *Alrededores de Milpa Alta* (*Near Milpa Alta*), Pablo O'Higgins, oil on canvas, 1969
53. Pablo O'Higgins painting Hawai'i mural, with David Thompson, 1952
54. Pablo O'Higgins with David Thompson and Fred Tanimoto, Hawai'i, 1952
55. Mural detail, Chicano Park, San Diego

All photographs of Hawai'i murals taken by Steve Murin.

SELECTED PERMISSIONS

Materials from the Jean Charlot Collection, copyright the Jean Charlot Estate LLC. By permission of the Jean Charlot Estate LLC.

Bayley, Ed., *Letters of Katherine Anne Porter*, p. 67. Excerpt from Letter of Katherine Anne Porter, copyright © 1990 by Isabel Bayley. By permission of Grove/Atlantic, Inc.

David Jenkins, "The Union Movement, the California Labor School, and San Francisco Politics," an oral history conducted in 1987 and 1988 by Lisa Rubens, Regional Oral History Office, The Bancroft Library, University of California, Berkeley, 1993, pp. 47, 51. By permission.

M. Meyer and W. Sherman, *The Course of Mexican History*, p. 588 (7th Ed.) (New York: Oxford, 2002). By permission of Oxford University Press, Inc.

George I. Sánchez, *A Revolution by Education* (New York: Viking, 1936). By permission of Penguin Group USA (Inc.).

T. Michael Holmes, *Specter of Communism in Hawaii* (Honolulu: University of Hawai'i, 1994). By permission of University of Hawai'i Press.

Patricia Albers, *Fire, Snow: The Life of Tina Modotti* (Berkeley: University of California Press, 2002). By permission of University of California Press.

José Clemente Orozco, *The Artist in New York: Letters to Jean Charlot and Unpublished Writings (1925–1929)* (Austin: University of Texas Austin Press, 1974), translated by Ruth L.C. Simms, copyright © 1974. Courtesy of the University of Texas Press.

Photographs by Steven Murin © Steven Murin, 1952. By permission of Steven Murin.

Photograph of Tina Modotti, Jean Charlot, and Carlos Merida, taken by Edward Weston, by permission of Center for Creative Photography, Phoenix, Arizona, and Jean Charlot Collection, University of Hawai'i at Manoa Library, Honolulu.

Images by Byron Randall and Pele deLappe, by permission of artists.

Other quotes and reproductions per fair use doctrine, 17 U.S. Code, Section 107 through 118.

Front cover image: Pablo O'Higgins, 1952. Photograph by Steve Murin, by permission of Steve Murin

Back cover image: Pablo O'Higgins portrait, detail from the "Historical Mural" originally painted in March 1973 at Chicano Park, San Diego, California, USA. © Salvador Barajas, CPSC member. By permission.

NOTES

EPIGRAPH

1. Mexico Ministry of Labor, Introduction to a series of lithographs by Pablo O'Higgins, December 1973. Pablo O'Higgins Lithographs, accession no. 82-48, box 25, University of Washington Henry Art Gallery. Seattle Art Museum Archives.

PROLOGUE

1. E.g., El Foro Cultural Coyoacanese, Exposición—Homenaje, Pablo O'Higgins, September 4–30, 1978.
2. Diego Rivera, *Textos de Arte* (México, D.F.: Universidad Nacional Autónoma de México, 1986), 424–25.

CHAPTER 1 | SEATTLE, 1975

1. *Chicano* normally refers to a person born in the United States of Mexican ancestry residing permanently in the United States. See Raymund Paredes, "Teaching Chicano Literature: An Historical Approach," http://www9.georgetown.edu/faculty/bassr/tamlit/essays/chicano.html (accessed December 19, 2009).
2. Oscar Rosales Castaneda, "The Chicano Movement in Washington State 1967–2006," http://depts.washington.edu/civilr/Chicanomovement_part2.htm (accessed March 26, 2009).
3. John Caughlan's wife, Goldie Caughlan, remembers things differently. She said that in early 1975, Caughlan was helping her with her Spanish homework and suggested they go to Mexico. This reminded John Caughlan of Pablo O'Higgins, whom he met in 1945 when Pablo painted a mural in Seattle. Caughlan called Maestas to ask what had happened to the mural. Goldie Caughlan, interview by the author, Seattle, WA, August 15, 2009.
4. Report by the University's Physical Plant Department, March 4, 1975. It states that on February 20 a student named Ramon Benavidez asked Steven Nord, assistant vice president for Student Affairs, about the lost murals.
5. "Pablo O'Higgins: The Seattle Mural," handwritten draft press release in Henry Art Gallery Archive.
6. Ibid.
7. John Caughlan, memorandum to "Interested Individuals, Trade Unions & Other Organizations, re Pablo O'Higgins Hawaiian murals," December 12, 1981. John Caughlan archives, University of Washington, Seattle.
8. Van T. Morrison, To Whom it May Concern (undated). Archives of the Ship Scalers Union. "Since this is a work of art by a Chicano. . . ."
9. "Major Work of Art 'found' at U," *Seattle Post Intelligencer*, March 6, 1975 ("the Chicano muralist," "American-born Mexican artist").
10. Helga Prignitz, *El Taller de Gráfica Popular en México 1937–1977* (México, D.F.: Instituto Nacional de Bellas Artes, 1992), 214. Prignitz added that his relief prints were second rate. This often is not mentioned when the former praise is quoted.
11. Terry Goldblatt, interview by the author, Mill Valley, CA, May 3, 1989.
12. John Caughlan, telephone interview by author, Seattle, WA, September 17, 1991.
13. Jim Emerson, "Fresco, muralist returns to Seattle community . . . 20 years later," *UW Daily*, October 7, 1975.
14. Ibid.

15. John Caughlan interview.
16. Emerson, "Fresco."
17. John Caughlan interview.
18. "The way Paul O'Higgins lived was just the way all the others lived. None of them had much money. When they had any money they lent it to whoever needed some or shared it." Viola Patterson Oral History interview, Oct. 22–29, 1982, Archives of American Art, Smithsonian Institution.
19. Ibid.
20. John Caughlan interview.
21. Emerson, "Fresco."
22. John Caughlan interview.
23. Kathryn McCormick, telephone interview by the author, Seattle, WA, October 18, 2009.
24. Kathryn McCormick, interview by the author, Seattle, WA, August 15, 2009.
25. Ibid.
26. Daniel Gómez, interview by the author, Mexico City, May 30, 1990 (translated by Amparo Ventura). *Angustia* is the word he used.

PART 1 | CHILDHOOD

1. Elena Poniatowska and Gilberto Bosques, *Pablo O'Higgins* (México, D.F.: Banco Nacional de Comercio Exterior, 1984), 153. "Cuál era su bagaje de viajero solitario?—Era nada más que su corazón, en la aventura apasionada de la belleza, y su pensamiento buscando nuevos espacios de verdad." Translation by Julio César Tapia Guzmán.

CHAPTER 2 | PURITANS & COVENANTERS

1. Prignitz, 214 ("*se funden*," or meld).
2. Anita Brenner, *Idols Behind Altars* (New York: Dover, 1929), 319–20.
3. Patricia Albers, *Shadows, Fire, Snow: The Life of Tina Modotti* (Berkeley: University of California Press, 2002), 151.
4. Seattle Civil Rights and Labor History Project, Special Section Chicano Movement, http://depts.washington.edu/civilr/mecha_timeline.htm (accessed May 11, 2009).
5. Perry Robinson, telephone interview by the author, New Jersey, September 21, 2009. Robinson said, "I can see him to this day—a beautiful guy—Irish—he had an Irish accent."
6. Higgins in England was the diminutive of Hicke, which was a nickname for Richard. The Irish Higgins comes from O'Higgins or O hUigin, from *uiginn*, meaning *vikings*. Irish O'Higgins clan website, e-mail correspondence with author, 2006. The website specifically says that the Irish O'Higgins "has nothing to do with the similar English name of 'Higgins' which is derived from another source not connected in any way to the original Ó hUigín." http://www.ohigginsclan.com/welcome.htm (accessed March 27, 2009). Many O'Higginses lost their land in Ireland due to their "loyalty to their Catholic faith and their Gaelic traditions." Adding an *O* is usually done to "reaffirm some lost sense of identity," according to Dr. James O'Higgins-Norman, MGSI, chairperson, The O'Higgins Clan. E-mail correspondence with author, February 21, 2007. Dr. O'Higgins added, "If he added the O to his name he was def[initely] on the side of the Catholic nationalists in Ireland."
7. Interview in unknown publication in María O'Higgins's scrapbook.
8. Howard Rushmore, "Art," *Progressive Weekly People's Daily World*, February 4, 1939.

9. John Charlot, interview by the author, Honolulu, HI, November 2, 2009; Jean Charlot, "Art and Communication: The Example of José Guadalupe Posada," June 9, 1965, lecture delivered at Wayne State University, Detroit, Michigan. Jean Charlot Collection, University of Hawai'i.

10. Family history provided by Edward McKinley.

11. http://freepages.genealogy.rootsweb.ancestry.com/~smason/combined/fam04146.htm (accessed February 1, 2010).

12. María O'Higgins, interviews by the author, Mexico City, May 26–June 2, 1990.

13. Sons of the American Revolution, *National Year Book, 1914*, 291. http://www.archive.org/details/nationalyearbook1914sons (accessed December 2, 2009). Another relative fought in the American Revolution: William Higgins, born in 1739 in Medford, Massachusetts. His great grandfather, Richard Higgins, born 1613 in England, had come to the United States and settled in Plymouth, Massachusetts. Scotts-Cobb Family Tree, http://trees.ancestry.com/tree/330805/person/-2094475709 (accessed December 2, 2009). Richard's father was Robert Higgins, born in England in 1575. Family Tree in LDS Family History database. http://www.familysearch.org/eng/search/frameset_search.asp?PAGE=/eng/search/ancestorsearchresults.asp (accessed December 2, 2009).

14. The seminary, founded by Presbyterians, "worked across denominational lines to prepare clergy for the American frontier and foreign missions." Faculty participated in the great social movements of the time: the struggles against slavery and for women's suffrage, temperance, and reforms that uplifted the poor. Auburn was one of the first theological schools in the country to educate women and to enroll students from Asia. "About Auburn," http://www.auburnsem.org/about/welcome.asp?nsectionid=1&pageid=1 (accessed August 1, 2007).

15. Matthew A. C. Newsome, "The Migration of the Scots-Irish to Southwestern North Carolina," http://www.albanach.org/ulster.html (accessed February 20, 2007).

16. www.parkuniversity.edu (accessed February 20, 2007).

17. Biography of Samuel McAfee, Ancestry.com, http://trees.ancestry.com/pt/AttachStree.aspx?otid=2269532&opid=-1848638963&oid=24004c7c-6783-48cf-a284-2879eafda5b7&tid=1107042&pid=-603652780&act=set&npp=False (accessed June 20, 2009).

18. Family history provided by Edward McKinley.

19. The information on Greeley and Evans was generously provided by Peggy A. Ford of the Greeley Historical Society, via e-mail correspondence with author, February, 2007. According to James Oles, Alice McAfee's father was an industrialist from Denver. James Oles, *Walls to Paint On: American Muralists in Mexico 1933–36* (Doctoral dissertation, Yale University, 1995), 200, n. 16.

20. *Mayflower Quarterly*, http://www.alden.org/pilgrim_lore/whoheard.htm, states that Greeley said it to Josiah Grinnell, who, like Reverend Higgins, was a graduate of Auburn Theological Seminary married to a *Mayflower* Chapin. Grinnell went to Iowa and founded Grinnell College. While the Colorado town named Greeley that evolved from the Union colony remained dry until 1969, nearby Evans never enforced the temperance laws and it became the place to which Greeleyites escaped for a drink.

21. "Isabelle" McAfee Higgins's death certificate names her father as John McAfee, born in Scotland, and her mother as Mary Stephenson, birthplace unknown. Certificate of Death, State of California, March 28, 1912. Her first name is normally spelled Isabel.

22. Ian Ruskin, *From Wharf Rats to Lords of the Dock*, a play presented in Los Angeles by the Harry Bridges Project, 2005.

CHAPTER 3 | MORMONS & MINERS

1. Caughlan added, "This was pretty much the concept of the Communist Party rather than the Marxist concept of exploitation. The emphasis was on workers who work together rather than individual workers." John Caughlan interview.
2. In a 1939 interview with Howard Rushmore, Pablo said that he was born in San Francisco. In numerous books written by those observing the mural movement and interviewing the artists, Pablo was listed as born in California. E.g., Laurence E. Schmeckebier, *Modern Mexican Art* (Minneapolis: The University of Minnesota Press, 1939), 179; Museum of Modern Art, *Twenty Centuries of Mexican Art* (New York: MOMA, 1940), 187 ("Born San Francisco, California 1905"); *Pablo O'Higgins*, exhibition catalog (New York: John Levy Gallery, 1931, "Born in San Francisco"); Mildred Constantine, *Tina Modotti, A Fragile Life* (London: Paddington Press, 1975), 74 ("Pablo O'Higgins, an American painter born in San Francisco . . .").
3. Gladys, on October 10, 1910, married William Newton Glaeser, 25, of Reno, who worked as a bookkeeper for a restaurant, according to the U.S. Census, 1910.
4. Eduardo Espinosa Campos, *Pablo O'Higgins, Cronología de su obra gráfica* (*Pablo O'Higgins: Chronology of his Graphic Work*, or "Campos Chronology"), http://discursovisual.cenart.gob.mx/dvwebne08/documentos/doceduardo.htm (accessed September 13, 2009), quoting Juan Baigts, "O'Higgins, limpio de corazón [O'Higgins, Pure of Heart]," *Excélsior. Diorama de la cultura*, México, September 21, 1980.
5. Byron Randall, interviews by the author, February 24, October 28, and November 1, 1991, and other dates. Randall and I, and later Pele deLappe, became friends, and met many times in Tomales and Petaluma to talk about Mexico, art, Communism, and Pablo.
6. E.g., *El Minero* (*The Miner*), lithograph, 1949 (in Poniatowska and Bosques, 150); *La huelga de Cananea* (*The Cananea Strike*), linocut, 1947 (in *Pablo O'Higgins: Voz de lucha y de arte* [México, D.F.: UNAM-Gobierno del Distrito Federal–Gobierno del Estado de Nuevo León–Fundación Cultural María y Pablo O'Higgins, A.C., 2005], 23); *Minero* (*Miner*), lithograph, 1974 (in *Humanidad recuperada, obra gráfica de Pablo O'Higgins*, or *Humanity Regained, Graphic Works of Pablo O'Higgins* [México, D.F: Fundación Cultural María y Pablo O'Higgins, A.C. Gobierno de Distrito Federal, 2006], 74).
7. Oles, *Walls*, 207 (Pablo organized miners); María O'Higgins interviews (Pablo organized strike).
8. Richard S. Van Wagoner, *Mormon Polygamy, A History* (Salt Lake City: Signature Books, 1998), 158–170.
9. Historical Record 6:226; Andrea Moore Emmett, *God's Brothel* (San Francisco: Pince-Nez Press, 2004), 21.
10. Van Wagoner, 157, n. 10.
11. Federal Writers' Project, Utah, *A Guide to the State* (New York: Hastings House, 1945), 120.
12. Richard H. Peterson, *The Bonanza Kings: The Social Origins and Business Behavior of Western Mining Entrepreneurs, 1970–1900* (Lincoln and London: University of Nebraska Press, 1971), 21.
13. Federal Writers' Project, Utah, 78.
14. Federal Writers' Project, Utah, 84.
15. Experience of author and siblings growing up in Salt Lake City.
16. Kansas State Historical Society, Sixth Biennial Report, 102, http://www.archive.org/stream/6biennialreport00kansuoft#page/102/mode/2up/search/higgins (accessed December 2, 2009).

17. Utah Heritage Society, *Historic Buildings Along South Temple* (Salt Lake City: Utah Heritage Society, 1980), 1; Federal Writers' Project, 84.
18. *Salt Lake Tribune*, April 7 and 8, 1890.
19. http://www.ci.slc.ut.us/info/area_info/salt_lake_city.htm (accessed May 30, 2007).
20. Salt Lake City's population rose 116 percent between 1880 and 1890, from 20,800 to 44,800. The cost of city lots doubled between 1886 and 1891. In 1889, the Salt Lake Rapid Transit Company installed an electric railway. Electric lighting and telephones had arrived by the late 1880s as well. Between 1890 and 1930, the addition of nearly 100,000 more people strained the city's amenities and services. Salt Lake City website, http://www.ci.slc.ut.us/info/area_info/salt_lake_city.htm (accessed January 29, 2007).
21. Federal Writers' Project, Utah, 78–85.
22. This led the way for fundamentalist Mormon polygamist groups that prosper in the U.S. West, Canada, and Mexico to claim that they are practicing the "true" Mormon religion.
23. Experience of author and siblings at East High School.
24. *Harper's*, May 15, 1858, 312.
25. Wain Sutton, *Utah—A Centennial History*, vol. 2 (New York: Lewis Historical Publishing Company, Inc., 1949), 877.

CHAPTER 4 | ALICE MCAFEE HIGGINS

1. María O'Higgins interviews (Sundays).
2. John Caughlan interview.
3. María O'Higgins interviews.
4. Charles and Blanche sold the Eureka newspaper and moved to Pacific Grove, California, after Hazel's death, then returned to Utah.
5. 1900 U.S. Census data, http://www.census.gov/Press-Release/www/1999/cb99-ff17.html (accessed April 7, 2009).
6. *Salt Lake City Directory*, 1893–95 (Salt Lake City: R.L. Polk & Co., 1893); Noble Warrum, *Utah Since Statehood* (Chicago–Salt Lake City: The S.J. Clarke Publishing Co., 1919), 366–68.
7. O. N. Malmquist, *The Alta Club* (Salt Lake City: The Alta Club, 1974), 88. It later moved to its current location on South Temple and State Street.
8. *Utah Since Statehood.* According to the city directories, in 1890, Edward Higgins and his wife, Lida, shared a home with Will and Isabel as well as John McAfee. Three years later, Edward's family was living at 238 E. 4th So. with two "boarders"—his sister Lucy, then 24 years old, the same age as Lida, and Lida's sister Alice McAfee, who was 28. Edward's brother Charles and his family lived in the rear of the building. John J. McAfee lived a few blocks away at 128 W. 300 So. Charles McAfee, who may have been a relative, roomed at 205 So. State. Lucy Higgins and John McAfee worked as typesetters for the newspaper.
9. Miriam B. Murphy, "Development of Brighton Resort," *History Blazer*, July, 1996, http://historytogo.utah.gov/utah_chapters/mining_and_railroads/developmentofbrightonresort.html (accessed April 5, 2009); *Salt Lake City Directory*, 1893; discussions about procedures with Salt Lake Historical Society staff (September 9, 2009), and San Diego Historical Society staff (October 23, 2009).
10. *Salt Lake Tribune*, April 7, 1890.
11. 1900 data from U.S. Census, http://www.census.gov/Press-Release/www/1999/cb99-ffl7.html (accessed April 7, 2009).

12. Elizabeth M. and William Sagstatter, *The Mining Camp Speaks* (Denver: BenchMark Publishing of Colorado, 1998), 142–43.
13. On March 29, 1945, the *Park Record* (Park City, Utah) referred to him as "the inimitable Will C. Higgins."
14. Ronald W. Walker, "The Panic of 1893," http://www.uen.org/ucme/media/text/ta000663.txt (accessed December 6, 2009).
15. Ibid.
16. Census records for 1900 place the family in Nephi, but Edward Higgins's professional biography says that he practiced law in Cedar City before becoming a judge. *History of the Bench and Bar* (Salt Lake City: Interstate Press Assn., 1913), 148.
17. "A Legacy of Dedication," www.cedarcity.com, http://www.cedarcity.com/history.html (accessed December 8, 2009).
18. Warrum, 368; *Utah Press Association: A Century Later* (Salt Lake City: Utah Press Association, 1996) (re: Will a judge); "Statehood Day, January 6, 1896," *The Broad Ax*, January 4, 1896.
19. Edward and Alice were married in Cedar City on November 9, 1896. "Death of Judge E.V. Higgins," *Salt Lake Mining Review*, August 15, 1926. Reverend Corydon Higgins died five months after Lida's death, on August 21, at age 71.
20. National Academy of Sciences of Azerbaijan Institute of Archeology and Ethnography, *Azeris: A Historical Ethnographic Essay* (Azerbaijan: Chashioglu & ANA Press, 2005), 190.
21. Author interview with visitor from Iraq.
22. "Pioneer Jurist Suddenly Dies: Barrister Heard Famous Utah Mine Litigation, Practiced Law Here," *Salt Lake Tribune*, August 7, 1926, 22. The Utah Supreme Court's decision in *Mammoth Mining Co. v. Grand Central Mining Co.* is published at 29 Utah 490 and 83 Pac. 648.
23. "Death of Judge E. V. Higgins," 17.
24. Higgins's obituary in the *Salt Lake Mining Review* lists 1902–07 as the dates Higgins practiced with Edward Senior; the *Salt Lake City Directory* lists the Higgins and Senior firm from 1904–1906.
25. In 1916, Higgins advertised in his brother's paper, the *Salt Lake Mining Review*, as practicing in the areas of "mining, irrigation and corporate law." In 1925, he listed "corporation and mining practice a specialty." *Salt Lake Mining Review*, August 30, 1916; May 15, 1925.
26. It stayed in print until 1929. Utah Digital Newspapers, University of Utah, http://www.lib.utah.edu/digital/unews/slmr.html (accessed January 28, 2007). Re readers: *Salt Lake Mining Review*, September 16, 1912, 22, http://www.scribd.com/doc/7831499/SLMR-1912-09-15 (accessed December 2, 2009).
27. http://udn.lib.utah.edu/slmr/image/91833.pdf
28. http://udn.lib.utah.edu/slmr/image/91829.pdf

CHAPTER 5 | SALT LAKE CITY AND EL CAJON

1. "Cuando O'Higgins hace contacto con Diego, es porque dos figuras descubren sus afinidades a pesar de no conocerse personalmente. Ambos habían entregado su vida a la causa de los trabajadores [When Pablo made contact with Diego, it was because two people discovered their affinities even though they didn't know each other personally. Both had dedicated his life to the cause of the worker]." Alberto Híjar, *Pablo O'Higgins: Apuntes y Dibujos de Trabajadores* (Monterrey, México: Secretaría de Educación y Cultura, 1987), 19.

2. José Juárez Sánchez, "An Artistic Commitment," catalog of exhibit, Dolores Olmedo Patiño Museum, Mexico Cultural Institute, Washington, D.C., 1995.
3. Mónica López Velarde Estrada, Curaduría e Investigación, Museo Soumaya, www.museosoumaya.com.mx/navegar/anteriores06/febrero/poh.html (accessed March 25, 2009).
4. Alma Reed, *The Mexican Muralists* (New York: Crown Publishers, Inc., 1960), 113.
5. "ILWU Memorial Association presents, Murals by Pablo O'Higgins," brochure, October, 1952, reprint, March, 2005.
6. Caption from an art exhibit, Labor & Leisure, at the University of Hawai'i Art Gallery, March 2004.
7. Salt Lake City directories, 1904–1909. For the first year or so of his life, Pablo lived in the house he was born in, at 1356 South 500 East, a half block from Liberty Park. Charles and Blanche Higgins had lived next door. The *Salt Lake City Directory* for 1907 (reflecting 1906 data) says next to Edward Higgins's name, "moved to El Cajon." Edward Higgins is back in the directory for 1909 (1908 data), residing at 144 So. 11th East.
8. San Diego County city directories, 1904–09.
9. In 1917, the directory for San Diego city lists Edward V. and Alice M. at 3360 30th Street, and Edward as "Wood, Higgins & Wood." *San Diego County Directory*, 1917, 533.
10. Conversation with John Hannibal, longtime resident, at El Cajon Historical Society, October 24, 2009.
11. One Mexican source indicated it was predestined for Pablo to become Mexican because Utah had originally been part of Mexico. Miguel León-Portilla, "El Mundo indígena de Pablo O'Higgins," *Voz de la lucha*, 48.
12. Victor Geraci, "El Cajon 1900," *Journal of San Diego History*, Volume 36, Number 4, http://www.sandiegohistory.org/journal/90fall/elcajon.htm (accessed April 6, 2009).
13. Ibid.
14. Stagecoach Display, San Diego Historical Society, San Diego, October 23, 2009.
15. *San Diego County Directory*, 1908, 664–67; San Diego Historical Society Photo Archives, El Cajon, Books 1–6.
16. *Salt Lake City Directory*, 1909, 1910.
17. Ibid.
18. "Carta de O'Higgins a su madre," title of publication unknown, 13.
19. Records from Longfellow Elementary School, with the notation that Pablo entered the third grade there, after having transferred from Irving.
20. Phyllis Vetter, interviews by the author, 1990–2009.
21. Vetter interviews.
22. Francisco Reyes Palma, "Chronology," in Poniatowska and Bosques, 155. It is unlikely Edward Higgins was ever a judge in California. He was not a member of the State Bar of California, and was listed as residing in San Diego County for only three years (the directories of 1917–1919; he was listed as an attorney during 1917 and 1918). For every year that he is not present in the San Diego directories, he is present in Salt Lake City directories. His obituaries say nothing of him having been a judge outside of Utah. Scholar James Oles calls Frances Reyes Palma "one of the leading historians of O'Higgins's career." Oles, *Walls*, 201.
23. Mitsue Thompson, interview by author, Honolulu, HI, October 18, 1988 (pianist); María O'Higgins interviews (practiced).
24. Yvonne Templin, interview by author, La Jolla, California, July 22, 1991.
25. Palma Chronology.

26. E-mail correspondence with www.prcua.org, January 31, 2007; also, http://info-poland.buffalo.edu/classroom/paderewski/tg.html; http://www.usc.edu/dept/polish_music/PMJ/issue/4.2.01/paderewskiappeals.html.d
27. Ibid.
28. http://www.nebraskahistory.org/exhibits/doll_show/information.htm
29. Poniatowska and Bosques, 8–9.
30. Alejandro Acevedo Valenzuela, "Sinfónias Plásticas de Pablo O'Higgins," *12 la guía de Novedades*, November 4, 1983.
31. Randall interviews.
32. María O'Higgins interviews.
33. Palma Chronology, in Poniatowska and Bosques.

CHAPTER 6 | EDWARD VANDENBURG HIGGINS

1. Edward H. McKinley, telephone interview by author, Pasco, WA, August 25, 1991.
2. Ibid.
3. "Pioneer Jurist," *Salt Lake Tribune*, August 7, 1926.
4. Gibbs Smith, *Joe Hill* (Layton: Peregrine Smith Books, 1969), 107 (E. V. Higgins is listed as the first of two assistant attorneys general assigned to the case). Most of the research on the Joe Hill case comes from Smith's book. See also Philip Sheldon Foner, *The Case of Joe Hill* (New York: New World, 2004), 55. Professor James Oles is the only scholar, to my knowledge, who has mentioned this fact in his writing on Pablo.
5. Oles, *Walls*, 199–200. "The fear of such connection seems the most plausible explanation for the adjustment to his surname."
6. Smith, 63 (lost job).
7. Smith, 15.
8. Smith, 107.
9. Smith, 155, 179.
10. Smith, (quoting the *Salt Lake Herald-Republican*, October 1, 1915), 155.
11. *World*, Nov. 20, 1915.
12. *Salt Lake City Directory*, 1916, 400, reflecting 1915 data, showing E. V. Higgins residing at 37 H Street and working as an assistant attorney general at the State Capitol Building. Pablo's school records confirm that he lived at 37 H Street in the 1914–15 school year (Utah School Register, Longfellow School, 1914–15). The register lists Longfellow School at the corner of J Street and First Avenue, one block from the Higgins home, at H Street between South Temple and First Avenue. In the previous year's directory, E. V. Higgins is at the same address and same job, but Roger Higgins is listed as boarding at 566 First Avenue, the family's prior home. (*Salt Lake City Directory,* 1915, 466.)
13. Will was publishing the *Mining Review*; Charles was engaged in mining in Nevada; and Edward, even while working at the Attorney General's Office, advertised as a mining attorney. *History of the Bench and Bar in Utah*, 148 (E. V. Higgins a Republican).
14. "Utah Labor Leaders Resent A.F.L. Action," *Salt Lake Tribune*, Nov. 17, 1915, 14.
15. *Salt Lake Tribune*, November 14, 1915, 28.
16. Smith, 169.
17. School records provided by Utah Historical Society, May 7, 2009.
18. The Governor's Office was in the City and County Building until November 6, 1915, when it moved to the newly constructed State Capitol building. *Salt Lake Tribune*, November 6, 1915, 16 (the move occurred the night of November 6). The attorney

general's office was also relocated to the State Capitol—the *Salt Lake City Directory* for 1915 lists E. V. Higgins's office address as the Capitol Building.
19. Roger Higgins's obituary states that he was assistant to Arthur Barnes when he was attorney general of Utah. Barnes was attorney general 1909–1916. *Salt Lake Tribune*, November 6, 1928, 28.
20. Byron Randall interviews.
21. http://www.archive.org/stream/reportoncommunis00unit (assessed September 9, 2009). The activities scrutinized were regarding the American Continental Congress for Peace in Mexico City in September, 1949, and the first assassination attempt on Leon Trotsky.
22. It is possible that there was an estrangement between Edward Higgins and his family or Pablo. The 1920 *Salt Lake City Directory* lists Edward V. Higgins living at one address and Paul, age 16, at another. The home he lived in at 1533 9th East was not owned by any family members.

CHAPTER 7 | WORLD WAR I

1. May, 1915.
2. *Salt Lake Tribune*, September 15, 1918 (menu); September 17, 1918 ("death knell,"); September 8, 1918 (ads).
3. *San Diego County Directory*, 1917, 533; *San Diego County Directory*, 1918, 458.
4. Palma Chronology in Poniatowska and Bosques.
5. *San Diego County Directory*, 1917, 533; 1918, 458; and 1919, 447. (In the 1917 directory, Woods Higgins & Wood is at "716 Central Mortgage Building, 1015 1st.") The 1918 directory lists Wood & Wood as a firm, so likely Edward V. Higgins was on his own.
6. S. T. Black, *History of San Diego County* (Chicago: The S.J. Clarke Publishing Company, 1913), 383.
7. Ibid., 384–84.
8. http://www.westminstercollege.edu/library/digitization/yearbook.cfm (accessed February 2, 2007).
9. "Lawyer Meets Sudden Death," *Salt Lake Tribune*, November 6, 1928.
10. "Military Bases in San Diego—World War I (1914–1920)," University of San Diego, http://history.sandiego.edu/gen/local/kearny/page00d.html (accessed April 20, 2009).
11. Ibid.
12. "Balboa Park History," Richard Amero Collection, in San Diego Historical Society database, http://search.blossom.com/geturl?&o=0p&i207&KEY=isis+theater&URL=http://www.sandiegohistory.org/amero/notes-1918.htm (accessed April 17, 2009).
13. "On 17 October 1917 the 145th Field Artillery of Utah was inducted into federal service. They were sent to Camp Kearny, California where they remained for about a year in training. While in California 369 men were taken out of the regiment and sent as replacements in American front line units in Europe. There were several casualties among this group. In August 1917 the 145th started its move to Europe and ended up at Camp De Souge near Bordeaux, France. They trained for front line duty and were making preparations to move to the front when the Armistice ended the war." Utah National Guard records at Utah Historical Society Archives, http://www.utahguard.com/history.html. "Family's new home": *San Diego County Directory 1919*, 447; the dwelling no longer exists; it has been replaced by a cluster of stucco condominiums. San Diego High School was a high school and a junior college. One of Pablo's classmates was Leland G. Stanford, grandson of the California governor and founder of Stanford

University, who later wrote several volumes of histories of the bench and bar of San Diego County, none of which mention Edward V. Higgins. San Diego High School yearbooks, 1918–22. Stanford was president of his high school's sophomore class.
14. Voting records, www.ancestry.com (accessed July 13, 2009).
15. Cindy Baxman, "History of the Mexican Revolution," University of Arizona, http://history.sandiego.edu/gen/projects/border/page03.html (accessed April 21, 2009).
16. Jim Duffy, "The Blue Death," Johns Hopkins Public Health, Fall 2004, http://www.jhsph.edu/publichealthnews/magazine/archive/Mag_Fall04/prologues/index.html (accessed December 21, 2009). The author suggests that previous estimates of 20 million deaths were low and that it actually killed 50 million, or as many as 100 million.
17. Richard Crawford, "1918 Spanish Flu epidemic held San Diego in its grip," *San Diego Union Tribune*, November 13, 2008, http://copleynews.com/uniontrib/20081113/news_1ez13history.html (accessed April 16, 2009).
18. *Salt Lake Tribune*, November 11–18, 1918, front pages and obituaries.
19. Crawford, "1918 Spanish Flu."

CHAPTER 8 | AN ART EDUCATION

1. Swanson, Vern G., Robert S. Olpin, and William V. Seifrit, *Utah Painting and Sculpture* (Layton, Utah: Gibbs Smith, 1997), 41–42; Jeff Anderson, The Paris Art Mission, a presentation at BYU–Idaho, http://www.byui.edu/Presentations/transcripts/majorforums/2006_01_19_andersen.htm (accessed April 21, 2009). The missionaries were John Hafen, Lorus Pratt, and John Fairbanks.
2. Ibid.
3. It appears that Roger stayed at the home in San Diego. The 1919 county directory lists Roger as living there, along with his parents; in the 1920, 1921, and 1923 directories, Roger is listed as living in San Diego but at other addresses.
4. "James Harwood," Utah Artists Project, University of Utah, Marriott Library, http://www.lib.utah.edu/portal/site/marriottlibrary/menuitem.350f2794f84fb3b29cf87354d1e916b9/?vgnextoid=93551df6f1a08110VgnVCM1000001c9e619bRCRD&vgnextfmt=nomenu (accessed April 20, 2009).
5. Ibid.
6. Robert S. Olpin, introduction to *A Basket of Chips: the Autobiography of James Taylor Harwood* (Salt Lake City: Signature Books, 1985), http://www.signaturebooks.com/basket.htm (accessed April 2, 2009).
7. "Lee Greene Richards," Springville Museum of Art, http://www.springvilleartmuseum.org/collections/browse.html?x=artist&artist_id=7 (accessed April 20, 2009).
8. Swanson, Vern G., William V. Seifrit, and Robert S. Olpin, *Artists of Utah* (Layton, Utah: Gibbs Smith, 1999), 40.
9. Byron Randall interviews.
10. Robert K. Murray, *Red Scare, A Study in National Hysteria, 1919–1920* (New York: McGraw-Hill, 1964).
11. Records indicate that Pablo may have lived at an address other than that of his parents during his first year of high school at East High School in Salt Lake City. The *Salt Lake City Directory* and East High records list Paul Higgins as living at 1533 9th East, and his father's address as 47 8th East. According to county property records, the 9th East address was not property owned by the Higgins or McAfee family, nor does the

Salt Lake Directory list any Higgins or McAfee family member other than Pablo living at the address. The next year's directory lists Pablo's father as living at 265 5th Avenue; Pablo is not listed. This would have been Pablo's second year of high school, which, according to school records, he spent in San Diego. The directory for his last year of high school shows Pablo and his brother, Roger, living at the E. V. Higgins residence on 5th Avenue. The 1920 and 1921 Salt Lake City directories list Edward Higgins as living in Salt Lake City. From 1920 to 1923 the *San Diego Directory* lists Roger as the only Higgins living in San Diego County.

12. María O'Higgins interviews.

13. Pablo's picture did not appear in his senior yearbook.

14. East High School records, 1921–22.

15. "LeConte Stewart," Springville Art Museum, ttp://springvilleartmuseum.org/collections/browse.html?x=artist&artist_id=26 (accessed April 20, 2009).

16. Swanson, et al., *Utah Painting and Sculpture*, 120.

17. Richard P. Christenson, "Utah artist strived to 'capture the light,' " *The Deseret News*, June 10, 1990.

18. James Swensen, e-mail correspondence with author, December 22, 2009.

19. Discussions with Mary Muir, professor of art at University of Utah, January 12, 1992.

20. 15 Bytes e-zine.

21. John Charlot interviews.

22. Pablo's name never appears in the San Diego County directories, though Roger's does for the years 1920, 1921, and 1923. In 1919, Roger's employer is listed as the Cuyamaca Club, and his work as "clk," clerk; for 1920, his employer is Ralph Hamlin, Inc. Employment information for the other years is not listed.

23. Palma Chronology in Poniatowska and Bosques.

24. Poniatowska and Bosques, 8.

25. María O'Higgins interviews.

26. The *Salt Lake Directory* for 1922 lists Edward, Paul, and Roger, living at 265 Fifth Avenue, a large Victorian home. The 1923–26 editions list Edward as living at 6 French Apartments (50–56 E. 600 So). 1924 also lists Edward as owning the home on 5th Avenue, so perhaps he rented it out. In 1926, Roger is also listed as living in the French Apartments. Wives are listed in the San Diego directories but not in the Salt Lake directories.

27. Bruce Kammerling, "San Diego Landscape Painters," *Journal of San Diego History*, http://search.blossom.com/geturl?&o=0p&i207&KEY=san+diego+academy+of+art&URL=http://www.sandiegohistory.org/journal/2001-3/imagesbraun.htm (accessed April 17, 2009).

28. "Painting Ladies," *The Journal of San Diego History* 32, no. 3 (Summer 1986) (accessed April 17, 2009).

29. Martin E. Peterson, "An Overview of San Diego Artists," *The Journal of San Diego History*, Summer 2001, Volume 47, Number 3, http://search.blossom.com/geturl?&o=0p&i207&KEY=san+diego+academy+of+art&URL=http://www.sandiegohistory.org/journal/2001-3/overview.htm (accessed April 17, 2009).

30. Bruce Kammerling, telephone interview by author, November 11, 1992.

31. Rushmore, "Art." Re: Communist Party controlling paper: David Jenkins, "The Union Movement, the California Labor School, and San Francisco Politics," an oral history conducted in 1987 and 1988 by Lisa Rubens, Regional Oral History Office, The

Bancroft Library, University of California, Berkeley, 1993, http://bancroft.berkeley.edu/ROHO/collections/subjectarea/ics_movements/labor.html (accessed April 23, 2009) ("David Jenkins oral history").

32. E.g. Yang Jiang, *Six Chapters from my Life "Downunder,"* trans. Howard Goldblatt (Seattle: University of Washington Press), 111.

33. Pablo O'Higgins, interview with Dr. and Mrs. Lester C. Walker, March 21, 1974, Jean Charlot Collection, University of Hawai'i ("O'Higgins–Lester interview"). Pablo was asked about Charlot, "Was he connected with the Art Students League then?" He answered, "I don't know. We would go to see the exhibitions. He didn't . . . . There was no mention of any . . . . I was more like a visitor. I wasn't interested in being in any league or, you know? Because when you're talking with a painter about your own work, you're not talking about are you a member of this or are you a member of that. So I didn't know, but we were living together for four [months] . . . and I didn't see any league there."

34. James Swensen, e-mail correspondence with author, December 22, 2009. See also, Leonard J. Arrington, *Great Basin Kingdom Economic History of the Latter-Day Saints 1830–1900* (Salt Lake City: University of Utah Press, 1993).

35. Rushmore, "Art." Schmeckebier, 179 ("[B]orn 1904 in San Francisco"); MOMA, 187 ("Born San Francisco, 1905").

36. María O'Higgins interviews.

37. Taller de Gráfica Popular, *Doce Años de obra artistica colectiva* (México, D.F: La Estampa Mexicana, 1949), "1922–23: [Pablo] studied in the San Diego Academy of Art, earning his living as a topographer's assistant." Poniatowska, *Tinisima*, 129 (Vidali worked as longshoreman).

38. See Chapter 40.

39. "ILWU Memorial Association presents Murals by Pablo O'Higgins," *March of Labor*, June 1953. Nor did Mitsue Thompson, in my interviews with her, mention Pablo working as a longshoreman. Her husband arranged the mural project and O'Higgins had dinner with them five nights a week during the six months he was in Hawai'i.

40. Terry Goldblatt interview, 1989; Byron Randall interviews; Mitsue Thompson interview; David Jenkins, interview by author, San Francisco, October 4, 1988.

41. Jessica Mitford, *A Fine Old Conflict* (New York: Knopf, 1977), 77.

42. Ibid.

43. Palma Chronology in Poniatowska and Bosques.

44. Juan Tablada, "Diego Rivera," *The Arts*, October, 1923.

45. "The ILWU Memorial Association Building Murals by Pablo O'Higgins" states that he "[s]pent a year at the San Diego Academy of Art"; *Pablo O'Higgins: Un Artista de su Pueblo*, exhibition catalog (Monclova, Coahuila: Museo Biblioteca Pape, 1989), states that he studied there "1922–23."

46. *Doce Años*, Pablo O'Higgins biography.

47. Thomas Albright, "The Mural is the Message," *San Francisco Chronicle*, November 11, 1975.

48. Oles, *Walls*, citing Guillermo S. Rivas [Howard S. Philips], "Pablo O'Higgins," *Mexican Life* 12, no. 2 (Feb. 1937).

49. Armin Haab, *Mexican Graphic Art* (Teufen, Switzerland: Arthur Niggli, Ltd., 1957), 103–26.

50. O'Higgins–Lester interview, Jean Charlot Collection, University of Hawai'i.

51. Poniatowska and Bosques, 9.

52. Palma Chronology in Poniatowska and Bosques. One wonders how reliable mail delivery would have been in 1924 between Salt Lake City and Northern Mexico.
53. Tablada, "Diego Rivera."
54. María O'Higgins interviews.
55. O'Higgins–Lester Interview, Jean Charlot Collection, University of Hawai'i.
56. Ibid.
57. Palma Chronology in Poniatowska and Bosques.
58. O'Higgins–Lester interview, Jean Charlot Collection, University of Hawai'i. ("And then about six months later is when I started working with Diego.")
59. Pablo O'Higgins, "Art," *People's World.*
60. U.S. average income: http://local.aaca.org/bntc/mileposts/1924.htm (accessed April 25, 2009).
61. "My qualifications for writing this book," November 3, 1976, Archives of Emmy Lou Packard, Smithsonian Archives of American Art, Series No. 5 ("Packard Archives"), Notes on Mexico, 1971–82, Reel 5816.
62. Ibid.

PART TWO: THE REVOLUTIONARY YEARS

CHAPTER 9 | POST-REVOLUTIONARY MEXICO

1. Museo Biblioteca Pape, *Pablo O'Higgins—Un artista de su pueblo*, exhibition catalog (Monclava, Coahuila: Museo Biblioteca Pape, 1989), 13. Foncerrada's father worked for the railroad and gave them free tickets to Mexico City. They stopped in Queretero and met Robert Montenegro, who suggested they stay in Hotel Guardiola in the capital. Oles, *Walls*, 201, referring to interview with María O'Higgins.
2. Ibid.
3. http://www.Hawaii.edu/jcf/OthersOnJC/OHIGinterv.htm (accessed on January 17, 2007).
4. E. Zúniga Herrera, D. Hernández, and J. Martínez Manautou, "History of the Population of Mexico," Mexico City, Mexico, Academia Mexicana de Investigación en Demografía Médica, 1987, 1, http://www.popline.org/docs/0835/052145.html (accessed November 6, 2009).
5. Peter N. Sterns, *The Industrial Revolution in World History* (Boulder: Westview Press, 1998), 159–60.
6. Híjar, *Apuntes*, 21.
7. Article 33: "Foreigners are those who do not possess the qualities determined in Article 30. They have the right to the guarantees of Chapter I of the first title of this Constitution, but the Executive of the Union has the exclusive right to expel from the national territory, immediately and without necessity of judicial proceedings, all foreigners whose stay it judges inconvenient. Foreigners may not, in any manner, involve themselves in the political affairs of the country." Supreme Court of Justice of the Nation, Political Constitution of the United Mexican States (Mexico City: 2005), 81.
8. "His Mexico Wealth $75,000, Says Fall," *New York Times*, January 18, 1920.
9. Daniela Spenser, *The Impossible Triangle: Mexico, Soviet Russia and the United States in the 1920s* (Durham and London: Duke University Press, 1999), 17.
10. Héctor Aguilar Camín and Lorenzo Meyer, *In the Shadow of the Mexican Revolution: Contemporary Mexican History, 1910–1989* (Austin: University of Texas Press, 1993), 82.

CHAPTER 10 | THE ARTISTIC REVOLUTION

1. Margaret Hooks, *Tina Modotti: Radical Photographer* (Cambridge: Da Capo, 1993), 77 (description of house).
2. Poniatowska and Bosques, 7 (arrival).
3. Antonio Rodríguez, *A History of Mexican Mural Painting* (New York: Putnam, 1969); J. Charlot, *The Mexican Mural Renaissance* (New Haven and London: Yale University Press, 1967), 40–45.
4. Shifra Goldman, *Contemporary Mexican Painting in a Time of Change* (Austin: University of Texas Press, 1977), 1–4; A. Rodríguez, *A History*, 148–53; Rafael Carrillo, *Mural Painting of Mexico* (México, D.F.: Panorama, 1981), 91. The trend toward social realism and against "bourgeois" art appeared in the literary world as well as the visual arts. For example, the *New Masses*, a literary journal for works with social themes and a "proletarian realism," was launched in New York in the 1920s. It denounced Marcel Proust as the "master-masturbator of bourgeois literature." Harvey Klehr, *The Heyday of American Communism* (New York: Basic Books, Inc., 1984), 72.
5. Originals of the oversize newspapers can be read at the Hoover Institution Archives, Stanford University. A famous photograph by Tina Modotti shows workers reading *El Machete*. Re Comintern: Albers, 129.
6. A joke would surface along the lines that when an Indian was hungry, Vasconcelos would fetch him a copy of the classics.
7. James M. Wechsler, "Mexicanidad," in *Mexico and Modern Printmaking, A Revolution in the Graphic Arts, 1920 to 1950*, ed. John Ittmann (Philadelphia: Philadelphia Museum of Art, 2006), 184.
8. Salvador Jiménez, interview by author, Salt Lake City, October 29, 2009.
9. John Charlot, e-mail correspondence with author, February 22, 2010.
10. Tina Martin interviews.
11. Bertram Wolfe, *The Fabulous Life of Diego Rivera* (New York: Scarborough House, 1990), 188 (re Lupe's rudeness to guests).
12. Albers, 128.
13. *El Universal*, July 14, 1924, http://chnm.gmu.edu/worldhistorysources/unpacking/newsanalysis.html (accessed April 19, 2009).
14. Irma Vega de Bijou, interview by author, Los Angeles, October 22, 2009, recalling Rafael Carrillo talking about Modotti's sexy walk.
15. Albers, 132–33.
16. Albers, 127.
17. Karen Thompson, "Jean Charlot, Artist and Scholar," http://libweb.Hawai'i.edu/libdept/charlotcoll/J_Charlot/charlotthompson.html (accessed November 2, 2009).
18. Ibid.
19. Tina Martin interviews.
20. Michael K. Schuessler, "Frances Toor and Mexican Folkways," *InsideMexico* (March 2008), http://www.insidemex.com/people/people/frances-paca-toor-and-mexican-folkways (accessed May 12, 2009).
21. Alfredo Zalce interview by John Charlot, July 27–28, 1971 ("Zalce–Charlot interview"), Jean Charlot Collection, University of Hawai'i.
22. Susannah Glusker, *Anita Brenner* (Austin: University of Texas Press, 1998), 33; re Bertram and Ella Wolfe: Alicia Azuela, "*El Machete* and *Frente a Frente*," *Art Journal* 1, March 22, 1993, 2.
23. MacKinley Helm, *Mexican Painters* (New York: Harper & Brothers, 1941), 42.

Guerrero assisted Rivera on numerous murals, including the Anfiteatro Bolívar in 1922. Ibid.

24. Ione Robinson, 98.

25. Hooks, 161 (re Orozco not being Communist).

26. Jean Charlot, *Mexican Mural Renaissance* (New Haven and London: Yale University Press, 1967), 114.

27. Founders Society Detroit Institute of Art, *Diego Rivera—A Retrospective* (New York: W.W. Norton, 1986), 56; Hayden Herrera, *Frida* (New York: Harper & Row, 1983), 114.

28. José Clemente Orozco, *Autobiografía* (México, D.F.: E.D. ERA, 1981).

29. Brenner, 252-57.

30. Founders Society, *Diego Rivera—A Retrospective*, 118.

31. Cynthia Newman Helms, ed., *Diego Rivera, A Retrospective* (New York: W.W. Norton, 1986), 59.

32. Zalce–Charlot interview.

33. Charlot ultimately painted nine decorative shields and three murals: *Cargadores (Burden Bearers)*, *Lavanderas (Washerwomen)*, and *Danza de los Listones (Dance of the Ribbons)*. Karen Thompson, "Jean Charlot, Artist and Scholar," http://libweb.Hawai'i.edu/libdept/charlotcoll/J_Charlot/charlotthompson.html

34. Susan L. Aberth, Ph.D., "Rufino Tamayo," http://www.christies.com/Lotfinder/lot_details.aspx?intObjectID=5261958 (accessed November 6, 2009). Dr. Aberth reports that Tamayo was not a full-blooded Indian but a mestizo.

35. Zalce–Charlot interview.

36. Ibid.

37. Ione Robinson, *A Wall to Paint On* (New York: E.P. Dutton, 1946), 99.

38. Ibid.

CHAPTER 11 | RIVERA'S ASSISTANT

1. Karen Thompson, "Jean Charlot," The Jean Charlot Collection, University of Hawai'i, http://libweb.Hawai'i.edu/libdept/charlotcoll/J_Charlot/charlotthompson.html (accessed September 13, 2009).

2. Viola Patterson oral history.

3. Little is known about what Foncerrada did in Mexico or how long he stayed. According to María, he did not ultimately devote himself to the arts. María O'Higgins interviews.

4. Poniatowska and Bosques, 8.

5. Ibid.(played at her house)

6. O'Higgins–Lester interview, Jean Charlot Collection, University of Hawai'i.

7. Karen Thompson, "Jean Charlot."

8. O'Higgins–Lester interview.

9. Ibid.

10. Ibid.

11. *Un artista de su pueblo*, 17.

12. María O'Higgins interviews.

13. Glusker, 45.

14. O'Higgins–Lester interview.

15. http://www.Hawai'i.edu/jcf/OthersOnJC/MorseJohnIntroSpan.htm

16. Palma Chronology in Poniatowska and Bosques.

17. Híjar, *Apuntes*, 21.

18. Robinson, 99.
19. Wolfe, 189.
20. Patrick Marnham, *Dreaming With His Eyes Open—A Life of Diego Rivera* (New York: Knopf, 1998), 188.
21. Lourdes Uranga López, *El tema campesino en la pintura de Pablo O'Higgins (*Chapingo: Universidad Autónoma de Chapingo, 1987), 17.
22. O'Higgins–Lester interview.
23. Marnham, 193.
24. Bebe Fenstermaker, "Conversation With Emily Edwards," *San Antonio Society Newsletter*, 4th Installment (July–August, 1980), in Jean Charlot Collection, University of Hawai'i.
25. "Una Exposición Muy Mexicana," *Tiempo*, August 18, 1950; translation by Joel Hancock.
26. Poniatowska and Bosques, 12.
27. J. Givner, 148–49 (mixed paints); E. López, *Conversations with Katherine Anne Porter* (New York: Little Brown, 1981), 63 (euphemism).
28. Poniatowska and Bosques, 9.
29. Mitsue Thompson interview.
30. Poniatowska and Bosques, 9.
31. Various interviews noted herein.
32. Yvonne Templin interview.
33. Randall interviews. Luis and Lea Remba also said he had a "naïvete." Luis and Lea Remba, interview by author, Los Angeles, October 22, 2009.
34. Yvonne Templin interview.
35. Terry Goldblatt interviews.
36. Yvonne Templin interviews.
37. María O'Higgins interviews.
38. George Gutekunst, telephone interview by author, Pagosa Springs, Colorado, May 10, 1989.
39. Poniatowska and Bosques, 8.
40. Ibid., 8–9.
41. Ibid.
42. María O'Higgins interviews; Kathryn McCormick interviews; Miguel Orozco, telephone interviews by the author, September 3 and October 16, 2009.

CHAPTER 12 | PAUL BECOMES PABLO

1. María vehemently denied Pablo was ever a member of the Communist Party, in 1990, but in a 2004 interview she said, "like most intellectuals of his day, he joined the Communist party," http://lists.isber.ucsb.edu/pipermail/reformanet/2004-April/012172.html (accessed April 25, 2009).
2. Híjar, *Apuntes*, 261 (re date when Pablo joined the PCM); V. Schultize, "Pablo O'Higgins," *Salt Lake Tribune*, December 8, 1988, and Byron Randall interviews (re Partido Popular Socialista).
3. Spenser, 44.
4. Letizia Argenteri, 101.
5. Ibid., 102.
6. Ibid.
7. Spenser, 63.

8. Frank B. Kellogg, "U.S. Intervention in Central America: Kellogg's Charges of a Bolshevist Threat," memorandum, January 1927, http://historymatters.gmu.edu/d/4987 (accessed September 13, 2009).
9. Robinson, 86–87. Robinson said that Modotti unpacked Robinson's clothes, looking at her dresses "like a nun who had renounced all worldly possessions."
10. David Craven, *Art and Revolution in Latin America 1910–1990* (New Haven: Yale University Press, 2001), 20.
11. Igor Golomstock, *Totalitarian Art* (Great Britain: Icon Editions, 1990), 31–32. See also, L. Cohen, *The Cultural-Political Traditions and Developments of the Soviet Cinema, 1917–1972* (New York: Arno, 1974), 29.
12. Bill Holyoak, interview with the author, Salt Lake City, October 30, 2009, regarding Mormon family history.
13. Granville Hicks, *John Reed: The Making of a Revolutionary* (New York: The MacMillan Company, 1936), 133–35.
14. *Taller de Gráfica Popular a Cien Años del Primero de Mayo del Movimiento Obrero*, exhibition catalog 10 (México, D.F.: Universidad Autónoma Metropolitana, undated).
15. Noah Arthur Bardach, "Post-revolutionary Art, Revolutionary Artists—Mexican Political Art Collectives, 1921–1960: Grupo de Pintores 30–30!, Liga de Escritores y Artistas Revolutionarios (L.E.A.R.) and the Taller de Grafica Popular (T.G.P.)" (Ph.D. diss., University of Sussex, 2008), 274.
16. "A los tres años de edad me llevaron mis padres a vivir a San Francisco, California. Tres o cuatro años más tarde radicamos en San Diego. Ahí conocí a muchos mexicanos y aprendí el español," http://discursovisual.cenart.gob.mx/dvwebne08/documentos/doceduardo.htm, quoting *Autor desconocido*, "Camino a un mundo major," D.F., México, February 15, 1953 (accessed May 9, 2009).
17. Juan Baigts, "O'Higgins, limpio de corazón," http://discursovisual.cenart.gob.mx/dvwebne08/documentos/doceduardo.htm, quoting *Excélsior*. Diorama de la cultura, México, September 21, 1980.
18. "Youthful S.F. Artist Paints Mexico Murals," *San Francisco Chronicle*, June 25, 1933.
19. San Francisco is given as his birthplace in catalogs for Mexico and Its People, An Exhibition of Painting by Pablo O'Higgins, at Associated American Artists Gallery in New York in 1943, and at John Levy Galleries in New York in 1931, with the biographical statement written by Frances Flynn Paine, who promoted Mexican art for the Rockefellers. The *San Francisco Chronicle* followed his career, always reporting that he was born in San Francisco. "Youthful S.F. Artist Paints Mexico Murals," *San Francisco Chronicle*, June 25, 1933. Mexican publications also referred to him as born in San Francisco. "Una Exposition muy Mexicana," *Tiempo*, August 18, 1950.
20. María O'Higgins interviews (pronunciation explanation).
21. Zalce–Charlot interview.
22. Apparently the worst thing a Northern Irelander can call a native Irish person is a "dirty Mexican." I found this slur deep in the pages of Wikipedia for Northern Ireland where people post their disagreement with Wiki's articles.
23. Edward Kantowicz, *The Rage of Nations* (Grand Rapids: Wm. B. Eerdmans Publishing Co., 1999), 246.
24. Jules Heller, *Codex Méndez* (Phoenix: University of Arizona Press, 1999), 24. "[I]t seems reasonable to believe that the man's surname was, somehow, related to that of that great Chilean liberator, Bernardo O'Higgins."
25. Oles, *Walls*, 199, n. 14, referring to Oles's interview with María O'Higgins.

26. Jean Charlot, "Art and Communication: The Example of José Guadalupe Posada," June 9, 1965. Lecture delivered at Wayne State University, Detroit, Michigan, Jean Charlot Collection, University of Hawai'i. "This is by Pablo O'Higgins. It's a curious name, but he's a direct descendant of the famous Bernardo O'Higgins, who is the George Washington of Latin America."
27. John Charlot interview.
28. Oles, *Walls*, p. 200, n. 16, citing María O'Higgins.
29. Anita Brenner called him "an Irishman 'gone Mexican,'" and Patricia Albers said Tina Modotti spent time with "her husky blond Irish-American friend Pablo O'Higgins." Anita Brenner, 320. Albers said, "donning sandals and serapes, he refashioned himself as Pablo O'Higgins, Mexican painter and, within a couple of years, creed-bound Communist." Albers, 150–51. Anita, who professed that having been born in Mexico she had an affinity for the underdog, would have believed that an "O'Higgins" too came from underdog ancestry.
30. Frances Reyes Palma, Chronology ("Palma Chronology"), in José Juárez Sánchez, "An Artistic Commitment," catalog of exhibit, Dolores Olmedo Patiño Museum, Mexico Cultural Institute, Washington, D.C., 1995.
31. O'Higgins–Lester interview.
32. Farmer: http://www.museoblaisten.com/english.asp?myURL=%2F02asp%2FEnglish%2FartistDetailEnglish.asp&myVars=artistId%3D140 (accessed April 15, 2009). And a "farmwoman": http://graphicwitness.org/group/tgpohiggins.htm (accessed April 15, 2009). María said that after her husband's death, Alice went to live with family or family friends in Southern California. The family had a daughter who was very young. She later recalled holding Alice's gloved hand as Alice took her to exhibits and concerts. She said these were some of her best memories of her childhood. María O'Higgins interviews.
33. Robinson, 126-27. Freeman was referring to Carleton Beals.
34. Pablo O'Higgins, letter to Joseph Freeman, undated, Hoover Institution Archives, Stanford University.
35. Rafael Carrillo, interview by author, Mexico City, May 29, 1990 (translation by Amparo Ventura).
36. Edward Higgins's death certificate gives his cause of death as "nephritis, chronic, with hypertension and uraemia" and lists hypercarditis as contributing.
37. Albers, 154 (train to San Francisco a five-day trip).
38. Affidavit by Native American to Explain Protracted Foreign Residence; Affidavit by Naturalized American to Overcome Presumption of Noncitizenship, sworn and signed on December 15, 1941, by Paul Higgins in Mexico City.
39. Some biographies say that Pablo had his first exhibits as an artist in San Francisco in 1925 and 1927 at the Art Center Gallery. The exhibit or exhibits in the mid-1920s, likely group shows with artists from Mexico, may have been at the Modern Gallery, which later changed its name to the Art Center. It was founded by Otis Oldfield and Yun Gee "as a vanguard exhibition space." Gee, around the same time, also founded the "Chinese Revolutionary Artists' Club." Derrick R. Cartwright, "A Chronology of Institutions, Events, and Individuals," in *On the Edge of America: California Modernist Art 1900–50*, ed. Paul J. Karlstrom (Berkeley: U.C. Press, 1996), 279.
40. "Death of Judge E. V. Higgins," *Salt Lake Mining Review*, August 15, 1926.

CHAPTER 13 | TINA MODOTTI

1. Byron Randall interviews.
2. O'Higgins–Lester interview.
3. Hooks, 75 (re home).
4. Constantine, 75–76.
5. Vetter interviews.
6. The area of her face is conspicuously blank. Dolores del Río may have interrupted the sitting. María O'Higgins interviews.
7. Albers, 138.
8. Hooks, 98.
9. Glusker, 68–69, 71.
10. Albers, 151.
11. Albers, 150.
12. Albers, 157.
13. *Roses*, 1924.
14. Hooks, 104–10; Albers, 145–46.
15. Hooks, 114.
16. Wolfe, 189.
17. Albers, 156; Johnson, 15.
18. Poniatowska, *Tinisima*, 43 (Modotti learned songs about Joe Hill in the factory where she worked in San Francisco).
19. Albers, 158.
20. Albers, 158–59.
21. Albers, 161.
22. Hooks, 131.
23. Albers, 167.
24. Albers, 151.
25. George Gutekunst interview (closest friends); Byron Randall interviews.
26. Mildred Constantine, telephone interview by author, London, August 16, 1991.
27. Hooks, 248.
28. Albers, 151.
29. María O'Higgins interviews. María did not meet Pablo or travel in the artistic circles of Mexico City until 1959, however.
30. Albers, 117.
31. Albers, 167.
32. Hooks, 133–36.
33. Alexandra Kollontai, forward in *Red Love*, English ed. (New York: Seven Arts Publishing Company, 1927), www.marx.org (accessed May 25, 2009).
34. O'Higgins–Lester interview.
35. Mitsue Thompson interview.
36. Byron Randall interviews. Stirling Dickinson was also revered by the common people in the countryside. "When he went to the ranchos, the kids would rush out as soon as they saw the van and hug him when he got out." John Virtue, *Model American Abroad, a Biography of Stirling Dickinson* (Port Orchard: Windstorm Creative, 2008), 231, quoting Dickinson's driver.
37. Virginia Stewart, *45 Contemporary Mexican Artists* (Stanford: Stanford University Press, 1951) 87–88 ("All the neighbors came to love and care for the bachelor").

38. Seymour Kaplan, telephone interviews with the author, Santa Rosa, CA, June 18, and 21, July 6 and 21, 2009.
39. Yvonne Templin interview.
40. Ibid. Templin said it was "generally known" that Pablo was a homosexual. Randall echoed the "asexual" description.
41. Byron Randall interviews.
42. Yvonne Templin interview.

CHAPTER 14 | MEXICAN COMMUNIST PARTY

1. Hooks, 131.
2. Wolfe, 82; Hooks, 132.
3. Herrera, 85.
4. Hooks, 132.
5. Albers, 179 ("to simplify life").
6. Hooks, 142. Brenner later hired Tina to photograph Orozco's murals, and had the same problem with Tina feeling she could print from the negatives and sell them.
7. Wolfe, 215–6, 229.
8. Wolfe, 245.
9. Albers, 167.
10. Albers, 170–71.
11. Albers, 124 (re sundresses); Poniatowska, *Tinisima,* 120 (flowers).
12. Albers, 171 (renounced, quoting Dos Passos).
13. Robinson, 127.
14. Hooks, 161 (moved in).
15. Hooks, 136.
16. Albers, 179.
17. Albers, 171–72.
18. Hooks, 139.
19. Alberto Híjar called O'Higgins an "exemplary Communist." Alberto Híjar, interview by author, Mexico City, June 1, 1990 (translated by Amparo Ventura).
20. John Caughlan interview ("enthusiastic").
21. Daniel Gómez interview.
22. Alberto Híjar interview. María is president of the Fundación Cultural María y Pablo O'Higgins, which promotes Pablo's work and legacy.

CHAPTER 15 | CULTURAL MISSION

1. In *Doce Años* Pablo says he worked as a cultural missionary in 1929–30.
2. Zalce–Charlot interview.
3. Lloyd Hughes, *The Mexican Cultural Mission Programme Monograph on Fundamental Education* (Paris: UNESCO, 1949).
4. Millán, 234; Oles, *Walls*, 211.
5. George I. Sánchez, *A Revolution by Education* (New York: Viking, 1936), 68.
6. Hughes, 70.
7. G. Sánchez, 70.
8. Hughes, 70.
9. G. Sánchez, 75.
10. Hughes, 69.
11. Hughes, 64–65.

12. G. Sánchez, 83–84.
13. G. Sánchez, 77.
14. Miguel Orozco interviews.
15. *Voz de la lucha*, 116.
16. For example, John Charlot interview.
17. Sergio R. Blanco, "Valoran energía de Pablo O'Higgins," *Reforma*, February 10, 2005. "Alrededor de su persona había un halo de luz. . . . [Around him was a halo of light. . . .]" See also Poniatowska and Bosques, 9.
18. Salvador Jiménez, interview by author, Salt Lake City, October 19, 2009.
19. G. Sánchez, 83.
20. Palma Chronology in Poniatowska and Bosques, 155.
21. Ibid.
22. Maria O'Higgins interviews; Oles, *Walls*, 207.
23. María O'Higgins interviews.
24. Palma Chronology in Poniatowska and Bosques, 156.
25. Robinson, 81.
26. M. Meyer and W. Sherman, *The Course of Mexican History*, 7th ed. (New York: Oxford, 2002), 588.
27. Marcela de Neymet, *Cronología del partido comunista Mexicano, primera parte, 1919–1939* (México, D.F.: Ediciones de Cultura Popular, 1981), 71.
28. María O'Higgins interviews.
29. *Un artista de su pueblo*, 18.
30. Enrique Krauze, *Mexico: A Biography of Power* (New York: Harper Collins, 1997), 403.
31. Palma Chronology in Poniatowska and Bosques.
32. Palma Chronology in Poniatowska and Bosques. Palma also says Pablo was in hiding in Tehuantepec for some time because of the persecution of Communists and his status as a foreigner.
33. November 5, 1928, per death certificate.
34. "Lawyer Meets Sudden Death," *Salt Lake Tribune*, November 6, 1928, 28.

CHAPTER 16 | MODOTTI TRIAL

1. Hooks, 151 (law student).
2. Hugh Thomas, *Cuba*, 588.
3. Albert Híjar interview.
4. Albers, 211.
5. Wolfe, 230–31.
6. Glusker, 124–25; Charlot devout, letters of Zohmah Charlot. Zohmah says when they were courting and she realized how devout Jean was, she had to go outside for air. Transcript of diary of Zohmah Charlot, Friday, July 17, 1931, Jean Charlot Collection, University of Hawai'i.
7. Herrera, 86.
8. Tina Martin interviews.
9. José Clemente Orozco, *The Artist in New York: Letters to Jean Charlot and Unpublished Writings, 1925–1929,* tran. Ruth L. C. Simms (Austin: University of Texas Press, 1974), 40.
10. Ibid.
11. Albers, 211.
12. Glusker, 33 (re coffee); Zohmah Charlot, *Mexican Memories [1931]* (Honolulu:

Privately published, 1989, 1993), 30.
13. Poniatowaka, *Tinísima*, 49-50.
14. Poniatowska, *Tinisima*, 137.
15. Hooks, 189.
16. Albers, 176.
17. Herrera, 100.

CHAPTER 17 | SPLIT WITH RIVERA

1. The Sixth Congress (Sixth International) promised that Communism would solve all of the world's suffering: it would "abolish all forms of exploitation and oppression of man by man," "the misery of enslaved classes, and a wretched standard of life generally will disappear," "the last vestige of the social inequality of the sexes will be removed," "all measures of coercion will expire," and "culture will become the acquirement of all." The Programme of the Communist International. Comintern Sixth Congress 1929, III. The Ultimate aim of the Communist International—World Communism, http://www.marxists.org/history/international/comintern/6th-congress/ch03.htm (accessed June 2, 2009). The Sixth International advocated "[f]omenting world revolution." Anne Applebaum, *Gulag* (New York: Anchor Books, 2003), 129.
2. Charles James Stephens, "Communism in Mexico, 1919–1940" (Thesis for MA in International Relations at the University of California, undated), 55.
3. Stephens, 66, quoting a speech given by Siqueiros in Buenos Aires at the First Latin American Communist Conference.
4. Ibid., 66.
5. Stephens, 62–69.
6. Stephens, 74. "This abortive revolt proved disastrous for the Mexican Communists. *El Machete* and *El Libertador* were suppressed. The Party was weakened through the subsequent purges. Its hold on the peasant leagues was shattered. Its position with the Government became precarious. The Party nonetheless, continued in its hostility thereby incurring the wrath of the Mexican authorities."
7. Constantine, 167.
8. W. Laquer, ed., *Fascism, A Reader's Guide* (Berkeley: University of California Press, 1976).
9. Pablo wrote in an undated letter to Joseph Freeman, "I separated from Rivera before and during the preparation of [National] palace walls painting . . . ." Joseph Freeman Archives, Hoover Institution Archives, Stanford University.
10. Herrera, 102 (Rivera expelled from party October, 1929).
11. Alberto Híjar interview.
12. Ibid.
13. Robinson, 110–11.
14. Ibid. Freeman later denied he was a member of the Mexican Communist Party or presided over this meeting. Joseph Freeman Archives, Box 180, Folder 5, Hoover Institution Archives, Stanford University.
15. Robinson, 111.
16. Albers, 231.
17. Nathaniel Gardner, "Benita Galeana y el Taller de Gráfica Popular: Ilustraciones, propaganda, y el pasar del tiempo," University of Glasgow, http://www.ajlas.org/v2006/paper/2008vol21no404.pdf (accessed May 24, 2009).
18. Benita Galeana, *Benita* (Pittsburg: Latin American Literary Review Press, 1994), 15.

19. Founders Society, *Diego Rivera—A Retrospective.*
20. Byron Randall interviews.
21. See Chapter 20, n. 11.
22. Herrera, 201.
23. María O'Higgins interviews.
24. A. Rodríguez, "An International Workers Movement," University of Virginia, American Studies Department, http://xroads.virginia.edu/~MA02/rodriguez/rivera/Communist.html (accessed May 9, 2009).
25. Pablo O'Higgins letter to Jean Charlot, May 28, 1945. Pablo O'Higgins letter to Jean Charlot, October 8, 1945.
26. Campos Chronology.
27. The Fellowship, www.gf.org (accessed September 26, 2009).
28. Albers, 228.
29. Freeman was in Mexico on October 15, and by November 20, both he and Robinson were in New York. Robinson, 116–118.
30. Robinson, 124.
31. This letter does not appear to be in the Joseph Freeman archives at the Hoover Institution Archives, Stanford University.
32. Robinson, 125. See also Chapter 20, n. 4.
33. Lucretia Blow Le Bourgeois Van Horn, born 1882, had studied at the Art Students League and the Académie Julian in Paris.

CHAPTER 18 | MEXICO/U.S. LOVE AFFAIR

1. Joan Givner, *Katherine Anne Porter, A Life* (New York: Simon & Schuster, 1982), 230; Darlene Harbowz Unrue, *Katherine Anne Porter* (New York: Library of America, 2008), 127. Pablo gave piano lessons to Porter for six weeks in 1930.
2. Porter made this acerbic comment in a February 11, 1931, letter to Josephine Herbst. Pablo was at the time in New York drawing sketches for the *Daily Worker.* Referring to some Communists in Mexico who lived in poverty but borrowed money from friends who were "silly enough to work for the capitalist system," Porter says she has "advised several of these to go to Moscow and get their bottoms spanked." Letters, 35. Porter may have portrayed a bit of Pablo in her character of David Scott in her 1962 novel, *Ship of Fools* (Boston: Little, Brown, 1962). David is an American artist from Colorado who lives in Mexico, works as a miner, and is learning Russian. He spends the voyage to Europe in steerage, sketching poor peasants, to the chagrin of his bourgeois girlfriend who finds his subject matter tired and repetitive.
3. Glusker, 138.
4. Ibid., 120.
5. In 1926, Charlot published an article about Posada, "Un precursor del movimiento de arte mexicano" ("A Precursor to the Mexican Art Movement"), in Mexico's *Revista de Revistas.* A Chronology: José Guadalupe Posada, Jean Charlot Collection, University of Hawai'i Library, http://libweb.Hawaii.edu/libdept/charlotcoll/posada/posadachronos.html. Pneumonia: http://libweb.Hawaii.edu/libdept/charlotcoll/J_Charlot/charlotmcvicker.html (accessed May 24, 2009).
6. Glusker, 54, 71–72.
7. Glusker, 71. This was the cause for the ultimate demise of the working relationship between Anita and Frances.
8. O'Higgins "Datos Biográficos," in Organization of American States (OAS), Pablo

O'Higgins file, Washington, D.C.

9. Alicia Azuela, *Art Journal*, March 22, 1993.

10. See James Oles, *South of the Border* (Washington, D.C: Smithsonian, 1993).

11. Hooks, 198. Anita said in a letter to Weston, "I hear Tina is again a martyr."

12. Francis V. O'Connor, "The Influence of Diego Rivera on the Art of the United States During the 1930s and After," in *Diego Rivera* (New York: W.W. Norton, 1986), quoted in *Latin American Spirit*, 185.

13. Klehr, 84.

14. Ibid.

15. Palma Chronology in Poniatowska and Bosques.

16. Innis Shoemaker, "Crossing Borders—The Weyhe Gallery and the Vogue for Mexican Art in the U.S. 1926–1940," in Ittmann, *Mexico and Modern Printmaking*, 45–46.

17. Consulate affidavit.

18. Thompson, "Jean Charlot" (accessed May 27, 2009).

19. The 1930 Census shows Charlot living in Manhattan with Lowell Houser, age 27, an artist/illustrator whom he had met in Mexico and worked with on a dig in the Yucatan. http://libweb.Hawai'i.edu/libdept/charlotcoll/J_Charlot/charlotmcvicker.html. On the census, Charlot lists both parents as born in France and his profession as archeology. He entered the U.S. at Laredo with his destination New York on October 24, 1928, with his mother, Ana, and $400 in his pocket. He arrived again in New York by ship from Veracruz, Mexico, on August 30, 1931. http://search.ancestry.com/cgi-bin/sse.dll?gl=ROOT_CATEGORY&rank=1&new=1&so=1&MSAV=1&msT=1&gss=ms_f-2&gsfn=jean&gsln=charlot&ne=2 (accessed May 1, 2009).

20. In New York, Charlot's work was shown in a Mexican government–sponsored group exhibition at the Art Center in 1928, and in a retrospective at the Art Students League in 1930.

21. Pablo O'Higgins, Exhibition Catalog (New York: John Levy Gallery, 1931).

22. Ibid.

23. "Final Show in Mexican Series, *New York Times*, May 17, 1931 ("The final exhibition in the Mexican series held this season by the John Levy Galleries opened yesterday and will remain open until May 30. It consists of works by Pablo O'Higgins . . . .")

24. Palma Chronology, Poniatowska and Bosques.

25. O'Higgins–Lester interview. This story appears in many publications. Notes from an exhibit of Pablo's in Aguascalientes in April, 1982, indicate he mentioned it then as well, but gave the place of the manifestation as Battery Park, New York. Notes on Aguascalientes, Mexico, April 16, 1982, Archives of Emmy Lou Packard.

26. "A Pablo no le importaba correr riesgos con tal de obtener un apunte directo . . . . (Pablo didn't mind taking risks in order to obtain a direct sketch . . . .)" in Poniatowska and Bosques, 156; also, Uranga López, *El tema campesino*, 32, "de regreso a Mexico ... casi pierde el barco (on the return to Mexico he almost missed the ship)."

27. Diary of Jean Charlot, 1931, and Paintings Catalog ("May 16—To Mexico to live with Pablo"), Jean Charlot Collection, University of Hawai'i.

28. *Daily Worker*, March 28, 1931.

29. For an in-depth analysis of these drawings, see Leonard Folgarait, "O'Higgins y el *Daily Worker*, 1931," *Voz de la lucha*, 69.

30. Rosalio Negrete (aka Russell Blackwell), whom Pablo and Abel Plenn, Anita's cousin, visited in New York in 1931, wrote in a letter to Diego Rivera that Pablo was "mas Stalinista que la Chingada—especialmente Plenn." Glusker, 171, n. 26.

31. *Doce Años.* Maximum honor: Alberto Híjar, "Contribución política," *Voz de la lucha*, 40.
32. Leonard Folgorait, "O'Higgins y el *Daily Worker*, 1931," *Voz de la lucha*, 81, 87.
33. Palma Chronology, Poniatowska and Bosques.
34. Patricia Rosales y Zamora, O'Higgins, "Ejemplo para jóvenes pintores: su viuda" ("Example for Young Painters: His Widow"), *Excelsior*, March 13, 1985. "[*U*]n *cuadro que Pablo vendio a Diego Rivera en 1931, para que el primero pudiera asistir a un congreso en Estados Unidos*" ("a painting [or work of art] that Pablo sold to Diego Rivera in 1931, so that he could attend a conference in the United States").
35. Z. Charlot, *Mexican Memories [1931]*, 19 (re: date Jean Charlot met Pablo and Jean).
36. *Zohmah Charlot Diary*, August, 27, 1931, Jean Charlot Collection, University of Hawai'i.

CHAPTER 19 | MOSCOW

1. Some biographies refer to Pablo as Pablo Esteban O'Higgins, though his middle name was Barton. His grandmother's maiden name was Stevenson; this is likely the name that got turned into Esteban.
2. Also in 1931, Pablo's work was included in a group show of 135 pieces by 28 Mexican artist in Los Angeles at the Plaza Art Center on Olvera Street. Karlstrom, ed., *On the Edge*, 127.
3. Bayley, 67.
4. Albers, 263–64; Unrue, 127.
5. David Jenkins oral history, 186.
6. Stout, 56.
7. Stout, 94.
8. These descriptions are based on the reports of visitors to the Soviet Union in the early 1930s, who were routinely escorted to see the best of the country. Martha Dodd, *Through Embassy Eyes* (New York: Harcourt Brace, 1939); César Vallejo, *Rusia en 1931: Reflexiones al pie del Kremlin* (Madrid: Ulises, 1931).
9. Dodd, *Through Embassy Eyes*, 190.
10. Stout, 98.
11. Stout, 82.
12. Rafael Carrillo interview.
13. Robert Conquest, *The Harvest of Sorrow—Soviet Collectivization and the Terror-Famine* (New York: Oxford University Press, 1986), 326.
14. María O'Higgins interviews.
15. Wolfe, 217–21.
16. The article was published in *Arts Weekly* in March 1932, and reprinted by Alberto Misrachi in the June 1932 edition of *Sinthesis.*
17. Hooks, 82, 141, 146 (Guerrero sent to Lenin School).
18. Randall interviews.
19. The descriptions in this section about Pablo meeting Modotti and Vidali are gleaned from Poniatowska's excellent fictionalized account of Modotti's life, *Tinísima*, and descriptions in Modotti biographies of her activities in Russia.
20. Albers, 146 (Comintern organization).
21. It is unclear whether Vidali and Modotti were in a relationship when Pablo arrived.
22. Vidali's position, as stated in Poniatowska, *Tinisima*, 190.
23. Hooks, 213.

24. Hooks, 219–20.
25. Constantine, 168.
26. Stout, 144.
27. Stout, 144.
28. Letter from Jean Charlot to Zohmah Day, March 4, 1933.
29. Seymour Stern, "Introduction to Synopsis of 'Que Viva México,' " *Experimental Cinema* 5 (New York: 1934).
30. Albers, 264.
31. Another effort is in the works to re-edit the footage. Lutz Becker, e-mail correspondence with author, June 29, 2009.
32. Stout, 56. Modotti had many excuses for abandoning photography once in the USSR. One was bad light, another the unavailability of the right film. Albers, 262–63.
33. Modotti had been called a "Kollontai type" by 23-year-old poet Kenneth Rexroth, who added, "she terrified me." Albers, 217–18.

CHAPTER 20 | A HORNET'S NEST

1. Robinson, 197.
2. Robinson, 197.
3. *New Masses* 7, February 1932, http://xroads.virginia.edu/~ma04/hess/RockRivera/newspapers/NewMasses_02_1932_2.html (accessed September 13, 2009).
4. "Battle of the Century," Marion Greenwood oral history, http://www.aaa.si.edu/collections/oralhistories/transcripts/greenw64.htm. "Snowballed": "The Communist controversy over Rivera in America began well before the Rockefeller Center incident. In February of 1932, Joseph Freeman wrote an article in *New Masses* under the pseudonym of Robert Evans entitled, "Painting and Politics: The Case of Diego Rivera." "In this corner," American Studies at the University of Virginia, http://xroads.virginia.edu/~MA04/hess/RockRivera/mainframe5.html (accessed September 13, 2009).
5. Reuben Kadish, 21, and Philip Goldstein [Philip Guston], 22. *Time*, April 1, 1935. In a letter from Siqueiros, who was in New York, to Pablo and "other comrades," dated April 20, 1934, Siqueiros recites his past art projects, apparently in response to a questionnaire Pablo sent him a month earlier. Getty Research Institute, Los Angeles.
6. Oles, *Walls*, 233, quoting Pablo O'Higgins's letter to Marion Greenwood, undated, Marion Greenwood Archives. Oles notes that O'Higgins adds the cryptic note to the end of the letter, "Tell Siqueiros I'll write him and that the comrades got his communication." Ibid., n. 114. Siqueiros's letter to Pablo had opened, "Pablo O'Higgins y demas camaradas (Pablo O'Higgins and the rest of the comrades)."
7. Oles, *Walls*, 234, quoting Pablo O'Higgins letter to Marion Greenwood, June 12, 1934, Marion Greenwood Archives.
8. Joseph Freeman archive, undated typewritten page 6, Box 180.
9. Freeman letter to Morris Topchevsky, July 14, 1933, Joseph Freeman Archives, Hoover Institution Archives, Stanford University, Box 180.
10. Abel Plenn letter to Joseph Freeman, July 29, 1933, Joseph Freeman Archives, Box 180.
11. Pablo O'Higgins letter to Joseph Freeman, undated, Joseph Freeman Archives, Hoover Institution Archives, Stanford University. Also, Emmy Lou Packard, in an August 1974 document, wrote, "Pablo O'Higgins is about to start a fresco in the Palacio Nacional, having completed a series of lithographs commissioned by the government

to honor the trade-unions." Draft document beginning "Driving through Mexico," with note "Emmy Lou Aug 74", Emmy Lou Packard Archives.

12. Robinson, 107.
13. Robinson, 112–14.
14. Ibid., 127.
15. James Bloom, "About Joseph Freeman," University of Illinois, http://www.english.illinois.edu/maps/poets/a_f/freeman/about.htm (accessed September 19, 2009).
16. Robinson, 124-25.
17. "With Pablo, things were either right or wrong." Goldie Caughlan interview.
18. Pablo was described in 1931 "más Stalinista que la chingada" (hard-core Stalinist). Glusker, 171, n. 26. Robinson, 98 (ardent). Poniatowska, *Tinisima*, 128 (Modotti selling photographs to *New Masses*).
19. Poniatowska, *Tinisima*, 136–37.
20. Byron Randall interviews.
21. Alberto Híjar interview.
22. Pablo O'Higgins letter to Joseph Freeman, undated, Joseph Freeman Archives, Hoover Institution Archives, Stanford University, Box 180.
23. David Jenkins oral history, 47, 51.
24. David Jenkins oral history, 152.
25. Ibid. The U.S. formally recognized the USSR in 1933 after Roosevelt took office. U.S. State Department, "Recognition of the Soviet Union," www. http://www.state.gov/r/pa/ho/time/id/86555.htm (accessed November 11, 2009).
26. John W. Wright, ed., *2003 New York Times Almanac* (New York: Penguin, 2003), 109.
27. The Communist Party was, and has always been legal in the U.S. T. Michael Holmes, *The Specter of Communism in Hawaii* (Honolulu: University of Hawaii Press, 1994), 6.
28. M. Stanton Evans, *Blacklisted by History* (New York: Random House, 2007), 52.
29. Barry Carr, *Marxism and Communism in Twentieth Century Mexico* (Lincoln: University of Nebraska Press, 1992), 110, n. 8, quoting Joseph Starobin, *American Communism in Crisis 1943–1957* (Berkeley: University of California Press, 1972), 52.

CHAPTER 21 | RETURN TO MEXICO

1. E.g., Oles, *Walls,* 233 (quoting Pablo O'Higgins letter to Siqueiros).
2. E. Alberto, "Conversación con Pablo O'Higgins." Even on his short visit Pablo sensed a very charged atmosphere, "presaging the revolution in which Villena would play a vital part." Villena had been sentenced to death for his role in a strike against Gerardo Machado, but escaped to the U.S. and went to Russia to seek a cure for his tuberculosis. Carolina Hospital and Jorge Cantera, *A Century of Cuban Writers in Florida: Selected Prose and Poetry* (Sarasota: Pineapple Press, 1996), 81.
3. Galeana, 146.
4. Galeana, 15.
5. Stout, 47.
6. Marnham, 186 (describing the reaction to Bertram Wolfe throwing Rivera out of the Communist Party in 1925).
7. Pablo contributed a lithograph of Galeana teaching. Nathaniel Gardner, "Benita."
8. Wolfe, 353.
9. Galeana, 131.
10. Oles, *Walls*, 210-12.
11. Poniatowska and Bosques, 156.

12. Juan O'Gorman, *Autobiographia* (México, D.F.: DGE Editions S.A, 2007), 110–11. O'Gorman said Pablo was an excellent artist, of high quality, if not a bit forgotten. He said he had high esteem and admiration for Pablo and Méndez.
13. Jean Charlot, *Guía de los frescos de varios artistas en las escuelas primarias* (México, D.F.: Toor Studios, 1945).
14. "Youthful S. F. Artist Paints Mexico Murals," *San Francisco Chronicle,* June 25, 1933.
15. Palma Chronology in J. Sánchez.
16. Oles, *Walls*, 208.
17. Oles, *Walls*, 210. Translation by Julio César Tapia Guzmán.
18. Oles, *Walls*, 233.

CHAPTER 22 | THE LEAR

1. María says it was planned in Pablo's studio at Belisario Domínguez 43, 16th floor. Híjar, *Apuntes*, 262.
2. Millán, 171–72.
3. R. Tibol, *Historia general del arte de México* (México, D.F.: Editorial Hérmes, S.A., 1964), 182.
4. Members included Rivera, Siqueiros, Rufino Tamayo, Manuel Alvarez Bravo, Xavier Guerrero, Carlos Mérida, and writers Octavio Paz, German List Azurbide, Carlos Pellicer, and José Mancisador. Bardach, "Post-revolutionary Art," 120, n. 235–39. Composer Silvester Revueltas became leader of the group, and Carlos Chávez, whom Pablo would later try to introduce to U.S. songwriter Earl Robinson, was involved as well. Ibid., 122.
5. Poniatowska and Bosques, 156.
6. Bardach, 117.
7. Alicia Azuela, *Art Journal*, March 22, 1993, 1.
8. Azuela, 4.
9. *Time*, August 29, 1938.
10. Bardach, 135.
11. Bardach, 125. Bardach notes that in carrying out its objectives the LEAR was not terribly concerned with accuracy: "[T]he LEAR also seems to be willing to say whatever was necessary to advance their agenda without being overly concerned with factual accuracy. For example, the articles of *Frente a Frente* aren't peppered with citations or references. If one accepts the proposal that the LEAR's goal was to produce effective political propaganda, then truth and accuracy aren't, in the end, of primary concern." 128, n. 255.
12. David Alfaro Siqueiros, "Rivera's Counter-Revolutionary Road," *New Masses*, May 29, 1934.
13. Bardach, 158-61.
14. Ibid.
15. Wolfe, 341.
16. Bardach, 159. Bardach points that this cover, depicting an event at Bellas Artes far beyond the knowledge of the *campesinos* and workers, the purported audience of *Frente a Frente*, shows that the publication was really aiming at other intellectuals.
17. Alberto Híjar interview.
18. Friedrich E. Schuler, *Mexico Between Hitler and Roosevelt* (Albuquerque: University of New Mexico Press: 1998), 60.
19. Rushmore, "Art."

20. Ibid.
21. James Oles, *Las hermanas Greenwood en Mexico*, (México, D.F.: Circulo de Arte, Consejo Nacional Para la Cultura y las Artes, 2000), 5.
22. Palma Chronology in Poniatowska and Bosques, 157.
23. Oles, *Walls*, 290.
24. Marion Greenwood oral history interview, January 31, 1964, 3, Archives of American Art, Smithsonian Institution, http://www.aaa.si.edu/collections/oralhistories/transcripts/greenw64.htm (accessed May 2, 2009).
25. For extensive information on the murals, see Oles, *Walls*.
26. Craven, 64.
27. Beatriz González, Dir., *Pablo O'Higgins: Voz de lucha y arte* (Mexico: TV UNAM, 2005). Translation by Julio César Tapia Guzmán.
28. Oles, *Las hermanas Greenwood*, 7. Oles notes that Ione Robinson assisted Rivera on his National Palace murals, and Isabel Villaseñor assisted Alfredo Zalce on a mural.
29. Greenwood oral history.
30. Oles, *Walls*, 229–47. Oles also points out that the contracts for the mural were with individual artists, not LEAR.
31. Greenwood oral history.
32. Isamu Noguchi, *A Sculptor's World* (New York and Evanston: Harper Row, 1968).
33. Herrera, 200.
34. "Art: Mexican Market," *Time*, July 22, 1935.
35. Greenwood oral history, 2.
36. Oles, *Walls*, 246-47.

CHAPTER 23 | THE SPANISH CIVIL WAR

1. Wolfe, 341 ("painter for millionaires").
2. Herrera, 202.
3. Bardach, 117, n. 229 (list of those present).
4. Prignitz, 34.
5. Ralph M. Pearson, "These Prints and the Public," *Graphic Works of the American 30's* (New York: Da Capo, 1977), 7.
6. Ibid.
7. Oles, *Walls*, 210 (hygiene).
8. Galeana, 153.
9. Galeana, 154.
10. Galeana, 154–56.
11. Palma Chronology in Poniatowska and Bosques ("Pablo never had a weapon in his hands").
12. Herrera, 182.
13. Herrera, 200.
14. Herrera, 200–1.
15. Tina Martin interviews.
16. Abraham Lincoln Brigade Archives (ALBA), http://www.alba-valb.org/volunteers/paolino-sarti. When they later tried to enlist to serve in WW II, the U.S. government labeled them "pre-mature antifascists" and questioned their loyalty to the U.S. The countries who signed the nonintervention pact also banned, but did not succeed in stopping, these volunteers.
17. Ibid.

18. Albers, 288–89.
19. Albers, 289.
20. Albers, 301, 294.
21. Pablo also participated in the second collective exhibition of LEAR, in the National Library's lobby in Mexico City. Palma Chronology in Poniatowska and Bosques.
22. Craven, 58.
23. Meyer and Sherman, 584.

CHAPTER 24 | STALIN/TROTSKY SCHISM

1. Diego later recreated it at the Palace of Fine Arts (Palacio de Bellas Artes) in Mexico City, where it can be seen today. The Rockefeller mural controversy was depicted in Tim Robbins's film *The Cradle Will Rock*.
2. Rafael Carrillo interview.
3. Herrera, 201.
4. Ibid.
5. Interviews with Tina Misrachi Martin, Salt Lake City, 2005-09.
6. Glusker, 161–62.
7. Glusker, 162–63.
8. Interviews with Tina Misrachi Martin, Salt Lake City, 2005–09.
9. Herrera, 204.
10. "Trotsky, Stalin & Cárdenas," *Time*, January 25, 1937, http://www.time.com/time/magazine/article/0,9171,770539-2,00.html (accessed January 23, 2010).
11. Wolfe says that on June 10, 1936, the party, through the editors of *El Machete*, then headed by Rafael Carrillo, had apologized for ignoring his art. Wolfe, *Fabulous Life*, 237. This peace offering was rescinded and Rivera remained an enemy of the party until after the assassination of Trotsky, when, according to Wolfe, "both Party and painter found it convenient to make up." Ibid., 239. Herrera, 204.
12. See note 10.
13. Dmitri Antonovich Volkogonov and Harold Shukman, *Trotsky: The Eternal Revolutionary*, tran. Harold Shukman (New York: Simon and Schuster, 1996), 385.
14. Volkogonov and Shukman, 395.
15. Prignitz, 46.
16. Palma Chronology in Poniatowska and Bosques.
17. Miguel Hernández and Ted Genoways, *The Selected Poems of Miguel Hernández* (Chicago: University of Chicago Press, 2001), 110.
18. Prignitz, 46; Palma Chronology in Poniatowska and Bosques (Pablo's work).
19. Bardach, 115.
20. Bardach, 114 (30 members), 119 (hundreds of members); Millán, 193 (350 members).
21. Craven, 59.
22. Ibid.
23. Wechsler, "Propaganda Gráfica," in Ittmann, ed., 65–67.
24. Ibid, 62.
25. Krauze, 592.
26. Alicia Azuela, "*El Machete* and *Frente a Frente*," *Art Journal*, March 22, 1993.
27. Bardach, 165.
28. Bardach, 178.
29. Bardach, 115.

CHAPTER 25 | THE TGP

1. "Pablo O'Higgins, Conciencia y Política," *Humanidad recuperada*, 94.
2. Lincoln Cushing, *A Contracorriente* 5, no. 3 (Spring 2008), 257–62, www.ncsu.edu/project/acontracorriente, http://www.docspopuli.org/articles/CaplowReview.html (accessed June 13, 2009). Cushing cataloged the TGP's work for UC–Berkeley's Bancroft Library.
3. Conversation with Noah Bardach, August 7, 2009.
4. http://www.docspopuli.org/ (accessed June 12, 2009).
5. Wechsler, "Mexicanidad," in Ittmann, 67.
6. Ibid.
7. Daniel C. Lienau, telephone interview by author, Santa Rosa, CA, June 18, 2009.
8. Raquel Tibol, *Gráficas y Neográficas en México* (México, D.F.: Secretaría de Educación Publica, 1987), 70. (Translation by Joel Hancock.)
9. Poniatowska and Bosques, 22. They also tended to be from working-class or *campesino* backgrounds. A. Haab, *Mexican Graphic Art.*
10. Lyle Williams, "Evolution of a Revolution: A Brief History of Printmaking in Mexico," in Ittmann, 16.
11. Maria O'Higgns interviews; Prignitz, 215. E.g., *Cárdenas Informa al Pueblo*, linoleum, 1939. Palma Chronology in J. Sánchez.
12. Poniatowska and Bosques, 18.
13. Elena Poniatowska, "Leopoldo Méndez, cien años de vida," *La Journada*, en honor a Leopoldo Méndez. Centenario, http://www.aceroarte.com/colección/Leopoldo_Méndez_venganzapueblos.htm, Referencia Internet, Información (septiembre 2004) www.jornada.unam.mx/2002/may02/020523/02aa1cul.php?printver=1 (accessed June 26, 2009).
14. *Voz de la lucha*, 116.
15. Elena Poniatowska, "Leopoldo Méndez, cien años de vida," *La Journada*, supra; re: Pablo, Byron Randall interviews; Seymour Kaplan interviews.
16. Heller, 10.
17. Noah Bardach, telephone interview with author, Los Angeles, July 19, 2009.
18. Ibid.
19. Ibid.
20. Haab, 7.
21. Elena Poniatowska, "Leopoldo Méndez, cien años de vida," *La Journada*, supra (re Méndez's life).
22. Bardach, 172.
23. Poniatowska and Bosques, 19; Herzog, 54.
24. Cushing website.
25. Helm, 189–90.
26. Museo Biblioteca Pape, 10–11.
27. O'Higgins–Lester interview.
28. Rushmore, "Art."

CHAPTER 26 | THE FIGHT AGAINST FASCISM

1. Lilyan Tregob, interview by the author, Menlo Park, California, March 15, 1999. Tregob said that she introduced Rivera to Emma Hurtado, who became his art dealer in 1946, and his wife in 1955, a year after the death of Frida Kahlo. Hurtado, publisher of *Esta semana*, a publication for tourists, said she met Rivera when she asked him to

do an illustration for a book she was to publish. Wolfe, *The Fabulous Life of Diego Rivera*, 407. Tregob, who had studied theater at Columbia University, came to Mexico in the late 1930s to work for an American theater company and stayed for ten years. "Lilyan Tregob," *Palo Alto Weekly*, August 20, 2003, http://www.paloaltoonline.com/weekly/morgue/2003/2003_08_20.obits20ja.html (accessed December 31, 2009).

2. Jean Charlot, "José Guadalupe Posada and His Successors," in *Posada's Mexico*, ed. Ron Tyler (Washington, D.C.: Library of Congress; Fort Worth: Amon Carter Museum of Western Art, 1979), 51.

3. Exhibit of works of the Taller de Gráfica Popular, Bronx Museum, New York, 1990; Virginia Stewart, *45 Contemporary Mexican Artists* (Stanford: Stanford University Press, 1951); Bardach, 186–9; Wechsler, "Propaganda Gráfica," in Ittmann, 69 (re "Comintern-affiliated").

4. Bardach, 192.

5. Palma Chronology in Poniatowska and Bosques, 161.

6. *Voz de la lucha*, 19. (http://www.gráficamexicana.com/Catalog_Viewer.asp?dir=filtered&filter=artist&fname=Pablo&lname=O'Higgins). In the biography of Pablo included in *Doce Años*, it states that in 1936 he was "Sub-chief of Department of Graphics of the Museum of Industry, Mexico."

7. Calendario de la Universidad Obrera de México 1938, 1937. Pablo created, for May, *En la época de la represión, 1o de mayo de 1933*. For July, *Buitres fascistas sobre España. 18 de julio 1938* [sic]." And for October, *Se van derrumbando los opresores del indígena.*

8. Bardach, 188.

9. Bardach, 201.

10. Albers, 298.

11. Joseph H. L. Schlarman, *Mexico—a Land of Volcanos from Cortes to Alemán* (Kronenberger Press, 2007), 581, quoting Associated Press, April 2, 1928.

12. This figure was negotiated down from the $450 claimed ($200 million by U.S. companies and $250 by British companies). M. Meyer and W. Sherman, 604–5.

13. "Openings of the Week: Paul O'Higgins—Paintings and lithographs. Bonestell Gallery. (Feb. 16–March 2)," *New York Times*, February 16, 1939.

14. Palma Chronology, Poniatowska and Bosques.

CHAPTER 27 | SEEDS OF DOUBT

1. Mark Vallen, "Pele deLappe: RIP," Art For A Change, October 9, 2007, http://art-for-a-change.com/blog/2007/10/pele-delappe-rip.html (accessed October 10, 2009).

2. Byron Randall interviews.

3. Not surprisingly many American Jews left the Communist Party when it became friendly with Nazi Germany.

4. David Jenkins oral history, 184.

5. Stephens, 207, n. 17.

6. David Jenkins oral history, 186. Jenkins also cites as the party's issues with Roosevelt his refusal to recognize Spain, the steel strike, and that he wouldn't admit Jewish refugees into the U.S., resulting in many of their deaths. Ibid., 275.

7. Carr, 69.

8. Don M. Coerver, Suzanne B. Pasztor, Robert Buffington, *Mexico* (Santa Barbara: ABC-CLIO, 2004), 108.

9. Between 1939 and 1941 the PCM membership fell from 35,000 to 14,000. It is likely that this was due as much to the disillusionment with the Nazi-Soviet pact as to the

PCM purge." Stephens, 207, n. 17. "By May 1941 . . . the Mexican Communist Party had become a negligible factor in the political life of the Mexican Nation." (Stephens, 236.)
10. James M. Wechsler, "Propaganda," in Ittmann, 70. Wechsler says the TGP expressed this in a print by Alfred Zalce, *Calaveras vaciliadoras de la Guerra.* The word *vaciliadoras* is translated as "*shaky*," but Mexico native and professional interpreter Efraín Méndez and retired Mexican consul Salvador Jiménez believe that in this context it is more likely to mean *joking*, as between friends.
11. Albers, 322.
12. Poniatowska, *Tinísima.*
13. Albers, 320.
14. Elena Poniatowska, "Mujeres mágicas," *Journada UNAM*, www.jornada.unam.mx/1997/06/12/poniatowska.html (accessed May 8, 2009).
15. Albers, 319.
16. Albers, 320.
17. Albers, 320.
18. *Alien Registration Act* or *Smith Act*, *U.S. Code,* Title 18 (1940), § 2385.
19. Evans, 75–76.
20. Pele deLappe, *A Passionate Journey Through Art & the Red Press* (Petaluma, CA: 2000).
32. Pele deLappe, interviews with the author, Tomales CA, Petaluma, CA.
21. Skovgaad; deLappe, *A Passionate Journey,* 32.
22. Rushmore, "Art."
23. Rushmore testified at the HUAC's 1947 hearings on "Red Hollywood," naming as Communists Edward G. Robinson, Charlie Chaplin, playwright Clifford Odets, and screenwriters Dalton Trumbo and John Henry Lawson. In 1958, Rushmore shot and killed his wife and himself in a New York cab. Jay Maeder, "Turncoat: the Estrangements of Howard Rushmore, January 1958 Chapter 282," *New York Daily News*, February 26, 2001. 24. A document from the U.S. State Department says that Pablo was in the U.S. from November 1939 to March 1940.
24. Taller de Gráfica Popular, *El Pueblo de México y sus enemigos de 1935-39* (México, D.F., 1939)
25. Compare Dmitri Volkogonov, *Trotsky: The Eternal Revolutionary* (New York: The Free Press, 1996), 451–52 (corner, face), with The Trotsky Museum, Mexico City (against wall, toe).
26. Herrera, 295.
27. Bardach, 216 (Chávez Morado, Méndez president).
28. Antiguo Colegio de San Ildefonso, Mexico, D.F., http://www.sanildefonso.org.mx/expos/211004a/hogigins02.swf (accessed June 27, 2009).
29. Luis and Lea Remba interview.
30. Volkogonov, 455.
31. Rafael Carrillo interview.
32. Luis and Lea Remba interview.
33. Philip Stein, *Siqueiros: His Life and Works*, (New York: International Publishers, 1994), 133.
34. Robert Payne, *The Life and Death of Trotsky* (New York: McGraw-Hill, 1977), 432.
35. Ibid.
36. Harvey Klehr, John Earl Haynes, and Alexander Vassiliev, *Spies: The Rise and Fall of the KGB in America* (New Haven: Yale, 2009), 477.
37. Pierre Broue of Grenoble, France, authority on Trotsky, correspondence with the

author, May, 1989.
38. Volkognov, 466.
39. "Mexico: Communazi Columnists," *Time*, June 3, 1940.
40. Juan Alberto Cedillo, *Los Nazis en México* (New York: Random House, 2007).
41. Wechsler, "Propaganda Gráfica," in Ittmann, 71.
42. Ibid.
43. Byron Randall interviews. Pablo remained a member until 1947.
44. Bardach, 182–83.
45. Wechsler, in Ittmann, 71.
46. Helga Prignitz-Poda, "Pablo O'Higgins: un cuarto de siglo en el TGP," *Voz de la lucha*, 113.
47. Byron Randall interviews.

CHAPTER 28 | A MEXICAN ARTIST

1. Sometimes it is said he was the only "non-native Mexican" included. http://artsellerexchange.com/artists/ohiggins_prime_include.html.
2. Rosa Rolanda, Andrés Blaisten Museum, www.museoblaisten.com/english.asp?myURL=%2F02asp%2FEnglish%2FartistDetailEnglish%2Easp&myVars=artistId%3D64 (accessed November 6, 2009).
3. MOMA, 187, 189.
4. Ibid., 185.
5. The U.S. could not get enough of Mexican art and especially that of Rivera during the war years. Bertram Wolfe's biography of Rivera, *Diego Rivera, His Life and Times*, had just been published in New York, as had Jean Charlot's *Art from the Mayans to Disney. Modern Mexican Art* by Lawrence Schmeckebier came out in 1939. Rivera spent much of 1940 painting for thousands of fans and spectators at the 1940 Golden Gate International Exhibition in San Francisco, assisted by Emmy Lou Packard, who would later marry Byron Randall and come to know Pablo and Maria.
6. Prignitz, 67.
7. Campos Chronology.
8. Bardach, 208.
9. Prignitz, 67.
10. Bardach, 217–19.
11. T.R. Fehrenbach, *Fire and Blood: A Bold and Definitive Modern Chronicle of Mexico* (New York: Collier Books, 1973), 608; Krauze says 1945, and the wording changed to a "democratic and national" education, Krauze, 507.
12. Fehrenbach, 606–09.
13. deLappe, *A Passionate Journey*, 35.
14. Princeton University Library Digital Collections, http://diglib.princeton.edu/view?_xq=pageturner&_type=book&_doc=%2Fmets%2Fgc061.mets.xml&_inset=0&filename=gc061%2F00261.jpf&_start=47&_index=73&_count=73&47=1&div1=47 (accessed February 25, 2009).
15. http://www.gráficamexicana.com/Catalog_Viewer.asp?dir=filtered&filter=year&year=1941 (accessed April 27, 2009).
16. Bardach: Sindicato Mexicano de Electricistas, 22 de diciembre ... célula Cura Hidalgo P.C. de México, 1942.
17. Fehrenbach, 608.
18. Irma Vega de Bijou, interview by the author, Los Angeles, CA, October 22, 2009.

19. He was rejected because he was underweight, but he was given a position with Rockefeller's Inter-American Affairs office and was paid a $2,400 annual salary for dressing as a Mexican peasant (he was 6' tall) and walking the beaches of Mexico looking for signs of Germans or Japanese. Virtue, 94–101.
20. Vittorio Vidali, *Colección crónicas y testimonios "Retrato de mujer"—Una vida con Tina Modotti* (Puebla: Universidad Autónoma de Puebla, 1984) (translation by Joel Hancock).
21. In April 1943, U.S. President Roosevelt met with Camacho to encourage Mexico to participate more fully in the war efforts. To get the public excited about the idea, on March 5, 1942, Camacho had the Mexican Air Force, Fuerza Aerea Mexicana (FAM), stage a dramatic simulation of an air attack near Mexico City with AT-6's and A-24B's. The response was overwhelming and Camacho announced that Mexico would fight in WW II, with the air force leading the effort. Volunteers came from all over Mexico to serve the mission in many capacities. The FAM flew longrange sorties over Formosa and provided important support in the liberation of the Philippines in 1945.
22. Méndez, *Mariscal Timichenko*, 1942.
23. "Architecture," Bauhaus Archive Museum of Design, http://www.bauhaus.de/english/bauhaus1919/architektur/index.htm (accessed November 26, 2009).
24. Bardach, 224.
25. Ibid. (never before viewed).
26. Ibid., 224.
27. Bardach, 228.
28. Bardach, 229.
29. Ibid.
30. *Voz de la lucha*, 199.
31. Palma Chronology, Poniatowska and Bosques.

CHAPTER 29 | NOT MEXICAN ENOUGH

1. La Estampa Mexicana, "presents 13 lithographs in color and black and white of the Mexican artists," 1943.
2. Campos Chronology, quoting Sarmiento Anaya, "Palabras de Pablo O'Higgins," *Excélsior.* Diorama de la cultura, México, 8 de diciembre de 1957. Whereas Pablo normally took several sessions to create a lithograph, this one he did in one. He called it *A Man*, but Diego Rivera referred to it as *Un hombre del siglo XX*, in a statement for a 1956 exhibit of Pablo's work, and said that it was an enlightening expression of Mexican easel painting emerging from mural painting. Campos Chronology, 1939. Several versions: Another was in his studio in 1990 when I visited.
3. Octavio Paz, *The Labyrinth of Solitude* (New York: Grove Press, 1994).
4. Palma Chronology in Poniatowska and Bosques.
5. Oles, *Walls*, 245, n. 152, referring to the contracts for the Abelardo Rodríguez murals.
6. Mexico and its People, An Exhibition of Painting of Pablo O'Higgins, exhibition catalog (New York: Associated American Artists, 1943).
7. "Una Exposition Muy Mexicana," *Tiempo*, August 18, 1950 (quoting *Tiempo*, Oct. 16, 1942).
8. Charlot ancestry: "Family Background," http://www.jeancharlot.org/onJC/books/BIO%20WEB%20PUB/BIO%20I%202%20FAMILY%20BACKGROUND.htm (accessed December 5, 2009).
9. www.zalce.com (accessed November 28, 2009).
10. See James Oles, *South of the Border* (Washington, D.C: Smithsonian, 1993).

11. Helm, 195.
12. Rafael Carrillo interview.
13. Alice O'Higgins, letter to Pablo, n.d.
14. *Artists of Utah*, 120.
15. Even when I was in high school in the 1970s at East High, the school Pablo attended, career day never included artists. Art was considered a hobby. At East High in the 1970s, young men were expected to go to college and become doctors, lawyers, accountants, and businessmen. Young women were expected to take college courses in early childhood education or teaching. (My sisters and I were dissuaded from attending good colleges thereby taking a seat that a boy could have.) It can't have been more progressive when Pablo attended.
16. Zalce interview, Jean Charlot Collection, University of Hawai'i.
17. Rafael Carrillo interview.
18. Preface, *Voz de la lucha.*
19. Joel Hancock, interview with the author, Salt Lake City, September 21, 2009.
20. Miguel León-Portilla, "El Mundo indígena de Pablo O'Higgins," *Voz de lucha*, 49.
21. María said, "Siendo Pablo artista tan ligado a nuestros problemas y a nuestra realidad, algunas veces fue cuestionado como extranjero e inclusive le suspendieron una obra de la que [sic] ya tenía avanzado el proyecto . . . parecía que tantos años de trabajo intenso, pintando y viviendo como mexicano, no eran suficientes." (Pablo, being an artist so tied to our problems and our reality, sometimes he was questioned as to his being a foreigner and even had a project suspended that he had already begun . . . it seemed that so many years of intense work, painting and living like a Mexican were not sufficient). Uranga López, *El tema campesino*, 42. (Translation by author.)
22. From the 1930s to her death in 1951, Alice Higgins lived in Los Angeles. Her health never prevented her from traveling (she was on a trip from Los Angeles to the San Francisco Bay Area to visit her niece when she died at age 84).
23. This situation brings to mind the story of Emma McCune, a young white British upper-class woman who married a Nuer guerilla commander for the Sudan People's Liberation Army. According to biographer Deborah Scroggins, even though she held a British passport, she was perplexed when she was treated as a white woman and not as a Nuer. Deborah Scroggins, *Emma's War* (New York: Viking, 2004).
24. Lesley Corn, M.A., F.G.B.S., "World War II Fourth Registration Draft Cards: A Newly-Released 20th-Century Resource for 19th-Century Research," New York Genealogical and Biographical Society, http://www.newyorkfamilyhistory.org/modules.php?name=sections&op=printpage&artid=107(accessed December 26, 2009).
25. Pablo O'Higgins, letter to Jean Charlot, January 2, 1943, Jean Charlot Collection, University of Hawai'i.
26. Palma Chronology in Poniatowska and Bosques.
27. *The New York Times*, February 7, 1943.
28. *Art News*, February 1, 1943, 27. Other U.S. artists who worked at the TGP did the same thing, but not expecting to "become Mexican." Frank Rowe whimsically signed his name Francisco (or Pancho) Rosa.
29. Pablo O'Higgins, letter to Jean Charlot, April 27, 1943, in Jean Charlot Collection, University of Hawai'i.

CHAPTER 30 | TEHRAN ACCORD

1. Pablo's letters to Jean Charlot, in Jean Charlot Collection, University of Hawai'i.
2. Pele deLappe, "Pablo O'Higgins, A Fresh Wind from Mexico," *People's Daily World*, February 14, 1949.
3. The Palma Chronology (in Poniatowska and Bosques) says Pablo came to the U.S. in 1945 and worked as a welder in San Francisco shipyards out of a moral duty to fight fascism from his country of origin. It says that six months later, he was discovered to be an artist and was given the commission in Seattle. Interestingly, another chronology, which follows the aforementioned one almost verbatim, omits mention of any wartime work. Híjar, *Apuntes*, 263. It has also been put this way: "[Pablo] returnó a su país de origen para sumarse al esfuerzo bélico ([Pablo] returned to his country of origin to join in the war efforts)." María Luisa Sabau García, "México en el mundo de las colecciónes de arte," Universidad Nacional Autónoma de México, Consejo Nacional para la Cultura y las Artes (Mexico City: 2002), 143. Leticia López Orozco, "Los murales de O'Higgins: una ensananza historica," *Voz e la Lucha*, 103 (1945); *Virginia Stewart, 45 Contemporary Mexican Artists* (Stanford: Stanford University Press, 1951), 87 ("In 1945, on one of his infrequent trips back home . . ."). In his 1950 biography in the TGP publication *Doce Años*, he says he worked as a welder in the San Francisco shipyards for six months in "1944–45." The Campos Chronology says that in 1945 Pablo came to the U.S. to work as a welder in the shipyards of San Francisco using his familiarity with and ability to weld, which he had used in creating encaustics, and he thus contributed to the defeat of fascism. Six months later, his artistic background was discovered and he was hired to paint the Seattle mural. In an essay in a 2005 publication, Prignitz (now Prignitz-Poda) says that in 1944, "Pablo was in Los Angeles to be close to the workers of the U.S. in wartime, and he worked in a port where he also observed and collected ideas and sketches for his murals." Prignitz-Poda, "Pablo O'Higgins," *Voz de la lucha*, 121.
4. Poniatowska and Bosques, 22 (translation by Bernardo Flores-Sahagún).
5. Palma Chronology in Poniatowska and Bosques.
6. The last draft required men aged 18–44 living abroad to register between November 16 and December 31, 1943. See Chapter 29, n. 24. Pablo was then 39. It would be interesting to learn whether Pablo registered, however, these records are not open to the public.
7. John Skovgaad, "The California Labor School," http://zpub.com/gaw/wordpress/wp-content/labor_school_/laborschool-.html (accessed March 25, 2009).
8. Carol Cuenod, telephone interview with the author, San Francisco, September 1, 2009.
9. Carr, 113, citing Earl Browder, *The Road Ahead to Victory and Lasting Power* (New York: Workers Library Publishers, 1944), 62.
10. Carr, 123–25.
11. Carol Cuenod, interview with the author, San Francisco, California, April 16, 2007.
12. Emerson, "Fresco," UW Daily, October 7, 1975.
13. Byron Randall interviews; John Caughlan interview; George Gutekunst, interview by author, Sonoma, California, June 6, 1997.
14. Uranga López, 28–29.
15. Pablo O'Higgins, letter to Earl Robinson, November 15, 1946.
16. David Jenkins oral history, 206.
17. Rushmore, "Art."
18. Tomás Zurián, "El color como medio expresivo en la obra litográfica de Pablo

O'Higgins" (Color as an Expressive Medium in the Lithography of Pablo O'Higgins), *Humanidad recuperada*, 127.

19. "Libros Latinos," http://www.libroslatinos.com/cgi-bin/libros/96074.html (accessed September 6, 2009); Campos Chronology.

20. Julio Moreno, *Yankee Don't Go Home!* (Chapel Hill: University of North Carolina Press, 2007), 53.

21. Stephen R. Niblo, *Mexico in the 1940s* (Wilmington: SR Books, 2000), 333. Re Rockefeller investment: Stanton L. Catlin, oral history interview, July 1–September 14, 1989, Archives of American Art, Smithsonian Institution.

22. The same film was shown in Santiago, Chile. The "publicity agents of Disney" coordinated the cultural exhibitions with openings of the Disney film and children's events in a manner rarely seen at the time. Catlin oral history.

23. Campos Chronology.

24. *Doce Años*, Introduction (invasion); Bardach, 222-23.

25. Prignitz, 90. "Probablemente este cartel no fuera una obra maestra, pero salvó al Taller de perder su local y le evitó la quiebra. Por otra parte indica una clara tendencia hacia la representación simplificada de la historia."

26. Elena Poniatowska, "Mariana Yampolsky," http://www.marianayampolsky.org/texto_homenaje_engl.html (accessed February 14, 2010).

27. Prignitz-Poda, "Pablo O'Higgins," *Voz de la lucha*, 121.

28. Uranga López, 28–29; Leticia López Orozco, "Los murales de O'Higgins: una ensenanza historica," *Voz de la lucha*, 103.

29. David Jenkins oral history, 213.

30. Though this letter is undated, the content indicates it was 1945, as it discusses the situation the Charlots would face when looking for an apartment on their return to Mexico, which was in summer 1945. John Charlot, in an article he wrote, places the date of 1945 on this letter as well. See John Charlot, "Una carta inedita de José Clemente Orozco para Jean Charlot, con extractos de cartas de Pablo O'Higgins," *Parteaguas* (Winter 2008), 92.

31. Pablo O'Higgins letter to Jean Charlot, October 8 [1945], Jean Charlot Collection; Jean Charlot Paintings Catalog, University of Hawai'i.

32. Physical Plant report March 4, 1975; Notes on Pablo O'Higgins, Henry Art Gallery Archives, accession 82–48, box 25, University of Washington.

33. *Oakland Tribune*, July 1, 1945; Pablo O'Higgins file, Henry Art Gallery Archives, University of Washington. Pablo was interviewed in Seattle in September, 1945. Oles, *Walls*, 199, citing Fair Taylor, "Pablo O'Higgins, People's Artist, Completing Murals," *The New World* [Seattle], September 27, 1945.

34. "En la época de la Segunda Guerra Mundial, siente el deber cívico de colaborar con su país en la lucha contra Hitler, contra el fascismo, por ello decide ir a los Estados Unidos. Va siéndose mexicano, dejando en México sus afectos, sus amigos, su trabajo, pues era maestro en La Esmeralda. Dejó todo lo que lo ligaba al lugar donde se vive, va a San Francisco, consigue trabajo como soldador en un barco. Como soldador! Con lo importante que eran sus ojos…." Uranga López, *El tema campesino*, 28–29. María continued, saying "Fue a trabajar como un ciudadano más, a cumplir con el deber de colaborar con su país en la época en que hombres y mujeres están en Guerra. Pero alguien al irle a pagar o algo así, lo reconoció y le preguntó si era O'Higgins el pintor y le dijo con asombro que qué estaba haciendo ahí. Después del incidente, le pidieron que pintara un mural, para el Sindicato de Limpiadores de Quillas de Barcos en Seattle

Washington. Pablo fue una persona civicamente muy elevada. (He went to work like any other citizen to fulfill his duty to collaborate with his country in the time when its men and woman were at war. But someone went to pay him or something and recognized him, and asked if he was O'Higgins the painter and asked with surprise what he was doing there. After this, he was asked to paint the mural, for the Ship Scalers Union in Seattle .... Pablo was a person with a very elevated sense of civic duty.)" Ibid.

35. In an interview after Pablo's death, María O'Higgins was asked if Pablo lived as a revolutionary ("vivió como un revolucionario?") María said, no, "not in the sense of having a pistol in his belt," but then described that he went to the U.S. during World War II "out of a moral duty to fight the war against fascism from his country of origin." Uranga López, *El tema campesino*, 28. (Note that the Campos Chronology cites L.P., "Mural mexicano en Seattle," *Revista de América*, ca. 1945.)

36. Steve Murin, interview by the author, Honolulu, HI, November 5, 2009.

37. Mituse Thompson interview.

38. Steve Murin interview.

39. Sally J. Clark, "Mural mixes politics, art and history," *Seattle Post Intelligencer,* December 2, 1977, 12 (paid $2,000). At the time when the federal minimum wage in the U.S. was 40 cents an hour, or $3.20 a day (http://www.dol.gov/ESA/minwage/chart.htm, accessed November 2, 2009) and in Mexico for a worker was 1.90 pesos a day (Carr, *Communism in Mexico*, 202).

40. Author's interviews with Byron Randall, John Caughlan, George Gutekunst, David Jenkins, Mitsue Thompson, and Terry Goldblatt.

41. Byron Randall interviews; John Caughlan interview.

42. Bardach, 223.

CHAPTER 31 | THE LAST HURRAH OF COMMUNISM

1. The ILWU had its roots in the bloody workers' riot of May 1934, when Australian Harry Bridges led longshoremen in a work slowdown, leading to a three-day general strike that left streets deserted and essentially shut down the city. On July 5, 1934, the police tried to break up the strike. A riot spread from Pier 38 and two men were killed. The strike was seen as a victory to the labor movement in the U.S. and made Bridges a hero. It led Bridges to create the ILWU.

2. Longshoremen now make as much as $130,000 a year. Carl Nolte, "Anniversary of a Dark Day," *San Francisco Chronicle*, July 4, 2009, www.sfgate.com.

3. David Jenkins oral history, 145.

4. Ibid., 176.

5. Ibid., 174.

6. Ibid., 174.

7. Ibid., 175–76.

8. Ibid., 180.

9. Ibid., 167, 181; Johnson, 49 (African-American).

10. David Jenkins oral history, 181.

11. Re "peak": John Skovgaad, "The California Labor School," http://zpub.com/gaw/wordpress/wp-content/labor_school_/laborschool-.html (accessed March 25, 2009); Jenkins oral history.

12. Mark Dean Johnson, ed., *At Work: The Art of California Labor* (San Francisco: San Francisco Historical Society Press, 2003), 49; Skovgaad, *California Labor School.*

13. Pele deLappe interviews.

14. deLappe, *A Passionate Journey*, 38.
15. David Jenkins oral history, 190.
16. Dorothy Walker, "Labor School seeking post-war unity," *San Francisco News*, May 16, 1944; David Jenkins oral history, 185.
17. David Jenkins oral history, 165. In 1929, as chairman of the Council of People's Commissars, Soviet Foreign Minister Vyacheslav Molotov showed American journalists for radical newspapers around Moscow, greeting them with the *Internationale* and impressing them so much they promised to "tell the workers of America how the workers of the Soviet Union live and how they are creating a new life." Applebaum, *Gulag*, 76, citing 1920 visit; Molotov attended the San Francisco U.N. opening. The Secretary-General of the entire U.N. conference was Alger Hiss, who would later be accused of espionage. Stanley Meisler, "U.N. Looks Back at Founding 50 Years Ago," "In San Francisco," *Los Angeles Times*, reprinted in *The Seattle Times*, June 26, 1995. If Pablo's dates were correct in the letter he sent to Earl Robinson, he would have been in San Francisco for this event, the high point of which was a reception for the revolutionaries, put on by the Labor School. David Jenkins oral history, 164.
18. David Jenkins oral history, 200.
19. Johnson, ed., *At Work*, 50.
20. Carol Cuenod interview, 2007; Pablo helped get the TGP five exhibits in the United States, 1944–45: San Francisco, Boston, New York, Chicago and Seattle. Prignitz, 439.

CHAPTER 32 | SEATTLE, 1945

1. Dick Clever, "Ship Scalers: A union's half century of turmoil, tragedy and triumph," *The Seattle Times*, May 2, 1982.
2. Ibid., quoting Don Del Castle.
3. Laura Flores, "Pablo O'Higgins: Pintura y Cambio Social," *Metamórfosis, Northwest Chicano Magazine of Art and Literature* IV, no. 2, col V, no. 1 (1982/1983), 27. "Hallie Donaldson . . . se entero del proyecto (aun nebuloso en cuanto a la forma concreta que debia tomar) a traves de Del Castle, representante de los limpiadores de quillas ante la misma Federación, y sugirió la contratención de O'Higgins, de cuyo trabajo ella tenía conocimiento, para que pintara el mural." (Hallie Donaldson . . . learned of the project [though nebulous in terms of what form it would take] through Del Castle, representative of the ship scalers before the same Federation [Donaldson was a member of the American Federation of Teachers] and suggested they contract with O'Higgins, whose work she knew, to paint the mural). Worked with TGP: http://www.gráficamexicana.com/Catalog_Viewer.asp?dir=filtered&filter=artist&fname=Hallie&lname=Donaldson (accessed June 9, 2009). Attorney John Caughlan, who was involved with the Ship Scalers Union in 1945, said, "I met Pablo in 1945. There was a teacher who is now dead, at a Seattle high school, Hallie Donaldson, who traveled to Mexico and knew Pablo. She suggested an appropriate memorial to the Ship Scalers/Dry Docker [who worked] during the war might be a mural in the Mexican muralist style in the Ship Scalers Hall on 3rd Street. The treasury was full so they decided to do it." John Caughlan interview.
4. Dick Clever, "Ship Scalers," 10.
5. http://dailyuw.com/2002/1/30/letters-to-the-editor/ (accessed August 23, 2009).
6. Daniel C. Lienau, telephone interview by author, Santa Rosa, CA, September 30, 2009.
7. Ibid.

8. Gerda Katz, telephone interview with the author, Los Angeles, CA, July 12, 2009.
9. Daniel Lienau interview.
10. *San Mateo Times*, April 28, 1944.

CHAPTER 33 | EARL ROBINSON

1. Ross Reider, "Earl Hawley Robinson (1910–1991)," HistoryLink.org ssay 2029, November 22, 1999, http://www.historylink.org/index.cfm?DisplayPage=output.cfm&File_Id=2029 (accessed April 16, 2009).
2. Ibid.
3. Michale Denning, *The Cultural Front* (Brooklyn: Verso, 1998), 115.
4. Reider (accessed September 24, 2009). In 1940, during the Soviet-Nazi Non-aggression Pact, Robinson wrote music for a film, *Says Youth*, opposing U.S. involvement in the war in Europe. The following year he received a Guggenheim. "Education: Guggenheim Fellows," *Time*, March 31, 1941. Singer Paul Robeson, who was an All-American athlete, Columbia Law graduate, and Shakespearean actor as well as a singer, was also a suspected Communist with a fat FBI dossier because of his leftist beliefs. The TGP's respect for him is shown in a portrait of him that Leopoldo Méndez created in 1953–54, showing a smiling Robeson with a dove in his hands. Above him are chains that he has broken out of.
5. Bruce Eder, *All Movie Guide*, http://www.answers.com/topic/earl-robinson (accessed September 26, 2009).
6. María recalled being with a group of friends standing around the piano singing the song while Robinson played. Everyone, including Pablo, knew the words, she said. Yet Robinson certainly never knew that Pablo's father was involved in the Joe Hill case. Nor did Maria. And when I mentioned it, she initially adamantly denied it and said that Pablo did not know anything about his father's role in the case. María O'Higgins interviews.
7. Roberto Maestas, interview by the author, Seattle, WA, August 12, 2009.
8. Perry Robinson, telephone interview by author, Jersey City, NJ, September 21, 2009.
9. Ibid.
10. Perry Robinson interview.
11. John Caughlan interview.
12. Pele deLappe, "Pablo O'Higgins, A Fresh Wind from Mexico," *People's Daily World*, February 14, 1949.
13. Pablo O'Higgins, letter to Earl Robinson, January 13, 1946.
14. Ibid., November 15, 1946.
15. Truman referred to it several times in his March 3, 1947, speech in Mexico City.
16. "Well, the Sons of the American Revolution were going around to all the contributors of the Labor School, identifying me as Communist." David Jenkins oral history, 268. A 1991 FOIA request on Pablo, and a follow-up request in 2009, revealed that in 1942, mail sent to Pablo from someone named Helen Selles, in the U.S., was intercepted by the United States National Censorship Office. No reason was given. WW II records describe Leo J. Selles of New York as missing, with a death date of May 1946, and lists his widow as Helen Selles, 24 Broom St., New York. www.ancestry.com, http://search.ancestry.com/cgi-bin/sse.dll?rank=1&new=1&MSAV=1&msT=1&gss=angs-g&gsfn=leo&gsln=selles&ne=2&pcat=ROOT_CATEGORY&h=89481&recoff=1+3+23&db=WWIIcasualties&indiv=1 (accessed March 2, 2009).
17. *¡Victoria! Los artistas del Taller de Gráfica Popular nos unimos al júbilo de todos los trabajadores y hombres progresistas de México y del mundo por el triunfo del glorioso Ejército Rojo y de las armas*

de todas las naciones unidas sobre la Alemánia nazi, como el paso más trascendente para la destrucción total del fascismo! http://www.gráficamexicana.com/Catalog_Viewer.asp?dir=filtered&filter=year&year=1945

18. Pablo O'Higgins, letter to Earl Robinson, January 13, 1946.
19. Kevin Allen Leonard, *The Battle for Los Angeles* (Albuquerque: University of New Mexico Press, 2006) 102-7.
20. Pablo O'Higgins, letter to Earl Robinson, January 13, 1946.
21. Shareen Blair Brysac, *Resisting Hitler: The Life and Death of an American Woman in Nazi Germany* (New York: Oxford University Press, 2000), 218, quoting Jurgen Kuczynski.
22. Harvey Klehr, et al, *Spies*, 437.
23 Peter Max Ascoli, Julius Rosenwald, *The Man Who Built Sears, Roebuck and Advanced the Cause of Black Education in the American South* (Bloomington, University of Indiana Press, 2006), 256.
24. Glenn Fowler, "Martha Dodd Stern Is Dead at 82; Author and an Accused Soviet Spy," *The New York Times*, August 29, 1990 (re source of Stern money).
25. K. Vanden Heuvel, "Grand Illusions," *Vanity Fair*, Sept. 1991, 248.
26. Yvonne Templin interview, 1992.
27. Ibid.
28. Brysac, 395.
29. Pablo O'Higgins, letter to Earl Robinson, November 15, 1946.
30. Diana Anhalt, *A Gathering of Fugitives: American Political Expatriates in Mexico 1948–1965* (Santa Maria, CA: Archer Books, 2001), 34.
31. Rebecca M. Schreiber, *Cold War Exiles in Mexico* (Minneapolis: University of Minnesota, 2008), xi, quoting former U.S. Secretary of State Dean Acheson.
32. The Steins arrived in Mexico in 1948. Anhalt, 30–31.
33. Pablo O'Higgins, letter to Earl Robinson, November 14, 1946.

PART THREE | THE CULTURAL YEARS

1. Viola Patterson, Oral History interview, October 22, 1982, Archives of American Art, Smithsonian Institution.

CHAPTER 34 | A NEW REVOLUTION

1. Palma Chronology, J. Sánchez.
2. Pablo O'Higgins, letter to Earl Robinson, January 13, 1946.
3. Untitled document in University of Washington Henry Art Gallery, "Pablo O'Higgins Lithographs" file, quoting Alma Reed, *The Mexican Muralists* (New York: Crown, 1960).
4. The U.S. government did something similar: In the late 1970s, U.S. President Jimmy Carter told U.S. residents to turn down their thermostats to conserve (meaning use less) energy. In 1980, when Ronald Reagan came into office, through the Code of Federal Regulations, he changed the definition of conservation from using less energy to not wasting it—in other words, crank the heat, just make sure it's not leaking out through drafty windows and doors.
5. Krauze, 528.
6. Octavio Paz, introduction to *Massacre in Mexico*, by Elena Poniatowska (Columbia: University of Missouri Press, 1975), xiv–xv.
7. Ibid.
8. Bardach, 275, quoting Poniatowska, "Los 60 años de Leopoldo Méndez," 18 (translation by Efraín Méndez).

9. Though the TGP did produce the materials, and Alemán won, my father recalls seeing few campaign materials for Alemán in Mexico City the summer of 1946, but "abundant campaign signs and posters for his opponent Ezequiel Padilla." Bill Vogel, interview with the author, Salt Lake City, November 12, 2009.
10. Bardach, 242.
11. Boullosa, "Their Boots Were Made for Walking: El Taller de Gráfica Popular," http://www.wordswithoutborders.org/?lab=BoullosaBoots# (accessed July 9, 2009), 5.
12. Pablo O'Higgins, letter to Earl Robinson, November 15, 1946.
13. Ibid.
14. Bardach, 241.
15. Bardach, 230.
16. Williams, "Evolution of a Revolution," in Ittmann, 16.
17. Herzog, 56.
18. Seymour Kaplan interviews.
19. Prignitz, 429.
20. Schreiber, 149, quoting Willard Motley.
21. Krauze, 524.
22. Krauze, 557.
23. Carr, 183.
24. Victoria Schultize, "Pablo O'Higgins," *Salt Lake Tribune*, December 8, 1988; Rafael Carrillo interview.
25. Bardach, 123, n. 245.
26. Noah Bardach, telephone interview with the author, Los Angeles, July 19, 2009.
27. Bardach, 255.
28. Karl M. Schmitt, *Communism in Mexico: A Study in Political Frustration* (Austin: University of Texas, 1965), 80.
29. Martin C. Neelder, *Mexican Politics: The Containment of Conflict* (Santa Barbara: Greenwood Press: 1995), 59.
30. Bardach, 273.
31. Schmitt, 80; Palma Chronology, Poniatowska and Bosques.
32. Krauze, 593.
33. Palma Chronology in Poniatowska and Bosques.
34. Bardach, 253.
35. Bardach, 255.
36. Bardach, 271.

CHAPTER 35 | TGP SHAKEUP

1. Boullosa, 6.
2. Boullosa, 4; Krauze, 574.
3. Boullosa, 4.
4. Pablo O'Higgins letter to Earl Robinson, September 2, 1947.
5. Krauze, 595.
6. Ibid.
7. Secret police, Anhalt, 99; petroleum, Anhalt, 99, n. 5, citing Barry Carr re the U.S. government's Four Point program.
8. Krauze, 595.
9. Bardach, 246.
10. Ibid.

11. Bardach, 243.
12. Bardach, 232.
13. Bardach, 238.
14. Seymour Kaplan interviews.
15. Tibol, *Gráficas*, 152.
16. Ibid.
17. Ibid., 158.
18. http://www.graficamexicana.com/Catalog_Viewer.asp?dir=filtered&filter=year&year=1947 (assessed July 3, 2009).
19. Pablo O'Higgins, letter to Jean Charlot, Nov. 3, 1947, Jean Charlot Collection. "Sobre mi propio trabajo, estoy dissatisfecho [sic]—pues he pintado poco aquí en el estudio y no he podido organizar la necesaria rit o de trabajo. Lo poco he hecho no me conviene." (Translation by author.)
20. Ibid.
21. Ibid. "En el caballete no he podido iniciar algun trabajo nuevo que me anime realmente." (Translation by author)

CHAPTER 36 | THE TGP IN CALIFORNIA

1. Biberman painted a portrait of Paul Robeson. Biberman, his wife, and his brother were all named as Communists by a witness before HUAC. His brother went to jail. Mark Vallen, "Edward Biberman Revisited," June 22, 2009, http://art-for-a-change.com/blog/category/mexican-muralism (accessed September 1, 2009).
2. Lived with Méndez: http://web.utk.edu/~gumbo/speakers.html (accessed September 25, 2009).
3. Pablo O'Higgins letter to Earl Robinson, September 2, 1947.
4. Prignitz, 123.
5. Ibid.
6. Prignitz, 93.
7. Prignitz, 123.
8. Prignitz, 124.
9. Ibid.
10. Rowe, 5. In March 1947, U.S. President Truman initiated loyalty oaths, requiring that public employees swear that they were not and had never been members of any organization advocating for the overthrow of the U.S. government. Frank Rowe, who worked in the Taller in Mexico City in 1946, lost his job as an art teacher at San Francisco State University in 1950 when he refused to sign the oath required of all California State employees. This began a 20-year battle to get the loyalty oath overturned and a 27-year battle to be reinstated in his job. His story is in: Frank Rowe, *The Enemy Among Us* (Sacramento: Cougar Books, 1980).
11. Schreiber, 174, quoting Richard Fried.
12. Pablo O'Higgins, letter to Earl Robinson, September 2, 1947.
13. George Gutekunst interview, 1997.
14. A chronology of Pablo's work says that he, "Participó con una litografía en el concurso interno del TGP sobre el tema 'Retrato de Víctor Marco Antonio,' líder estadunidense que sufrió persecuciones durante el macartismo" (Participated with a lithograph in an internal contest of the TGP regarding the theme "Portrait of Victor Marco Antonio," a U.S. student leader who suffered persecution during the McCarthy era). Campos Chronology. It would be interesting to know if a copy has survived.

15. David Jenkins oral history, 205.
16. David Jenkins oral history, 207.
17. Carr, *Communism in Mexico*, 134–35.
18. The party membership card said "Travelers Club." T. Michael Holmes, *Specter of Communism in Hawaii* (Honolulu: University of Hawai'i, 1994), 184.
19. Holmes, 7.
20. Evans, *Blacklisted*, 622, n. 8.
21. Anhalt, 18.
22. Anhalt, 66.
23. Carol Wells, interview by author, Los Angeles, CA, July 9, 2009.
24. Brysac, 370.
25. http://www.paulrobesonfoundation.org/biography.html (accessed September 11, 2009).
26. Pablo O'Higgins, letter to Jean Charlot, April 19 [1948], Jean Charlot Collection, University of Hawai'i; re *Picture Book*, Karen Thompson, "Jean Charlot," Jean Charlot Collection, University of Hawai'i, http://libweb.Hawai'i.edu/libdept/charlotcoll/J_Charlot/charlotthompson.html (accessed November 6, 2009). It does not appear that Kistler printed any of Pablo's work. Lynton Kistler, Oral History Transcript 1988–89, UCLA Oral History, http://www.archive.org/details/fineartslithogra00kist (accessed November 9, 2009).
27. Pablo O'Higgins, letter to Jean Charlot, April 19, [1948], Jean Charlot Collection, University of Hawai'i.
28. Ibid., December 27, 1947.
29. "Randall encouraged cooperation among his fellow artists, forming the Artists' Guild of San Francisco, of which he was the first president, as well as the Arts Association (also in San Francisco) which successfully lobbied for public money for the arts. An avowed Communist. . . ." Margi Gómez, "Byron Randall: The Mendocino Years," http://www.realestatemendocino.com/pdfs_editorials/editorial_469print.pdf (accessed November 3, 2009). During the 1940s, he was very active as the founder of the Artists Guild of San Francisco and co-chairman of a group which acquired a grant to stage the first open-air art show in the city. Chris Samson, "Artist finds his place in the country," http://home.comcast.net/~2samsons/Chris/Writing/Artists/randall.html (accessed November 3, 2009).
30. Prignitz, 124 (full image). Inaugural address, Prignitz-Poda, "Pablo O'Higgins," *Voz de la lucha*, 122.
31. Prignitz, 124.
32. Ibid.
33. Ibid., 122–24. They produced calendars from 1953 to 1957, as well as a publication, "A Graphic History of the Negro People in America." Ibid., 124, n. 172.
34. Ibid., 125.
35. Seymour Kaplan interviews.
36. Schrieber, 51. In the U.S., artists moved too toward abstract expressionism. Frank Rowe saw it as a retreat from the exposure of social realism in light of the loss of personal liberties during the McCarthy era. Rowe, 89.
37. Seymour Kaplan interviews.
38. "Como yo esperaba no conseguí la aplicación del Guggan y Jean, agradezco sumamente tu ayuda—lo siento es haber molestado a mis amigos—perdiendo tiempo en una cosa inútil—y no lo voy a hacer otra vez." (Translation by author.)

39. The Chouinard Foundation, "About Nelbert Chouinard," http://www.chouinardfoundation.org/nelbertchouinard (accessed February 4, 2010).
40. Pablo O'Higgins letter to Jean Charlot, April 19, 1948.
41. Ibid.

CHAPTER 37 | CALIFORNIA LABOR SCHOOL

1. Carol Cuenod interview, 2009.
2. Skovgaad, *The California Labor School.*
3. George Hitchcock, letter to "Dear Friend," December 20, 1948, archives of California Labor School, Labor Archives and Research Center, San Francisco State University.
4. Image from California Labor School archives, Labor Archives and Research Center, San Francisco State University, provided by Carol Cuenod.
5. Pele deLappe, "Pablo O'Higgins, A Fresh Wind from Mexico," *People's Daily World*, February 14, 1949.
6. Byron Randall and Pele deLappe interviews.
7. Rowe, 10–11.
8. deLappe, *A Passionate Journey*, 41.
9. Ibid.
10. Ibid., 42
11. David Jenkins oral history, 191.
12. Ibid., 172 (classes). The party also, historically, had forbidden "open homosexuals" to be members. Ibid., 126.
13. Jenkins appeared before the Tenney Committee in Oakland at the courthouse in early November, 1947. Jenkins oral history, 230.
14. Johnson, ed., 51.
15. David Jenkins oral history, 209.
16. Ibid., 186–87. The government had also taken away W. E. B. DuBois's U.S. passport (Ibid., 205). Communist leaders such as Jenkins were told they might go into hiding. He did not, but others went underground.
17. Johnson, ed., 68.
18. U.S. Department of State, "Report on the Communist "peace" offensive, a campaign to disarm and defeat the United States (1951)," 66–67.
19. Virtue, 153.
20. Virtue, 160.
21. Virtue, 152–4.
22. Carol Cuenod interviews.
23. U.S. State Department Report, 66–67. "Assisting O'Higgins with congress arrangements was Dr. Esther Chapas, who was formerly a collaborator of Jacques Mornard, alias Frank Jacson, the assassin of Trotsky. Also taking an active part were such well-known Latin-American Communists as Lombardo Toledano, Diego Rivera, Narciso Bassols, Fernando Bamboa [sic], and Alfaro Siqueiros [sic], of Mexico . . . Lázaro Pena and Juan Marinello of Cuba; Salvador Ocampo and Pablo Neruda, exiled from Chile; and Solano, secretary general of the Panamanian Communist Party."
24. "The congress decided to establish an artists' section to utilize the talents of craftsmen in Mexico and four cities in the United States (Los Angeles, Chicago, New York and San Francisco) for the publication of a bimonthly magazine. Active in the promotion of this project were Lilli Anne Killen Rosenberg and Victor Arnautoff of

San Francisco, Peggy Craft of Chicago, Antonio Fransoni of New York, and Leopoldo Méndez and Pablo O'Higgins of Mexico City." The report goes on to list the people in the U.S. supporting the peace congress as including Thomas Mann, Dorothy Parker, Clifford Odets, Marion Greenwood, Martha Dodd, Waldo Frank, Dashiell Hammett, Albert Maltz, Anton Refrieger, and Max Weber.

25. Given that the State Department now had the information on the peace congress, it is likely that Pablo was watched during this stay in the U.S. It is odd that multiple FOIA requests have not turned up a larger file on Pablo (Carol Cuneod's was in the hundreds of pages, of which 90 or so were blacked out).

26. Anhalt, 19, 44–45.

27. Seymour Kaplan interviews.

28. Nancy Rowe, e-mail correspondence with author, June 16, 2009.

29. The gallery was founded in 1948 by Victor Selinsky, a recent graduate of Otis Art Institute, and his business partner Manny Singer. It was destroyed in a fire (Byron Randall suspected arson) and reopened on La Cienaga. Paul Kantor Oral History, UCLA Oral History Program (Los Angeles: University of California, 1982), 154, http://www.archive.org/stream/paulkantororalhi00kant#page/n327/mode/2up, (accessed August 1, 2009).

30. Victor "Vic" Selinsky, artist biography, www.askart.com/askART/studio/studio.aspx?studio=11010321 (accessed July 8, 2009). Artists who worked with the TGP exhibited there, including Morton Dimondstein, Selinsky's Otis classmate, in 1954, after two years at the TGP in Mexico. Ibid.

31. Goldman, 129.

32. Art historian Shifra Goldman noted O'Higgins's influence in a work of his former student, Francisco Corzas, which portrayed a group of workers drinking in a bar. Goldman, 128.

33. Daniel Gómez interview.

34. The ratio is usually approximately 5:8.

35. R. Meyer, *A Dictionary of Art Terms and Techniques* (New York: Thomas Y. Crowell Co., Inc., 1969); B. Myers (ed.), McGraw-Hill Dictionary of Art (New York: McGraw-Hill, 1969); Byron Randall interviews ("bones").

36. Daniel Gómez interview.

37. Palma Chronology in Poniatowska and Bosques; funded by the government, Herzog, 78.

38. Prignitz-Poda, 125–26.

39. Bardach, 173.

40. Bardach, 194, 221, 255, 276, and 272, quoting Hannes Meyer.

41. Bardach, 279.

42. *Chopin creando su tema de las baladas*, 1949; *Chopin y el pueblo polaco*, www.gráficamexicana.com.

43. Prignitz, 132.

CHAPTER 38 | AN EXPATRIATE COMMUNITY

1. Schreiber, 67, n. 28.
2. Schreiber, xi–xii.
3. Schreiber, 202.
4. Anhalt, 89.
5. Anhalt, 115 (Article 33)

6. Diana Anhalt, telephone interview by the author, Atlanta, Georgia, February 7, 2010. Anhalt said the Mexican authorities mainly carried out the wishes of the U.S. in terms of whom to deport.
7. Anhalt, 114.
8. Anhalt, 116.
9. Anhalt, 119.
10. Virtue, 153; e-mail correspondence with Diana Anhalt, March 18, 2010, referring to her correspondence with Dickinson (re train, dispute).
11. Virtue, 90. "O'Higgins, who was Stirling's house guest at the time . . . became one of the country's leading artists." Virtue, 139.
12. Virtue, 163-67. Anhalt, however, says that the Sobells were deported on August 16th. E-mail correspondence with author, March 18, 2010.
13. Virtue, 165.
14. Anhalt, 109.
15. Anhalt, 110 (author's translation); Schreiber, 67.
16. Virtue, 166–67.
17. "Una Exposición muy Mexicana," *Tiempo*, August 18, 1950. (According to the article the exhibit opened the Monday of the prior week.) Krauze quotes *Tiempo*'s founder, Martín Luis Guzmán, as refusing to print anything other than the official report of the Alemán government's brutally breaking up a meeting in support of an opposition candidate, leaving people dead. He says that Guzmán said he had the "obligation to mutilate and deform the truth" if necessary to promote his publication's political objectives. Krauze, 582.
18. *Tiempo*, August 18, 1950.
19. Joel Hancock, interview by the author, Salt Lake City, September 21, 2009. Hancock grew up in Mexico City in the 1950s and attended the American School in Mexico City with many expatriate children.
20. Mauricio Devaux, "La Exposición de Pablo O'Higgins," *Excelsior*, August 27, 1950.
21. Schreiber, 69, n. 46.
22. Salvador Jiménez, interview by the author, Salt Lake City, October 29, 2009.
23. Krauze, 582.

CHAPTER 39 | A "SUBVERSIVE ORGANIZATION"

1. The same allegations were contained in the Sixth Report of Un-American Activities in California, also dated 1951.
2. Prignitz, 143, n. 207, refers to a 1977 conversations with those artists.
3. Herzog, 75, 79. Mariana Yampolsky, a U.S. citizen who joined the TGP in 1944 and became a Mexican citizen in 1954, does not appear to have had any problems as a U.S. citizen in Mexico during this time.
4. Conversation with Carol Leadenham, Assistant Archivist for Reference, Hoover Institution Archives, Stanford University, January 28, 2010.
5. A law went into effect in 1952 requiring U.S. citizens to have a passport if they are to enter or leave the U.S. See Jaffe, "The Right to Travel: The Passport Problem," 35 Foreign Affairs 17. "[I]t was first made a requirement by § 215 of the Act of June 27, 1952, 66 Stat. 190, 8 U.S.C. § 1185, 8 U.S.C.A. § 1185, which states that, after a prescribed proclamation by the President, it is 'unlawful for any citizen of the United States to depart from or enter, or attempt to depart from or enter, the United States unless he bears a valid passport.'" *Rockwell Kent and Walter Briehl, Petitioners, v. John Foster*

Dulles, Secretary of State, June 16, 1958, 2 L.Ed.2d 1204; 357 U.S. 116; 78 S.Ct. 1113.

6. Paul P. Kennedy, "Passport Ruing Shifted in Mexico," *New York Times*, June 29, 1958. The State Department, in 1952, had denied U.S. citizen Rockwell Kent a passport he requested to travel to Europe, on the grounds that he refused to sign an affidavit regarding his involvement with the Communist Party. This precedent continued until January 1958, when the U.S. Supreme Court overturned the case.

7. Former President Richard Nixon, in 1973, suggested abortion was "necessary" when "you have a black and a white." "On Nixon Tapes, Ambivalence Over Abortion, Not Watergate," *The New York Times*, June 23, 2009, http://www.nytimes.com/2009/06/24/us/politics/24nixon.html?_r=1 (accessed September 10, 2009).

8. Noah Bardach, conversation with author, re interview of Elizabeth Catlett, December 6, 2006.

9. Schreiber, 200. Herzog says, "Once she became a Mexican citizen in 1962, she did not attempt to reenter the U.S. until 1971. . . . Her [1961] trip to Washington to make this speech was her last until 1971, because her Mexican citizenship meant that her country of origin could now bar her from entry." Herzog, 108. Schrieber, however, says, "after becoming a Mexican citizen in 1962, Catlett continually was denied a visa to enter the United States." Schreiber, 212. "The U.S. government's persistent refusal to give her a visa in the 1960s and early 1970s was based on the provision of the Immigration and Nationality Act of 1952 that prohibited those the government perceived as 'Communists' from entering the country." Schreiber says after being denied a visa in 1970, Catlett attended a conference by phone. Ibid.

10. Prignitz says that according to Catlett, in July 1956, 76 TGP works were confiscated in customs for being anti-American. The works were en route to Garelick's Gallery in Detroit. A court ordered that some could be displayed. Prignitz, 143, n. 207.

11. Daniel Gómez interview.

12. Campos Chronology.

13. Daniel Gómez interview.

14. The autopsy revealed "emphysema of chest" as a contributing condition.

15. The Mexican Cultural Institute of New York, "Embracing Mexico," May 11, 2007 http://www.lavitrina.com/artman/publish/article_182.shtml (accessed February 14, 2010).

16. Daniel C. Lienau interview.

17. The U.S. Supreme Court reversed, but the legal battles continued until 1958, when he was issued a U.S. passport.

18. Prignitz, 150–51.

19. "Exposiciónes individuales" and "Exposiciónes colectivas," OAS files, Washington, D.C.

20. Prignitz, 142.

21. Prignitz, 143, n. 205.

22. *Time*, September 14, 1953, http://www.time.com/time/magazine/article/0,9171,858259-8,00.html (accessed August 29, 2009).

23. Tina Martin interviews.

24. Krauze, 590.

25. Krauze, 589.

26. Krauze, 593.

27. Boullosa, 7.

28. Bardach, 266-67, citing Prignitz, 163 (re national culture).

29. Craven, 57, citing Pablo González Casanova, *La democracia en Mexico.*
30. Prignitz, 140.
31. Herzog, 94–5; Prignitz, 140.
32. Bardach (garbage can), Méndez, then Pablo: Bardach, conversation with the author, re interview with Arturo García Bustos, December 4, 2006.
33. Krauze, 558. The award was given in 1951.

CHAPTER 40 | THE HAWAI'I MURALS

1. John Charlot, telephone interview with the author, Honolulu, November 4, 2009.
2. Steve Murin interview.
3. Moray Epstein, "Left-Wing Artist Is Sought For ILWU Building's Mural," *Honolulu Star-Bulletin*, March 14, 1952 (preference).
4. Steve Murin, interview with the author, Honolulu, November 5, 2009.
5. Louis Goldblatt oral history, 413.
6. Pablo O'Higgins, letter to Lou Goldblatt, December 17, 1951, in files of ILWU, Honolulu, Hawai'i.
7. Ibid., December 18, 1951.
8. Jack W. Hall, letter to Pablo O'Higgins, December 17, 1951, in files of ILWU, Honolulu, Hawai'i.
9. Steve Murin interview.
10. Pablo O'Higgins, letter to Lou Goldblatt January 19, 1952.
11. Ibid. Nowhere in many files of materials and news clips about the mural and about Pablo in the ILWU library is there any mention of him having worked as a longshoreman when living in San Diego. Rather, the articles talk of how he spent three months visiting union members throughout the islands to learn about their work and lives.
12. George Gutekunst interview, 1989.
13. At the time, a longshoreman in Local 142 made $1.88 an hour. So if Pablo worked for six months for eight hours a day, he was making $4.16 an hour. Rae Shiraki, ILWU Local 142 librarian, e-mail correspondence with author, November 4, 2009, re longshoreman wages, citing "Hawai'i Stevedore Straight Time Wage Rates" chart in brochure for the 40th Anniversary of the 1949 Longshore Strike, September 4, 1989.
14. John Charlot interview, November 2, 2009.
15. Jack Hall, letter to Pablo O'Higgins, February 7, 1952.
16. Jack Hall, letter to Lou Goldblatt, February 28, 1952.
17. "The Story of the Murals, the Muralist at Work," *ILWU Reporter*, October 22, 1952, 1–2.
18. Morey Epstein, "Left-Wing Artist Is Sought for ILWU Building's Mural," *Honolulu Star-Bulletin*, March 14, 1952.
19. Louis Goldblatt oral history, 403.
20. Phil Meyer, "Mural embodies isle labor struggle," *Honolulu Star-Bulletin*, October 5, 1987.
21. Steve Murin interview.
22. Devout Catholic, art: Bronwen Solyom, curator, Jean Charlot Collection, interviews with the author, University of Hawai'i Manoa Library, Honolulu, November 4–5, 2009.
23. Per date of photo of Pablo on Moloka'i, ILWU Mural Archives, Honolulu.
24. Mitsue Thompson said, "David's artistic abilities did not come out until he started working with Pablo." Mitsue Thompson, interviews. *ILWU Reporter*, April 23, 1952 (arrival), June 25, 1952 (Thompson leave), July 30, 1952 (Diego); Mitsue Thompson

interview (driving around); Steve Murin interview (leg).

25. Charlot diaries, April 17, 1951, May 1, 1951, May 19, 1951, September 19, 1951, and September 22, 1951.

26. Steve Murin interview.

27. Oles, *Walls*, 257, n. 180.

28. Mitsue Thompson interview.

29. T. Oshiro, letter to Pablo O'Higgins, October 14, 1952, ILWU Local 142 archives.

30. Alejandro Acevedo Valenzuela, "Sinfónia plásticas de Pablo O'Higgins," *12 la guía*, January 14, 1983.

31. Holmes, 190. The others were former schoolteacher John Reinecke; Jack Kimoto and Koji Ariyoshi of the *Honolulu Record*; Jim Freeman, a mechanic; Charles Fujimoto, alleged party head; and Eileen Fujimoto, secretary of Local 136 of the ILWU.

32. Rae C. Shiraki, Library Services Coordinator, ILWU Local 142, Honolulu, e-mail correspondence with author, November 9, 2009.

33. Stephen Schwartz, "Article Says Bridges Was a Communist," *San Francisco Chronicle*, November 6, 1992.

34. Mitsue Thompson interview.

35. Steve Murin interview.

36. Ibid.

37. Mike Leidemann, "Laborious Art," *The Honolulu Advertiser*, September 28, 2001.

38. Mitsue Thompson interview.

39. "The Story of the murals—the muralist at work," *ILWU Reporter*, October 22, 1952.

40. Carl Damaso, letter to Scott Matheson, November 5, 1979, archives of the ILWU Local 142.

41. Scott Matheson, letter to Carl Damaso, November 12, 1979.

42. Postcard invitation; Terry Goldblatt interviews, 1989, 1992.

43. David Jenkins, telephone interview with the author, San Francisco, October 4, 1988.

44. Nancy Rowe, e-mail correspondence with author, August 23, 2009.

45. Carol Cuenod, telephone interview, San Francisco, September 1, 2009.

46. The letter appears to be responding to correspondence from the State Department to the governor, dated September 5, 1952. This letter was obtained pursuant to the author's FOIA request, October 21, 1991.

47. Letter David Thompson to Pablo O'Higgins, December 3, 1952.

50. The large lithograph arrived folded up, in a manila envelope. Rae Shiraki, Library Services Coordinator, ILWU Local 142, Honolulu, Hawai'i, conversation with the author, November 3, 2009.

CHAPTER 41 | EXECUTIONS AND EXILES

1. Stephan Thernstrom, Ann Orlov, and Oscar Handlin, *Harvard Encyclopedia of American Ethnic Groups* (Cambridge, Mass: Harvard, 1980), 746.

2. Anhalt, 40. Between 1945 and 1966 the U.S. instituted deportation proceedings against 15,000 "subversive aliens" and deported 250. Ellen Schrecker, *The Age of McCarthyism* (Basingstoke: Palgrave McMillan, 2002), 55.

3. Anhalt, 40.

4. Krauze, 606–09.

5. Krauze, 608.

6. Anhalt, 130, calm.

7. Rowe, 105. The executions inspired him to begin teaching a children's art class on

Saturdays at the California Labor School. Rowe, 102–03, 105. In September 1953, when the Rowe family moved from the Mission to Santa Rosa, they were followed by the FBI. When they later moved to Sacramento, the FBI showed up there as well. Ibid., 105.
8. K. Vanden Heuvel, "Grand Illusions," *Vanity Fair*, September, 1991.
9. Ibid.; Harvey Klehr, et al, *Spies*, 431-45.
10. Anhalt, 89.
11. Anhalt, 52.
12. K. Vanden Heuvel, "Grand Illusions," *Vanity Fair*, September, 1991. Randall and Templin confirmed that Dodd became Pablo's "lover and patron." Byron Randall interviews; Yvonne Templin interview.
13. Byron Randall interviews.
14. Yvonne Templin interview. María O'Higgins denies he had seizures and the existence of a trust fund, but did say that he fell from a scaffold in 1960.
15. K. Vanden Heuvel, "Grand Illusions."
16. Mark Vallen, "Diego Rivera: Glorious Victory!" Art For A Change, October 5, 2007, www.art-for-a-change.com/blog/2007/10/diego-rivera-glorious-victory.html.
17. Krauze, 622; supported by the TGP, Schreiber, 179.
18. Anhalt, 88.
19. "The Roundup," *Time*, November 1, 1954.
20. Sydney Gruson, "Mexico Is Prodded to Clean Up Reds," *The New York Times*, July 20, 1954.
21. Herzog, 83–84.
22. Herzog, 87.
23. Noah Bardach, conversation with the author, re Catlett interview, December 6, 2006.
24. Herzog, 87, n. 39.
25. Herzog, 102.
26. Herzog, 103.
27. Prignitz, 160.
28. Prignitz, 160. She also says it was 12 prints.
29. Most publications in Mexico do not mention the fate of these prints, only that the prints "had the destination of the magazine *Freedom*." See, e.g., Eduardo Espinosa Campos, "Trabajos de ilustracion," *Voz de la lucha*, 150.
30. Schreiber, 173, n. 7.
31. Angel Picon, "El Muralismo, Bajo el Pincel de Pablo O'Higgins," *Novedades*, January 23, 1954.
32. Schreiber, 213, n. 40.
33. Bardach, 249.

CHAPTER 42 | TGP INTERNAL CONFLICTS

1. Bardach, conversation with the author, re interview with Catlett, December 6, 2006.
2. Bardach, conversation with the author, re interview with Alfredo García Bustos December 4, 2006.
3. See Note 1. In reflecting on the demise of the TGP, Catlett mentioned Méndez "taking off with the archives of the Taller," and her discomfort with Méndez, the unequivocal head of the Taller and mentor of the younger artists, in 1962, when he was 60 years old, leaving his wife, Andrea, with whom Taller members were close, to live with a young model whom he had met in his teaching job at La Esmeralda. Also, Elena Poniatowska, "Leopoldo Méndez, cien años de vida," *La Jornada*, May 23, 2002.

4. Bardach, 123, n. 245. The PP supporters were Mariana Yampolsky, Adolfo Mexiac, Ángel Bracho, Alberto Beltrán, Fanny Rabel, and Ignacio Aguirre. Members of the more militant PCM were Arturo García Bustos, Francisco Mora, Elizabeth Catlett, Guillermo Monroy, Antonio Pujol, Luis Arenal, Mercedes Quevedo, and Oscar Fria.
5. Bardach, 258-59.
6. Ibid., 258.
7. Ibid., 265.
8. Prignitz, 167 (estampas religiosas).
9. Ibid.
10. Prignitz, 157. Translation by Julio César Tapia y Guzmán. On February 17, 1952, Siqueiros had had a reconciliation with Rivera, celebrated by nearly 100 artists, government officials, and the expatriate community in the garden of María Asunsolo's home in the wealthy Pedregal neighborhood of Mexico City. Anhalt, 91.
11. Bardach, 264–65.
12. Lyle Williams, "Evolution of a Revolution," in Ittmann, 19–21.
13. Prignitz, 158–59.
14. Ibid., 159.
15. Bardach, 265.
16. Prignitz, 159.
17. Ibid.
18. Ibid., 159, n. 238.
19. Ibid., 160.
20. Byron Randall interviews.
21. Prignitz, 161.
22. Emmy Lou Packard, "Notes on Rivera Frescoes at Golden Gate International Exposition, San Francisco, 1940," July 1958, 5, Packard Archives.
23. Prignitz, 161.
24. Prignitz, 171, n. 276.
25. Prignitz, 163.
26. Bardach 242, citing Prignitz 103.
27. Prignitz, 163.
28. Prignitz, 166.
29. Oles, *Walls*, 233, n. 115.
30. David Jenkins oral history, 231.
31. Carol Cuenod, telephone interview with the author, San Francisco, September 1, 2009.
32. David Jenkins oral history, 231.
33. Rowe, 106.
34. Mitford, 272.
35. Rowe, 106.
36. Ibid.
37. Krauze, 592.
38. David Jenkins oral history, 190.
39. Bardach, conversation with the author, re Catlett interview, December 6, 2006.

CHAPTER 43 | DEPORTATIONS

1. Anhalt, 147–48.
2. Anhalt, 150, re Cuba.

3. K. Vanden Heuvel, 256.
4. *Nevada State Journal*, Reno, April 21, 1957. "Mr. & Mrs. W.C. Higgins returned last week from a tour of Mexico where they visited their cousin . . . . Sister Gladys accompanied them."
5. Herzog, 78.
6. Herzog, 78.
7. "Mexico: Red Haven," *Time*, September 9, 1957, http://www.time.com/time/magazine/article/0,9171,893629,00.html (accessed August 29, 2009). Ironically, William Burroughs contributed to this depiction by describing Mexico as a place where one could "live like a Prince." Schreiber, 166, quoting William Burroughs. The Beats were in Mexico to drop out of "U.S. consumer-driven society." Ibid.
8. Anhalt, 154.
9. Anhalt, 154–55.
10. "Red contra espias a lo largo de la frontera—500 hombres viligan para evitar que aquellos escapan de México."
11. Anhalt, 156.
12. Anhalt, 157.
13. Anhalt, 158–59.
14. Anhalt, 159.
15. Krauze, 617-23.
16. Ibid.
17. Schreiber, 191–92. Alemán had purged Communists from the oil, rail, and mining unions in 1948–51, and, to cooperate with the U.S. during the cold war, declared the PRI "staunchly anti-Communist," and purged Communists from government. Writers Octavio Paz and Carlos Fuentes joined the strikers. Krauze, 623–24.
18. Krauze, 638.
19. Bardach, 266–68.
20. Anhalt, 171.
21. Schreiber, 187 (mentioning John Bright).
22. Anhalt, 172.
23. Ibid., 174. Rebecca Schreiber, however, says that Catlett's three children were all United States citizens. *Cold War Exiles*, p. 267.
24. Anhalt, 173.
25. Anhalt, 173–74.
26. Schreiber, 191, n. 90.
27. Schreiber, 191.
28. Ibid., quoting an article by Manuel Camin titled, "Ninguno debe quedar en el país" (No one should remain in the country), *Ultimas Noticias de Novedades*, September 10, 1958.
29. Anhalt, 176.
30. Anhalt, 177.
31. Halperins: Anhalt, 178; James C. McKinley, Jr., "Maurice Halperin, 88, a Scholar Who Chronicled Castro's Career," *New York Times*, February 15, 1995, http://www.nytimes.com/1995/02/12/obituaries/maurice-halperin-88-a-scholar-who-chronicled-castro-s-career.html (accessed November 24, 2009).
32. Bardach, 256.
33. Bardach, 269.
34. Anhalt, 169–70, quoting Alonso Aguilar. Writer Enrique Krauze notes that

López Mateos, the Partido Popular's presidential choice, did not limit his repression to expatriates and strikers: Siqueiros went to jail for nearly all of López Mateos's administration for violating Article 45, the crime of "social dissolution." Krauze, 637.
35. Bardach, 269, citing Prignitz.
36. Schreiber, 70. Anhalt says that Catlett, having lived in Mexico more than five years, would have already become an *inmigrado*. E-mail correspondence, March 18, 2010.
37. Anhalt, 139-40.
38. Anhalt, 225.
39. Anhalt, 89–90.
40. Anhalt, 108.
41. Anhalt, 139.
42. Anhalt, 177.
43. Anhalt, 143, Jorge Espinosa de los Reyes.
44. Schreiber, 47. "In 1951, with letters of recommendation from Pablo O'Higgins and Diego Rivera, John Wilson applied for and received a grant from the Institute of International Education in 1951, which enabled him to remain in Mexico."
45. Schreiber, 73, n. 70.
46. Schreiber, 173, n. 6.
47. Schreiber, 69, quoting Maltz letter.
48. Anhalt, 178.
49. Ibid., 180.
50. Ibid.
51. Anhalt, 181–82.
52. Anhalt, 197.

CHAPTER 44 | LA RUPTURA

1. As early as 1952, groups began forming against the "official political art" of social realism. Goldman, *Contemporary Mexican Painting*, 35. The protest did not find widespread support until the late 1950s.
2. *Ruptura 1952–1965*, Catálogo de la exposición (México, D.F.: INBA/SEP, 1988), 86–87.
3. Bardach, 285.
4. Bardach, 169.
5. Bardach, 179.
6. Author's visit to O'Higgins home, 1990.
7. A good understanding of the polemics in the graphics area may be obtained from Raquel Tibol's book *Gráficas y Neográficas en México* (México D.F.: SEP/UNAM, 1987). The criticisms mentioned are discussed on pages 128, 137, 152, and 155.
8. R. Tibol, *Documentación Sobre El Arte Mexicano* (Advertencia) (México, D.F.: Fondo de Cultura Economica, 1974) 8. Siqueiros, in 1958, advocated a return to the stance of the Sindicato in 1923: "to face the state and declare they are betraying the Revolution's essential program in cultural materials and we are going to fight along with the people to correct this inadequate march." Ibid., 100.
9. Re: funeral: Alberto Ruy-Sánchez, "New Forms for a Century's End," *Through the Path of Echoes—Por Camino de Ecos*, exhibition catalog (New York: Independent Curators, Inc., 1990).
10. A. Haab, 7.
11. The Sociedad Mexicana de Grabadores, founded in 1947, sought to provide "premises which can be used by all members, to promote exchange of views and

experiences, arrange group exhibitions, allowing the members every kind of scope for their personal liberty." Armin Haab, 9. José Julio Rodríguez, a member of the Sociedad, said, "The TGP has a preferred theme, their members are all alike in their love for themes dealing with social topics or propositions . . . . If I went to the TGP, I'd have to abandon my preferences of a poetic or romantic nature . . . ." R. Tibol, *Gráficas*, 155.
12. *Pablo O'Higgins—Un Artista de Su Pueblo*, 26.
13. Pablo O'Higgins, "Art," *People's World*, February 4, 1939.
14. Luis Ruis Caso (Centro National de Investigación, Documentación e Información de las Artes Plásticas, INBA), "Pablo O'Higgins. Entre la leyenda y la polemica," *Voz de la lucha*, 165–74.
15. Ibid., 169.
16. See Chapter 1, note 10.
17. Craven, 69 (Daumier); Macario Matus, "Los retratos de O'Higgins," *Humanidad recuperada*, 89.

PART FOUR | THE SOLITARY YEARS

1. María O'Higgins, interviews with the author, Mexico City, 1990.

CHAPTER 45 | MARÍA

1. Poniatowska and Bosques, 154. Translation by Julio César Tapia Guzmán.
2. Yvonne Templin interview.
3. Byron Randall interviews; Miguel Orozco interviews.
4. Seymour Kaplan interviews.
5. Poniatowska and Bosquez, 26. The mural in Veracruz had the theme "From the Primitive Pre-Hispanic Agricultural Work to the Current Industrial Petroleum Development." Palma Chronology in Poniatowska and Bosques.
6. Ibid.
7. Announcement/invitation in Jean Charlot Collection. The back includes a handwritten note: "Saludos a Toda la familia! P."
8. Randall interviews.
9. Guadalupe Elósegui, "Entrevista a María O'Higgins," *El Porvenir*, April 28, 2008. She did not recall how long she worked for the Defense of Women office.
10. Randall interviews. Early in their marriage Pablo and María supported the Cuban Revolution, support that later would cause María visa problems. This was, however, a mainstream cause in Mexico: when Castro announced his intention to become premier of Cuba, on July 26, 1959, to a crowd of hundreds of thousands in Havana, former Mexican President Cárdenas was at his side.
11. Uranga López, 48.
12. *Voz de la lucha*, unnumbered last page.
13. Several articles appeared in *U.S. News & World Report* in 1960, singling out members of the "American Communist colony in Mexico," one with the heading, "The Underground Railroad—to Russia."
14. Yvonne Templin interview ("promising art career"); Byron Randall said, "She thought she'd given up a big art career to devote herself to Pablo." Byron Randall interviews.
15. María O'Higgins interviews.
16. Byron Randall interviews.
17. María O'Higgins interviews.
18. Ibid.

19. Rafael Carrillo interview; María said Pablo let her design the house—he wanted only a studio with lots of light, María O'Higgins interviews.
20. Poniatowska & Bosques, 13.
21. Terry Goldblatt interview, 1989.
22. Maria O'Higgins interviews.
23. Noah Bardach, telephone interview, July 19, 2009; Bardach quotes Elena Poniatowska as referring to Méndez's "poverty, his infinite poverty, because he was never able to escape poverty. Nor did he try to escape," Bardach, 273-74, quoting Poniatowska, "100 Años de Leopoldo Méndez."
24. Pablo O'Higgins, interview March 21, 1974, Jean Charlot Collection, University of Hawai'i.
25. María O'Higgins interviews (re: finances).
26. Uranga López, 28–29.
27. María O'Higgins interviews.
28. María O'Higgins interviews. María did not mention any of the rest of it: "The man, whose sexual attributes are principally courage and strength, should and will give protection, food, and guidance to the woman. The woman, whose principal attributes are abnegation, beauty, compassion, perspicacity and tenderness, should and will give her husband obedience, pleasure, assistance, consolation and counsel, always treating him with the veneration due to the person who supports and defends her." Alan Riding, *Distant Neighbors* (New York: Vintage, 1986), 348.
29. Elizabeth Catlett had a stronger reaction in her interview with Bardach. She made it clear she was never a friend of María, she was a friend of Pablo, and said that María "did a very ugly thing to me." Bardach, re December 6, 2006, interview with Catlett.
30. Yvonne Templin interview.
31. Byron Randall interviews.
32. Emmy Lou Packard, interview with author, San Francisco, CA, May 3, 1989.
33. Luis and Lea Remba interview; translations, María Rendón, Irma Vega de Bijou.
34. Mildred Constantine, telephone interview by author, London, August 16, 1991.
35. Terry Goldblatt interview, 1992.
36. María O'Higgins interviews.

CHAPTER 46 | MEXICAN CITIZENSHIP

1. Bardach, 250.
2. Goldman, 36.
3. Ibid. Some art historians, including Shifra Goldman, believe the U.S. government and capitalistic interests orchestrated this change. Goldman, 27–35.
4. Goldman states, "Within the two-year period between 1958 and 1960, the confrontation between social realism and its major counterstyle, abstract expressionism, became so acute that it splintered the art world . . . ." Ibid. She sees these two exhibitions—the 1958 and the 1960 Inter-American Biennial shows—as microcosms of the controversy. Goldman, 31–26; *Cuadernos de Bellas Artes*, January 1961.
5. Goldman, 30 (re Cuevas); Armin Haab, *Mexican Graphics* (Teufen, Switzerland: Arthur Niggli, Ltd., 1957), 8 (re Méndez).
6. SEP/INBA, *Ruptura*, 82, 91.
7. Palma Chronology in Poniatowska and Bosques.
8. Prignitz, 179–80.
9. Schreiber, 210.

10. Prignitz, 180.
11. Goldman, 201, n. 32; Schmitt, 144.
12. Herzog, 111.
13. Selva Hernández, "Leopoldo Méndez y el Fondo Editorial de la Plástica Mexicana," *Cenidiap*, revista digital, http://discursovisual.cenart.gob.mx/dvweb12/entorno/entselva.htm (accessed October 11, 2009).
14. Prignitz, 180.
15. Ibid., re "Méndez faction"; Bardach, 268 (supported the candidacy).
16. Herzog, 111.
17. Ibid.
18. Bardach, conversation re Catlett interview, December 6, 2006.
19. Alberto Beltrán, Mariana Yampolsky, Iker Larrauri, Adolfo Mexiac, Fanny Rabel, and Andrea Gómez also left. Ibid.
20. Conversation with Noah Bardach, August 7, 2009.
21. Hernández, "Leopoldo Méndez."
22. Schreiber says that Catlett and Mora both left the Taller in 1964 after TGP member Luis Arenal brought López Mateos to the TGP to solicit funding from his government. Schreiber, *Cold War Exiles*, 210. She says López Mateos "wanted to be known for his support of the arts." Ibid.
23. Virtue, 224.
24. Herzog, 109. Catlett had trouble visiting the U.S. even as late as 1971. After much effort, she was allowed to attend an exhibit of her work that year but her travel in the U.S. was monitored. Herzog, 108-09.
25. Herzog, 79.
26. María O'Higgins interviews, Mexico City, 1990. It is sometimes suggested that he did not ask for it, but a Mexican diplomat who served in Europe, Latin America, and the U.S. from 1968 to 2008, told me that this would not happen, that it must be requested. Salvador Jiménez, interview with the author, Salt Lake City, October 19, 2009. Kathryn McCormick said that Pablo and María told her that Pablo had been granted Mexican citizenship for his mural work, long before he met María, and gave her the impression that this was a rarity. Kathryn McCormick interviews.

CHAPTER 47 | 1960s

1. "Official Report Released on Mexico's 'Dirty War,' " George Washington University National Security Archive, November 21, 2006, "accused three Mexican presidents of a sustained policy of violence targeting armed guerrillas and student protesters alike, including the use of 'massacres, forced disappearance, systematic torture, and genocide.' The report makes clear that the abuses were not the work of individual military units or renegade officers, but official practice under Presidents Díaz Ordaz (1964–1970), Echeverría (1970–1976) and López Portillo (1976–1982)," http://www.gwu.edu/~nsarchiv/NSAEBB/NSAEBB209/index.htm (accessed February 14, 2010).
2. "Era una persona muy solitaria, muy compañera, no le causaba problemas participar conmigo en lo que hubiera que hacer en la casa. Al terminar el día hacíamos un balance de lo que se hizo y lo que quedaba por resolver. Esto fue muy importante, tal vez más que las afinidades sociales o políticas que pudieron existir entre nosotros desde un principio." Uranga López, 48.
3. *Cuadernos de Bellas Artes*, August 1961.
4. Ibid., October 1961.

5. Poniatowska, *Massacre in Mexico* (La Noche de Tlatelolco, estimated 325 dead); Salvador Jiménez interview, October 29, 2009 (CIA).
6. Byron Randall interviews; Terry Goldblatt interview, 1989.
7. Byron Randall interviews.
8. Terry Goldblatt interview, 1992.
9. Leticia López Orozco, "La Plástica de Pablo O'Higgins," in *Pablo O'Higgins, Construyendo vidas* (México, D.F.: Fundación Cultural María y Pablo O'Higgins, 2005), 13. "[S]in perder de vista los sucesos del 'dia' que acontecian en Mexico y en el mundo."(Translation by Bernardo Flores-Sahagún.)
10. Emily Edwards, Letter to Zohmah and Jean Charlot, October 18, 1965, in Jean Charlot Collection, University of Hawai'i.
11. Ibid.
12. María O'Higgins interviews.
13. Luis Remba, telephone interview by the author, July 16, 2009, Los Angeles, CA ("very close"); Luis and Lea Remba interview (travel).
14. Luis and Lea Remba interview.
15. A. Sen, *Identity and Violence, the Illusion of Destiny* (New York: W.W. Norton, 2006), 38.
16. Ibid., 30.

CHAPTER 48 | ANGUSTIA

1. Boullosa, 6.
2. Palma Chronology, J. Sánchez.
3. Kate Doyle, "The Corpus Christi Massacre: Mexico's Attack on its Student Movement, June 10, 1971," *Proceso*, June 10, 2003, http://www.gwu.edu/~nsarchiv/NSAEBB/NSAEBB91/ (accessed September 9, 2009).
4. Ibid. Also, Chagoya oral history. Re 1971 riots: "And I had to run for my life in that one. There was a point when we got confronted by paramilitary groups that had bamboo sticks with knives at the end of the bamboo. And they were just coming at us." Chagoya recalled that there were "paramilitary gangs . . . in all the high schools, not only ours, even in Coyoacán" (where Pablo and María lived).
5. Daniel Gómez interview.
6. Interview with Byron Randall, Tomales, CA, November 1, 1991.
7. Daniel Gómez interview.
8. *Campesina de Toluca* (*Peasant Woman of Toluca*), reproduced in Prignitz, 214, appears to be the same image in an oil painting.
9. Orozco and McCormick interviews. His teacher, LeConte Stewart, had been the same way. His son later recalled that Stewart would be hours late for social occasions his wife planned, because he had been off painting; he often arrived back home after the guests had left. Tom Alder, "Tales of LeConte Stewart," *15 Bytes, Artists of Utah*, e-zine, http://www.artistsofutah.org/15bytes/06dec/06dec.pdf (accessed April 17, 2009). "My father was an eccentric, but he was absolutely dedicated to his art. He put it first—sometimes before his family."
10. María O'Higgins interviews, Mexico City, 1990.
11. Daniel Gómez interview.
12. María O'Higgins interviews, Mexico City, 1990.
13. Daniel Gómez interview.
14. Daniel Gómez interview.
15. For example, in his 1979 lithograph *Madre tierra*, a maguey plant seems to radiate

from a woman's head like a crown. Observations by students Antonio Coria and Stephanie Swasey at exhibit of O'Higgins works, Salt Lake City, Utah, 2010.
16. Daniel Gómez interview.
17. *Pablo O'Higgins, Un Artista de su Pueblo*, 39.
18. Byron Randall interview, Tomales, CA, November 1, 1991. Méndez's death was followed in months by the suicide of another former Taller member, Celia Calderon. R. Tibol, *Gráficas and Neográficas*, 175.

CHAPTER 49 | MIGUEL

1. Miguel Orozco interviews.
2 Ibid.
3. Orozco used the term, "Ser humano."

CHAPTER 50 | MUJER DE ARMAS TOMAR

1. Irma Vega de Bijou, interview by the author, Los Angeles, CA, October 22, 2009.
2. Ibid.
3. Emmy Lou Packard, letter to Pablo and María O'Higgins, May 28, 1973, Packard Archives.
4. Emmy Lou Packard, letter to Rick Tejada-Flores, July 29, 1981, Packard Archives.
5. Pablo and María O'Higgins, letter to Emmy Lou Packard, June 16, 1974, Packard Archives.
6. Luis and Lea Remba interview.
7. Ibid.
8. Luis Remba interview.
9. Tina Martin Interviews.
10. Philip Stein, *Siqueiros: His Life and Work* (New York: International Publishers, 1994), 133.
11. María O'Higgins interviews.
12. See Kurt Heinzelman, Ed., *The Covarrubias Circle* (Austin: University of Texas, Austin, 2004), 118.
13. Luis and Lea Remba interview.

CHAPTER 51 | SEATTLE, 1975

1. Roberto Maestas interview.
2. Emmanuel C. Montoya, telephone interview by author, Oakland, CA, Oct. 8, 2009.
3. Goldie Caughlan interview.
4. Ibid.
5. John Caughlan, letter to author, December 5, 1991. He said, "I have no idea whether you'll get any FOIA [Freedom of Information Act] info re Pablo. I'm quite sure you'll get something on Maria, however, if you include INS in your request (the Seattle office at least) and the dope on her must be tied to Pablo somehow, so I guess I do have an idea that you'll get something." (INS is now ICE.)
6. "Future Exhibitions" memo, Sept. 17, by "RG," in Henry Art Gallery Archives, 82–48, Box 25.
7. Goldie Caughlan interview.
8. John Caughlan interview.
9. Roberto Maestas interview.
10. Albright, "The Mural."

CHAPTER 52 | WUTHERING HEIGHTS

1. Goldie Caughlan interview; Kathryn McCormick interviews.
2. John Caughlan interview.
3. Kathryn McCormick interviews.
4. Steve Murin interview.
5. Holmes, 219–20.
6. Kathryn McCormick interviews.
7. Miguel Orozco interviews.

CHAPTER 53 | FRIENDS

1. Carl Damaso, letter to Pablo O'Higgins, September 23, 1981, archives of ILWU Local 142.
2. Ibid.
3. Flores Castro, translation of letter to Mrs. A. McElrath, August 14, 1991, archives of ILWU, Local 142.
4. Committee of Concern, Pablo O'Higgins' Hawaiian Frescos, letter to Carl Demaso, September 2, 1981, ILWU Archives. It is highly unlikely that a drawing by Pablo sold for $16,000 in 1981.
5. "Hawai'i's economy was controlled by a handful of families," ILWU Local 142, http://www.ilwulocal142.org/new159/index.php?option=com_content&view=article&id=76&Itemid=121 (accessed November 7, 2009).
6. Emmy Lou Packard, letter to Mary Ellen, May 1, 1982, Packard Archives.
7. Notes to discuss with Rupert García, February 26, 1981.
8. Notes on Aguascalientes, April 16, 1982, Packard Archives.
9. Emmy Lou Packard, letter to Mary Ellen, May 1, 1982.
10. María O'Higgins interviews, Mexico City.
11. Terry Goldblatt interview, 1989.
12. Emmy Lou Packard, letter to Pablo and Maria, April 8, 1983.
13. Emmy Lou Packard interview. Her archives include a letter to Pablo and María from Byron Randall, her ex-husband and Pablo's close friend. In his lively handwriting, Byron asks Pablo if there was a problem when Emmy Lou left their home. He says that Emmy Lou made a quip about a friend stealing Pablo's books, and that Pablo had suspected that Emmy Lou had taken some of his books. Byron Randall, letter to Pablo and María O'Higgin, June 25, 1982. Packard Archives.

CHAPTER 54 | PABLO

1. Daniel Gómez interview. He would not answer why, perhaps because María was present in this interview and had become upset when he talked about Pablo's painting demonstrating anguish.
2. Miguel Orozco interviews.
3. María O'Higgins interviews.
4. *Pablo O'Higgins, Un Artista de su Pueblo*, exhibition catalog, 1.
5. Martha Zamora, letter to Mrs. Emmy Lou Packard, undated. Her archives contain another odd letter, handwritten from Zamora to Packard, dated October 10, 1983, apologizing that economist and historian Jesús Silva Herzog has not died yet. Packard Archives.
6. Daniel Gómez interview.

CHAPTER 55 | LEGACY

1. Pamela Jane Ferree, "The Murals of Chicano Park, San Diego, California," San Diego State University, 1994, http://www.chicanoparksandiego.com/murals/history.html (accessed October 16, 2009).
2. History of Chicano Park, from Kevin Delgado, "A Turning Point: The Conception and Realization of Chicano Park," undated submission for the Bruce Kammerling Award: Art and Artists, San Diego Historical Society.
3. Salvador Barajas, e-mail correspondence with author, November 24 and 25, 2009.
4. Víctor Ochoa, e-mail correspondence with author, November 24, 2009.
5. Art Hazelwood, California in Relief: A History in Wood and Linocut Prints, July 25–September 20, 2009, at the Hearst Art Gallery of Saint Mary's College; Emmanuel C. Montoya, telephone interview with the author, Oakland, CA, October 16, 2009.
6. "Amen siempre a México, como antes de ustedes lo amaron con ternura y pasión, Pablo O'Higgins o Luis Buñuel . . . .," Entrega el Presidente Vicente Fox Cartas de Naturalización, Fox Governmental Website, February 28, 2005, http://fox.presidencia.gob.mx/actividades/orden/?contenido=16949&imprimir=true (accessed November 22, 2009).

BIBLIOGRAPHY

BOOKS

Aguilar Camín, Héctor, and Lorenzo Meyer. *In the Shadow of the Mexican Revolution: Contemporary Mexican History, 1910–1989*. Austin: University of Texas Press, 1993.

Albers, Patricia. *Fire, Snow: The Life of Tina Modotti.* Berkeley: University of California Press, 2002.

American Artists' Congress. *Graphic Works of the American Thirties: A Book of 100 Prints.* New York: Da Capo, 1977.

Anhalt, Diana. *A Gathering of Fugitives: American Political Expatriates in Mexico 1948–1965.* Santa Maria, CA: Archer Books, 2001.

Applebaum, Anne. *Gulag.* New York: Anchor Books, 2003.

Arrington, Leonard J. *Great Basin Kingdom Economic History of the Latter-Day Saints 1830–1900.* Salt Lake City: University of Utah Press, 1993.

Ascoli, Peter Max, and Julius Rosenwald, *The Man Who Built Sears, Roebuck and Advanced the Cause of Black Education in the American South.* Bloomington: University of Indiana Press, 2006.

Black, S.T. *History of San Diego County.* Chicago: The S.J. Clarke Publishing Company, 1913.

Brenner, Anita. *Idols Behind Altars.* New York: Dover, 1929.

Brysac, Shareen Blair. *Resisting Hitler: The Life and Death of an American Woman in Nazi Germany.* New York: Oxford University Press, 2000.

Carr, Barry. *Marxism and Communism in Twentieth-Century Mexico.* Lincoln: University of Nebraska Press, 1992.

Carrillo A., Rafael. *Mural Painting of Mexico.* México, D.F.: Panorama, 1981.

Cedillo, Juan Alberto. *Los Nazis en México.* New York: Random House, 2007.

Charlot, Jean. *Guía de los frescos de varios artistas en las escuelas primarias.* México, D.F.: Toor Studios, 1945.

Charlot, Jean. *The Mexican Mural Renaissance.* New Haven and London: Yale University Press, 1967.

Coerver, Don M., and Suzanne B. Pasztor, *Mexico.* Santa Barbara: ABC-CLIO, 2004.

Cohen, Louis Harris. *The Cultural-Political Traditions and Developments of the Soviet Cinema, 1917–1972.* New York: Arno, 1974.

Conquest, Robert. *The Harvest of Sorrow—Soviet Collectivization and the Terror-Famine.* New York: Oxford University Press, 1986.

Constantine, Mildred. *Tina Modotti, A Fragile Life.* London: Paddington Press, 1975.

Craven, David. *Art and Revolution in Latin America 1910–1990*. New Haven: Yale University Press, 2001.

deLappe, Pele. *A Passionate Journey through Art & the Red Press* (Petaluma: Pele deLappe, 2000)

de Neymet, Marcela. *Cronología del partido comunista Mexicano, primera parte, 1919–1939*. México, D.F.: Ediciones de Cultura Popular, 1981.

Denning, Michael. *The Cultural Front*. Brooklyn: Verso, 1998.

Dodd, Martha. *Through Embassy Eyes*. New York: Harcourt Brace, 1939.

Evans, M. Stanton. *Blacklisted by History*. New York: Random House, 2007.

Federal Writers' Project. *Utah, A Guide to the State*. New York: Hastings House, 1945.

Fehrenbach, T. R. *Fire and Blood: A Bold and Definitive Modern Chronicle of Mexico*. New York: Collier Books, 1973.

Foner, Philip Sheldon. *The Case of Joe Hill*. New York: New World, 2004.

Fundación Cultural María y Pablo O'Higgins. *Pablo O'Higgins, Construyendo vidas* [Constructing lives]. México, D.F.: 2005.

Fundación Cultural María y Pablo O'Higgins, A.C. *Humanidad recuperada, obra gráfica de Pablo O'Higgins* [Humanity regained, graphic works of Pablo O'Higgins]. México, D.F: Gobierno de Distrito Federal, 2006.

Galeana, Benita. *Benita*. Pittsburgh, PA: Latin American Literary Review Press, 1994.

Givner, Joan. *Katherine Anne Porter, A Life*. New York: Simon & Schuster, 1982.

Glusker, Susannah. *Anita Brenner*. Austin: University of Texas Press, 1998.

Goldman, Shifra. *Contemporary Mexican Painting in a Time of Change*. Austin: University of Texas Press, 1977.

Golomstock, Igor. *Totalitarian Art*. Great Britain: Icon Editions, 1990.

Haab, Armin. *Mexican Graphics*. Teufen, Switzerland: Arthur Niggli, Ltd., 1957.

Harwood, James T. *A Basket of Chips: the Autobiography of James Taylor Harwood*. Salt Lake City: Signature Books, 1985.

Haynes, John Earl, Harvey Klehr, and Alexander Vassiliev. *Spies: The Rise and Fall of the KGB in America*. New Haven: Yale University Press, 2009.

Heinzelman, Kurt, ed. *The Covarrubias Circle*. Austin: University of Texas, Austin, 2004.

Heller, Jules. *Codex Méndez*, Phoenix: University of Arizona Press, 1999.

Helm, MacKinley. *Mexican Painters*. New York: Harper & Brothers, 1941.

Helms, Cynthia Newman, ed. *Diego Rivera: A Retrospective*. New York: W.W. Norton, 1986.

Hernández, Miguel, and Ted Genoways. *The Selected Poems of Miguel Hernández*. Chicago: University of Chicago Press, 2001.

Herrera, Hayden. *Frida*. New York: Harper & Row, 1983.

Hicks, Granville. *John Reed: The Making of a Revolutionary*. New York: MacMillan, 1936.

Híjar, Alberto. *Pablo O'Higgins: Apuntes y dibujos de trabajadores*. Monterrey, México: Secretaría de Educación y Cultura, 1987.

History of the Bench and Bar. Salt Lake City: Interstate Press Association, 1913.

Holmes, T. Michael. *The Specter of Communism in Hawai'i*. Honolulu: University of Hawai'i, 1994.

Hooks, Margaret. *Tina Modotti: Radical Photographer*. Cambridge: Da Capo, 1993.

Horne, Gerald. *Class Struggle in Hollywood, 1930–1950: Moguls, Mobsters, Stars, Reds, and Trade Unionists*. Austin: University of Texas Press, 2001.

Hospital, Carolina, and Jorge Cantera, eds. *A Century of Cuban Writers in Florida: Selected Prose and Poetry*. Sarasota, Florida: Pineapple Press, 1996.

Hughes, Lloyd. *The Mexican Cultural Mission Programme Monograph on Fundamental Education*. Paris: UNESCO, 1949.

Ittmann, John, ed. *Mexico and Modern Printmaking, A Revolution in the Graphic Arts, 1920 to 1950*. Philadelphia: Philadelphia Museum of Art, 2006.

Jiang, Yang. *Six Chapters from My Life "Downunder."* Translated by Howard Goldblatt. Introduction by Jonathan Spence. Seattle: University of Washington Press, 1988.

Johnson, Mark Dean, ed. *At Work: The Art of California Labor*. San Francisco: San Francisco Historical Society Press, 2003.

Kantowicz, Edward. *The Rage of Nations*. Grand Rapids: Wm. B. Eerdmans Publishing Co., 1999.

Karlstrom, Paul J., ed. *On the Edge of America: California Modernist Art 1900–1950*. Berkeley: University of California Press, 1996.

Klehr, Harvey. *The Heyday of American Communism*. New York: Basic Books, 1984.

Kollontai, Alexandra. *Red Love*. (Forward to the English edition.) New York: Seven Arts Publishing Company, 1927.

Krauze, Enrique. *Mexico: A Biography of Power*. New York: Harper Collins, 1997.

Laquer, W., ed., *Fascism, A Reader's Guide*. Berkeley: University of California Press, 1976.

López, E. *Conversations with Katherine Anne Porter*. New York: Little Brown, 1981.

Marnham, Patrick. *Dreaming With His Eyes Open—A Life of Diego Rivera*. New York: Knopf, 1998.

McGraw-Hill Dictionary of Art. New York: McGraw-Hill, 1969.

Meyer, B., ed. *A Dictionary of Art Terms and Techniques.* New York: Thomas Y. Crowell Co., Inc., 1969.

Meyer, M., W. Sherman, and S. Deeds. *The Course of Mexican History.* 7th ed. New York: Oxford University Press, 2002.

Mitford, Jessica. *A Fine Old Conflict.* New York: Knopf, 1977.

MOMA. *Twenty Centuries of Mexican Art.* New York: Museum of Modern Art, 1940.

Moore-Emmett, Andrea. *God's Brothel.* San Francisco: Pince-Nez Press, 2004.

Moreno, Julio. *Yankee Don't Go Home!* Chapel Hill: Univ. of North Carolina Press, 2007.

Murray, Robert K. *Red Scare, A Study in National Hysteria, 1919–1920.* New York: McGraw-Hill, 1964.

National Academy of Sciences of Azerbaijan Institute of Archeology & Ethnography. *Azeris: A Historical Ethnographic Essay.* Azerbaijan: Chashioglu & ANA Press, 2005.

Needler, Martin C. *Mexican Politics: The Containment of Conflict.* Santa Barbara: Greenwood Press: 1995.

Niblo, Stephen R., *Mexico in the 1940s.* Wilmington: SR Books, 2000.

Noguchi, Isamu. *A Sculptor's World.* New York and Evanston: Harper Row, 1968.

O'Gorman, Juan. *Autobiographia.* México, D.F.: DGE Editions S.A, 2007.

Oles, James. *Las hermanas Greenwood en Mexico.* México, D.F.: Circulo de Arte, Consejo Nacional Para la Cultura y las Artes, 2000.

Oles, James. *South of the Border.* Washington, D.C.: Smithsonian, 1993.

Orozco, José Clemente. *The Artist in New York: Letters to Jean Charlot and Unpublished Writings (1925-1929).* Austin: University of Texas Austin Press, 1974.

Orozco, José Clemente. *Autobiografía.* México, D.F.: E.D. ERA, 1981.

Payne, Robert. *The Life and Death of Trotsky.* New York: McGraw-Hill, 1977.

Peterson, Richard H. *The Bonanza Kings—The Social Origins and Business Behavior of Western Mining Entrepreneurs, 1970–1900.* Lincoln and London: University of Nebraska Press, 1971.

Poniatowska, Elena. *Massacre in Mexico.* Columbia: University of Missouri Press, 1975.

Poniatowska, Elena. *Tinisima.* New York: Penguin, 1992.

Poniatowska, Elena, and Gilberto Bosques. *Pablo O'Higgins.* México, D.F.: Banco Nacional de Comercio Exterior, 1984.

Porter, Katherine Anne. *Ship of Fools.* Boston: Little, Brown, 1962.

Prignitz, Helga. *El Taller de Gráfica Popular en México 1937–1977.* México, D.F.: Instituto Nacional de Bellas Artes, 1992.

Reed, Alma. *The Mexican Muralists.* New York: Crown Publishers, Inc., 1960.

Riding, Alan. *Distant Neighbors.* New York: Vintage, 1986.

Rivera, Diego. *Textos de Arte.* México, D.F.: Universidad Nacional Autónoma de México, 1986.

Robinson, Ione. *A Wall to Paint On.* New York: EP Dutton & Co., 1946.

Rodríguez, Antonio. *A History of Mexican Mural Painting.* New York: Putnam, 1969.

Rowe, Frank. *The Enemy Among Us.* Sacramento: Cougar Books, 1980.

Sabau García, María Luisa. *México en el mundo de las colecciónes de arte.* México, D.F.: Universidad Nacional Autónoma de México, Consejo Nacional para la Cultura y las Artes, 2002.

Salt Lake City Directory, 1893–1930. Salt Lake City: R.L. Polk & Co., 1893–1930.

Sánchez, George I. *A Revolution by Education.* New York: Viking, 1936.

Schmeckebier, Laurence E. *Modern Mexican Art.* Minneapolis: University of Minnesota Press, 1939.

Schrecker, Ellen. *The Age of McCarthyism.* Basingstoke: Palgrave McMillan, 2002.

Schreiber, Rebecca M. *Cold War Exiles in Mexico.* Minneapolis: University of Minnesota Press, 2008.

Schuler, Friedrich E. *Mexico Between Hitler and Roosevelt.* Albuquerque: University of New Mexico Press, 1998.

Scroggins, Deborah. *Emma's War.* New York: Viking, 2004.

Sen, A. *Identity and Violence, the Illusion of Destiny.* New York: W.W. Norton, 2006.

Sons of the American Revolution. *National Year Book, 1914.* http://www.archive.org/details/nationalyearbook1914sons.

Spenser, Daniela. *The Impossible Triangle: Mexico, Soviet Russia and the United States in the 1920s.* Durham and London: Duke University Press, 1999.

Stein, Philip. *Siqueiros: His Life and Works.* New York: International Publishers, 1994.

Sterns, Peter N. *The Industrial Revolution in World History.* Boulder: Westview Press, 1998.

Stewart, Virginia. *45 Contemporary Mexican Artists.* Stanford: Stanford University Press, 1951.

Sutton, Wain. *Utah—A Centennial History*, Vol. 2. New York: Lewis Historical Publishing Company, Inc., 1949.

Swanson, Vern G., Robert S. Olpin, and William V. Seifrit. *Utah Painting and Sculpture.* Layton, Utah: Gibbs Smith, 1997.

Swanson, Vern G., William V. Seifrit, and Robert S. Olpin. *Artists of Utah.* Layton, Utah: Gibbs Smith, 1999.

Thernstrom, Stephan, and Ann Orlov. *Harvard Encyclopedia of American Ethnic Groups.* Cambridge, Mass: Harvard University Press, 1980.

Tibol, Raquel. *Documentación sobre el arte mexicano.* México, D.F.: Fondo de Cultura, 1974.

Tibol, Raquel. *Gráficas y neográficas en México.* México D.F.: SEP/UNAM, 1987.

Tibol, Raquel. *Historia general del arte de México.* México, D.F.: Editorial Hérmes, S.A., 1964.

Tyler, Ron, ed. *Posada's Mexico.* Washington, D.C.: Library of Congress; Fort Worth: Amon Carter Museum of Western Art, 1979.

UNAM, *Pablo O'Higgins: Voz de lucha y de arte.* México, D.F.: UNAM–Gobierno del Distrito Federal–Gobierno del Estado de Nuevo León–Fundación Cultural María y Pablo O'Higgins, A.C., 2005.

Unrue, Darlene Harbowz. *Katherine Anne Porter.* New York: Library of America, 2008.

Utah Heritage Society, *Historic Buildings Along South Temple.* Salt Lake City: Utah Heritage Society, 1980.

Utah Press Association: A Century Later. Salt Lake City: Utah Press Association, 1996.

Vallejo, César. *Rusia en 1931: Reflexiones al pie del Kremlin.* Madrid: Ulises, 1931.

Vidali, Vittorio. *Colección crónicas y testimonios "Retrato de mujer"—Una vida con Tina Modotti.* Puebla: Universidad Autónoma de Puebla, 1984.

Virtue, John. *Model American Abroad, a Biography of Stirling Dickinson.* Port Orchard: Windstorm Creative, 2008.

Van Wagoner, Richard S. *Mormon Polygamy, A History.* Salt Lake City: Signature Books, 1998.

Volkogonov, Dmitri Antonovich, and Harold Shukman. *Trotsky: The Eternal Revolutionary.* Translated by Harold Shukman. New York: Simon and Schuster, 1996.

Warrum, Noble. *Utah Since Statehood.* Chicago–Salt Lake City: The S.J. Clarke Publishing Co., 1919.

Wolfe, Bertram. *The Fabulous Life of Diego Rivera.* New York: Scarborough House, 1990.

CHAPTERS IN A BOOK

Espinosa Campos, Eduardo. "Trabajos de ilustracion." In *Pablo O'Higgins: Voz de lucha y de arte.*

León-Portilla, Miguel. "El Mundo indígena de Pablo O'Higgins." In *Pablo O'Higgins: Voz de lucha y de arte.*

López Orozco, Leticia. "Los murales de O'Higgins: una enseñanza historica." In *Pablo O'Higgins: Voz de lucha y de arte.*

O'Connor, Francis V. "The Influence of Diego Rivera on the Art of the United States During the 1930's and After." In Helms, *Diego Rivera.*

Pearson, Ralph M. "These Prints and the Public." In American Artists Congress, *Graphic Works of the American Thirties.*

Prignitz-Poda, Helga. "Pablo O'Higgins: un cuarto de siglo en el TGP." In *Pablo O'Higgins: Voz de lucha y de arte.*

Ruis Caso, Luis. "Pablo O'Higgins. Entre la leyenda y la polemica." In *Pablo O'Higgins: Voz de lucha y de arte.*

Shoemaker, Innis. "Crossing Borders—The Weyhe Gallery and the Vogue for Mexican Art in the U.S. 1926–1940." In Ittmann, *Mexico and Modern Printmaking.*

Wechsler, James M. "Mexicanidad." In Ittmann, *Mexico and Modern Printmaking.*

Williams, Lyle. "Evolution of a Revolution: A Brief History of Printmaking in Mexico." In Ittmann, *Mexico and Modern Printmaking.*

ARTICLES

Aberth, Susan L., Ph.D. "Rufino Tamayo." http://www.christies.com/Lotfinder/lot_details.aspx?intObjectID=5261958 (accessed November 6, 2009).

Acevedo Valenzuela, Alejandro. "Sinfónias plásticas de Pablo O'Higgins." *12 la guía de Novedades*, November 4, 1983.

Alberto, E. "Conversación con Pablo O'Higgins." (unknown publication)

Albright, Thomas. "The Mural is the message." *San Francisco Chronicle*, Nov. 11, 1975.

Alder, Tom. "Tales of LeConte Stewart." *15 Bytes, Artists of Utah.* http://www.artistsofutah.org/15bytes/06dec/06dec.pdf (accessed April 17, 2009).

Azuela, Alicia. "*El Machete* and *Frente a Frente.*" *Art Journal*, March 22, 1993.

Baigts, Juan. "O'Higgins, limpio de corazón." *Excélsior. Diorama de la cultura*, México, September 21, 1980.

Baxman, Cindy. "History of the Mexican Revolution." University of Arizona. http://history.sandiego.edu/gen/projects/border/page03.html (accessed April 22, 2009).

Blanco, Sergio R. "Valoran energía de Pablo O'Higgins." *Reforma*, February 10, 2005.

Bloom, James. "About Joseph Freeman." University of Illinois. http://www.english.illinois.edu/maps/poets/a_f/freeman/about.htm (accessed November 12, 2009).

The Broad Ax. 1896. "Statehood Day, January 6, 1896."

Castaneda, Oscar Rosales. "The Chicano Movement in Washington State 1967–2006." http://depts.washington.edu/civilr/Chicanomovement_part2.htm (accessed March 26, 2009).

Charlot, John. "Una carta inedita de José Clemente Orozco para Jean Charlot, con extractos de cartas de Pablo O'Higgins." *Parteaguas* (Winter 2008).

Christenson, Richard P. "Utah artist strived to 'capture the light.' " *The Deseret News*, June 10, 1990.

Clark, Sally J. "Mural mixes politics, art and history." *Seattle Post Intelligencer*, December 12, 1977.

Clever, Dick. "Ship Scalers: A union's half century of turmoil, tragedy and triumph." *The Seattle Times*, May 2, 1982.

Crawford, Richard. "1918 Spanish Flu epidemic held San Diego in its grip." *San Diego Union Tribune*, November 13, 2008. http://copleynews.com/uniontrib/20081113/news_1ez13history.html (accessed April 16, 2009).

Cuadernos de Bellas Artes. January 1961.

Cushing, Lincoln. *A Contracorriente* 5, no. 3 (Spring 2008): 257–62. www.ncsu.edu/project/acontracorriente. http://www.docspopuli.org/articles/CaplowReview.html (accessed June 13, 2009).

deLappe, Pele. "Pablo O'Higgins, A Fresh Wind from Mexico." *People's Daily World*, February 14, 1949.

Devaux, Mauricio. "La Exposición de Pablo O'Higgins." *Excelsior*, August 27, 1950.

Doyle, Kate. "The Corpus Christi Massacre: Mexico's Attack on its Student Movement, June 10, 1971." *Proceso*, June 10, 2003. http://www.gwu.edu/~nsarchiv/NSAEBB/NSAEBB91/ (accessed September 9, 2009).

Duffy, Jim. "The Blue Death." *Johns Hopkins Public Health* (Fall 2004) http://www.jhsph.edu/publichealthnews/magazine/archive/Mag_Fall04/prologues/index.html (accessed December 21, 2009).

Elósegui, Guadalupe. "Entrevista a María O'Higgins." *El Porvenir*, April 28, 2008.

Emerson, Jim. "Fresco, muralist returns to Seattle community . . . 20 years later." *UW Daily*, October 7, 1975.

Epstein, Morey. "Left-Wing artist is sought for ILWU building's mural." *Honolulu Star-Bulletin*, March 14, 1952.

Evans, Robert [Joseph Freeman]. "Painting and Politics: The Case of Diego Rivera." University of Virginia. http://xroads.virginia.edu/~MA04/hess/RockRivera/mainframe5.html (accessed September 13, 2009.

Fenstermaker, Bebe. "Conversation With Emily Edwards." *San Antonio Society Newsletter*, 4th installment, July–August, 1980.

Ferree, Pamela Jane, "The Murals of Chicano Park, San Diego, California." San Diego State University, 1994. http://www.chicanoparksandiego.com/murals/history.html (accessed October 16, 2009).

Flores, Laura. "Pablo O'Higgins: Pintura y Cambio Social." *Metamórfosis, Northwest Chicano Magazine of Art and Literature* IV, no. 2, col. V, no. 1 (1982/1983).

Fowler, Glenn. "Martha Dodd Stern Is Dead at 82; Author and an Accused Soviet Spy." *The New York Times*, August 29, 1990.

Gardner, Nathaniel. "Benita Galeana y el Taller de Gráfica Popular: Ilustraciones, propaganda, y el pasar del tiempo." University of Glasgow. http://www.ajlas.org/v2006/paper/2008vol21no404.pdf (accessed September 35, 2009).

Geraci, Victor. "El Cajon 1900." *Journal of San Diego History* 36, no. 4. http://www.sandiegohistory.org/journal/90fall/elcajon.htm (accessed April 6, 2009).

Gruson, Sydney. "Mexico is Prodded to Clean Up Reds." *The New York Times*, July 20, 1954.

Harpers. May 15, 1858.

Hernández, Selva. "Leopoldo Méndez y el Fondo Editorial de la Plástica Mexicana." *Cenidiap.* Revista digital, http://discursovisual.cenart.gob.mx/dvweb12/entorno/entselva.htm (accessed October 11, 2009).

Herrera, E. Zúniga, D. Hernández, and J. Martínez Manautou. "History of the Population of Mexico." Mexico City, Mexico, Academia Mexicana de Investigación en Demografía Médica (1987): 1. http://www.popline.org/docs/0835/052145.html (accessed November 6, 2009).

ILWU Reporter. 1952. "The Story of the murals—the muralist at work." October 22.

Jaffe, "The Right to Travel: The Passport Problem." 35 *Foreign Affairs* 17.

The Journal of San Diego History 32, no. 3. "Painting Ladies." (Summer 1986).

Kammerling, Bruce. "San Diego Landscape Painters." *Journal of San Diego History.* http://search.blossom.com/geturl?&o=0p&i207&KEY=san+diego+academy+of+art&URL=http://www.sandiegohistory.org/journal/2001-3/imagesbraun.htm (accessed April 17, 2009).

Kennedy, Paul P. "Passport Ruling Shifted in Mexico." *New York Times*, June 29, 1958.

Kilduff, Marshall. "A Political Power Behind the Scenes." *San Francisco Chronicle*, January 15, 1977.

"A Legacy of Dedication." http://www.cedarcity.com/history.html (accessed December 8, 2009).

Leidemann, Mike. "Laborious Art." *The Honolulu Advertiser*, September 28, 2001.

Leonard, Kevin Allen. *The Battle for Los Angeles.* Albuquerque: University of New Mexico Press, 2006. www.pbs.org/wgbh/amex/zoot/eng-timeline/timeline2.html (accessed August 19, 2009).

Maeder, Jay. "Turncoat: the Estrangements of Howard Rushmore, January 1958 Chapter 282." *New York Daily News*, February 26, 2001.

Mayflower Quarterly. "Who Heard That? Pilgrim Lore." http://www.alden.org/pilgrim_lore/whoheard.htm (accessed November 2, 2009).

McKinley, James C. Jr. "Maurice Halperin, 88, a Scholar Who Chronicled Castro's Career." *New York Times*, February 15, 1995. http://www.nytimes.com/1995/02/12/obituaries/maurice-halperin-88-a-scholar-who-chronicled-castro-s-career.html (accessed November 24, 2009).

Meisler, Stanley. "U.N. Looks Back at Founding 50 Years Ago," In San Francisco, *Los Angeles Times,* reprinted in *The Seattle Times*, June 26, 1995.

Meyer, Phil. "Mural embodies isle labor struggle." *Honolulu Star-Bulletin*, October 5, 1987.

Murphy, Miriam B. "Development of Brighton Resort." *History Blazer*, July 1996. http://historytogo.utah.gov/utah_chapters/mining_and_railroads/developmentofbrightonresort.html (accessed April 5, 2009).

New Masses, February 1932. http://xroads.virginia.edu/~ma04/hess/RockRivera/newspapers/NewMasses_02_1932_2.html (accessed September 24, 2009).

New York Times. 1920. "His Mexico Wealth $75,000 Says Fall." January 18.

New York Times. 2009. "On Nixon Tapes, Ambivalence Over Abortion, Not Watergate." June 23. http://www.nytimes.com/2009/06/24/us/politics/24nixon.html?_r=1 (accessed September 5, 2009).

Newsome, Matthew A. C. "The Migration of the Scots-Irish to Southwestern North Carolina." http://www.albanach.org/ulster.html (accessed February 20, 2007).

Nolte, Carl. "Anniversary of a Dark Day." *San Francisco Chronicle*, July 4, 2009. www.sfgate.com (accessed July 25, 2009).

Palo Alto Weekly. 2003. "Lilyan Tregob." August 20. http://www.paloaltoonline.com/weekly/morgue/2003/2003_08_20.obits20ja.html (accessed December 31, 2009).

Paredes, Raymund. "Teaching Chicano Literature: An Historical Approach." http://www9.georgetown.edu/faculty/bassr/tamlit/essays/chicano.html (accessed December 10, 2009).

Peterson, Martin E. "An Overview of San Diego Artists." *The Journal of San Diego History* 47, no. 3. (Summer 2001.) http://search.blossom.com/geturl?&o=0p&i207&KEY=san+diego+academy+of+art&URL=http://www.sandiegohistory.org/journal/2001-3/overview.htm (accessed April 17, 2009).

Ponce, Mildred. "The Protest of the Thirteen: the first thrust of Cuba's Young Intellectuals." *Cuba Now*. http://www.cubanow.net/pages/loader.php?sec=7&t=2&item=4525 (accessed June 26, 2009).

Poniatowska, Elena. "Leopoldo Méndez, cien años de vida." *La Journada*, en honor a Leopoldo Méndez. Centenario, http://www.aceroarte.com/colección/Leopoldo_Méndez_venganzapueblos.htm (Referencia Internet, Información (septiembre 2004). www.jornada.unam.mx/2002/may02/020523/02aa1cul.php?printver=16/29/09 (accessed June 29, 2009).

Poniatowska, Elena. "Mujeres mágicas." *Journada UNAM*. www.jornada.uam.mx/1997/06/12/poniatowska.html (accessed May 8, 2009).

Rodríguez, A. "An International Workers Movement." University of Virginia, American Studies Department. http://xroads.virginia.edu/~MA02/rodriguez/rivera/Communist.html (accessed May 9, 2009).

Rosales y Zamora, Patricia. "Ejemplo para jóvenes pintores: su viuda" (Example for Young Painters: His Widow). *Excelsior*, March 13, 1985.

Rushmore, Howard. "Art." *Progressive Weekly People's Daily World*, February 2, 1939.

Salt Lake Mining Review. September 16, 1912, 22. http://www.scribd.com/doc/7831499/SLMR-1912-09-15 (accessed December 2, 2009).

Salt Lake Mining Review. 1926. "Death of Judge E.V. Higgins." August 15.

Salt Lake Tribune. 1915. "Utah Labor Leaders Resent A.F.L. Action." November 17.

Salt Lake Tribune. 1918. Front pages and obituaries. November 11–18.

Salt Lake Tribune. 1926. "Pioneer Jurist Suddenly Dies: Barrister Heard Famous Utah Mine Litigation, Practiced Law Here." August 7.

Salt Lake Tribune. 1928. "Lawyer Meets Sudden Death." November 6.

San Francisco Chronicle. 1933. "Youthful S.F. Artist Paints Mexico Murals." June 25.

Schuessler, Michael K. "Frances Toor and Mexican Folkways." *InsideMexico*, March 2008. http://www.insidemex.com/people/people/frances-paca-toor-and-mexican-folkways (accessed May 12, 2009).

Schultize, V. "Pablo O'Higgins." *Salt Lake Tribune*, December 8, 1988.

Schwartz, Stephen. "Article Says Bridges Was a Communist." *San Francisco Chronicle*, November 6, 1992.

Seattle Post Intelligencer. 1975. "Major Work of Art 'found' at U." March 6.

Siqueiros, David A. "Rivera's Counter-Revolutionary Road." *New Masses*, May 29, 1934.

Stern, Seymour. "Introduction to Synopsis of 'Que Viva México.' " *Experimental Cinema* 5 (1934).

Thompson, Karen. "Jean Charlot." The Jean Charlot Collection, University of Hawai'i. http://libweb.Hawai'i.edu/libdept/charlotcoll/J_Charlot/charlotthompson.html (accessed September 13, 2009).

Tiempo. 1950. "Una Exposition muy Mexicana." August 18.

Time. 1937. "Trotsky, Stalin & Cárdenas." January 25. http://www.time.com/time/magazine/article/0,9171,770539-2,00.html (accessed August 29, 2009)

Time. 1940. "Mexico: Communazi Columnists." June 3.

Time. 1941. "Education: Guggenheim Fellows." March 31.

Time. September 14, 1953, http://www.time.com/time/magazine/article/0,9171,858259-8,00.html (accessed August 29, 2009).

Time. 1954. "The Roundup." December 1.

Time. 1957. "Mexico: Red Haven." September 9. http://www.time.com/time/magazine/article/0,9171,893629,00.html (accessed August 29, 2009).

El Universal. July 14, 1924. http://chnm.gmu.edu/worldhistorysources/unpacking/newsanalysis.html (accessed April 19, 2009).

Valenzuela, Alejandro Acevedo. "Sinfónia plásticas de Pablo O'Higgins." 12 *la guía*, January 14, 1983.

Vanden Heuvel, K. "Grand Illusions." *Vanity Fair*, September 1991.

Walker, Dorothy. "Labor School seeking post-war unity." *San Francisco News*, May 16, 1944.

Walker, Ronald W. "The Panic of 1893." http://www.uen.org/ucme/media/text/ta000663.txt (accessed January 3, 2009).

THESES AND DISSERTATIONS

Bardach, Noah Arthur. "Post-revolutionary Art, Revolutionary Artists, Mexican Political Art Collectives, 1921-1960: Grupo de Pintores 30-30!, Liga de Escritores y Artistas Revolutionarios (L.E.A.R.) and the Taller de Gráfica Popular (T.G.P.)." Ph.D. diss., University of Sussex, 2008

Oles, James. "Walls to Paint On: American Muralists in Mexico 1933-36." Ph.D. diss., Yale University, 1995

Skovgaad, John. "The California Labor School," http://zpub.com/gaw/wordpress/wp-content/labor_school_/laborschool-.html (accessed March 25, 2009).

Stephens, Charles James. "Communism in Mexico, 1919-1940." Master's thesis, University of California, undated

PAPERS PRESENTED

Charlot, Jean. "Art and Communication: The example of José Guadalupe Posada." Lecture delivered at Wayne State University, Detroit, Michigan, June 9, 1965. http://www.jeancharlot.org/writings/english/1965%20ART%20AND%20COMMUNICATION.htm (accessed November 1, 2009).

WEBSITES

Andrés Blaisten Museum. "Rosa Rolanda, 1895–1970." www.museoblaisten.com/english.asp?myURL=%2F02asp%2FEnglish%2FartistDetailEnglish%2Easp&myVars=artistId%3D64 (accessed November 6, 2009).

Antiguo Colegio de San Ildefonso, Mexico, D.F. "Pablo O'Higgins: Voz de lucha y de arte." Images from an exhibition and information about the artist's activism and artwork. http://www.sanildefonso.org.mx/expos/211004a/hogigins02.swf (accessed June 27, 2009).

Ask Art. Victor "Vic" Selinsky artist biography. www.askart.com/askART/studio/studio.aspx?studio=11010321 (accessed July 8, 2009).

Auburn Theological Seminary. "About Auburn." Overview of seminary founded by Presbyterians, now in New York. http://www.auburnsem.org/about/welcome.asp?nsectionid=1&pageid=1 (accessed August 1, 2007).

Autor desconocido. "Camino a un mundo major." February 15, 1953. http://discursovisual.cenart.gob.mx/dvwebne08/documentos/doceduardo.htm (accessed August 6, 2009).

Bauhaus Archive Museum of Design. "Architecture." http://www.bauhaus.de/english/bauhaus1919/architektur/index.htm (accessed November 26, 2009).

Chouiard Foundation. "About Nelbert Chouinard," http://www.chouinardfoundation.org/nelbertchouinard (accessed February 4, 2010).

Corn, Lesley, M.A., F.G.B.S. "World War II Fourth Registration Draft Cards: A Newly-Released 20th-Century Resource for 19th-Century Research." New York Genealogical and Biographical Society. http://www.newyorkfamilyhistory.org/modules.php?name=sections&op=printpage&artid=107 (accessed December 26, 2009).

Bruce Eder, *All Movie Guide*, http://www.answers.com/topic/earl-robinson (accessed May 4, 2009).

"Biography of Samuel McAfee." Ancestry.com, http://trees.ancestry.com/pt/AttachStree.aspx?otid=2269532&opid=-1848638963&oid=24004c7c-6783-48cf-a284-2879eafda5b7&tid=1107042&pid=-603652780&act=set&npp=False (accessed June 20, 2009).

Fox Governmental Website. "Entrega el Presidente Vicente Fox Cartas de Naturalización." February 28, 2005, http://fox.presidencia.gob.mx/actividades/orden/?contenido=16949&imprimir=true (accessed September 27, 2009).

Gómez, Margi. *Byron Randall: The Mendocino Years*. http://www.realestatemendocino.com/pdfs_editorials/editorial_469print.pdf (accessed September 36, 2009).

Orozco, Sylvia. "A Chronology: José Guadalupe Posada." Jean Charlot Collection, University of Hawai'i Library. http://libweb.Hawai'i.edu/libdept/charlotcoll/posada/posadachronos.html. Pneumonia: http://libweb.Hawai'i.edu/libdept/charlotcoll/J_Charlot/charlotmcvicker.html (accessed May 25, 2009).

Reider, Ross. "Robinson, Earl Hawley (1910-1991)." HistoryLink.org, Essay 2029, November 22, 1999, http://www.historylink.org/index.cfm?DisplayPage=output.cfm&File_Id=2029 (accessed September 13, 2009).

Salt Lake City Corporation. "Salt Lake City History: The City Takes Shape," http://www.ci.slc.ut.us/info/area_info/salt_lake_city.htm (accessed January 7, 2007).

Samson, Chris. "Artist finds his place in the country." Interview with Byron Randall. http://home.comcast.net/~2samsons/Chris/Writing/Artists/randall.htm (accessed May 2, 2010).

Springville Art Museum, "LeConte Stewart." http://springvilleartmuseum.org/collections/browse.html?x=artist&artist_id=26 (accessed April 20, 2009).

Springville Art Museum. "Lee Greene Richards." http://www.springvilleartmuseum.org/collections/browse.html?x=artist&artist_id=7 (accessed April 20, 2009).

U.S. State Department, "Recognition of the Soviet Union." http://www.state.gov/r/pa/ho/time/id/86555.htm (accessed November 11, 2009).

Utah Artists Project. "James Harwood." University of Utah, Marriott Library. http://www.lib.utah.edu/portal/site/marriottlibrary/menuitem.350f2794f84fb3b29cf87354d1e916b9/?vgnextoid=93551df6f1a08110VgnVCM1000001c9e619bRCRD&vgncxtfmt=nomenu (accessed April 20, 2009).

Utah Digital Newspapers, University of Utah http://www.lib.utah.edu/digital/unews/slmr.html (accessed January 4, 2009).

WEBLOGS

Vallen, Mark. "Diego Rivera: Glorious Victory!" *Art For A Change*, October 5, 2007. www.art-for-a-change.com/blog/2007/10/diego-rivera-glorious-victory.html (accessed August 5, 2009).

Vallen, Mark. "Edward Biberman Revisited." *Art for a Change*, June 22, 2009. http://art-for-a-change.com/blog/category/mexican-muralism (accessed September 1, 2009).

Vallen, Mark. "Pele deLappe: RIP." *Art for a Change*, October 9, 2007. http://art-for-a-change.com/blog/2007/10/pele-delappe-rip.html (accessed November 3, 2009).

INDEX

A

B

C

D

E

F

G

H

I

J

K

L

M

N

O

P

R

S

T

U

V

W

Y

Z

ABOUT THE AUTHOR

Susan Vogel is a freelance writer and journalist. In 1990, she received a grant from the Utah Humanities Council, which funded a portion of the research for this book. Vogel hold a B.A. in English from San Francisco State University and a J.D. from University of California, Hastings College of the Law. In 1977, she studied at the Universidad Nacional Autónoma de México in Mexico City. Her writing has appeared in regional, national, and international publications.